MW00322931

STAGING PERSONHOOD

Staging Personhood

Costuming in Early Qing Drama

Guojun Wang

Columbia University Press   *New York*

GEISS HSU
FOUNDATION

This publication was made possible in part by an award from the James P. Geiss and Margaret Y. Hsu Foundation and an Association for Asian Studies First Book Subvention award.

Material for the introduction, chapter 3, and appendixes of this book first appeared in Guojun Wang, "Absent Presence: Costuming and Identity in the Qing Drama *A Ten-Thousand* Li *Reunion*," *Harvard Journal of Asiatic Studies* 79, no. 1 (2019). Reprinted by permission of the author and the publisher.

Columbia University Press
Publishers Since 1893
New York   Chichester, West Sussex
cup.columbia.edu

Library of Congress Cataloging-in-Publication Data
Names: Wang, Guojun, 1982- author. | Wang, Guojun, 1982- Sartorial spectacle.
Title: Staging personhood : costuming in early Qing drama / Guojun Wang.
Description: New York : Columbia University Press, [2020] | Revision of author's thesis:
    Sartorial spectacle : clothing, identity, and the state in early Qing drama. |
    Includes bibliographical references and index.
Identifiers: LCCN 2019033435 (print) | LCCN 2019033436 (ebook) |
    ISBN 9780231191906 (cloth) | ISBN 9780231549578 (ebook)
Subjects: LCSH: Costume—China—History—Ming-Qing dynasties, 1368-1912. |
    Clothing and dress—China—History—Ming-Qing dynasties, 1368-1912. |
    Clothing and dress—Social aspects—China. | Theater—China—History—17th century. |
    Theater and society—China.
Classification: LCC GT1555 .W2776 2020 (print) | LCC GT1555 (ebook) |
    DDC 391.00951—dc23
LC record available at https://lccn.loc.gov/2019033435
LC ebook record available at https://lccn.loc.gov/2019033436

Cover image: Anonymous, *Wanshou tu* 萬壽圖, detail of a scroll, color on silk, 1799. Palace Museum, Beijing. Reprinted in *Putian tongqing: Qingdai wanshou shengdian*, ed. Gugong Bowuyuan (Beijing: Gugong chubanshe, 2015).

For Pengfei

Contents

Acknowledgments

This book is a product of my intellectual journey over the past decade, during which I received support from many teachers, colleagues, and friends. My deepest thanks go to Tina Lu for her faith in this project when it was still a curious assemblage of ideas, and for her unwavering support in every aspect of my academic career. For intellectual guidance during my PhD study, which first gave form to the book, I am grateful to Kang-I Sun Chang and other Chinese studies scholars with whom I crossed paths, including Mick Hunter, Paize Keulemans, Peter Perdue, Haun Saussy, David Sensabaugh, and Jing Tsu. In the past four years, Vanderbilt University has provided me with an extraordinary intellectual and institutional home. One can hardly ask for a more collegial environment than our Asian Studies Program. Gerald Figal, my program director, has been unstinting in his support. I thank, in particular, the Chinese studies scholars and program faculty Rob Campany, Peter Lorge, Tracy Miller, Ruth Rogaski, Ben Tran, and We Jung Yi.

Outside Yale and Vanderbilt, Li-ling Hsiao provided thoughtful suggestions in the project's incipient stage; Ling Hon Lam's lasting trust and support gave me courage to carry the project through. Stephen West, Mark Stevenson, and Andrea Goldman kindly made time for a book manuscript workshop that facilitated the completion of the manuscript. Catherine Swatek shared her collection of rare materials and commented meticulously on the manuscript. I also benefited from the insights of Liana Chen, Ann Waltner, Paola Zamperini, and Judith Zeitlin. Through invited lectures, I was fortunate to share the project with colleagues at the University of Minnesota Twin Cities, the University of Chicago, Indiana University Bloomington, and Hong Kong Baptist University. During two memorable visits to the Minneapolis Institute of Art, I was able to study its collection of early Chinese theater costumes.

During the summer of 2016, Hu Siao-chen hosted my visit to Academia Sinica, where I collected fresh materials critical for enriching the manuscript. In Taiwan, conversations with Lin Li-yueh, Yi Jolan, and Cheng Yu-Yu familiarized me with relevant scholarship in the Chinese academic world; while in Beijing, Qin Wenbao generously shared his expert knowledge on Chinese theater costumes with me on an unforgettable rainy night. My abiding gratitude is reserved for Guo Yingde, who selflessly taught me about traditional Chinese drama and philology and has provided enduring support ever since.

My former schoolmates at Yale were also a source of intellectual pleasure and inspiration. I cherish the conversations with Yun Bai, Jesse Green, Fu-ming Lee, Yiwen Li, Jessica Moyer, Casey Schoenberger, Rosa Vieira de Almeida, Paul Vierthaler, Mengxiao Wang, and Huasha Zhang. Cheow Thia Chan has read every single piece of my scholarly writing; our writing group with Wei Luo, Yu Luo, and Pengfei Zhao sustained me whenever I was in dire straits. I remember Yuanfei Wang's comforting words and food at a time when they were most needed. My former classmates at Beijing Normal University, especially Chen Jiani, Li Xiaolong, Li Zhiyuan, Ma Sicong, Wang Yongen, Wang Yuyu, Xie Yan, Xie Yongjun, Xu Qingjiang, and Zhang Jingqiu, have offered timely assistance at different stages of the book project.

Nicholas Williams read through all the translations of Chinese texts in this book. His loyalty to Chinese poetry keeps reminding me of my initial commitment to this profession as I wander along various paths seeking my own understanding of the Chinese tradition. Jessica Moyer tirelessly answered my questions about translation. Wonhee Cho went through the romanization of Korean names and titles. My editor Kim Singletary has not only revised my prose but also helped tighten and sharpen my arguments. I thank the wonderful librarians I have worked with: Tang Li's early assistance in acquiring rare books made it possible for me to write some of my dissertation chapters; I cannot thank Yuh-Fen Benda enough for going out of her way to acquire resources essential for my research and for rushing to my help at last-minute notices; and I remember all the hours Chris Benda spent—with patience, precision, and expertise—in fixing the manuscript's notes and references. Needless to say, I am solely responsible for any remaining errors in the book.

A Prize Fellowship from the Council on East Asian Studies at Yale University aided the completion of the dissertation that grew into this book. A Provost Research Studios Award at Vanderbilt University supported a workshop on the draft manuscript. Vanderbilt University also generously granted two periods of research leave, which were funded by, respectively, a Henry Luce Foundation/ACLS Postdoctoral Fellowship in China Studies and a Dean's Faculty Fellowship from the College of Arts and Science at Vanderbilt University. Financial support for the publication of this book comes from the James P. Geiss and Margaret Y. Hsu Foundation Publication Subvention Award; the Association for Asian Studies First Book Subvention; the Brooks McNamara Publishing Subvention from the American Society for Theatre Research; and the Vanderbilt University Publication Subvention Grant.

At the publishing stage, it is my pleasure and honor to acknowledge help from Jennifer Crewe, Christine Dunbar, and Christian Winting at Columbia University Press for their understanding, efficiency, and professionalism.

Back home, I am deeply indebted to my parents, Wang Shumin and Yang Yurong, who still live in the northern Chinese village named Little Ice Valley where I grew up. I am also grateful to my brother Wang Guochen for taking care of them while we are oceans and nations apart. During our difficult time of transitions, my parents-in-law, Zhao Gui and Liu Huimin, twice offered their time to help with childcare, which enabled me to finish the dissertation and the book manuscript with relative ease. Phil Carspecken and Barbara Dennis have not only guided me in reading critical theories but also made Bloomington, Indiana, a home for us.

Pengfei Zhao, my partner in both life and scholarly pursuit, has saved me from despair countless times and has always challenged me to be intellectually adventurous. Our shared life is enriched by many conversations about our common academic interests, ranging from Tang poetry, to Hegelian philosophy, to clothing and dead bodies, to sent-down and returned youths during the Cultural Revolution, all of which have, directly or indirectly, shaped the current book. Our daughter Iris grounds me in everyday life while I pursue lofty ideas through reading and thinking. With love and appreciation, I dedicate this book to Pengfei for trusting me as a scholar and a person.

Costuming as Method

Around the year 1694, the aging scholar and playwright You Tong 尤侗 (1618–1704) completed an autobiography with captioned illustrations.[1] One illustration represents the premiere of his drama *Celestial Court Music* (*Juntian yue* 鈞天樂) performed almost four decades prior in 1658 by his private household troupe to entertain his father (figure 0.1).[2] In what can be assumed to be the main hall of You Tong's home, he, his father, and a group of guests watch the performance at the moment a successful cohort of imperial examination candidates makes its public procession, which corresponds to the second scene in the latter half of the play.[3]

As a rare illustration of an early Qing dramatic performance and audience, this image from You Tong's autobiography highlights several important tensions surrounding vestimentary and costume codes associated with the change to Manchu rule. Most starkly, it reveals a disparity between ethnically coded dress on- and offstage. The picture includes two types of clothes for the male characters—those in the style of the Ming dynasty (Han style) and those in the style of the Qing dynasty (Manchu style). Among the eight fully depicted members of the audience, seven wear unmistakable Manchu-style clothing marked by a gown with narrow sleeves and a cap with tassels.[4] Four members show their thin queues, a clear sign of the enforcement of Manchu hairstyle. By contrast, the costumes of the performers in the procession are in the traditional

FIGURE 0.1 Woodblock illustration showing premiere of You Tong's drama *Celestial Court Music*. Judith Zeitlin, Yuhang Li, and Richard A. Born, eds., *Performing Images: Opera in Chinese Visual Culture* (Chicago: Smart Museum of Art, University of Chicago, 2014), 141.

Han style because theatrical costumes in the Ming–Qing period were based on everyday clothes of the Ming dynasty.[5] The four troupe musicians, especially the one dressed as a scholar, are also wearing Han-style clothing likely because they have just performed or are about to perform onstage in a different scene.[6] The picture depicts Manchu clothing as the dress code for the social space and Han clothing for the performance space. The differentiation of dress codes in and around performance spaces constituted a distinguishing feature of theatrical life in early Qing China, a feature that has continued to reverberate in the aesthetics of traditional theater down to the present day.

In addition to the performance space, the image indicates another space reserved for Han clothing. Whereas all the other audience members, including You Tong himself—likely to the right in the back row—wear Manchu-style clothes of the Qing dynasty, You's father, seated in the middle of the back row, wears traditional Han-style clothes of the Ming dynasty. The father's outfit would have violated regulations regarding hair and dress in early Qing China given the requirement that all of the empire's Han Chinese males adopt and conform to Manchu hairstyle and clothing practices. The only explanation for the anachronism is that the father had passed away by the time the picture was produced and, as a dead person, was depicted as a Ming subject wearing traditional Chinese clothing. The theatrical performance was about stories set in the historical past, and You Tong's deceased father also belonged to the past. As demonstrated in the picture, Manchu clothing takes up the space of reality, of the present; Han clothing is assigned for the space of the past, the theatrical, the imagined. Through clothing, the image shows a social world that cannot be represented onstage and a performance space that cannot extend into the social world. In traditional China, clothing was indicative of social status, ethnicity, political regime, and different cultural traditions. In the Ming dynasty, costumes used in theatrical performances corresponded with Ming state attire as well as with the millennia-long sartorial tradition especially solidified by Confucian culture. In Qing China, that sartorial tradition was banished to the stage.

Staging Personhood is about theatrical costuming. I use "clothing" and "clothes" in reference to items of apparel in society, "costumes" in reference to pieces of clothes used in drama and theater, and "costuming" in reference to the theatrical appropriation of body and clothing in drama texts, performances, and different types of visual representations. The book asks a two-sided question: how did the Ming–Qing transition influence costuming as theatrical practices and how, in turn, did costuming enable the production of different types of personhood in early Qing China? Focusing on a group of dramas composed in the latter half of the seventeenth century, this book fulfills three tasks: it revisits a selected body of early Qing literature; it introduces an interdisciplinary perspective to understand the relations between literary writing and individual identities; and it develops costuming into a critical method for the study of highly unstable performance texts. Examining the case of early Qing drama, this study shows that theatrical costuming in traditional China was rarely a static affair. Instead, it was in constant interaction with historical changes and personal experiences and was often a means of negotiating disrupted personhood at a time when the world and the stage were simultaneously entangled and detangled. This introduction further explicates theatrical costuming as a hermeneutic entry to early Qing society and discusses the methods and materials of this study.

UNSTAGEABLE WORLD: CLOTHING AND COSTUMING IN EARLY QING CHINA

Together, natural environment, seasonal changes, textile technologies, gender, and social status shaped the material form and social use of clothing in traditional China. Dorothy Ko succinctly summarizes the cultural significance of clothing particularly for the literati class: "Correct attire—headdress, dress, and shoes—was the quintessential expression of civility, culture, and humanity, all being ramifications of *wen*."[7] In addition to being a symbol of civilization, clothing also served as a political language embodying lines of authority and power. Records about clothing abound in historical documents, including Confucian ritual classics, dynastic histories, encyclopedias, and literary writings.[8] Dynastic transitions almost always involved a change in clothing and dress codes in correlation with cosmological beliefs. Upon the establishment of a dynasty, the new government would choose one of five colors, corresponding to the five basic elements (*wuxing*) in the culture's correlative cosmology, to be the basic color for state attire and government paraphernalia. The state would continue to issue protocols regarding attire for people of different social status. Dressing against those protocols was considered not only an infringement of political order but also a disturbance of heavenly order.[9]

The sartorial spectacle shown in You Tong's image was a direct consequence of the Ming–Qing transition around the mid-seventeenth century. During the Manchu invasion into central China, Manchu rulers forced Han Chinese (nonclerical males) to shave their heads and change to Manchu clothing.[10] Manchu dress regulations in the early Qing period comprised two parts: shaving the head to leave only enough hair for a thin queue and the substitution of Manchu-style clothing for Han-style clothing. The Manchu conquest thus brought clothing and hairstyle into the center of ethnic contention.[11] For Han Chinese people whose traditional culture placed great value on the intactness of the body, shaving the head was one of the greatest insults—a form of punishment, *kun* 髡—up until the Qing dynasty.[12] In response to Manchu rulers' determination to exercise the policy, Han Chinese revolted in many areas of southern China. Records relating to the enforcement of and resistance to this policy abound in early Qing documents, in particular in *Veritable Records of the Shunzhi Emperor* (*Shizu Zhanghuangdi shilu* 世祖章皇帝實錄, basic version issued in 1667), which recounts events in the Shunzhi reign from the perspective of the Manchu court. As Lin Li-yueh's 林麗月 study shows, remnant subjects of the Ming dynasty invented a variety of ways to preserve their hair (in part at least) and their Han-style clothing (in remote areas, for example).[13]

As the Manchu regime continuously reformed and regulated the attire of its subjects, the topic of ethnic clothing remained sensitive even after the Qing dynasty had consolidated its rule. A century into the new dynasty, a scholar in Jiangxi province was still subject to capital punishment for openly remarking in his writings on the clothing policy.[14] Beginning in the mid-Qing period, discourse and resistance against the Manchu dress regulations gradually waned, until the final decades of the nineteenth century, when the Manchu hairstyle again became a target of anti-Manchu movements.[15] Even today, the master narrative in the Han-clothing movement still regards the Manchu dynasty as a time of unprecedented rupture in the history of Chinese clothing and treats Manchu clothing as the "evil other" to the sartorial tradition of the Han Chinese.[16]

From the perspective of the Manchu rulers, clothing—both Manchu-and Han-style—served as a way to consolidate political control and spread state ideology. On the one hand, forcing male Han Chinese to abandon their traditional dress and hairstyle constituted a symbolic way to demand their submission to the Manchus.[17] On the other hand, studies in the so-called new Qing history show that clothing was an effective way for the Manchus to formulate, express, and maintain their ethnic identity. In contrast to loose robes and wide sleeves, Manchu clothing features boots, trousers, and jackets essential for their equestrian and archery practices—key elements of the "Manchu Way."[18] To maintain an ethnic distinction in dress, the early Qing government prohibited Chinese men from wearing certain Manchu-specific items such as apparel made from fur and prohibited bannerwomen from modeling themselves after the fashion of Han Chinese women.[19] As studies show, Manchu-style clothing, as much as Manchu identity, was not a static existence but a historical entity in the making throughout and beyond the Ming–Qing transition.

Early Qing clothing policy, however, cannot be reduced to a replacement of Han clothing by Manchu clothing. Instead, the sartorial order involved a complex structure and was primarily a mechanism of differentiating between dominant and subordinate cultures. Although Manchu clothing prevailed and Han clothing was prohibited in daily life, Han-style clothes did not cease to exist in society. Hair and dress regulations applied mainly to adult males, as women and children were largely exempted from those regulations along with Buddhist and Daoist monks, who continued to wear robes developed in the Ming dynasty. Even though adult males had to wear Manchu-style clothes, families were permitted to bury them in ritualistic clothes of the Han style after they passed away.[20] The Manchu state designated different dress codes for different spaces within early Qing society, creating a sartorial landscape with Manchu clothing as an arch symbol of state power and Han clothing as a symbol of defeat and submission. In no other historical context of traditional China did clothing play such an important role in mediating interpersonal communication and shaping one's gender, ethnic, and cultural identities.

Traditional Chinese drama lies at the very nexus between Manchu and Han cultures and between literature and history. Perceiving theatrical performance to be a depraved practice of the Han Chinese tradition, the Manchu rulers prohibited Manchu people from theatergoing as well as the employment of Manchu clothing in popular drama performances. Meanwhile, they allowed theater to continue displaying Han-style costumes onstage, despite the ban on Han clothing in society.[21] Chapter 1 shows that Manchu clothing was largely absent on the early Qing stage outside the court. This special phenomenon has significant connotations for our understanding of Chinese theater and history. Before the Qing dynasty, clothing in everyday life—for different ethnic groups—found its way into theatrical costumes. The complicated dress regulations in seventeenth-century China produced a unique sartorial landscape: offstage, Manchu clothing prevailed; onstage, costumes in the Han style remained.[22] Early Qing society and early Qing theater became two distinct spaces featuring different dress codes.

Lu Eting 陸萼庭 summarizes three types of violations in drama identified by the Qianlong and Jiaqing emperors in the late eighteenth and early nineteenth centuries: stories about the Ming–Qing transition, "incorrect" accounts of the Song and Jin confrontation, and the use of Qing state attire and other absurd representations.[23] An edict regarding dramas on current affairs issued by the Jiaqing emperor in 1806 reads, "If the story refers to current affairs, however, and authors fabricate stories as they like, thus confusing public opinion, then this contravenes the ban on commoners discussing state affairs. . . . From now on, if anybody dares to compile a drama referring to current affairs, once they are found out, they will be certainly punished severely with no pardon."[24] The emperor's edict clearly points out the prohibition against dramatizing events in the Ming–Qing transition and in Qing society. The spirit iterated in the decree reflects the Manchu emperors' animosity toward the representation of contemporary politics in theatrical works, a disfavor that continued up to the nineteenth century.

In this book I use the expression "unstageable world" to describe the early Qing society that was segregated from the performance space. It refers to the difficulty of representing Manchu clothing onstage as well as that of representing early Qing society in theatrical practices. Throughout Chinese history, almost all "conquest dynasties" forced Chinese people to conform to their ethnic clothing and hairstyles, but the Manchu Qing dynasty was the only regime to stringently enforce the policy.[25]

Further, although traditional China witnessed continuous antitheatrical discourses and practices, the Manchu Qing dynasty was the only regime that regulated theatrical costumes along ethnic and gendered terms. The sartorial changes in seventeenth-century China involved a process of disrupting and reassembling the body and different styles of clothes. Body and clothing, accordingly, encapsulated a special realm of experience that reflected the negotiations over ethnic and gender identities during the Ming–Qing transition. As my study shows, the unstageable world of early Qing China promises a unique case for us to understand the relations between clothing, costuming, identity, and history.

This book explores the ways in which early Qing individuals grappled with historical and sartorial changes through theatrical costuming. Although the Manchu hair and dress regulations have long been a scholarly focus in studies of Chinese history, literature, and art, the special role of costuming in early Qing drama has thus far received little scholarly attention. Challenges in exploring the question include the scarcity and inaccessibility of evidence about early Qing drama performances because of the natural deterioration of material costumes over time and the political sensitivity of the dynastic transition in early Qing society. As a result, many theater scholars assume that Qing drama simply inherited the costuming practices of Ming drama, and they tend to regard the Ming and Qing dynasties as one continuous period in the development of Chinese drama. If we consider only the material formats of theatrical costumes, that proposition is largely valid since theatrical performances in the Qing dynasty inherited and developed the principal practices of the Ming dynasty. If we consider the dynamic between clothing on- and offstage, however, we notice a significant rupture during the dynastic change.

The world-stage relationship has been a perpetual theme in traditional Chinese drama. A number of studies have illuminated the pervasiveness of theatricality in late imperial Chinese society.[26] Art historian Jonathan Hay suggests there were "three structural principles of worldmaking" in urban theater beginning in the Song dynasty—namely, the stage space generated outwardly from the performer's body, the oscillating boundary between the observed world and the observers, and shifting places in chainlike scenes of a drama.[27] In contrast to the permeability between the world and the stage in different cultures worldwide, early

Qing China constitutes a unique case in which the world and the stage were clearly separated. By looking at the architecture of the stage in early Qing China, Sophie Volpp notes the increasingly less "soluble" boundary between stage and social space in seventeenth-century China: "The new prominence toward the end of the seventeenth century of commercial theaters with fixed stages in Beijing presumably fostered a sense that the space of performance was more highly demarcated and that the social space of the audience was now less integrated with the space of performance."[28] Following Volpp's proposition, I suggest that the contrast between clothing on- and offstage in early Qing China conspicuously indicates a separation between the social and the theatrical. Instead of discussing the worldly stage, I focus on a historical moment when a large part of the world, especially the dominant dress code, was rendered unstageable.

COSTUMING THE UNSTAGEABLE WORLD

Staging Personhood addresses a puzzle regarding early Qing drama: when the world was rendered unstageable, was it still possible for dramas to represent contemporary society? The answer lies in the careful selection and interpretation of theatrical materials enabled by the lens of costuming. Just as scholars have studied theater both as stage performances and as a mode of representation in late imperial China, in this book I suggest two understandings of theatrical costuming. In the strict understanding of the concept, "costuming" means the production and stage use of costumes. Modern scholars usually use *xiqu fushi* 戲曲服飾, a phrase coined in the twentieth century, in reference to costumes of traditional Chinese theater. Neither *xiqu* nor *fushi* has a ready equivalent in classical Chinese. Scholars of Chinese theater have identified a cluster of references to the clothes used onstage throughout Chinese history. Those terms include *qiemo* 砌末 in the Song–Yuan period, *chuanguan* 穿關 in Ming drama, and *chuandai* 穿戴 in court performances and *xingtou* 行頭 in commercial performances of the Qing dynasty.[29] The absence of a consistent name does not indicate that theatrical costuming was a trivial matter. Rather, the changing references show that theatrical practitioners continuously explored the potential capacities of costuming over time.

Current studies of *xiqu fushi* have focused on two questions: what were the material formats of theatrical costumes in traditional China, and how were those costumes coupled with different role types and characters onstage? Some recent studies represent synchronic and diachronic approaches to traditional Chinese theater costumes. Alexandra B. Bonds has provided a systematic introduction to the costumes used in Beijing opera as a means to visually communicate received aesthetic and cultural traditions.[30] Song Junhua's recent survey of the history of Chinese theatrical costumes focuses on the changing formats of costumes and the shifting ways of using them onstage. With respect to the Ming–Qing transition, Song stresses the continuity in theatrical costumes between the two dynasties.[31] Attention to costumes has also engendered important studies of European theatrical traditions. For example, using Shakespeare's plays as examples, Robert Lublin shows that costuming produced prominent visual codes for sex, social station, religion, and foreignness on the early modern English stage.[32]

The narrow understanding of costuming serves as a background for this book. With no ambition to address general costume history, *Staging Personhood* maintains a focus on a single dimension of costuming at a very specific historical juncture: the ethnic connotations of theatrical costumes, primarily for male characters, during the Ming–Qing transition in mid-seventeenth-century China—namely, how the nascent sartorial system of Manchu clothing interacted with theatrical performances. The introduction, chapter 1, and the epilogue include discussions about this narrowly defined costuming.

However, since Manchu clothing did not readily appear in stage performances in early Qing China, costume-based studies prove inadequate in dealing with issues about clothing and dressing in early Qing drama. I am more concerned with a broad definition of costuming that corresponds to the ambit of theatrical representation in Ming–Qing China. Different from costume-based approaches, the second understanding of costuming involves dressing, undressing, and crossdressing—different modes of associating bodies and clothing—in all kinds of theatrical practices. Using flower guides (*huapu* 花譜) in nineteenth-century Beijing as an example, Mark Stevenson has coined the term "epitheatre" to describe "forms of social life and literature that exist as an extension or effect of performances or performance spaces."[33] Costuming can be considered a typical epitheatrical practice because it extends beyond the stage use of costumes to include textual and visual representations of body and clothing in response to and in negotiation with the sartorial changes in society. The broad understanding of costuming enables us to probe the boundaries between page, stage, and the social world in early Qing China.[34]

This book further suggests that costumes and costuming can be understood as representing two opposite relations between the social world and theatrical practices in early Qing China. Seen from the contrast between clothes and costumes, the world and the stage were separated. Yet theatrical costuming was still able to probe worldly affairs because costuming transcended the boundaries of the stage and penetrated spaces for textual and visual representation. Although Manchu clothing was taboo on the early Qing stage, it was nevertheless represented in some early Qing drama texts, which opens a window for scholars to investigate theatrical responses to the intrusion of Manchu clothing. What is more, theatrical costuming in early Qing China not only dealt with the intrusive Manchu clothing but also responded to the changes in the traditional Han-style clothes of the Ming dynasty. Costuming thus provides an alternative space in which early Qing society can be represented and contested. When historical changes rendered the world unstageable, costuming rendered the unstageable world perceptible.

Staging Personhood is concerned less with the material specifications of theatrical costumes than with actual and symbolic processes of integrating bodies, clothes, and personhood in theatrical practices. Rather than explicating the meaning of the visual codes associated with Manchu clothing, chapter 1 discusses the general absence of Manchu clothing on the early Qing stage, which, I argue, led the existing Han-style costumes to be ethnically and politically charged. The four case studies that follow are based on an examination of drama scripts; at the same time they consider visual and performance records that shed light on the possible use of costumes in actual performances. Although usually not taken into account by costume studies, those very phenomena unveil the entanglements between literature and history in early Qing China.

COSTUMING, PERSONHOOD, AND PRODUCTION ANALYSIS

When talking about literature and personhood in early Qing China, one might assume that discussion would focus on the authors of literary works. Indeed, scholars in traditional China developed sophisticated theories related to understanding the authorial mind through reading his or her writings.[35] It has been widely discussed how the Ming–Qing transition led some Han Chinese scholars to express their traumatic experiences through writings and artistic works. Scholars have explored the same question through reading early Qing dramas. As Wilt Idema notes, "No genre of literature provided a better opportunity to express the conflicting emotions concerning the collapse of the Ming and the subsequent conquest of the Chinese world by the Manchu Qing than drama."[36] Many studies of early Qing drama focus on the *yimin* group—remnant subjects of the Ming dynasty—and try to explain how that identity is embodied through different literary representations. Those studies tend to treat theatrical works as a form of authorial expression similar to poetry and thus might be referred to as the expression model of drama studies.[37] In line with seeking authorial intention, scholars also try to connect the represented characters in a drama with actual persons in society.[38]

Certainly early Qing literature provides precious materials for us to study personal experiences and expressions in response to the dynastic change. However, treating early Qing drama as playwrights' voices creates a few problems. Scholars of literary studies are all too familiar with the complicated relations between authors and their works. The genre of drama, in particular, allows and requires the author to hide the authorial voice. Regarding early Qing literature, we frequently face the lack of adequate information about the authorship of a certain drama. Even when a drama's authorship can be authenticated, there is still a distance between the author's mind and the written texts. Since the Manchu regime rendered writing politically sensitive, many early Qing writers consciously maintained a distance between themselves and their written works. As discussed by Kang-I Sun Chang, the scholar Wu Weiye 吳偉業 (1609–1672) constructed a "mask" in his poems and dramas as a way to create "an objectivity and a distance from the subject matter."[39] Chang describes the mask as a dramatic vehicle Wu transposed into the poetic tradition. The inherent distance between a playwright and the characters in his or her works discourages the practice of reading the characters in a drama as projections of the author's self. Meanwhile, a focus on Ming loyalists highlights political allegiance and ethnic belonging particularly among male scholars who voiced their sentiments through written words. It tends to overshadow the multiplicity of one's roles in society as a political subject, family member, and expert in different fields. Therefore, the expression model of studying early Qing literature falls short of the sophistication needed to understand theatrical works.

To complicate the issue of authorial intention, I propose a method that hinges on costuming, borrowing insights from Michel Foucault and production analysis in theater studies. Discussing what he refers to as the author function, Foucault argues that "such a name permits one to group together a certain number of texts, define them, differentiate them from and contrast them to others. In addition, it establishes a relationship among the texts."[40] By questioning the immediate association between texts and the authorial mind, Foucault suggests two different approaches in studying various types of writings. First, one can study the "modes of existence" of discourses—the "modes of circulation, valorization, attribution, and appropriation of discourses."[41] Second, one can study the relationships between discourses and their authors—not as real individuals but as positions that "can be occupied by different classes of individuals."[42] Rather than valorizing or ignoring the author, Foucault proposes studying the intricate connections between texts and their purported authors as well as how those connections influence the existence of those very texts.[43]

The questions raised in Foucault's article, when coupled with traditional Chinese philology, prove especially fruitful for the study of early Chinese drama. In her book about the reproduction and reception of early (primarily Yuan-dynasty) song drama in the Ming and early Qing periods, Patricia Sieber delineates two types of relations between authors and their works—what she refers to as attestatory authorship and reproductive authorship.[44] Sieber's study shows how a canonical author such as Guan Hanqing was constructed in late imperial China and how the "author function" was performed by playwrights, editors, commentators, and readers in the process of producing theatrical works.[45] Foucault's propositions about the author function are also helpful for understanding theatrical works in early Qing China. Under the names of certain authors, early Qing dramas circulated as manuscripts, prints, visual representations, and stage performances. The author holds together a group of materials across periods and genres, which allows us to explore costuming in those disparate practices.

Instead of the authors or authorial intentions, in this book I am more concerned with the individual and collective identities involved in various theatrical practices. I use the concept of "personhood" to refer to the state, meaning, and requirements of being a person specifically in the context of early Qing China, an era when the issue of personhood became a keen concern for Han Chinese people in general and literati scholars in particular. To explore the relations between costuming and personhood, I borrow and refine the method of production analysis. Judith Milhous and Robert Hume define production analysis as "interpretation of the text specifically aimed at understanding it as a performance vehicle— 'reading with a directorial eye.'"[46] Thus defined, production analysis focuses on drama scripts instead of actual performances. Starting from this definition, Andrew Sofer studies theatrical props as textual devices, performance vehicles, and material entities.[47] Sofer further develops production analysis to consider theatrical factors he refers to as dark matter, the invisible aspects of performance texts.[48] Sofer's studies maintain a balance between analysis of drama scripts and that of actual performances.

Like Sofer, I consider costuming in a wide range of theatrical practices, especially those found in the fissures between different editions of a drama, between dramas on the page and their executions onstage, and between what can and what cannot be performed. Some of the dramas discussed in this book were closely related with stage performance—they provided possibilities of stage executions or were the result of performance adaptations. Others, however, were produced as texts for reading rather than performance. On some occasions, early Qing drama scripts explicitly employed Manchu clothing, rendering the plays unstageable. On others, stage performances indirectly invoked Manchu hairstyle and clothing, moments that could not be written into drama scripts. Production analysis, therefore, allows for the exploration of actual performances as well as of textual details that were impossible to stage in early Qing China.

I refine and use the concept of production analysis to also address the production of theatrical scripts, a highly unstable corpus of literature in traditional China. Discussing Renaissance literature and theater, Stephen Orgel succinctly notes the instability of literary texts: "What scientific bibliography has taught us more clearly than anything else is that at the heart of our texts lies a hard core of uncertainty."[49] The early Qing dramas discussed in this book pose a similar challenge: some of them do not have authenticated authors; others exist as woodblock prints produced decades or centuries after their composition; and still others exist only as manuscripts and diffuse fragments. Oriented toward producing an authoritative text closest to the original author's edition, traditional Chinese philology often proves inadequate in studying scattered and fragmented performative texts. In response to these challenges, the book regards drama scripts as traces of textual and performance productions. It pays equal attention to the printed texts and marginal writings, textual fragments, performance records, and meaningful absence.

The production of theatrical works, in turn, involves a cluster of persons.[50] Early Qing dramas first afford nuanced analysis of the represented characters in theatrical works. For instance, the theatrical activities of bestowing, changing, and displaying clothing at a public celebration in You Tong's *Celestial Court Music* produce a successful examination candidate in the celestial world. Focusing on *Peach Blossom Fan* (*Taohua shan* 桃花扇), Tina Lu explores how the crumbling of the Ming dynasty endangered the stability of individual identities. Stephen Owen offers similar observations and points out the productive functions of naming and dressing in the same drama.[51] Likewise, the four case studies in this book focus on represented characters in drama texts, paying special attention to those characters when they travel between spaces within a text, spaces in different media, and social spaces revolving around a text.

Just as costuming spans different modes of theatrical practices, the persons discussed in this book include represented characters as well as actual people who participated in producing, reading, watching, discussing, and even censoring dramas. Whenever possible, the book examines the authorial practices in producing certain theatrical works. The perspective of costuming allows us to see the roles of an author beyond the writer of a playscript. For example, in addition to being the composer of the original manuscript, You Tong performed the role of a director and personally instructed his household troupe for the performance in 1658;[52] in producing the illustration and poetic caption, You acted as a commissioner of a project of cultural memory. Through playwriting, publishing, staging, and textual-visual representation, You Tong created multilayered relations with different forms of the drama he initially composed.

As some of the case studies in the following chapters show, the productions of scripts and performances involved different parties apart from the authors. With regard to Kong Shangren's *Peach Blossom Fan*, for example, the printed play includes a few dozen commentating and dedicatory poems in the beginning section that were composed by Kong's acquaintances. In the case of *Chaste Lady Hai* (*Hai Liefu chuanqi* 海烈 婦傳奇), the drama was printed more than a century after its composition by a group of local literati scholars with no personal association with the original author. As different parties collaborating to produce an extant text, those persons together fulfill the author function.

Whereas drama scripts involve authors, commentators, and readers, theater performances bring actual performers and their costumes into practices of costuming. In a drama performance, the practices of costuming associate costumes with the bodies of different performers. Again, take You Tong's picture for example. Although the three successful examination candidates are dressed in official uniforms for male scholars, in the actual performance it could as well be female actors who performed these characters onstage. Some of the dramas discussed in this book, such as *Lovebirds Reversal* (*Dao yuanyang* 倒鴛鴦), feature the theme of cross-dressing.[53] Other venues of performance involved complicated issues regarding gender and ethnicity: for example, the imperial troupe in the Manchu palace included eunuchs, whose gender identity was ambiguous; the Manchu rulers prohibited Manchu people from performing onstage, leaving the theatrical space primarily for Han Chinese. As far as performers are considered, theatrical costuming on the early Qing stage encompassed the combination of costumes and performers of particular genders and ethnic identities.

Theater audiences are also an essential part in the production of theatrical works, especially within the sartorial landscape of early Qing China. The audiences of early Qing dramas included men and women, scholars and the illiterate public, and people in different areas of the Manchu empire. A large part of the performances discussed in this book took place in private households. Audiences would occasionally include women, although in most cases they were excluded.[54] Other drama performances took place in public with larger and more heterogeneous audiences, just like in certain European theatrical traditions. Stephen Greenblatt points out two aspects that render Shakespearean theater collective practices: "The theater is manifestly the product of collective intentions" and "the theater manifestly addresses its audience as a collectivity."[55] Similar to the Shakespearean theater, drama performances in Qing China necessarily involved audiences as active participants. Because of the contrast in clothing on- and offstage, the audience became an integral part of costuming at the site of the drama performance. Both audiences' and performers' clothing created meaningful sartorial spectacles.

Staging Personhood develops a method significantly different from the existing model that treats literature as venues of identity expression. The analysis in this book focuses on the specific practices of costuming in drama scripts while probing possible connections between those practices and the playwrights, their scholar-writer communities, the audiences, and the role of the Manchu state. Whereas questioning the view of early Qing literature as expressions of *yimin* identity, this book does not simply argue for the instability and multiplicity of identity—what some social scientists call clichéd constructivism.[56] Neither is the book a study of self-fashioning through language as exemplified in Stephen Greenblatt's study of Renaissance literature.[57] What I propose in this book is essential to a different order of analysis—it brackets reified identities and examines the meaning-generating capacity of theatrical costuming. The analysis does not start from a preassumed identity of an intentional author; nor does it regard body and clothing as the exterior or the reflection of a certain interior world. Rather, it examines the dissociation and reassociation of different bodies and clothes in theatrical works—for men and women, Manchu and Han, the living and the dead—and places those practices of costuming into the sartorial landscape of early Qing society. This approach calls for equal attention to persons, clothes as objects, and acts of dressing and undressing. As is shown in the following chapters, different modes of costuming separate as well as conflate the social and the theatrical world, creating a matrix in which different persons and different aspects of personhood are located. Put simply, costuming is not a way of expressing a certain identity but one of producing multiple aspects of being a person.

MATERIALS: CENSORSHIP AND *SHISHI JU*

The topic of Manchu hair and dress regulations remained taboo throughout early Qing China. Most of the existing discussions on the topic by early Qing scholars are in the genres of poetry and prose, especially biographical notes. Except for a handful of titles such as the novel *Qiaoshi* 樵史 and the short fictional biography "Mister Painting His Hairnet" (Hua wangjin xiansheng zhuan 畫網巾先生傳), few pieces of early Qing literature provide detailed descriptions of the Manchu hair and dress regulations. Although the poetry and prose writings allow us to see how early Qing scholars wrote about the poignant experiences of shaving their heads and changing their clothing, they seldom touch on the more nuanced ways in which different clothes were separated from or assimilated with the human body. Among various ways of tackling the changing clothes and hairstyles, theatrical costuming provides a vibrant space to experiment with different ways of connecting the body and different types of clothes.

Early Qing dramas on current affairs, or *shishi ju* 時事劇, best serve the purposes of this study because these dramas include the most direct responses to contemporary history through theatrical representation. The two terms "historical drama" (*lishi ju* 歷史劇) and "drama on current affairs" (*shishi ju*) indicate contrasting possibilities for understanding the relations between theatrical works and historical events. Whereas *lishi* indicates a distance between a play and the story it represents, *shishi* signals proximity between them.[58] Playwrights of early Qing China were left with a legacy of dramatizing current affairs. Some recorded theatrical performances of the pre-Qin and Han dynasties were based on stories in society; many of the existing Yuan dramas directly feature social life and political events in the Yuan dynasty.[59] In the late Ming period, playwrights frequently adapted contemporary events, often political, into *chuanqi* dramas to be read and staged.[60] The term *shishi* was also frequently employed by Ming literati scholars in their drama critiques.[61]

Representing contemporary history in theatrical works became politically sensitive in early Qing China. The Manchu rulers and government were attentive to the content of dramas written and performed, especially those with direct or implicit references to society. Besides the representation of current events, most of the plays about military conflicts between central China and ethnic people to the north also became politically sensitive in the early Qing period. For example, despite the rich repertoire of Yuan and Ming plays about the Yang family fighting the Khitan invasion, the Qing dynasty did not see large-scale performances of such dramas until the eighteenth century.[62] Considering themselves descendants of the Jurchen people, the Manchu rulers were especially attentive to plays about the Song–Jin confrontation.[63]

Literary scholars and historians have discussed numerous cases of personal calamity caused by writings, or literary inquisition (*wenzi yu* 文字獄). In a recent study, Wang Fan-sen 王汎森 uses the word *feng* 風 ("wind" or "air," quoting early Qing scholar Gong Zizhen 龔自珍) to describe literary censorship in the Qing dynasty, which, he suggests, had a widespread capillary effect and incurred self-repression among scholar-writers.[64] Although focusing on cases in the Qianlong reign, Wang's study shows that literary inquisition and the practice of self-censorship were pervasive throughout the early decades of the Qing dynasty. As my case study in chapter 3 demonstrates, drama censorship in Qing China existed as a certain kind of shared knowledge rather than in the form of written codes.[65]

The explicit and implicit censorship on drama significantly influenced the extant repository of early Qing plays. Scholars have counted about thirty extant dramas based on current affairs in the last century of the Ming dynasty.[66] The first century (1640s–1730s) of the Qing dynasty saw the production of about four hundred *chuanqi* dramas and three hundred *zaju* dramas.[67] The trend of dramatizing current affairs continued into the first decades of the Qing dynasty. However, almost all the dramas directly centering on the Manchu massacres of Han Chinese are lost, and only about a dozen extant plays feature the Ming–Qing transition, most of which are set against the backdrop of peasant rebellions led by Li Zicheng and Zhang Xianzhong.[68] Several other dramas from the same period feature events from early Qing society. Produced under conditions of political oppression, early Qing dramas generally avoided direct comment on contemporary history. A convenient strategy to camouflage the relevance between a drama and current society is to change the historical setting to another dynasty or adopt the genre of fantastical literature.[69] After the publication and ensuing censorship of *Peach Blossom Fan* in the early eighteenth century, the number of dramas based on current affairs plummeted. The interest in composing such dramas resumed only in the late Qing period, in a completely different social setting.

Despite the sartorial limitations on different theatrical practices, early Qing playwrights still probed possible ways to represent clothing and the personal experiences related to the forced changes in early Qing society. In most cases, the plays discussed in this book are the only existing examples that directly represent Manchu hair and dress regulations (*Lovebirds Reversal*); confrontation between the Manchu government and Han Chinese (*A Ten-Thousand-Li Reunion* [*Wanli yuan* 萬里圓]); and the systemic change in the meaning of clothing (*Peach Blossom Fan*). Some of them employ costuming to probe the potential theatrical meanings of Manchu and Han clothing, while others make efforts to circumvent the issue of costuming. Although these cases do not represent the majority of existing dramas, they illustrate the known body of dramas on Ming–Qing transition that remain missing.

As the book reveals, theatrical works in early Qing China were produced in response to social reality and conditioned by the intricate relations between stage and society. Further, in early Qing dramas, the contemporary/present was not a given entity. Theatrical works provided alternative ways to differentiate between the past and the present, not least through costuming. Discussing contemporary operas during the decades of Ming–Qing transition, Paize Keulemans notes, "It is, however, precisely the way these contemporary operas engage with recent political affairs that makes them important, distinguishing them from the opera that either preceded or followed."[70] *Staging Personhood* explores how early Qing dramas responded to the new sartorial landscape in early Qing China—with the novel category of Manchu clothing and a new hierarchy of clothing based on gender and ethnicity.

In studying dramas based on current affairs, I draw attention to important facets of theatrical costuming in which historical events can be invoked. These facets include drama plots, costume instructions, prop lists, paratextual materials, performance records, and visual representations of theatrical themes. Costume instruction remained a marginal issue for drama composition during the early developments of Chinese drama and theater. When literati playwrights composed dramas in the Yuan and early Ming dynasties, they focused on the arias of the libretto, leaving stage execution—and even dialogue—to individual troupes and actors.[71] It was the increasing literati participation in drama performance in the late Ming and early Qing period that brought costuming to a central position in drama composition and performance. By the Ming–Qing period, a large percentage of drama texts, either as manuscripts or woodblock prints, included significant quantities of costume instructions. Since their connections with stage performance vary, the costume instructions in these plays do not necessarily reflect stage use of costumes.

Theater scholars have also studied visual materials and actual garments related to theatrical performances. For the Song–Jin–Yuan period, the materials included murals, paintings, and engravings on brick structures such as tombs and temples.[72] Woodblock drama prints in the Ming–Qing period include a repository of illustrations inspired by stage performances, including the use of costumes.[73] The same period saw the appearance of a group of texts with registers of theatrical costumes, providing more systematic information about costumes used in drama performances.[74] In the late Qing period, there appeared a new genre of representation known as *xihua*, or "play paintings," which represent popular scenes from the stage. These representations reveal different venues through which clothing was theatrically and artistically appropriated. The prism of costuming allows us to treat drama not as a text with a single master narrative but as an ensemble of textual, visual, and material elements—a space for the conversation between elements on the page, on the stage, and even those absent from both.

CHAPTER ORGANIZATION

The chapters of the book discuss costuming as a special sector of the sartorial system and as textual and performance practices. Chapter 1 delineates the changing modes of interaction between clothing on the stage and clothing offstage around the Ming–Qing transition. It also discusses different interpretations of such sartorial spectacles in the eyes of different audiences. It outlines the social context in which the theatrical practices discussed in the case studies took place. The book's main body comprises four case studies of theatrical works that follow a chronological order based on the time of the dramas' composition. Chapter 2 studies *Lovebirds Reversal,* which depicts a scholar who exchanges clothes with a girl to avoid shaving his head during the Manchu invasion. Composed and published immediately after the Manchu conquest, the drama shows how the ethnic conflicts influenced not only male scholars but also gender relations at large. The drama, together with other plays by the author, showcases some of the earliest attempts to represent the Manchu conquest through theatrical costuming. The chapter suggests that dressing across Manchu and Han ethnic styles problematizes the topos of cross-dressing in Chinese drama, a threat to gender stability during the dynastic transition.

Examining *A Ten-Thousand-Li Reunion,* chapter 3 focuses on the bodies and clothes of the male members in a Chinese family. It begins by noting a surprising absence of costume instructions in *Reunion* and continues to show that different scenes of the drama use different methods to dress characters as members of a family and subjects of changing states. Moving away from the male body and clothing, chapter 4 focuses on the semiological meaning of women's bodies and clothing. It discusses two early Qing dramas about a chaste lady who stitched her entire outfit together to prevent a sexual assault before committing suicide. In a close reading of the descriptions of the chaste lady's stitched clothes, body, coffin, statue, and shrine, I argue that theatrical costuming turned the woman's socially constructed body into a vehicle for mediating ethnic conflicts experienced during the dynastic change.

After three case studies of individual persons during the dynastic change, chapter 5 examines the changing nature of Ming state attire as represented in *Peach Blossom Fan.* Completed half a century after the fall of Ming, the drama provides a historical reflection with a panoramic view of the dynastic change. The chapter reveals the process through which Ming state attire is theatricalized—its banishment to the theatrical realm and the historical past and its separation from the bodies of

Ming subjects. *Peach Blossom Fan*, as theater scholars have argued, marked the peak and the end of a period in the history of Qing drama. Likewise, the practices of costuming centering around that drama symbolized the end of a historical period when costuming and personhood were specifically intertwined.

The epilogue explores the changing relations between costuming, personhood, and the state by tracing the emergence of Manchu clothing in drama throughout the Qing dynasty. As it reveals, both drama and Manchu clothing were associated with certain perceptions of groupness. The tension and interaction between them indicate shifting relations between Manchus, Han Chinese, and China transitioning from an empire to a nation-state.

The chronological order of the chapters helps us understand changing modes of interaction between Han Chinese and the intruding Manchu culture—from initial encounter to confrontation, reconciliation, and, finally, integration. Critiquing different types of diachronics in the studies of Chinese art history, Jonathan Hay suggests a disjunctive diachronics that would "contribute to a kaleidoscopic representation of the Chinese past—the only kind of historiographic representation that can do justice to our currently evolving state of knowledge."[75] Although the case studies in this book are in chronological order, I do not attempt to suggest a version of theater history that accords with the history of the Qing dynasty. Instead, different chapters use different combinations of materials to address specific aspects of costuming. The selected cases, in turn, address the interweaving between gender and ethnicity, individual males, individual females, and collective memory. The epilogue and some chapters use materials ranging from the early to late Qing era. They demonstrate the lasting impact of the dynastic and sartorial transitions that transpired in mid-seventeenth-century China. The choice of method and materials determines that the book is not dealing with a body of anti-Manchu writings with a coherent theme or voice. Rather, I endeavor to show the subtleties of costuming and inconsistencies in personhood that do not necessarily reflect the progress of Qing history.

Scholars of traditional Chinese theater such as Beijing or *kun* opera (also known as *kunqu* 崑曲, originating in Jiangsu province and boasting a history of more than five hundred years) tend to stress the ahistorical nature of theatrical performances, especially in the use of costumes; yet scholars of early Qing literature tend to read dramas as direct responses to and representations of the Ming–Qing transition. This book challenges and complicates both views. Placed into the context of the Ming–Qing transition, theatrical costuming turns out to be a volatile site reflecting and resisting historical changes. The Manchu conquest severed the existing connections between clothing in society and costumes onstage, consequently producing opportunities for theatrical costuming to negotiate these fissures. Early Qing history has more to do with costuming than current studies of theatrical costumes tend to indicate. Thus, I suggest that theatrical costuming is a uniquely productive means for the study of state and individuals in early Qing history, and that this interpretive framework allows us to better understand the Ming–Qing transition as a reconfiguration of the sartorial system, a policing of theatricality, and a transformation of individual identities.

CHAPTER ONE

Ways to Dress and Ways to See

The ancient Chinese costume is now very exactly represented on
the stage of their theatre, to which it is exclusively confined.

—JOHN FRANCIS DAVIS, *THE CHINESE*

In 1836, John Francis Davis (1795–1890), a translator of Chinese novels
and plays and the future governor of Hong Kong, published an encyclo-
pedia about Chinese history and culture. In it, he provided a concise
introduction to policies regarding hair and dress during the Ming–Qing
transition and an incisive comment on the role of theater in preserving
traditional Chinese clothing.[1] Davis noticed that traditional Chinese
clothing was not only "very exactly represented on the stage" but also
"exclusively confined" to it. His observation was based on his personal
experiences in China as well as his knowledge of Chinese history.
Although the book was published in the nineteenth century, his brief
comment captured the role of theater as a unique sartorial space in the
Qing dynasty. Davis's words epitomized the exile of Han clothing to the
stage in early Qing China. This chapter explicates the process of that exile
and its impact on different theatrical practices.

This chapter is about the relationship between costuming as stage
practice and costuming as audience experience. The materials referred
to in this chapter illustrate the two understandings of theatrical costuming laid out in the introduction. The first half examines stage use of
clothing, showing how the sartorial transition in seventeenth-century
China altered preexisting relations between clothing and costuming. The
second half demonstrates that different theater audiences experienced
sartorial spectacles in divergent ways. Together, the two parts clarify how

the intrusion of Manchu clothing and the concurrent dress regulations altered the practices and perceptions of theatrical costuming in Qing China. As this chapter suggests, the representational relation between stage costumes and Ming attire was a construct enabled by the dynastic transition and experienced by different audiences.

THE INTERACTION BETWEEN CLOTHING AND COSTUMING BEFORE THE QING DYNASTY

When discussing a certain type of traditional Chinese performance, scholars tend to stress the ahistorical nature of the costumes used. For example, in her seminal studies of traditional costumes in Beijing and *kun* opera, Liu Yuemei 劉月美 discusses the costumes and other props as well as different principles for using them onstage.[2] Liu's studies highlight the material dimension of theatrical costumes and their stage use based on gender and role types. In a recent English study of Beijing opera costumes, Alexandra Bonds more clearly points out the "absence of time" in stage use of Beijing opera costumes. She writes, "While the stage pictures give the impression of Chinese historical dress, in actuality, very little of what appears onstage replicates reality. The costumes developed specifically to suit the needs of the actors, enhancing movement and the nature of the characters and roles, and to create an image of utmost beauty."[3] As Bonds explains, existing Beijing opera performances use the same set of costumes for a certain role type despite the changing historical periods, seasons, and locations for theatrical characters that role type performs. That feature is best reflected in the saying, "One would rather wear tattered [costumes] than incorrect ones" (寧穿破不穿錯), which refers to the strict and stylistic prescriptions in place regarding the use of theatrical costumes. Besides discussing the stylistic and aesthetic dimensions of traditional Chinese theater costumes, Song Junhua has provided a thorough survey of historical changes in Chinese theater costumes from the pre-Qin down to the late Qing periods.[4] As Song's study demonstrates, the ahistorical nature of theater costumes in traditional Chinese drama has been the very result of historical developments for more than a millennium. In this chapter I focus on one aspect of the historical changes in theatrical costuming—the ethnic dimension.

To understand the position of theatrical costuming in the early Qing sartorial landscape, we first need an outline of the modes of interaction between clothing and costuming throughout Chinese history. The issue touches on the relation between onstage and offstage clothing and the relation between stage costumes and different ethnic clothes. One of the earliest records of theatrical acting in Chinese history reveals an inherent connection between clothing in performance and clothing in society.[5] In the story of Jester Meng 優孟 in the Warring States period, Meng impersonates the deceased Sunshu Ao 孫叔敖 (also known as Wei Ao; fl. 601 BCE), the former prime minister of the state of Chu, in front of King Zhuang of Chu. The king, startled by Sunshu's reappearance and moved by his subsequent conversation with Sunshu, bequeathed land and property to Sunshu's son. The *Shiji* 史記 version of the story reads, "[Meng] then copied Sunshu Ao's cap and gown and imitated Sunshu's manners and ways of talking" (即為孫叔敖衣冠，抵掌談語).[6] In this account, Sunshu Ao's cap and gown refer to a set of costumes modeled after Sunshu's clothes when he was alive. The two sets of clothes worn by Sunshu and Meng epitomize a derivative relation between clothing and costuming in traditional China: theatrical costumes originated from everyday clothes and on many occasions were used in imitation of those clothes. The derivative relation between clothing and costuming lasted throughout the history of Chinese theater that followed.

From the Tang dynasty to the Ming dynasty, official uniforms and everyday clothes went through continuous reformations. Meanwhile, theatrical costumes in each era readily adapted to the changing fashion in daily life. Performances in the Tang dynasty included plays with acting and conversation (*kebai xi* 科白戲) and plays with dancing and singing (*gewu xi* 歌舞戲). In the adjutant play (*canjun xi* 參軍戲), a type of *kebai xi*, the *canjun* role featured a green costume following the style of Tang official uniforms. Plays such as *Tayao niang* 踏搖娘, *Lanling wang* 蘭陵王, and *Botou* 撥頭, examples of *gewu xi*, employed caps and gowns based on official Tang uniforms and other items based on the clothes of ordinary people in Tang society. The costumes in both types of performances were modeled after clothes in everyday life. At the same time, some items of performance costumes found their way into social use—for instance, the headgear *jin* 巾.[7] These examples indicate the porous boundaries between everyday clothes and performance costumes in the early development of Chinese theater.

By the Song–Jin–Yuan period, Chinese theater had developed into its full-fledged form, with elaborate arias and dialogues and a well-developed system of stage performance including musical accompaniment, costumes, and props. Major performance genres included *zaju* 雜劇 and *nanxi* 南戲. The *zaju* performances in the Song dynasty saw the appearance of different role types. One of these role types, the uniformed official (*zhuanggu* 裝孤), usually employed a set of costumes including a gown with wide sleeves and a waist belt, a double-crowned headdress with bent wings (*futou* 幞頭), black leather boots, and a court tablet to be held with both hands—all of which resembled the dress of an official in the Song court. Other primary items employed in *zaju* performances of the Song dynasty included theater-style head wraps (*hunguo* 諢裹) and loose gowns (*kuanshan* 寬衫). Likewise, *nanxi* performances in the Song dynasty employed white robes (*bailan* 白襴), green robes (*lülan* 綠襴), and a headscarf for the scholar characters.[8] Most of the costumes in these performances developed from the actual attire worn in Song society.

Given the fluidity between onstage and offstage clothing, the question of whether and how theatrical costuming appropriated ethnic dress—especially during the non-Han dynasties—invites speculation. Clothing in traditional China differentiated between different ethnic groups or what were thought to be different levels of civilization. As recorded in *The Analects*, Confucius said, "Had it not been for Kuan Chung, we might well be wearing our hair down and folding our robes to the left."[9] As this statement illustrates, different styles of hair and clothes were considered markers of barbarity or civilization.

Early conceptions of cultural differences developed into explicit expressions about ethnic distinctions. The Han Chinese ethnic identity was historically formed and constantly shifting, and it was not until the Northern Song dynasty (960–1127) that the Han Chinese ethnicity emerged in literati discourses. Together with the increasingly explicit expression of ethnicity in elite discourses and popular literature, clothing came to be a site of ethnic confrontation. Historians have used the term "conquest dynasties" to refer to the Khitan Liao dynasty, the Jurchen Jin dynasty, the Mongolian Yuan dynasty, and the Manchu Qing dynasty. During the long period of disruption known as the Song–Jin–Yuan transition, clothing was not only a cultural language for the Han Chinese but also a ritualistic language for the non-Han conquerors.[10] All the rulers of these conquest dynasties attempted to inflict their ethnic clothing and hairstyle on Han Chinese. Some of the regulations lasted for decades and greatly shaped clothing in daily life and in representations, such as paintings and sculpture. Even the statues of Confucius and his disciples were dressed in the "barbarian" way with their clothes folded to the left.[11]

Despite the distinctions among different ethnic styles of clothes, traditional China witnessed the continuous integration of clothing of different ethnic styles in society.[12] The cross-pollination between clothing of Chinese and that of non-Chinese origin led to the absorption of different ethnic clothing styles into the repository of theatrical costumes. Records show that performers in the Song dynasty employed clothing styles belonging to ethnic peoples in the north—in addition to the official and civilian styles of dress in Song territory. In a silk painting and a brick mural illustrating drama performances, an actress wears *diaodun* 釣墩 leggings. The wearing of *diaodun* was a Khitan and Jurchen practice prohibited by the Song government because of its ethnic nature.[13] However, drama performances were exempt from such regulations and could freely employ the item onstage.[14]

The coexistence of Chinese and non-Chinese clothing onstage continued into the Mongolian Yuan dynasty, when different styles of clothes from the previous Chinese dynasties and of different ethnic groups were synthesized.[15] Accordingly, the performance of Yuan *zaju* drama was furnished with a variety of choices for costuming, including theater costumes of the Song dynasty and ethnic clothes of the Mongolian, Khitan, and Jurchen peoples. In a widely studied Yuan-dynasty mural about a dramatic performance in northern China, some of the costumed performers wear clothing in the style of Chinese people in the Song dynasty, and one performer wears a Mongolian-style costume similar to the clothes of the troupe staff depicted in the mural.[16] The mural indicates that the costumes for *zaju* performances in the Yuan dynasty included garments from various sartorial traditions, Chinese and non-Chinese.

Countering ethnic influences, the Han Chinese rulers of the Ming dynasty, upon toppling the previous Yuan empire, embarked on a cultural campaign of eliminating Mongolian elements from various aspects of society and the sartorial system.[17] In the name of restoring the

Chinese attire of the Tang dynasty, the Hongwu emperor issued strict bans on Mongolian hairstyles, headgear, and other types of clothes. Corresponding to the sartorial reforms in society, theatrical costuming also went through a major transformation in its material configuration. Theatrical costumes of the Ming dynasty were modeled after clothes worn in Ming society.[18] For different role types, clothing could be adjusted according to the specific characters performed.[19] For example, in a *chuanqi* performance, the *sheng* role (male lead) usually features a set of dress called *jinmao* 巾帽, which included a dark robe with a round collar (*yuanling qingyi* 圓領青衣) for students, square headgear (*fangjin* 方巾) for senior scholars, and headgear with fluttering straps (*piaojin* 飄巾) for the unrestrained scholars in romantic stories.

Despite the dress regulations aimed at eliminating Mongolian influence, Ming attire incorporated sartorial elements from both the Chinese and Mongolian traditions, and the non-Chinese elements in clothing found their way into stage costumes in the Ming dynasty. A case in point is the Ming item of apparel referred to as *yesa* 曳撒, which was derived from the Mongolian *jisum* dress (質孫服).[20] After the fall of the Yuan dynasty, the garment became a ceremonial dress for eunuchs and other servants in the early Ming court. In court performances, however, it was widely used as a costume for military generals.[21] In other words, theatrical costumes in the Ming dynasty, although based largely on Ming state attire, still incorporated non-Chinese elements.

By the Ming dynasty, Chinese drama had developed sophisticated methods to represent non-Han characters through their clothing and hairstyle. For example, the Ming-dynasty anthology of *zaju* dramas *Maiwangguan chaojiaoben gujin zaju* 脈望館抄校本古今雜劇 includes costumes for Khitan, Jurchen, and Mongolian characters, providing a rare record of ethnic costuming before the Qing dynasty.[22] In an anonymous play titled *Shi tanzi da'nao Yan'anfu* 十探子大鬧延安府, the Song-dynasty official Fan Zhongyan 范仲淹 hosts a feast for a group of guests including Muslim, Jurchen, and Mongolian officials wearing ethnic clothing such as Muslim caps (*Huihui mao* 回回帽), Muslim beards (*Huihui biran* 回回鼻髯), fox-fur caps (*humao* 狐帽), and fur gowns (*maoao* 毛襖). In contrast, Fan Zhongyan and other Song officials wear apparel in the Chinese style, including the *futou* headgear, round-collar uniforms with rank badges (*buzi yuanling* 補子圓領), and official belts.[23] Since fur and leather were commonly used in non-Chinese clothing, many plays in this anthology list fur or leather apparel for the non-Chinese characters—such as leather gowns (*pi'ao* 皮襖), fur gowns (*maoao* 毛襖), and fox-fur caps with drooping straps (*lianchui humao* 練垂狐帽) for some Khitan characters.[24] Another play uses the Mongolian *gugu* cap (罟罟冠) as part of the costume for the wife of a non-Chinese general.[25] This Ming anthology also includes the Jurchen people, whom the Manchus considered their ancestors. In a play about the Song general Yue Fei's resisting the Jurchen invasion, Jin Wuzhu 金兀术 and other Jurchen generals wear fox-fur caps, fur gowns, and eggplant-shaped leather pouches, among other items.[26]

The preceding examples reveal a few important features pertaining to clothing and costuming in traditional China. Clothing distinguished ethnic groups from one another, but clothing of different ethnic styles also constantly interacted throughout Chinese history. From the Song dynasty to the Ming dynasty—a major period for the development of Chinese drama—theatrical costuming continuously drew from the real-life clothing of both Han Chinese and non-Han people. As clothes in daily life changed with dynastic transitions, theatrical costumes correspondingly incorporated new fashion as well as the clothing of different ethnic groups. In other words, the boundaries between onstage and offstage clothing were permeable. The stage prior to the Qing era was a space with a certain amount of freedom to experiment with clothing of different periods and ethnic groups. As a result, Chinese theater had formulated particular ways of representing ethnic characters using ethnic clothes. This brief survey of clothing and costuming in pre-Qing China helps clarify the importance of the Qing dynasty in shaping the meaning of clothing in drama and society.

MANCHU CLOTHING NOT FOR PLAY

How did the Ming–Qing transition influence the relations between clothing and costuming and the audience's various experiences of costuming? In what ways did these experiences shape their individual and collective identities? To discover the ways in which theatrical costuming in the Qing dynasty interacted with the spread of Manchu clothing in society, we first need to understand whether and how the Manchu government regulated theater and theatrical costuming. Historians of

Chinese theater have lauded the Manchu emperors' enthusiasm for Chinese drama. They have frequently noted the Kangxi emperor's familiarity with *kun* opera, his interest in watching drama performances during his southern inspection tours, and the fact that officials in southern China presented him with a troupe of *kunqu* performers.[27] Yet considered from a different perspective, Manchu rulers inherited and strengthened a number of antitheatrical discourses and practices. In ways similar to those found in European history, as surveyed in the work of Jonas Barish, antitheatrical practices and attitudes were continuous throughout much of Chinese history.[28] Scholars of Chinese theater have amassed a large body of materials regarding drama regulations and censorship.[29] Beginning as early as the pre-Qin period, Chinese moralists regarded performances staged for entertainment (as opposed to serving ritual needs) as corrupting and obscene. Administrations, local communities, and moralist scholars consistently voiced their aversion toward drama texts and performances down through the ages. Drama remained a marginal genre in Chinese literature, and drama performances were generally considered frivolous and unruly.[30] In addition, the Manchu rulers provided an ethnic explanation for their antagonism toward Chinese drama. In the same vein as Rousseau's wanting to protect the simple citizens of his hometown, Geneva, from the corruption of theater, the Manchus endeavored to protect the innocent Manchus and Mongolians from the corruption of Han culture.[31]

The animosity toward Chinese drama based on ethnic concerns underpinned the Manchu government's policy regarding clothing for actors and theatrical performances. From the early to mid-Qing period, existing documents suggest a shift in focus regarding governmental control, one from clothing offstage to clothing onstage. In regulating actors' clothes, the Manchu government followed precedents set by previous dynasties. Viewing theatrical performance as a low profession, the changing governments in traditional China maintained regulations over the dress of performers. In the Jin and Yuan dynasties, theatrical performers offstage were required to respect the dress codes for commoners, whereas onstage they were allowed to wear embellished costumes.[32] The Ming government bolstered the distinction between clothes for performers and those for ordinary people. The Hongwu emperor issued a series of edicts over a period of two decades, one of which dictated, "In every-day life, performers in the Office of Music Instruction should wear green headgear so their attire will be differentiated from that of scholars and commoners."[33] These regulations were based primarily on people's social status, not their ethnic identities.

The Manchu regime developed dress regulations by imposing stricter rules on performers' routine dress. The early Qing government prohib-ited performers and other groups of low social status from wearing silk or fine fur in everyday life—materials reserved for people of higher social status.[34] At least one historical source provides specific information about actors' hairstyles in early Qing China. In 1653, two actors were arrested because they had not shaved their heads. The document records the two actors' plea: "We are actors willing to dress up as women onstage, so we have not shaved our heads. There are people like us in every prov-ince." The Shunzhi emperor immediately rejected their excuse, issuing an edict regarding the crime: "An edict issued earlier stipulates that those who do not shave their heads are to be executed. Was there ever an order that allowed actors to keep their hair?... Henceforth it is publicly stated and strictly commanded for all persons both inside and outside [the pal-ace] that whoever has not shaved his hair on account of being an actor should immediately shave it in accordance with the law."[35] Early Qing actors took the liberty of preserving their hair because of their identity onstage as female characters. The imperial edict accentuated a clear divi-sion between stage and routine life. Although actors continued to use Han-style costumes in drama performances, in daily life they were required to adopt the Manchu hairstyle and clothing. More than a cen-tury later (1784), the Qianlong emperor also issued edicts prohibiting actors from keeping their hair. In response, the governor of Suzhou reported that actors in Suzhou wore a hairnet (*wangjin* 網巾) made from real hair only onstage, and that all actors would shave their heads upon turning fifteen years old.[36]

If the Manchu administration demanded that actors dress like other male subjects offstage, how did it govern costuming onstage? Compared with the governmental regulations about clothing and hairstyles in soci-ety, we are left with few records relating to Manchu regulation of theat-rical costumes in the early Qing period. A group of official documents from the mid-Qing period reveal the Manchu government's rejection of the use of Manchu clothing onstage. In the late eighteenth century, the Qianlong emperor initiated a campaign to purge dramas in southern China. In the edict initiating the campaign (1780), the emperor wrote,

> I consider that certain playscripts may be in partial violation [of the regulations]. For example, in plays about events of the late Ming or the beginning of our own dynasty, there might be words and sentences pertaining to our dynasty. The entire corpus of such plays should certainly be inspected and censored. As to plays touching on the Southern Song and the Jin dynasties, their performances outside the court are frequently unreasonable to the extent of being counterfactual. When these plays circulate widely for a prolonged period, undiscerning people might regard the playscripts as recording facts. This is of special import. These plays should also all be inspected and censored.[37]

In the edict, the Qianlong emperor expressed his concerns about two aspects of plays: first, words and sentences (*ziju* 字句) touching on the Ming–Qing transition and the Song–Jin confrontation, and second, inappropriate performance (*banyan* 扮演) of these plays.

It is conceivable that any word pertaining to the Ming–Qing transition or other ethnic conflicts would be considered a violation (*weiai* 違礙).[38] In a 1780 report to the emperor, salt commissioner Yiling'a 伊齡阿 brought up the issue of costuming: "The scenes performed are derived largely from novels and drum songs. Occasionally, plays include events from the Southern Song, the Yuan, and the Ming dynasties. When the events relate to our current dynasty, the performances even use the clothing and colors of our own dynasty [*benchao fuse* 本朝服色]. The scripts are rather unorthodox."[39] *Fuse* refers to clothing and colors of the sumptuary code established by a dynasty upon its establishment. In the context of drama performance, the phrase *benchao fuse* translates as "attire of our dynasty." Manchu-style clothes in the Qing dynasty involved two different groups of apparel: those stipulated by the Manchu government and worn on official occasions and those worn by ordinary people in everyday life. It is probable that the Manchu emperor and officials were most concerned about Manchu official attire being represented in drama performances.

Yiling'a's report juxtaposes Manchu clothing, unorthodox words, and Song–Yuan–Ming history as reasons for censoring the dramas. Another record provides more information about the censoring of presenting Manchu clothing in drama. Nong Qi 農起, governor of Anhui, reported the result of drama censorship in 1781: "However, when performing nonspecific women from foreign countries in the late-Tang and Five Dynasties periods, the attire of our dynasty is employed inappropriately. There are also cases [of performance] that insult the sages or worthies of antiquity. Your subject has had them individually censored and prohibited them from being performed again."[40] Ming drama had employed ethnic dress such as the Mongolian *gugu* cap for non-Chinese women. Although Nong Qi did not mention specific titles, his report indicates that by the mid-Qing period Manchu women's clothing had occasionally been used to portray non-Han women. According to the report, the Manchu government not only prohibited the use of men's clothes in the Manchu style but also considered Manchu women's clothing as part of "the attire of our dynasty" and prohibited its use onstage.

Ye Xiaoqing points to two aspects of theatrical practices under censorship in the Qing dynasty: "The practice of non-Chinese characters in drama wearing Manchu costumes" and "any drama based on stories which supposedly occurred during the Qing."[41] The first part of Ye's proposition points to the ban on using Manchu clothing for non-Chinese characters. The second part of the quote refers to the censorship of dramas based on current affairs. Even in dramas on current affairs without reference to Manchu ethnicity, Manchu clothing appeared to be a major concern as well. In 1781, Hao Shuo 郝碩, governor of Jiangxi province, identified seven plays that violated the stated rules: "Among the three dramas singled out, *The Temple of the Red Gate* [*Hongmen si* 紅門寺] uses the attire of our dynasty, and the *Sheath of Heaven and Earth* [*Qiankun qiao* 乾坤鞘] draws on historical events during the Song and Jin dynasties—both dramas should be banned."[42] *The Temple of the Red Gate* was a popular drama in the Qianlong era. The play features renowned Qing governor Yu Chenglong 于成龍 (1617–1684), who, dressed in plain clothes, visits a Buddhist temple to uncover the crimes of an evil monk who has abducted and imprisoned women. As the governor's report indicates, in the performance, Yu (and perhaps other characters as well) was dressed in clothing of the Qing state—an official uniform in the Manchu style. The drama was censored simply because Manchu official attire was employed to represent a contemporary figure.

These scattered materials indicate that at least in the first one and a half centuries of the Qing dynasty, Manchu clothing remained front and center. In the early Qing period, the Manchu government was concerned primarily with hairstyles and clothing for men in society, including actors offstage. In the mid-Qing period, Manchu clothing became an explicit item to be censored from dramas. The fact that the Qianlong emperor exercised stricter control over drama scripts and performances indicates increasing theatrical practices that posed a threat to perceived Manchu identity.[43] Although we can find no legal code or official edict in early Qing China regarding the use of Manchu clothing onstage, it is conceivable that theatrical practitioners readily understood the sensitivity related to representing Manchu people and Manchu clothing onstage and thus avoided such representations.

Andrea Goldman discusses the Manchu state's efforts to impose ethnic segregation in the theater: "The ethnic and social heterogeneity of the crowds in the commercial playhouse caused anxiety in the eyes of the apartheid regime—a regime that viewed Manchu difference (and hence purity) as central to its claim to legitimacy."[44] This observation may help explain the mentality behind the Manchu government's regulation of theatrical costumes. Similar to the governmental effort to protect Manchu people from Chinese drama, Manchu rulers carefully policed the stage to separate Han clothing from Manchu clothing and that of other ethnic groups. In contrast to the Han Chinese, who considered Manchu clothing as part of an alien culture, the Manchu rulers regarded Manchu clothing as a symbol of their self-identity that needed to be kept out of Chinese drama.

WAS MANCHU CLOTHING USED ON THE EARLY QING STAGE?

Despite evidence of governmental prohibitions against using Manchu clothing in drama performances, whether or not certain types of Manchu clothing were adopted in early Qing drama remains an open question. To verify whether Manchu clothing was absent on the early Qing stage, we must examine extant costumes as material objects, records of court and commercial performances, and drama scripts—a project well beyond the scope of this book. In this chapter, I provide a brief survey of the stage use of Manchu clothing based on available documents about drama performances inside and outside the Manchu court.

In traditional Chinese drama performance there are two terms that involve Manchu-style clothing: *qingzhuang xi* 清裝戲 and *qizhuang xi* 旗裝戲. The former refers to any drama performance with any type of Manchu-style clothes; the latter refers specifically to Beijing opera performance featuring *qipao* and other pieces of Manchu women's clothes on the late Qing stage.[45] According to theater scholar Qi Rushan 齊如山, Beijing opera performance employed a number of items derived from Manchu clothing: *jianyi* 箭衣 or *jianxiu* 箭袖 (archer's robe, usually with horseshoe-shaped cuffs), *magua* 馬褂 (horse jacket), *qiumao* 秋帽 (autumn hat, based on the Manchu hat used in winter), *weimao* 緯帽 (based on the Manchu hat used in summer), and more generally *qizhuang* or *qiyi* 旗裝／衣 (Manchu dress).[46] It is Qi's opinion that Manchu-style costumes were a new fashion trend emerging toward the beginning of the twentieth century, not a practice passed down from earlier theatrical tradition.[47] Liu Yuemei, another expert on Chinese theater costumes, points out other costumes derived from Manchu clothing, such as *qimang* 旗蟒 (Manchu python robe), *bufu* 補服 (coat with a rank badge), and *longgua* 龍褂 (dragon gown).[48] These discussions provide clues for us to trace the possible use of Manchu clothing in Qing drama.

Figure 1.1 shows a set of theatrical jacket and skirt for onstage warriors modeled after the Manchu-style armor (*Manzhou jia* 滿洲甲) in Qing China. The bright yellow color and the python decoration indicate it was possibly worn by imperial guards. Many features of the costume resemble those of the Qianlong emperor's military armor as shown in *Qianlong Emperor in Ceremonial Armor on Horseback* (乾隆帝大閱鎧甲騎馬像), painted by the Italian Jesuit Giuseppe Castiglione (1688–1766, Chinese name Lang Shining). For example, both the costume and the imperial armor use fabric in lieu of metal for the convenience of performance—either theatrical or ritual.[49] Figure 1.2 shows another item of military costume. With the decoration of five-claw dragons and the employment of various choice materials, the costume was likely used in performances related to the emperor. Wang Hebei's 王鶴北 study suggests that such theater costumes were probably produced during the Kangxi

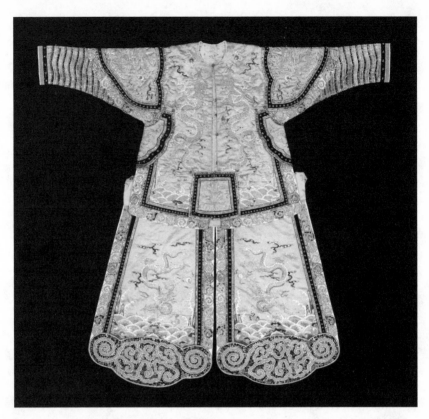

FIGURE 1.1 Theatrical jacket and skirt for a warrior, satin, Kangxi period. Minneapolis Institute of Art, accession no. 42.8.127a–e.

era and used in the early Qing court.[50] He also points out that costumes for the court troupe were produced by the Jiangnan General Manufacturing Bureau (Jiangnan Zhizao 江南織造), and that the costumes' materials and technical sophistication measured up to the court apparel produced by the same bureau.[51] Existing early Qing theater costumes in the Manchu style are largely military uniforms.[52] Although the costume in figure 1.1 is no longer commonly seen in *kun* or Beijing opera performances, the one in figure 1.2 could be an early example of the *kao* 靠 armor in Chinese drama performances.[53]

Despite existing pieces of costume attesting to the use of Manchu clothing onstage, Manchu clothing did not appear prominently in textual records of court performances. Court performances in the Qing

FIGURE 1.2 Theatrical jacket and skirt for a warrior, satin, Kangxi period. Minneapolis Institute of Art, accession no. 42.8.126a, b.

dynasty included three main types: ritual performances at agrarian or imperial festivals such as weddings and birthdays—usually in the form of short *zaju* dramas; grand plays in the form of lengthy *chuanqi* dramas; and selected scenes from popular dramas.[54] *Gugong zhenben congkan* 故宮珍本叢刊 includes a series of drama scripts for performance at ritual festivals in the court throughout the Qing dynasty. Some of these texts were used by the Bureau of Ascendant Peace (Shengping Shu 昇平署, the office in charge of entertainment within the Imperial Household) after 1827. The others could have been produced in the bureaus of Nanfu 南府 and Jingshan 景山 at a relatively early date.[55]

In the first type of performances, the costume instructions demonstrate that most performances at the Qing court used traditional costumes in the Han style. In a drama about a family festival, a scholar and his grandchildren wear caps and belts (*guandai* 冠帶) and scholarly dress with headgear (*jinfu* 巾服)—the Han-style dress for scholars.[56] In another play, an official appears wearing a black gauze cap (*wusha mao* 烏紗帽)— the Han-style uniform for officials in the Ming dynasty.[57] A more revealing example involves rulers from foreign countries paying their respects to the Qing court. In *A Gathering of Kings in an Era of Great Tranquility* (*Taiping wanghui* 太平王會), performed by the Shengping Shu, the *sheng* role is clothed in the Ming uniform of a round-collar robe with a gauze cap and a belt to perform the minister in the Office of Foreign Affairs (Huitong Guan 會同館).[58] As Ye Xiaoqing points out, "usually the tributary dramas had no particular reference to the current dynasty or current events."[59] As for the "barbarians" from the four directions, the playscript indicates that they can dress in whatever way desired and speak in foreign languages, meaning that there was not a prescribed way to dress these characters.[60]

Beginning in the Kangxi reign, the Manchu emperors commissioned the composition of "grand plays" (*daxi* 大戲) based on novels and tales from classical Chinese literature. This ceremonial repertoire was continuously expanded, edited, and performed throughout the Qing dynasty. One of the earliest grand plays is *Quanshan jinke* 勸善金科. According to Song Junhua's study of the plays' Qianlong edition, the Manchu court performances of the drama did not include any costume explicitly in the Manchu style except for the wide use of the archer's robe.[61] Likewise, a Qianlong edition of *Shengping baofa* 昇平寶筏, another grand play, includes no explicit reference to Manchu-style costumes.[62]

The third type of performance comprised selected scenes from popular dramas. We can gain an understanding of this type of performance by examining *Kangxi wanshou tujuan* 康熙萬壽圖卷, a scroll painting recording the celebrations for the Kangxi emperor's sixtieth birthday in 1713. Scholars have identified the staging of sixteen selected scenes portrayed in the scroll. Fourteen of these scenes were recorded in *A Register of Costumes* (*Chuandai tigang* 穿戴題綱), a document about court performances compiled in the nineteenth century.[63] My examination of these records confirms that early Qing court performances did not widely use Manchu-style clothes other than the archer's robe. Finally, an existing document from the Bureau of Internal Affairs (Neiwu Fu 內務府) lists the costumes employed by the imperial theater in the Qianlong era. Again, among 1,776 costume pieces, there are no costumes of Manchu ethnicity other than the commonly used archer's robe.[64]

The situation of costumes in popular theater largely accorded with that in court performances in early Qing China. *Patched White Fur* (*Zhui baiqiu* 綴白裘), a drama collection compiled in the Qianlong era, includes scenes popular on the early Qing stage. A majority of the plays in the anthology are part of the received repertoire before the beginning of the Qing dynasty. While the anthology was revised and expanded over time, it included an increasing number of plays composed and performed in the early Qing period. Similar to the court playscripts, *Patched White Fur* does not include any mention of costumes explicitly featuring Manchu-style clothing.

In all these documents, the archer's robe with horseshoe-shaped cuffs is the only piece of costume that frequently appears in early Qing drama scripts, especially those for court performances.[65] The Manchus regarded the archer's robe as one of the most representative pieces of their ethnic clothing. In Qing dramas, it was a typical costume for male soldiers.[66] If we compare the costumes in Ming dramas found in *Maiwangguan chaojiaoben gujin zaju* and those in Qing dramas such as *Quanshan jinke*, it is true that the archer's robe was an item widely used only in drama performances of the Qing dynasty.[67] However, whether this information testifies to the employment of Manchu clothing in Qing drama is debatable. For one thing, the Manchu-style archer's robe developed from a similar design in Mongolian dress of the Yuan dynasty and was not an item of the official Manchu clothes prescribed by the Manchu government. For another, Ming dramas had already made use of a similar item of costuming in texts and stage performances. For example, an garment referred to as archer's dress (*jianyi* 箭衣) had already appeared in some Ming-dynasty dramas.[68] Both *jianxiu* and *jianyi* were used for military characters, the possible difference being that *jianyi* in the Ming dynasty did not have the horseshoe-shaped cuffs, which in all likelihood were incorporated into theatrical costumes in the early Qing period.[69] Liu Yuemei explicitly holds that the *jianyi* costume in Beijing and *kun* opera originated from the *jianyi* used in Ming society and that Manchu elements were later added to the costume in the Qianlong era.[70]

What does all this information allow us to infer about early Qing costuming? Undeniably, Manchu clothing started to infiltrate the theatrical space: some Manchu garments, especially military uniforms, were employed in court performances; performances outside the court also occasionally used Manchu uniforms, leading to the emperor's explicit prohibition against the practice; sartorial elements bearing Manchu characteristics were also integrated with new designs in stage costumes. Just as in previous dynasties, clothing and costuming continued to cross-pollinate alongside the establishment of Qing rule. Meanwhile, the Manchu regime was attentive to the stage use of Manchu-specific state attire, especially official dress for men and women.

This brief foray by no means provides an exhaustive study of theatrical costumes in early Qing theater, but it suffices to suggest that Manchu clothing was used on a limited scale in court performances and was regarded as taboo in popular performances outside the court. The Manchu rulers' regulations pertaining to theatrical costumes were based on their understanding of self-other relations mediated by theater. Regarding theater as a realm of the Han Chinese, they assigned Han-style clothing as the dress code for the stage. Although they occasionally used Manchu clothing for a Manchu royal audience within the court, they believed it blasphemous for popular theater to tamper with sacred Manchu clothing.

The Manchu ruler's understanding of theater and costuming contradicted the costuming practices on the Shakespearean stage. As Robert Lublin points out, in Renaissance English theater, frequent references to apparel "nearly always mention contemporary items commonly worn in England" and "plays were rarely, if ever, costumed entirely in foreign fashions."[71] In world history, dress regulation has been a strategy of political rule in colonial contexts, such as sixteenth-century Ireland, eighteenth-century Scotland, and twentieth-century South Asia.[72] Yet in none of these cases was theatrical costuming specifically targeted. Thus, the Ming–Qing transition in mid-seventeenth-century China constitutes a rare case when theatrical costuming was problematized by ethnic relations.

MANCHUS AS THEATER AUDIENCE

With Manchu clothing prevalent in society and yet largely absent onstage, the Ming–Qing transition in mid-seventeenth-century China abruptly severed the connection between clothing and onstage costuming. The separation between the social and theatrical spaces created a complex sartorial landscape whose meaning was yet to be interpreted by different parties. Did the Manchus watch drama performances in the first place? If so, which group(s) among them watched these performances and how did they view onstage Han clothing? Andrea Goldman has provided a thorough account of the primary performance venues in Beijing in the eighteenth and nineteenth centuries and the state control of different types of border crossing enabled by these performance events.[73] Although Goldman's study focuses on the period after the 1770s, it, together with a limited amount of existing evidence, nonetheless affords a general understanding of Manchu people's view of theatrical costuming.

The Manchu government's regulation of drama enacted a segregation that paralleled a separation of ethnic communities. During the Qing dynasty, the majority of the Manchu people in Beijing and some garrison cities lived in Manchu cities (*Mancheng* 滿城), isolated from Han people.[74] In his tenth year on the throne (1671), the Kangxi emperor issued an edict to permanently prohibit the building of playhouses (*xiguan* 戲館) in the inner city.[75] The following Yongzheng emperor explicitly prohibited Manchu people from watching drama performances. An imperial edict issued in the second year of the Yongzheng reign (1724) discusses the livelihood of people belonging to the eight Manchu banners (*baqi Manzhou* 八旗滿洲). It reaffirmed the ban on Manchu people visiting performance sites and playhouses (*gechang xiguan* 歌場 戲館) and encouraged them to practice the Manchu language, horse riding, and archery (*Qingyu qishe* 清語騎射).[76] An imperial edict issued in the forty-fifth year of the Qianlong reign (1780) reemphasized the ban against Manchu people renting houses outside the inner city.[77] The Jiaqing emperor (1760–1820) continued to lament that innocent Mongolian people (allies of the Manchus) had been corrupted by detrimental Han doctrines and drama performances (1816).[78] These examples represent a large number of imperial edicts denouncing drama performance as a Han Chinese practice to be kept at bay, especially away from the Manchus. The edicts were collected as statutes in different types of official documents throughout the Qing dynasty.[79] They demonstrate the Manchu rulers' concern about theatrical performance not only in the capital of Beijing but also among Manchu and Mongolian communities statewide.

Although the Manchu rulers tried to keep drama performances away from the Manchu community except for a limited group within the imperial court, the effect of the bans was questionable.[80] As Goldman points out, "even as playhouses crept into the Inner City, high-ranking officials and bannermen crept into the Outer City playhouses."[81] A Qing official complained in a 1736 report, "Who imagined that nowadays once the playhouses are open, more than half of those indulging in drinking therein are bannermen."[82] We can infer from these documents that in the early Qing period, Manchu people, especially those in major cities of the empire, were not completely obstructed from experiencing drama performances in theater settings.

Manchu people enjoyed more freedom to watch drama performances at salons and temple fairs than inside a playhouse. Goldman's study shows that "Han, Banner, and Manchu households all hosted salon performances" during the Qing dynasty.[83] Considered by Goldman as "an extreme expression of salon performance,"[84] theater in the imperial palace resumed upon the founding of the Qing dynasty. Following the Ming, the early Qing government established the Office of Music Instruction (Jiaofang Si 教坊司) as part of the Ministry of Rites. During the Kangxi reign, the Manchu government established two institutes, Nanfu and Jingshan, to oversee drama performances within the court.[85] These imperial institutions were responsible for music and drama performances held for festivals, state ceremonies, and the entertainment of the imperial family.

Within the Manchu court, Han clothing for both men and women became a device for the amusement of Manchu rulers. Art historian Wu Hung has discussed early Qing portrait paintings in which the Yongzheng emperor and his twelve concubines are depicted in Han clothing, perceptively suggesting that the portraits symbolize "a defeated nation that was given an image of an extended feminine space with all its charm, exoticism, and vulnerability."[86] Just as the defeated Ming state was assigned the feminine space, traditional (male) Han clothing was relegated to the theatrical space. The feminine and the theatrical share the feature of being subordinate and inferior. From as early as the Kangxi era, the Manchu court recruited both eunuchs and performers from outside the palace to enact drama performances.[87] When these eunuchs wore Han-style costumes onstage to entertain the Manchu imperial

FIGURE 1.3 Stage characters bowing to the imperial carriage. Detail of *Wanshou tu* 萬壽圖, 1799, in *Putian tongqing: Qingdai wanshou shengdian* 普天同慶：清代萬壽 盛典, ed. Gugong Bowuyuan 故宮博物院 (Beijing: Gugong chubanshe, 2015), 78–79.

family, what the Manchu audience perceived was not Ming state attire but a defeated culture subjugated to Manchu power.

Besides commercial theater and salon performances, temple fairs in urban and rural settings provided opportunities for people of different genders and ethnicities to mingle as audience members of drama performances.[88] The festival in celebration of the Kangxi emperor's sixtieth birthday serves as an example of the display of traditional Chinese clothing in front of an ethnically mixed audience in public. As shown in figure 1.3, eight performers, dressed in Han-style costumes, are likely performing the Eight Daoist Immortals during the celebration of the Kangxi emperor's sixtieth birthday.[89] As the empress dowager's carriage passes by, the eight characters kneel down to pay their obeisance. If their onstage Han-style costumes represent traditional Han culture, the performers' submission to the Manchu imperial family would only strengthen the dominant role of Manchu culture and the forlorn situation of Han culture. This would appear to be the logic by which the Qing emperors allowed drama performances using Han clothing to continue—the stage was reserved for the conquered.

CHINESE EXPERIENCE OF THEATRICAL COSTUMING

If the Manchu strategy of relegating Han clothing to the theater was meant for Han Chinese to continually reexperience their defeat as an ethnic group, the Chinese audience interpreted theatrical costuming in varying ways. The late Qing scholar Xu Ke 徐珂 (1869–1928) provided a succinct observation to this effect: "Ever since entering the current dynasty, all men shave their heads and are dressed with gowns and jackets. Because dramas stage ancient events, they have roughly preserved the decorum of Han culture [*Hanguan weiyi* 漢官威儀]. Thus, they have largely remained unchanged over the past two centuries, although there have been frequent amendments and embellishments at any given time."[90] This entry, titled "Theatrical Costumes" (Xingtou 行頭), recapitulates the relation between theatrical costumes and traditional Chinese clothing throughout the Qing dynasty. It points out the changes in hairstyle and dress as a precondition for theater to sustain the sartorial tradition of pre-Qing China.

Written as a historical account at the end of the Qing dynasty, Xu's record does not provide information about possible emotional responses to theatrical costumes. For some Chinese intellectuals in the early Qing period, the theatrical world became the only space for authentic Chinese culture to exist. Some materials directly record Ming loyalists' experiences of watching drama performances. In 1644, the first year of the Qing dynasty, a Han Chinese scholar named Liu Cheng 劉城 (1598–1650), living in seclusion in his hometown, composed a series of fifty-two poems in conversation with his son. One of them reads as follows:

A PLAY PERFORMANCE

This drama is played by whom?
Red sandalwood clappers click night to morn.
Disparate emotions all combined for the moment,

Assorted poses left for the detached observer.
Prohibitions and taboo erase [barbarian] dance,
Leaving mere Han attire for gazing.
Few seated understand music as did Young Master Zhou,
Indulging themselves in fleeting joys and sorrows.

優戲

院本誰家奏，紅牙度夜闌。
群情皆假合，諸態落旁觀。
禁忌刪胡舞，留遺見漢冠。
周郎座上少，概是浪悲歡。[91]

Liu Cheng's poem preserves a rare record of the careful policing of the stage by the Manchus in the early years of the new dynasty. "Barbarian dance" refers to styles of dances that originated from ethnic peoples in northern China, most notably the famous "barbarian whirl." The barbarian whirl was originally a Sogdian dance associated with An Lushan in the Tang dynasty. In Yuan–Ming dramas, it referred to a specific type of dance performed by non-Chinese characters, usually those defeated by the Chinese. Thus barbarian dance in a drama performance was a highly charged symbol representing subdued northerners. While the first line of the third couplet mentions styles of dancing, the second line addresses clothing. The expression *liuyi* 留遺 (to leave behind) indicates a unique position of the stage in the sartorial landscape: the stage was the only space "left" for the display of Han attire. Together, the two lines in the couplet reflect a control over signs onstage—those associated with northerners became politically sensitive and the existing Han clothing triggered nostalgia among Ming loyalists.

Although both are about audience experiences, the two quatrains of the poem disclose two different ways of viewing and understanding the play performance. The first quatrain describes the spectators viewing the performance from a distance (*pangguan* 旁觀) and experiencing joy and sorrow through staged emotions and poses. Most of them, according to the author, did not decipher the true meaning of the performance. The word *jian* 見 in the third couplet indicates the author's active viewing of the theatrical costumes. Only the author and a few audience members

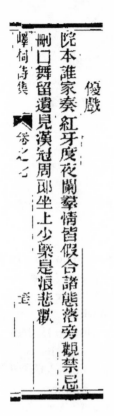

FIGURE 1.4 A woodblock page with Liu Cheng's poem "A Play Performance". Liu Cheng 劉城, *Yitong shiji* 嶧桐詩集, 1893, *juan* 7, 30a, in *Siku jinhuishu congkan* 四庫禁燬書叢刊 (Beijing: Beijing chubanshe, 2000), *jibu*, 121:621.

were able to ascertain the policing of symbols with ethnic connotations. The poem describes layers of feelings triggered by the play. Some audiences were moved by the play's music and plotline, while others, including the author, experienced sorrow over the changing states and clothes.

The author uses the phrase "prohibitions and taboo" (*jinji* 禁忌) to account for the excision of the barbarian dance. The word "taboo" captures the nature of drama censorship in the early Qing period. Liu's writings were published posthumously by his children in the 1670s, and later in the Qianlong era his works were banned because of their politically incorrect accounts of the Ming–Qing transition.[92] In a woodblock print of the book produced in 1893 (figure 1.4), the fifth line of the poem lacks the character for "barbarian" (*hu* 胡), which is replaced by an empty square indicating censorship of the poem. Although it is unclear when or how the character for *hu* was deleted, we can be certain that not only were barbarian dancing and clothing prohibited onstage but also censorship against writings on ethnicity lasted throughout the Qing dynasty.

Liu Cheng lamented that few people in the audience understood the political message embedded in the performance. Even if they did perceive the message, it would have been impossible for them to vocally communicate about it because of the topic's sensitivity. Writing at roughly the same time, a scholar, Li Shengguang 李生光 (b. 1595), openly expressed his admiration for the Han attire onstage.

WATCHING A DRAMA PERFORMANCE

How admirable are the singers and the dancers in the Pear Garden;
Their robes and caps kept neatly and properly in the antique style.
My breast full of desire "to keep the sheep for love of the ancient ritual,"
At the performance site, I can only nod my head in secret approval.

觀戲
堪羨梨園歌舞儔，衣冠楚楚舊風流。
一腔愛禮存羊意，但是逢場暗點頭。[93]

Poems of this kind show that some early Qing scholars considered theatrical costuming an isolated means for preserving traditional Chinese ritual and its embodiment in clothing. That perception, however, could be shared only in silence among those present at the performance.

According to one account, some Ming loyalists considered the theatrical world to be more desirable than the real world and became actors to preserve their Han-style clothing:

Wang Chenzhang was a great-grandson of Wang Zaijin, former minister of military affairs in the Ming dynasty. He was good at singing songs and boasted a handsome countenance. In his late years he lived in Yue city. In the *yiyou* year of the Shunzhi reign [1645], the provincial officials pressed him to change his clothes. Chenzhang convened a group of ten gentlemen in the community. Together, they abandoned their identity as Confucian scholars and became actors. People referred to them as the Ten-Gentlemen

Troupe since it was a theatrical group consisting of ten noblemen. A verse by Li Echen reads, "Each mister of the Ten-Gentlemen Troupe / in cap and gown of the former dynasty, bows to the tasseled crown."[94]

Even as actors, they still could not retain their hair and found solace only in the Han-style costumes used onstage. Such was their dismay with the banishment of Han-style clothing that the literati gentlemen chose a life of "self-exile" on the stage. The poetic commentary at the end of the piece imagines a performance by the ten gentlemen actors in which a crowned emperor receives the worship of his subjects wearing the attire of the former Ming dynasty (guguo). The last line alludes to a poem by the Tang-dynasty poet Wang Wei 王維, the first half of which reads as follows:

The crimson-capped watchman delivers the signal of dawn;
The apparel officer presents the fur robe with azure cloud.
Nine layers of heavenly gates open the palatial edifices;
Caps and gowns [of envoys] of myriad states bow to the tasseled
    crown.

絳幘雞人送曉籌, 尚衣方進翠雲裘。
九天閶闔開宮殿, 萬國衣冠拜冕旒。[95]

Wang Wei's poem describes the cosmopolitan empire of the Tang dynasty. The imperial dress in the poem symbolizes the refined culture and political power of Tang China and the envoys' clothes symbolize foreign countries in submission to China. In contrast to the cosmopolitanism seen in the poem, Li Echen's couplet describes a closed space of the stage. The garments on display are not the attire of tributary countries but rather the clothes of the former Ming dynasty. Although the story's authenticity is questionable, it reflects the special role of theater in the sartorial space of early Qing China and Chinese scholars' response to the phenomenon.

Beyond these scattered records, there are few substantial literati commentaries on the political meaning of theatrical costuming in early Qing China—the overall silence on the issue is indicative of its sensitivity in early Qing society. For Ming loyalists in early Qing China, Han-style clothing, either onstage or in society, would have immediately invoked political nostalgia for the defunct Ming dynasty, as witnessed by Korean visitors who dressed in a manner modeled after Ming attire.[96] Yi Yo 李澝 (1622–1658) noted that when he arrived in Beijing in 1656, "Upon seeing my attire in the eastern style, none of the Chinese people failed to become tearful."[97] The dress of the Korean visitors reminded early Qing Chinese of the state attire of the Ming dynasty. The cultural nostalgia triggered by clothes subsequently diminished. When another Korean envoy, Yi Tŏkmu 李德懋 (1741–1793), visited Beijing a hundred years later, he noticed a different situation. Surprised to see the foreigners' dress, many Chinese people surrounded them and laughingly pointed out, "[Their clothes] are identical to [those] in stage performances" (場戲一樣).[98] Yi promptly explained that Chinese people compared his clothing to theatrical costumes because all theater performers wore traditional clothes. For Chinese in the Qianlong era, the Korean attire, which used to be reminiscent of Ming attire, had by then become analogous with stage costumes. Han-style clothing, either onstage or on the bodies of Korean envoys, no longer invoked political nostalgia as in the early Qing era.

The connection between stage costumes and Ming state attire, however, was never entirely cut off. During the anti-Manchu rebellions in the eighteenth and nineteenth centuries—some of which were led by members of theatrical troupes—the rebel armies used theatrical costumes as makeshift uniforms. As Daphne Pi-Wei Lei points out, "Dressing up as Ming characters was a way for rebels to demonstrate their identity as true Chinese."[99] In 1904, when the revolutionary Chen Qubing 陳去病 wrote "On the Benefits of Drama" (Lun xiju zhi youyi 論戲劇之有益), he made a similar argument to claims offered by early Qing scholars, "The might and demeanor of Han culture [Hanguan weiyi] now exists only among actors in the Pear Garden."[100] Throughout the Qing dynasty, theatrical costuming served as an important medium for shaping the relationship between Manchus and Han Chinese. Theatrical costuming not only provided Han Chinese multifaceted experiences—such as the humiliation of defeat and nostalgia for past splendor—but also furnished anti-Manchu activities with models of dress.

The rupture between clothing and costuming in the early Qing period had long-lasting effects, not least for foreign visitors during their first encounter with Chinese theater. The records preserved from Korean envoys cited earlier illustrate the changing perceptions of stage costumes among Han Chinese from the early to the mid-Qing period. Other notes by Korean envoys reveal their complicated mentality when seeing theatrical costumes in Qing China.[101]

When the Korean envoy Kim Ch'ang-ŏp 金昌業 visited Qing China in 1712, he watched a series of drama performances in Yongping prefecture. At the end of his note, he discusses the significance of theater in preserving China's sartorial tradition: "What was worth admiring in the attire of the previous dynasties and the customs of the central plain is still presented [in the performance] today. This is probably the reason why the latter generations of Han people still admire the Chinese tradition. This point well illustrates why we still cannot do without actors."[102] By the early decades of the eighteenth century, most of the Ming loyalists who personally experienced the turmoil of the dynastic transition had passed away. In his note, Kim mentions the appreciation of Chinese traditions among the people he met and readily makes a connection between that cultural nostalgia and the Han-style costumes he witnessed onstage.

Most of the Korean envoys after Kim recorded paradoxical attitudes of despising and valuing theater. Traveling to Beijing in 1765, Hong Taeyong 洪大榮 recorded an anecdote that surprised and amused him: "We met about a dozen performers inside our lodgings carrying various instruments. They expressed the intention to buy hairnets from us. Since theater costumes retain the attire of the previous dynasty, the hairnets were indispensable. If someone among our group did not take care in storing them, they were frequently stolen."[103] The Korean envoy wrote in a mocking tone that the Chinese performers stole Korean hairnets to be used as part of stage costumes. The observation confirms the resemblance between theatrical costumes in early Qing China and the attire of the previous Ming dynasty. Hong particularly mentioned *wangjin*, a typical Ming-dynasty headgear the Manchu government prohibited from being used in society. Meanwhile, Hong describes Chinese actors as despicable thieves, in whose eyes Korean attire was little more than stage props. By simply juxtaposing the two phrases of "theater costumes" (*xichang zhuang* 戲場裝) and "attire of the previous dynasty" (*qianchao yiguan* 前朝衣冠) without any further explication, Hong's words capture the lamentable fate of Ming attire. Despite the disdainful attitude toward actors, Hong recognizes the important role of theater in Qing China: "The dramas are obscene and decadent and therefore must be banned by the imperial administration. However, following the fall of the land, [theater] preserves Han demeanor and ages of clothing for the remnant subjects to admire and for future rulers to emulate. It is thus no trivial matter."[104] Hong provides a typical narrative about the Korean envoy's view on the relation between theatrical costumes and Ming attire. In his narrative, stage costumes are no longer derivative from and thus secondary to clothing in society. Instead, costumes replaced actual clothes to be the only palpable signs of the Chinese sartorial tradition.

From a third-person perspective, a Korean envoy speculated on the Manchu rulers' purpose of regulating theater and costuming. Yi Hŏnmuk 李憲默 recorded watching a drama performance by the roadside in 1761: "We therefore know that stately demeanor also arises out of appropriate attire. The interpreters explained that the Qing people deliberately arranged such drama performances as a way to humiliate Han officials. However, should some true leaders rise [against the Qing] and attempt to restore the protocols established by the Hongwu emperor, are the protocols not present here? Are they not present here?"[105] Similar to Hong, Yi recognizes the political and cultural significance of theatrical costuming. As shown in the second half of the quote, the writer observed that the stage preserved a sanctuary for Ming culture that could be restored by true rulers in the future. Meanwhile, Yi recounted some Chinese or Korean interpreters' explanation that the stage performance was set up to humiliate Han Chinese. The paragraph discusses the relation between clothing, theater, and cultural dignity. In this context, the expression *hanguan* 漢官 carries a strong indication of Han-style clothing.[106] Although the author does not specify how theater was used to humiliate Han officials, the context indicates that the humiliation was directed toward Han clothing. Thus interpreted, the sentence appears to be one of the most explicit indications that the Manchu rulers allowed Han-style costumes to remain onstage as a way to embarrass Han Chinese.

Observations on theater abound in Korean envoys' diaries, which, from a visitor's perspective, illustrate the complicated mentalities of Han Chinese, Manchus, and Korean visitors regarding theatrical costuming in early Qing China. Ge Zhaoguang has discussed the Korean envoys' observation and imagination of theatrical costuming in Qing China. As he notes, whether it was Chinese people's intention to retain Han-style clothing onstage is debatable, but the Korean envoys, throughout much of Qing history, chose to believe and highlight the theater's role in preserving China's sartorial tradition.[107]

Japanese records echo what we see in the Korean documents. Nakagawa Tadateru 中川忠英 (1753–1830) sketched a Chinese stage when he visited Qing China. As shown in an image titled "A Theater Stage" (戲臺), the performers wear Han-style costumes, whereas the musicians are dressed in long gowns and caps with tassels—unmistakable Manchu-style clothing (figure 1.5).[108] The illustration is placed in a section of his miscellany labeled "Rituals of Worship" (祭禮) and follows an image of a temple. Like some Korean envoys, Nakagawa saw Chinese

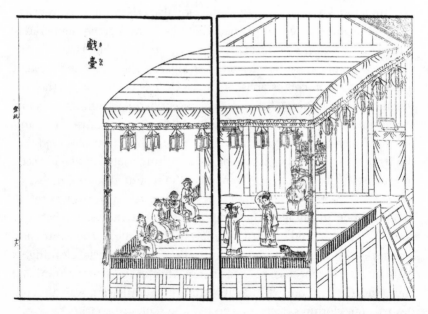

FIGURE 1.5 Image of a Chinese stage in the Qing dynasty. Nakagawa Tadateru 中川忠英, *Shinzoku kibun* 清俗紀聞, 1800, vol. 12, "Sairei" 祭禮, 15b–16a (repr., Taipei: Dali chubanshe, 1982), 522–23.

theater as a type of ritual performance rather than a tool for entertainment, and he left no explicit observations on the ethnic distinctions between the clothes of the performers and those of the troupe staff.

Compared with China's neighbors in Asia, European countries did not have as much official interaction with China during the eighteenth century, a period referred to by some as a blank space in Sino-Western relations.[109] Nevertheless, some documents offer glimpses of how Westerners perceived theatrical costuming in the Qing era. In 1793, the British Macartney Embassy visited China and was received by the Qianlong emperor in Chengde (Rehe), where members of the group watched a grand play performance. Sir George Macartney (1737–1806) described the performance as a mixture of "tragedies and comedies," some historical and others idealized, representing mainly the marriage between the earth and the sea. Macartney apparently saw no political messages embedded in the grand drama performances he witnessed, nor did he comment on the contrast between onstage and offstage clothing at the performance.[110] Other members of the delegation, however, have left some illuminating insights.

William Alexander (1767–1816), a member of the embassy, published more than one hundred paintings he produced during the trip to China. One of them depicts a female character onstage (figure 1.6). After pointing out that the female character was performed by either a boy or a eunuch since "women ha[d] been prohibited from appearing publicly onstage," Alexander continued, "The whole dress is supposed to be that of the ancient Chinese, and indeed is not very different from that of the present day."[111] In commenting on female clothing, Alexander pointed out the resemblance between clothing of the past and that of the present, as well as clothing onstage and that in society. In a book specifically about the costumes of China, Alexander included an image of a comedian—a military general (figure 1.7). At the end of the caption, he wrote, "The dresses worn by players are those of ancient times."[112] When commenting on male clothing, Alexander noticed the rupture between onstage and offstage clothing. His impression was shared by other members of the Macartney delegation. After watching a drama performance, Sir George Staunton (1781–1859) wrote, "The dresses worn by the ancient Chinese are still preserved in the drama."[113] Staunton immediately noticed that costumes onstage were different from clothing in society—as

CHINA- PLATE 30.

Published Jan 1 1814 by J.Murray, Albemarle Street

FIGURE 1.6 Portrait of a female Chinese actor. William Alexander, *Picturesque Representations of the Dress and Manners of the Chinese* (London: Bulmer, 1814), plate 30.

FIGURE 1.7 Portrait of a Chinese actor. William Alexander, "A Chinese Comedian," in *The Costume of China, Illustrated in Forty-eight Coloured Engravings*
(London: Miller, 1805).

noted by John Davis in the passage cited at the beginning of this chapter—although Staunton did not discuss the reasons for that difference any further.

John Barrow (1764–1848), an assistant to Staunton in the Macartney delegation, made some insightful comments on the contents and costumes of Chinese drama: "The subject of the pieces exhibited are, for the most part, historical; and relate, generally, to the transactions of remote periods: in which cases, the dresses are conformable to the ancient costume of China. There are others, however, that represent the Tartar conquest; but none built on historical events subsequent to that period. But the ancient drama is preferred by the critics."[114] Barrow's record aptly captured two distinct features of Chinese drama of the Qing dynasty. First, the author pointed out that theatrical costumes onstage remained in the traditional Chinese style, in contrast to the Manchu-style clothes used in society. Second, Barrow observed that the contemporary history following the Ming–Qing transition could not be readily represented in drama. Consequently, what the author witnessed onstage were things "historical," "ancient," and "remote."

Finally, when the Scottish photographer John Thomson (1837–1921) took a photo of a Chinese theater and published it in 1873, he added a special note: "The dresses usually worn are costumes belonging to the ancient Chinese dynasties, and the garb of the conquering mandarin is studiously avoided."[115] Thomson's explanation of the absence of Manchu clothing in the performance he saw might not reflect the actual situation in late Qing China, since Beijing opera and other types of performances had already started to employ pieces of Manchu clothing. However, his comment remains insightful in that it explains why throughout the Qing dynasty—and in the early Qing in particular—Manchu clothing remained inconvenient, if not impossible, to be used in stage performances.

Encounters between the Europeans and Chinese in many ways mirror the initial encounters between Han Chinese and Manchus during the Ming–Qing transition. The records from European visitors to China provide a third-party perspective on the connections between clothing and costuming in the Qing dynasty. They demonstrate that the banishment of traditional Chinese clothing to the stage was a pervasive phenomenon in Qing China, one easily perceivable by any audience of drama performance. In contrast to foreign visitors' marked observation on theatrical costuming, early Qing scholars remained almost silent about it in their writings. As some of the European visitors pointed out, the contemporary history of the Ming–Qing transition could not be readily represented in drama just as Manchu clothing in the early Qing era could not be easily employed onstage.

The audiences of early Qing drama did not simply observe the sartorial spectacles at theater performances. Their experiences transformed the self-understanding of those audiences. For example, the experiences of watching drama performance intensified the perception of ethnic tensions by Ming loyalists; the same activities awakened the Korean envoys about Korea's new role as a more authentic inheritor of the Confucian tradition; similarly, European visitors gained a refreshed understanding of Chinese history in comparison with their own through watching the display of costumes. Discussing the linkage between the visual experience of theater and image making in Chinese funerary culture, Jeehee Hong summarizes the power of spectacle: "Firmly anchored in the daily world of the living, spectacles experienced in this context offer audiences an opportunity to reflect on their own lives and perhaps provide them with fresh, unforeseen ways to reimagine, challenge, and re-create their lives."[116] Such power of theatrical spectacle was augmented in Qing China when costuming integrated the audiences into the sartorial spectacle at a drama performance. Costuming, via the production and perception of spectacles, shaped the personhood of its very audiences.

As this chapter has delineated, theatrical costuming occupied a special place in the sartorial landscape of Qing China. This landscape is profitably viewed from two perspectives: the changing relations between onstage and offstage clothing during the Ming–Qing transition and the different experiences of watching Han-style costumes onstage. In the interaction between clothing and costuming prior to the Qing dynasty, costumes onstage were subordinate and inferior to clothing in society. Whereas clothing functioned as part of the political and ritual systems, theatrical costumes belonged to a marginal arena; partly because of that, theatrical costuming enjoyed the freedom of employing different types of clothes from society. In the Qing dynasty, costumes onstage no longer mirrored clothes in society. Meanwhile, different parties viewed theatrical costuming in different ways. The meaning of costuming at an early Qing drama performance was not specified by the costumes on display but actualized through the experience and interpretation of the viewing audience.

The Ming–Qing transition was important for Chinese theater especially because it altered the relationship between clothing and costuming, giving rise to different sartorial experiences among its audiences. That unique feature of early Qing theater not only influenced the reception and perception of drama performance but also conditioned the ways in which early Qing playwrights employed the trope of costuming in their drama compositions. The following chapters of *Staging Personhood* demonstrate the scarcity of materials regarding Manchu people and Manchu clothing in theatrical works of the early Qing period. For playwrights in early Qing China, Manchu clothing was either too difficult to depict or still too foreign to be interpreted and represented through theatrical language. The case studies that ensue unpack different ways in which costuming shapes body and clothing and places a person into state, family, and gender relations.

CHAPTER TWO

Across Genders and Ethnicities

Therefore, I often imagine myself being a girl or being a lady.
As soon as one woman has a taste for the high bun, the others
in every quarter of the realm all admire and follow her. . . .
Yet now, I aspire to be a person that keeps his hair loose
but cannot; I aspire to be a lady or a girl but cannot.

—QU DAJUN, "A MAN WHO WEARS HIS HAIR IN A BUN"
(JIREN SHUO 髻人說)

In this quote, the anti-Manchu scholar Qu Dajun 屈大均 (1630–1696)
laments the loss of his hair in early Qing China by comparing himself
with a woman who could keep her long hair in a bun.[1] Qu's lament points
to a specific aspect of Manchu dress regulations in early Qing China—
the gender dimension. Whereas Chinese men were forced to adopt Manchu hairstyle and dress, Chinese women were largely exempt from such
rules. As Martin Huang points out, at times of dynastic transition, especially when China was ruled by a non-Han group, male Han Chinese
often experienced a gender identity crisis.[2] During the Ming–Qing transition, this identity crisis was directly related to gender-specific rules
about hairstyle and clothing. Although Qu's wish to impersonate a
woman to preserve his hair could not be fulfilled in early Qing society,
such imagining was precisely the theme of an early Qing drama about
cross-dressing. This chapter focuses on the gendered meaning of clothing as revealed in *Lovebirds Reversal* (*Dao yuanyang* 倒鴛鴦), an early
Qing drama composed by Zhu Ying 朱英 (b. ca. 1621) immediately after
the establishment of the Qing dynasty.[3]

In *Lovebirds*, a young scholar named Hua Jing 花鏡 and a young lady
named Shui Suyue 水素月 encounter each other when both are fleeing

battles between Manchu invaders and the remnant Ming army. When the Manchus force Chinese men to shave their heads, the scholar changes into the lady's clothing to avoid losing his hair. Meanwhile, the lady changes into the scholar's dress to avoid sexual assault. In the new dynasty, the lady, now a scholar, passes the imperial examination and assumes the uniform of the Manchu regime. After a series of accidental encounters, the couple's parents arrange for them to be married. However, they fail to recognize each other during the wedding and discover each other's real gender only after a sleepless night. Embedding the plot of dressing across ethnicities into a story of dressing across genders, *Lovebirds* is the only existing early Qing drama that foregrounds Manchu hair and dress control during the dynastic change, thus revealing details about the gendered consequences of Manchu hair and dress decrees not seen in other texts. This drama is one of a few that the author composed during the first years of the Qing dynasty, the other extant ones being *Disturbance at the Wu River* (*Nao Wujiang* 鬧烏江) and *Unicorn Pavilion Awaiting* (*Lin'ge dai* 麟閣待).[4] Together, these dramas depict a world in which new orders of ethnicity and gender are taking shape.

Zhu Ying's plays are some of the earliest theatrical works that explore such themes as Manchu hairstyle and clothing, body and cross-dressing, and gender relations. Costuming is a crucial tool with which the author structured his plays and depicted their characters. However, none of his existing plays is known to have been performed. These plays, especially *Lovebirds*, illustrate the imagined assemblage between bodies, clothing, and hairstyles in a theatrical setting. Only in these imagined practices could the author probe the nuanced relationship between sartorial history and theatrical representation.

MING–QING TRANSITION IN ZHU YING'S DRAMAS

Among early Qing playwrights, Zhu Ying was exceptional in that he directly described the Manchu invasion in several of his dramas. Scant existing materials about the author reveal that Zhu Ying hailed from Shanghai and moved to Nanjing after the dynastic transition.[5] *Disturbance at the Wu River* and *Lovebirds* each carries a preface dated 1650 stating that the place of the dramas' production was Hall of Chiming Jades (Yuxiao Tang 玉嘯堂), possibly the name of Zhu's study. The author's preface in *Lovebirds* also refers to characters from *Unicorn Pavilion Awaiting*, suggesting that the latter play had been completed by that time.[6] All his extant dramas make direct or indirect references to the Ming–Qing transition. Similar to *Lovebirds*, *Disturbance at the Wu River* depicts a world in which men impersonate women both onstage and in society, whereas *Unicorn Pavilion Awaiting* represents the military conflicts between the Manchu army and some pirates. As a rare group of dramas, they provide a theatrical panorama of the dynastic change, the sartorial transition, and the men and women who went through the upheavals.

Unicorn Pavilion Awaiting explicitly depicts naval warfare between the Qing government and some pirates—with clear indications of the Ming resistance movement in early Qing China. The author places in the *sheng* role (male lead) a high official in the Manchu government named Ji Bangfu 姬邦輔. As the first character to appear in the drama (scene 2), he wears an official uniform and a cap with a knob (*dingfu* 頂服)—the uniform of the Manchu government. He then introduces himself as a general from Liaodong 遼東 and is promoted by Nurhaci, one of the founding rulers of the Manchu regime. His costumes and self-introduction indicate that he is of the Manchu ethnicity. In the following scene, a clownish character appears wearing Manchu-style headgear and gown 滿巾袍 (*Man jinpao*). It is unclear what specific pieces of costume *Man jinpao* refers to because *jin* was not part of Manchu-style clothes in Qing society. In a script intended for reading rather than performance, the author simply introduces the idea that Manchu-style costumes be employed to perform certain characters. In contrast to the *sheng* role's Manchu-style uniform, the *xiaosheng* role (second male lead) features a Chinese scholar wearing traditional scholarly dress (*jinfu* 巾服; scene 3). Except for these places, the drama includes few other costume instructions. By assigning the *sheng* to a Manchu official wearing Manchu clothing, the drama effectively communicates Manchu dominance and Chinese scholars' inferior status in the new regime.

Other episodes in the drama further indicate that the story is set in the dynastic transition when the Qing army pacifies the entire country. Whereas the drama praises military generals who remain loyal to the Qing government when resisting pirate attacks, it also indirectly portrays the pirates as Ming loyalists. In scene 20, the leader of the pirates, Hai

Zhongbo 海中波 (literally, Waves in the Ocean), introduces himself as hailing from Nanjing and, after the dynastic change, actively plans to reclaim the lost land. When delivering a sacrifice to the sea, Hai Zhongbo invites "the two founders and ten succeeding emperors" (*erzu shizong* 二祖十宗) to receive the sacrifice, and his subordinates express their wish that "the legions of the Qing army will remain sound asleep" (清兵大隊 總酣夢; scene 20). The phrase "two founders and ten succeeding emperors" was commonly used in late Ming writings in reference to Ming-dynasty emperors.[7]

Unicorn Pavilion Awaiting is not a romantic play but one about a Manchu general winning a high position through military achievements against the remnant Ming army. The theme of the romance between a Chinese couple is subordinate to the theme of the Manchu pacification of China. Accordingly, the *sheng* is reserved for the Manchu general instead of the Chinese scholar—contravening the conventional character setup in traditional Chinese dramas. *Unicorn Pavilion Awaiting* does not represent Chinese resistance to the Manchu invasion. Instead, the Manchu conquest of southern China provides an opportunity for the Chinese couple to reunite.

Similar to *Unicorn Pavilion Awaiting*, *Lovebirds* is set in the background of the Manchu invasion. But the latter drama explores the difficulties of a Han Chinese scholar enduring the Manchu regulations over one's hairstyle. The geographical and temporal setting of *Lovebirds* resonates strongly with the author's own experiences during the Ming–Qing transition. *Lovebirds* was composed between 1645 and 1650, only a few years after the fall of Nanjing; all its characters are from the lower Yangzi delta.[8] At the beginning of *Lovebirds* (1645), the Manchu army has crossed the Yellow River and captured Nanjing, the capital of the Southern Ming government. During their escape to the ocean, the remaining Ming army loots the city of Changzhou and captures the heroine, Shui Suyue, and her sister. Moving on to the coastal city of Shanghai, they capture the hero, Hua Jing. The fleeing Ming army finally escapes to the sea and becomes pirates, in clear resonance with the pirates in *Unicorn Pavilion Awaiting*. Toward the end of the play, both the hero's and heroine's families move to Nanjing, now under Qing rule. In Nanjing, the children of the two families (two couples) quickly get married when the Manchu court issues an order for local governments to select beautiful girls to serve in the palace. The story spans about one year, from the fall of Nanjing to the reestablishment of order around 1645. The temporal and spatial setting of *Lovebirds* allows the playwright to carve out a niche that aptly reflects the complexity of clothing and gender during the dynastic change.

Lovebirds foregrounds Manchu hair and dress regulations, making them the direct trigger of its story about cross-dressing. Although Manchu regulations are usually referred to as "cutting hair and changing clothing," hair and clothing were, in fact, two different aspects of the policy. Within a month after conquering Nanjing in 1645, the Manchu general Dodo issued an order: "Everyone is ordered to have his hair cut within ten days. Those who comply are subjects of our country. Those who hesitate will be treated as equal to rebellious bandits. . . . As to clothing and hats, it is allowed that they be altered gradually."[9] About twenty days later, Dodo issued another order prohibiting the continued use of Ming clothing in Beijing, the Qing capital.

> Since officials and ordinary people have shaved their heads, they should also follow the dress code of our dynasty. . . . Recently it has been noticed that few militants and civilians inside and outside the capital abide by Manchu dress, and many still wear the former head-gear. This seriously contravenes the principle of uniformity and equality. Your ministry should immediately entrust the Shuntian prefect and the Censors of the Five Wards to issue decrees against this. Officials found accommodating the practice should be punished at the same time.[10]

As the documents show, at the time of the dynastic change, the Manchu government demanded Han Chinese shave their heads immediately while permitting officials and ordinary people to change their clothes at a slower pace. As Ge Zhaoguang points out, despite repeated prohibitions against wearing traditional Han-style clothing, both Manchu- and Han-style clothes were worn by officials and scholars in early Qing society for decades, and it was not until the 1670s that Ming attire for men finally disappeared from daily life.[11] Around 1645, society in southern China was undergoing a political as well as a sartorial transition. This historical context allowed the dramatist to probe the potential meanings of hair and clothing through theatrical works.

Cross-dressing had been a frequently employed trope in Chinese drama prior to the early Qing period. In most such dramas, the male and female characters resort to temporary dress in drag to overcome predicaments in their lives. In the end, they typically restore their original gender identities by simply donning their original clothing. This traditional trope faces a challenge in *Lovebirds*, a drama that spans the Ming–Qing transition, because posttransition men changed their clothing and hair to the Manchu styles. In the new sartorial order of the early Qing, was it possible for the cross-dressed couple to reassume their original clothing and gender identities? How did Manchu ethnicity influence the gendered meaning of clothing in a drama about cross-dressing? In the rest of this chapter I discuss three moments in the drama—the hero and heroine's encounter and cross-dressing, their subsequent changing of clothes, and the grand reunion—to unpack the costs and consequences of dressing across genders and ethnicities.

DRESSING ACROSS GENDERS

In traditional Chinese drama, cross-dressing usually involves a man, a woman, and their respective clothes. *Lovebirds* represents a special case in which the Manchu ethnic rule destabilizes the connection between these elements, calling into question the existing association of hair, body, gender, and different ethnic clothing. Through the hero's cross-dressing, we can see that the loss of scholarly dress emasculates the hero as well as the literati group he represents. At Hua Jing's first appearance, the stage instruction indicates that he wears a *Jinjin* 晉巾, an item of headgear that imitates the sartorial style of the Jin dynasty. Literati scholars in late Ming China invented a variety of headgear for self-fashioning, including Tang-style headgear (*Tangjin* 唐巾) and *Jinjin*.[12] Jin-style headgear was also widely used in Ming dramas to highlight such self-fashioning.[13] The Jin-style headgear in *Lovebirds* conveys the message that the hero models himself after the unrestrained literati of an ancient time, who were devoted to traveling and "pure talking" (*qingtan* 清談) instead of pursuing Confucian scholarship or an official career.

Hua Jing's monologue in the opening scene refers to the permeability between theater and social reality. He recites, "Puppets perform groundless worldly events; troupers stage human affection as if real" (scene 2). Chinese dramas frequently employ such expressions with reference to the theatrical nature of the world. Inserted into the hero's monologue, this line illustrates the function of his clothing, especially his headgear: in society, a scholar wears such a costume to represent a literatus unconcerned with mundane affairs; in the drama, an actor wears it to perform the role of such a scholar. In either case, the headgear itself suffices to indicate the hero's literati identity.

Whereas the outer garment defines the hero as a scholar in society, his hairstyle indicates his cultural and ethnic identity as a Han Chinese. In scene 4, the Ming army has plundered Shui Suyue's hometown, Changzhou, and taken her prisoner. Grasping the opportunity occasioned by the Manchu army's attack, Shui escapes and encounters Hua Jing (scene 7). At his urging, Shui borrows a set of Hua's clothes so that she can impersonate a man and avoid sexual assault. Just as the couple are about to embark on their travels together, two characters come onstage to pronounce the Manchu ordinance regarding hairstyle: "(Enter the *jing* and *wai* actors holding tablets and announcing the ordinance of shaving heads) Attention, everyone! If you want to keep your head, remove your hair; if you retain your hair, your head will be removed" (scene 7). The heroine encourages the hero to comply, but he refuses, referring to the Confucian prescription about physical intactness: "How can I accept this when I have received my hair and skin from my parents?" His reply epitomizes the mentality of Han Chinese people resisting the Manchu decree concerning hair: that it violated the basic principle of civility. Adopting a Manchu hairstyle would not only jeopardize the hero's literati identity—a shaved head would not befit Jin-style headgear—but also turn him into a barbarian.

As an alternative to shaving Hua's head, Shui Suyue suggests that Hua Jing change into her clothing and impersonate a woman, and he assents. As he changes clothes, Hua provides an explanation for his decision, singing, "My only hope is that both my parents will see me again." Moments earlier he had refused to shave his head because his parents bestowed to him his hair and body. Now, once more invoking his parents, he expresses his willingness to abandon his clothes to preserve his hair. The moment of cross-dressing introduces body, hair, and clothing as discrete aspects of a person. The hero's clothing defines his gender identity, his hair indicates his ethnic identity, and his body preserves his fundamental connection with his family. Clothing is the most exterior part of a person, followed by hair, and ultimately the body. Hua Jing of *Lovebirds* invokes an argument that serving his parents justifies the change of his clothing. The only problem is that when he dons female dress, he jeopardizes his very identity as a son.

Hua's second reason for abandoning his scholarly dress further reveals a paradox in his thinking. Assenting to Shui's suggestion, he adds, "What's more, quite a few men [*zhangfu* 丈夫] have transformed into women in today's world. Why should I be an exception?" (scene 7). The phrase *zhangfu* refers both to men and to masculinity as the major attribute of a man. The hero's apology indicates that he is willing to "transform" into a woman, which begs the question of whether his new identity allows him to continue to perform his roles as son and literati scholar.

The scholar's emasculation deepens as he acts as a cross-dressed woman. Soon after the cross-dressing takes place, the remnant Ming army captures the hero and detains him with other women to be sex slaves. Dressed as a woman, the hero's voice becomes completely feminized. He sings an aria with the heroine's younger sister, who has been detained in the same place: "(*Sheng* and *xiaodan*) Our hearts are determined. The fragrant heart will be hard to alter even in spite of physical compulsion and professed alarm. . . . Our tears stream down. This is not because feelings of romance are too deep but because the valiant spirit of a hero is not sufficient" (scene 8). The entire line uses a female voice, with only the last phrase indicating the hero's male identity. Apparently, the hero is a literati scholar "performing" a woman, but as the aria indicates, Hua is shedding tears while singing. The tears belie his claim to be a "hero." Is it acceptable for a male hero to cry over his misfortune? Is crying another trick he employs to perform as a woman? Or is he expressing true sentiments through a convenient female voice? The difficulty in answering these questions illustrates the difficulty in recognizing the hero's gender identity apart from his feminine clothing and voice.

Dressed in women's clothing, the hero must surrender all his male attributes, remaining a man only in his dreams. In scene 15, "Dream on Grass" (Caomeng 草夢), Hua Jing meets Shui Suyue in a dream, and the stage instructions indicate that he changes into scholarly dress (*jinfu*). Upon seeing the heroine in female dress, he warns her to be careful. When the Manchu army carries Shui away, he attempts to pursue but soon realizes that he has not cut his hair and then stops out of fear of the Manchu army. In his subconscious, Hua Jing still acts as a man wearing a man's clothing, but that identity ceases to be when he awakens to find himself in the world of the drama.

The hero has hoped that wearing female clothing would provide him a temporary sanctuary where he could preserve his hair. Unexpectedly, the clothing he dons simultaneously transforms his voice and body into female ones and turns him into a sexual object in the eyes of the Ming army. Earlier, the Manchu army posed a threat to his hair, a symbol of his cultural identity. Now the Manchu army saves him from being sexually besmirched by the Ming army, thus changing from the hero's enemy to his savior. Feminine clothing changes not only the hero's scholarly identity but also his relationship to the Manchu army.

In *Lovebirds*, the loss of scholarly dress triggers Hua Jing's emasculation. Whereas mentions of scholarly dress and headpiece (*jinfu*) refer to Hua's garments, other terms regarding hairstyle and clothing are used in the play to mock and criticize the emasculated literati group. Modern scholars have pointed out that cap and gown (*yiguan* 衣冠) became a politically charged term during the Ming–Qing transition, and literati discourses on *yiguan* reflected the crisis in their self-understanding as Confucian scholars and Ming subjects.[14] In its references to hair and *yiguan*, *Lovebirds* shows that the sartorial transformation relegated traditional Han-style hair and clothing to an inferior position and subjected them to mockery.

When captured, Hua Jing secretly talks to himself: "It's laughable that my cap and gown [*yiguan*] are turned into the makeup of melancholy and the scent of resentment" (scene 8). He uses *yiguan* here to refer to himself as a member of the literati group, but *Lovebirds* also depicts the entire literati community as being emasculated. It refers to the disasters during the dynastic change mainly through characters' narrations. In the opening scene of the second volume, a supporting character mentions the tragedy in passing: "How many wealthy nobles—perished and slaughtered, slaughtered and perished—nothing but a mound of black dirt. How many heroes—wronged and abused, abused and wronged—what's that saying about 'deities three feet above the head'? Whether wise or foolish, all cherish the hair more than skin" (scene 20). Although this speech points out that every person values his hair more than his body, none of the characters in the play lives up to that standard, as almost all of them willingly submit to the Manchu hair and dress regulations. The hero is the only character who attempts to preserve his hair, and he can do so only by hiding in women's clothing.

Instead of representing issues surrounding hair in a serious tone, the drama satirizes hair using the actions of a few clownish characters. In a scene about the imperial examination, a buffoonish character appears with a short beard to perform as an old student. He sings, "A fellow among the examination takers, I have a forehead emitting light. Though still young I have strands of white hair hanging from my head and prickly hair on both my weary cheeks. After all, it seems I'm better off not being capped: since I have not kept my hair, I'm spared the shaving knife" (scene 21). The aria describes an old man who has failed all his life to secure a degree. The first lines mock the student's advanced age, mockery that will be repeated in the scenes that follow. The last line refers to the Manchu hair regulation by way of a joke: the student is spared having his head shaved since he has not been capped as an adult—the true reason being that he is bald and unsuccessful in the examination. In contrast to the depictions of the tragic consequences of Manchu hair regulations during the Ming–Qing transition, *Lovebirds* reduces tragedy to farce.

The satire extends from hair to *yiguan*. Throughout the play several clownish figures perform as a group of literati. One of them is named Yi Guanzhong 伊官鐘, and in the preface to the drama, the author explains the connotation of the name: "His name is Yi Guanzhong. I don't know what a man of cap and gown [*yiguan*] he is."[15] A pun links the clownish character to the literati group in a clear satire of the latter. Other characters in the group repeatedly express their craving for the official titles embodied in official uniforms. In scene 2 Shu Sixi 倏思溪 remarks, "I, Shu Sixi, have harbored a deep affection for the two words *guan* and *mian* [official cap]. However, an ominous constellation hovers above me, blocking my fortunes." Toward the end of the play Shu Sixi once more recalls his experience of wearing a silk cap and a round-collar uniform (scene 26). The expression *guanmian* refers to the official Ming uniform, represented by the silk cap and round-collar dress and assigned to the clownish characters in the play.

The playwright further resorts to punning in his gendered satire of the *yiguan* group. In scene 6, a doctor is captured by the remnant Ming army. Unable to provide "treasures" upon demand, he is robbed of his clothing and laments, "The two words—*yi* and *guan* [醫官, "doctor"]—are clearly written on the golden plaque hanging high in my household. I've always heard people say that *yiguan* [doctor] can be used to defend against violence. Now I see that it's complete nonsense." The scene provides an ending poem immediately following his words: "Don't boast about fending off violence with *yiguan* [衣冠, "cap and gown"]; now my *yishan* [衣衫, "clothes"] have been ripped off like an unpalatable quince." Here *yiguan* 醫官 (doctor) puns with *yiguan* 衣冠 (literati group). The expression "fending off violence with *yiguan*" (*yiguan yubao* 衣冠禦暴) is derived from *The Book of Changes* (*Yijing* 易經), which prescribes that *yiguan* (civilization) can be used to ward off barbaric invasion.[16] By pointing out the inadequacy of *yiguan* to fend off violence, the poem reduces *yiguan* to *yishan*, an ordinary term for clothing, only to be removed from the doctor's body. *Yiguan* ceases to be the attire of literati scholars and is reduced to being a mere garment.

The poem uses "quince" (*mugua* 木瓜) as a metaphor for the literati group's dress, which immediately invokes the expression "deflowering" (*pogua* 破瓜). Comparing the doctor, a *yiguan* (doctor/literatus), to a quince, the poem potentially ridicules the literati group for being "deflowered" by violent armies. The metaphor also captures earlier scenes in which the hero is detained by the Ming army as a sex slave. Thus, Han literati have been assigned a female role, facing the threat of being raped by the Ming bandits, only to be rescued by the Manchu army.

Disturbance at the Wu River shows even more clearly Zhu Ying's satirizing of scholarly dress. One of the characters comments on the resemblance between theatrical performance and academic study: "Today, reading books is just like performing dramas.... One after another, [scholars] leap between destitution and prosperity as in a monkey show. Gains immediately compensate losses. Round collars and silk caps, black boots and waist belts—at such a time, one should seek an official title like this as soon as possible."[17] The garments named in this commentary are part of the official uniform in the Ming dynasty. The narrator refers to them as if they are theatrical costumes and compares the academic career to a monkey show. This commentary echoes the critique of the *yiguan* group in *Lovebirds*. *Disturbance at the Wu River* continues its critique of scholarly identity using theatrical costuming when a group of scholars form a troupe and participate in a performance contest. When one of them expresses reluctance to perform the *dan* (female lead), another scholar tries to persuade him: "Brother Tao, it's even more laughable that you mention the two words *yi guan*. In today's world, the *yiguan* group have grown accustomed to being as debased as those who wear skirts and hairpins."[18] Similar to *Lovebirds*, *Disturbance at the Wu River* associates cross-dressing in female clothing with the loss of literati identity.

To some extent, the entirety of *Lovebirds* addresses the issue of *yiguan*—the material apparel associated with the term, the literati identity it represents, and the gendered strategies of preserving it against the Manchu invasion. As a sublime symbol of Confucian culture, *yiguan* serves as the very reason the hero is willing to cross-dress and undergo subsequent suffering. Through the hero's character, *Lovebirds* indicates the impossibility of preserving the material existence of *yiguan*, and by way of the clownish characters, the play degrades *yiguan* to a nominal title. The satire in the drama turns *yiguan* into a sign of foiled masculinity, to be rescued by the cross-dressed heroine in a reconfigured sartorial system.

DRESSING ACROSS ETHNICITIES

As is typical of dramas of cross-dressing, both the hero and the heroine would normally have their original gender identities restored upon recovering their original clothing. *Lovebirds* problematizes this solution because in this instance men's clothing has undergone an ethnic reconfiguration immediately after the couple cross-dresses. In the earlier scenes, donning Shui Suyue's dress confers on Hua Jing the attributes of a woman. Shui Suyue undergoes a similar transformation when she adopts the hero's dress. Upon changing clothing, she sings, "I wash the dust off my hair and face" (洗塵髮面; scene 7). "Hair and face" is a metaphor for the female body, which is reshaped by a piece of men's attire. The scholarly dress serves not simply as a cover but also as a magical canopy that bestows upon the woman all the necessary attributes of a male scholar. In the rest of the drama, the heroine becomes an adopted son in the hero's family and a successful candidate in the imperial examination of the new state.

To become a scholar in the new dynasty, she will go through a sartorial transformation that reshapes her hair and clothing. As soon as the Manchu army announces the hair regulation, she says, "Since I have impersonated a man, it is unavoidable that I will shave my head" (scene 7). If donning scholarly dress changes her female body into a male one, shaving the head turns her hairstyle from that of Han Chinese into that of the Manchus, a further step in her deception. Shui Suyue indicates that shaving her head is only natural because she is impersonating a man. The theatrical nature of imposture renders head shaving an ambiguous activity, for both the woman and the man whom she performs. Hair—or cutting hair—demonstrates two entirely different meanings to the hero and heroine. For Hua Jing, losing his hair means losing his identity as defined within Confucian culture. For Shui Suyue, her hair and her entire outward appearance have been turned into a costume for performance. Cutting her hair, therefore, amounts to no more than an adjustment of her costume. Whereas the hero's hair and clothing position him in family and society, the heroine's hair and clothing serve merely the purpose of impersonation onstage. In contrast to the hero, who maintains Jin-dynasty headgear and an unshaved head in order to be a literatus, the heroine becomes a literatus based on her shaved head and borrowed dress. At that moment, although she wears a set of clothes belonging to the hero, her shaved head defines her as a scholar of the Manchu regime, an identity at a remove from that of the hero.

Equipped with Manchu hairstyle and Han-style scholarly attire, Shui Suyue continues to impersonate Hua Jing and represent the literati community in the new state. In scene 12 Hua Jing's father, Hua Zhao 花朝, living in Shanghai under Manchu rule, observes, "Fortunately, now a magistrate has been appointed in the county. As long as people shave their heads as instructed, soldiers are not allowed to harass them." Order is restored at the cost of the Chinese hairstyle. In the drama and in early Qing history, shaving the head was the most potent act of Chinese men's submission to the Manchus and, subsequently, their emasculation. The heroine's female body, coupled with the Manchu hairstyle and Ming scholarly dress, embodies the typical situation of a Ming scholar in transition to the Qing regime.

Ultimately, it is borrowed clothes that lead the heroine to the hero's family. After parting from Hua Jing, Shui Suyue encounters an acquaintance of the Hua family (scene 10). Mistaking her for Hua Jing because of her borrowed clothes, the gentleman brings her to Hua Jing's father. She claims to be Hua's friend and her borrowed clothing corroborates her story. As a result, Hua Jing's father adopts her as a son and sends her to school together with his second son. Up to this point, the scholarly dress the heroine has borrowed is the sole instrument defining her as a man and the single connection between her and the hero's family. In most traditional Chinese dramas, such a prop would be presented repeatedly throughout the drama, but in *Lovebirds* we lose track of Hua's clothing after Shui Suyue joins the hero's family. Once the borrowed dress allows the heroine to assume the social role of the hero it becomes unessential and never reappears or is mentioned again.

Having joined the hero's family, Shui Suyue proceeds in her role as a literati scholar. In traditional Chinese dramas of cross-dressing, the scholars usually overcome their predicament by succeeding in the imperial examination, which brings them official titles and uniforms. In the first half of *Lovebirds*, Hua Jing shows indifference toward the imperial examination because "the Manchu army has already crossed the Yellow River" (scene 2). After the Manchus capture Shanghai and Nanjing, social order is restored along with the examination. In scene 21, a scholar praises the justice exercised in the new dynasty's examination, which leaves no room for nepotism. Acting as a proxy for the hero, Shui Suyue diligently prepares for the imperial examination, declaring, "Originally I changed clothes [*yizhuang*] only temporarily to avoid the disaster. . . . Now I dedicate myself to literary study, freely following the *yiguan* group." In the first part of this line, the heroine uses *yizhuang* in reference to her clothing as a material object. In the latter part, she uses the term *yiguan* in reference to the literati group, with which she now identifies.

Under Manchu rule, both the heroine and the hero's younger brother become successful candidates in the examination. This common plot in dramas that feature cross-dressing is accompanied in this instance by an unusual detail of changes in clothing. The opening scene of the second volume introduces a new landscape featuring a new sartorial style. A group of gentlemen visit an earthen mound by the city wall and sing, "Strolling along, we have arrived at the city. . . . Spring fills our eyes— white headgear and narrow sleeves [*baijin xiaoxiu* 白巾小袖] in pursuit of the new fashion" (scene 20). The phrase "narrow sleeves" implies Manchu-style clothing in contrast to the wide sleeves typical of Han-style clothing, and "new fashion" (*shixing* 時興) indicates that Manchu clothing is now in vogue.

As these lines signal the increasing presence of Manchu clothing in daily life, scenes relating to the imperial examination provide an opportunity for public celebration of the Manchu uniform. Upon arriving at the examination site, the heroine is dressed in a black uniform with a round collar, the uniform of Ming officials and degree holders (scene 21). Right after she becomes a successful candidate, she appears in Manchu dress (*Manzhuang* 滿裝). This is one of the earliest usages of the phrase "Manchu clothing" in extant Chinese dramas. Scene 24, titled "Street Greeting" (Jieying 街迎), depicts the successful candidates marching in the street to receive public adulation. The drama emphasizes the setting as a public spectacle, as four successful candidates describe the event in an aria: "Behold! The crowd clamors like ants, all jealous of the prize candidate. Passersby on the street have all been alarmed. They rush to observe and compete to cast a look" (scene 21). With the words *du* 睹 and *qiao* 瞧, the aria highlights the visual aspect of the event. With joyous music and crowds of witnesses, the public festival resembles many others celebrating successful candidates in the examination. What distinguishes the scene from others is that it displays not only the successful candidates but also their newly assumed Manchu-style clothing.

As is conventional for *chuanqi* dramas, *Lovebirds* tempers a serious plot with episodes of farce. The scene of the public celebration starts by mocking a group of successful candidates wearing Manchu clothing. The drama includes two old candidates performed by clownish characters to contrast with the heroine and the hero's brother. The two old candidates appear wearing "Manchu clothing with a silver-knob cap" (*yinding Manzhuang* 銀頂滿裝). They explicitly sing about their Manchu headgear: "Silver flower pin, silver flower pin, sways and floats on the Manchu cap" (銀花插、銀花插、滿帽飄搖). Partly to describe their clothing and in part to ridicule their senility, two members of the audience sing, "Red lips flapping, white hair floating, new cap with a tin top, blue gown with black cuffs" (紅唇翻、白髮飄、錫頂的新帽，黑鉗的青袍). The red, white, blue, and black colors in the aria facilitate imagination of a spectacle with Manchu clothing on display. It could be out of ignorance that the audience mistakes the silver cap knob for one made from tin, but the misrecognition discloses the novelty of Manchu dress in the Chinese community. The phrase "black cuffs" (*heiqian* 黑鉗) invites special attention. In traditional China, *qian* 鉗 was a punishment in which an iron cuff was fastened to one's neck, hands, or feet.[19] This aria uses the expression in reference to either the collar or the horseshoe-shaped cuffs of the Manchu gown. As one of the earliest theatrical representations of Manchu clothing in Chinese drama, this episode shows how early Qing Chinese perceived Manchu clothing on public display, and how an early Qing drama could challenge Manchu authority through an oblique reference to Manchu attire.

At the same time, however, the scene depicts a ritualistic moment when Manchu clothing is celebrated. In contrast to the sarcasm in describing the two old candidates, the drama has the same audience express admiration for the heroine and her fellow scholar: "(*Fumo* and *jing*) The flourishing talent is of young age, with handsome looks. Nanjing people are indeed unconstrained: cropped gown and peacock cap [*jianpao quemao* 剪袍雀帽], with a silver flower quivering and swaying—they look as ethereal as flying immortals" (scene 21). Around 1645 and 1646, the Manchu government enacted regulations concerning the uniform of degree holders, requiring them to wear caps with gold and silver knobs and green gowns with blue rims.[20] The cropped gown and peacock cap mentioned in the aria indicate a Manchu-style uniform consisting of a robe with side openings and a cap decorated with peacock feathers. As the spectators point out, the heroine's handsome looks and the newly fabricated clothes render the heroine a supramundane immortal. The aria makes no explicit reference to Shui Suyue's queue in the Manchu style, but the newly adopted Manchu clothing alone empowers her and confirms her literati identity in the Manchu regime. Dressing across genders turns the heroine into a proxy for the hero. It is the female character who undergoes a change in hair and clothes and dresses across ethnicities. Although the hero takes shelter in women's clothing to avoid losing his hair, members of the literati group to which he belongs have abandoned their hairstyle and clothing in favor of Manchu ones.

Earlier on, the hero's scholarly dress turned the heroine into a son in the hero's family. Now the Manchu clothing transforms her into a scholar of the new state. Shui Suyue completes a second round of cross-dressing,

dressing in the Manchu style. The quasi-ritual moment integrates her body with Manchu clothing, further removing her from the hero's scholarly dress that she donned earlier. The Manchu clothing described here is not only something novel to the crowd in the drama but also a recent introduction in early Qing society in the 1640s. As a new item in the sartorial landscape, Manchu clothing opened the possibility for different theatrical interpretations: it could be worn by buffoonish characters for mockery or by leading characters for celebration.

In the drama, the successful examination candidates are the only characters wearing Manchu clothing. The audience at the grandiose public celebration still wear festive dress supposedly in the Han style. In a conversation, one gentleman comments on the other's clothing: "Since you are wearing a brand-new Daoist robe on your body, I guess you must be going over to deliver your congratulations" (scene 21). In this case, the Daoist robe, also named *xuezi* 褶子 onstage, does not mean the uniform of Daoist monks but rather the formal dress worn by Ming scholars in everyday life. Although the term "brand-new" (*cuxin* 簇新) indicates that the garment is of very recent production, the designation of a Daoist robe indicates that it still follows the old style of Ming clothing. The occasion constitutes a rare sartorial spectacle in the wake of the Manchu conquest, as sets of newly introduced Manchu clothing are placed at the center for public appreciation while a group of Chinese gentlemen assume their formal dress to pay their respects.

After the ceremony, the Manchu uniform is immediately integrated with traditional terms regarding scholarly dress. The heroine and the hero's brother praise their experiences as "the favor of the new robe" (*xinpao chong* 新袍寵). "New robe" simply refers to the state attire befitting their recently acquired degrees, with no indication of the newly introduced Manchu style. Referring to their success in the examination, the father, Hua Zhao, comments, "I am happy that today you have donned clothing of the time . . . removed your humble cloth and adopted a fine gauze gown." The term "gauze gown" (*luolan* 羅襴) refers to the official dress of successful candidates and had been traditional vocabulary associated with the Ming official uniform. The term "clothing of the time" (*shizhen* 時裀), however, indicates a new style of clothing different from that of the past. After the public celebration, those terms are seamlessly integrated with Manchu dress.

The public spectacle also constitutes a ritual of initiation that defines Manchu clothing as the new language of state power. Earlier in the play, a group of local gentlemen had served as city guards and prevented the hero's family from escaping, causing the family to disperse. Having witnessed the sartorial spectacle featuring the success of the hero's family, the guards become fearful of revenge. One of them pays his respects to the Hua family seeking reconciliation. He presents a gift list that reads as follows: "two pieces of patterned silk, a small pile of new tea, two boxes of ink sticks, and one Manchu cap" (scene 25). Silk, tea, and ink sticks were common gifts among literati scholars in late imperial China. The Manchu cap listed among them is introduced as a new item that signifies an official title as well as literati status. As the last item on the list, it appears to be the most important gift. Anthropologists have studied archaic societies where gifting is an important way to reciprocate and build social solidarity. In the case of *Lovebirds*, an item of Manchu apparel serves multiple functions: it mediates the interaction between a group of Han scholars; it conveys the visiting gentleman's acknowledgment of his inferiority since the Manchu cap can be worn only by the successful candidates in the Hua family; and, finally, the Manchu cap, a new symbol of power associated with the Manchu state, helps mitigate the conflicts that arose among Chinese scholars during the dynastic transition.

Upon donning the hero's dress, the heroine automatically obtains the social and political attributes of a male scholar. Men's clothing leads her into the Hua family to fulfill the tasks that Hua Jing has failed to fulfill, including passing the imperial examination. In the course of such changes, the heroine gradually abandons her hair as well as her borrowed clothes in favor of a set of Manchu clothing. Dressing across ethnicities poses a challenge to the scholar, who is hoping to redeem his original identity through restoring his clothes.

GRAND REUNION, OR STRANGERS AT HOME

Despite the tragedies, satire, and accidents, *Lovebirds* concludes with a grand reunion following the tradition of Chinese dramas. After a series of accidental encounters, Hua Jing is adopted by Shui Suyue's mother as a daughter. Hero and heroine, now in each other's home, are engaged to marry without knowing each other's true identity. When the truth is revealed, they change their clothing to accord with their original genders. In light of the previous changes in hairstyle and clothing, we have to ask, even if dressing across genders can be conveniently reversed, can dressing across ethnicities be reversed as well? With both the interior and exterior parts altered, will the hero and heroine still be able to reclaim their original selves?

In their "mistaken" gender identities, both the hero and heroine have lived in Nanjing for half a year after the dynastic change. Although the Manchu government has restored social order, and all have started a new life in peace, the hero and heroine are still constrained by their cross-dressed clothing. Lamenting his predicament, Hua Jing sings, "If I say I am a woman, how can anyone believe me? If I say I am a man, how can I bear that agony?" (scene 31). To become a man, he will have to undergo a painstaking process of transforming his body, including cutting his hair. Avoiding that process was the very reason for cross-dressing in the first place. In this new era, Hua finds himself in an exile defined by women's clothing.

Later on, the new government initiates a search for talented ladies to serve in the imperial palace. Fearing that her two daughters—Shui Suyue's younger sister and Hua Jing, now adopted as a daughter—will be enlisted, Madam Shui manages to arrange quick marriages for both of them to sons from the Hua family—namely, Hua Jing's brother and Shui Suyue. Whereas the previous public celebration served as an opportunity to display Manchu state attire, the wedding ceremony allows state attire to be integrated into the family ritual of marriage. Ever since her success in the examination, Shui Suyue has been wearing Manchu clothing on public occasions. In scene 32, the two grooms wear ceremonial dress (*da yifu* 大衣服) to attend the wedding. Despite the Manchu government's dress regulations, both Chinese brides and grooms were still allowed to wear Han-style dress at their weddings. It is possible that the couple, now temporarily donning Han-style wedding dress, would recognize each other on their wedding night. As we see in the drama, rather than prompting a reunion the Han-style clothing obstructs it.

On the wedding night, the two newlywed couples stay with the grooms' family, now located in Nanjing. The drama devotes an entire scene, "Waiting for Dawn" (Daidan 待旦), to describe the hero and heroine's reluctance to initiate a conversation. At one point, Hua Jing is about to speak when he suddenly recalls his female identity: "I had almost forgotten: I'm wearing women's clothing. How can I start a conversation with him?" (scene 33). His female garb dictates that the hero, as a woman, must follow the ritual codes forbidding a bride to initiate a conversation. The only obstacle on his return journey home, it appears, is a set of women's clothing. As a result, he finds himself a stranger in his own home. Although both wear traditional ceremonial dress in the Han style, they fail to recognize each other's true identity throughout the night. Only after Hua Jing returns to being a man in the new dynasty will the couple be able to properly reunite.

After the wedding night, both grooms remove their wedding garb and change into Manchu uniforms before paying the brides' family a ritual visit (scene 34). When they are with the brides' family, Shui Suyue's mother recognizes her the moment they meet.[21] Madam Shui balks, however, at her daughter's strange dress in a long aria consisting of seven questions, the last of which is, "Can it be a painting of Wang Qiang [Wang Zhaojun], mistakenly showing her wearing a Confucian cap?" (scene 34). "Confucian cap" (*ru guanmian* 儒冠冕) refers to the heroine's Manchu uniform as indicated in the scene's stage instructions. The mother sees no difficulty in associating the Manchu dress with existing terms of clothing, such as a Confucian cap. What befuddles the mother instead is her daughter's hair: "For what reason have you cut your hair to be neither a man nor a woman? How bitter is this for me, as if I were drunk, as if in a dream!" (scene 34). The mother uses the gender category of *nannü* to describe the girl's hair. Her criticism of being "neither a man nor a woman" is open to multiple readings. On the surface, the heroine has followed the Manchu regulation by shaving her head, leaving her with a male hairstyle that contradicts her true gender as a woman. On another level, the Manchu hairstyle itself fails to fall into any existing gendered categories of hairstyle. It is neither a conventional hairstyle for men nor a conventional hairstyle for women but a hairstyle for the Manchus.

The heroine's response more clearly indicates her hairstyle's ethnic features: "So I cut my hair to be neither a worldly person nor a girl/nun. How laughable that I carry both yin and yang on one body alone" (scene 34). This response indicates the difficulty of explicating the heroine's strange hairstyle using existing cultural categories. The phrase "nor a girl" (*feini* 非妮) uses the gender term *ni* 妮 to refer to the heroine's androgynous identity, which corresponds to the term *yinyang* in the latter half of the aria. This line directly responds to her mother's criticism that Shui Suyue is neither a man nor a woman. On the other hand, the character for *ni* 妮 (girl) can be read as a scribal error for *ni* 尼 (nun), which would constitute a contrasting parallel with *su* 俗 (worldly) in the phrase "neither a worldly person nor a girl/nun" (*feisu feini* 非俗非妮). The Manchu hairstyle for a man resembles that of a nun in that both barely keep any hair. Thus, the Manchu hairstyle lies between male and female genders and between the monastic world and the mundane world. Neither reading of the heroine's response, however, adequately captures the ethnic nature of her hairstyle. The mother's and daughter's conversation reveals the difficulty of integrating the Manchu hairstyle and clothing with a female body because the cap and the queue underneath would befit only a male degree holder in the Manchu regime. At the end of the scene, the mother sends her daughter inside to change her clothes. Conceivably, her hair will grow back over time, and she will assume traditional Chinese clothing for women on her female body.

How, then, will the hero remove his female dress and return to a male identity? At Hua Jing's new home in Nanjing, the father is equally surprised—not by the hairstyle but by his son's clothing.

WAI: Why are you wearing a girlish bun and phoenix hairpin? Why have you dressed up in a fiendish way to show such a sinister appearance?

SHENG: The other day I left the city to avoid the disaster. I heard that whoever refuses to shave his head would be executed. So in a hurry I was forced to change into women's clothing.

WAI: If that's the case, Lu, my son, quickly bring your brother inside to have his hair cut in the right style and his clothing changed into scholarly dress. And come out after that. (scene 35)

To the father, Hua Jing's cross-dressing is a sinister practice. Even for the purpose of preserving hair would such a decision not be justified. Dressing across ethnicities seems only natural—or, at least, more so than dressing across genders. At his father's order to shave his head, the hero makes no protest. Under this new sartorial order, only a male body and Manchu hairstyle are a legitimate combination. When the couple first changed their clothes, the hero twice referred to his parents as the reason why he would cross-dress to preserve his hair. By the end of the play, all his previous efforts end in vain since he ultimately cuts his hair at his father's urging.

Parents in traditional Chinese dramas often serve as protectors of the existing order. For example, by the end of *Peony Pavilion* (*Mudan ting* 牡丹亭), the father, Du Bao, still refuses to recognize his resurrected daughter, insisting that she is a ghost.[22] At the end of *Lovebirds*, the parents play an opposite role. Although the hero claims filial piety as the reason for his cross-dressing, his father disapproves and urges him to change to the Manchu hairstyle. Instead of serving as a guardian of the old order, the father acts as an advocate of the new. It is the father's demand that exculpates Hua Jing from failing to live up to his original promise.

Hua Jing's father asks that he change into scholarly dress with head-gear (*jinfu* 巾服), the same term used for the scholarly dress the hero wore at the very beginning of the drama. The stage instruction does not specify into which kind of clothes he changes. Can it be the scholarly clothing he gave to Shui Suyue earlier, which was lost after she entered the Hua family? Even if Hua Jing retrieves his old clothing, that very piece of garment has been abandoned by Shui in favor of the Manchu uniform. A man in the new era should have not only a male body and Manchu hairstyle but also Manchu clothing—the new language of power. We are certain, though, that the Manchu uniform, suitable only for a degree holder in the new dynasty, would not automatically befit the hero's body. After the ethnic transformation of clothing in the new dynasty, the cross-dressing between the couple cannot be readily reversed— either by restoring their original clothing or by exchanging what the couple are wearing upon their reunion.

In the final scene, the hero sings, "My *yiguan* is restored, and I have abandoned the fragrant powder." Hua Jing assumes that by abandoning fragrant powder—a symbol of female identity—his identity as one of the *yiguan* (literati) group will automatically be restored. He is not aware, however, that through the previous transformation the *yiguan* identity has been dissociated from the *jinfu* of the Ming dynasty and reassociated with the Manchu uniform of the Qing dynasty. In other words, there is no literati dress or literati identity to which he can return.

As shown in table 2.1, the heroine first abandons her clothing for men's scholarly dress and takes the hero's place in his family. The heroine then dons the uniform of Ming degree holders. As one among the literati scholars, she succeeds in the Qing-dynasty imperial examination and changes into a Manchu uniform. Her route of changing clothing replicates the process whereby Ming literati scholars submitted to Manchu rule and the Manchu sartorial system. It is also the female body that adopts the Manchu hairstyle. The hero, in a gender sanctuary, is exempt from the poignant experience of confronting Manchu rule and must inherit the reconfigured gender role only when he exchanges positions with the heroine at the end of the drama. The sanctuary preserves his hair, at the cost of his male identity. With his hair shorn and his original clothing abandoned, the cross-dressed hero will find himself forever a stranger in the new world. Discussing gender transgression during the Ming–Qing transition, Charlotte Furth writes, "If in these years the androgynous male body was the object of politically charged discourse suggesting its unfitness to represent the Confucian moral order, the asexual female body escaped from the ascription of deficiency when offered up as an icon of Confucian virtue uncompromised."[23] *Lovebirds* exhibits the relative tolerance of gender transgression for women that Furth discusses.

TABLE 2.1
Progression of changing clothing and hairstyle

	Clothing	Hairstyle
Heroine	female dress → the hero's scholarly dress → Han uniform (*yiguan*) → Manchu uniform → ceremonial attire (Han style) → Manchu uniform → female dress	female Han → male Han → male Manchu → female Han
Hero	scholarly dress → female dress → unknown	male Han → female Han → male Manchu

Cross-dressing creates a space for the hero to temporarily eschew a set of social changes. Discussing the romantic classic *The Western Chamber* (*Xixiang ji* 西廂記), Richard Strassberg coins the concept "lyric capsule" to describe "an enclosed realm located at the heart of the drama, a place where the conventional spatial, temporal and social relationships of the outside are suspended."[24] Another prime example of the lyric capsule is the garden scene in *Peony Pavilion* where Liu Mengmei 柳夢梅 and Du Liniang 杜麗娘 indulge in an intimate relationship unfettered by social and ethical principles.[25] Rather than a lyric capsule, *Lovebirds* creates a gender capsule that allows Hua to temporarily grapple with gender-specific regulations on hairstyle and cultural identities. Such a capsule is not free of social norms but is instead defined by the code of conduct for a young lady. It is a common plot in many *chuanqi* dramas that the hero must enter a feminine space and undergo some transformative experience before reclaiming his male identity. Different from these dramas, in *Lovebirds* the solution to the hero's predicament is imperfect, since he ultimately fails to preserve his hair or his scholarly clothing.

THE ETHNIC CHALLENGE TO CROSS-DRESSING

Rule by a non-Han ethnic group in Qing China posed an unprecedented challenge to the representation of gender in Chinese dramas, both on the page and onstage. Theater scholar Xu Wei 徐蔚 has identified 106 dramas from the Yuan through the Qing dynasties that include plots related to cross-dressing. A majority of these dramas feature male impersonation (women impersonating men), with only 17 featuring female impersonation.[26] In the vast majority of these dramas, the cross-dressed characters finally change back into their original clothing and reclaim their gender roles. By play's end, men are still men and women still women, with each group donning the clothing associated with their original genders.

An archetype of cross-dressing, the Mulan story is the theme of a series of Chinese dramas. Mulan cross-dresses to join the army and spares her father the arduous and dangerous task of enlisting. In Xu Wei's 徐渭 *zaju* drama *Female Mulan Goes to War on Behalf of Her Father* (*Ci Mulan tifu congjun* 雌木蘭替父從軍), Mulan unbinds her feet and changes into a military uniform with a felt hat before traveling to the battlefield. After returning home, she uses a secret family recipe to shrink her feet, changes back into her female dress, and marries a man. Her female body, female dress, and marriage secure her identity as a woman.[27] We see similar representations of gender restoration in dramas about female impersonation. In the late Ming drama *Record of a Book Gift* (*Zengshu ji* 贈書記), a couple assume each other's gender to avoid personal misfortune. For a while, the hero even stays in a Buddhist temple as a nun. Just as in *Lovebirds*, they are arranged to be married and fail to find out the truth during their wedding night. Only in the very last scene are they able to reclaim their original genders and clothing and hold their wedding ceremony one more time. A legitimate wedding, and thus a marriage, can consist only of a man and a woman wearing legitimate clothing based on their original genders.[28]

As Sophie Volpp has discussed at great length, *Male Queen* (*Nan wanghou* 男王后) is the only extant Chinese drama that intricately problematizes the relation between the genders of performers, role types, and characters in a story of cross-dressing. In this play a man, who regrets being born into a male body, accidentally becomes the concubine of a king. When the king discovers an affair between the male concubine and the king's sister, he grants them a marriage instead of exacting punishment. Rather than have the male concubine change into a silk cap and black boots—clothing for male officials—the king orders that the concubine continue to wear women's clothing as the groom at the wedding ceremony. The androgynous male concubine is ultimately shared by a man and a woman. Volpp uses the concept of "stage gender" to analyze the complicated relationship between the gender of a performer offstage, the gendered role type onstage, and the gender of a performed character in a drama.[29] In the case she discusses, the hair of the male and female performers facilitates gendered impersonation, since long hair could be used to perform both male scholars and female characters.

However complicated their plots, all these dramas assume a binary between men and women, hence their respective clothing. Even for a person with an ambiguous gender identity, she or he can still choose between men's and women's clothing; the categories of male and female

FIGURE 2.1 Drawing showing the costumes for a female actor impersonating a male scholar onstage. Zhongguo Xiqu Xueyuan 中國戲曲學院 and Tan Yuanjie 譚元傑, eds., *Zhongguo jingju fuzhuang tupu* 中國京劇服裝圖譜 (Beijing: Beijing gongyi mei-shu chubanshe, 1990), 324.

still suffice to sustain gender disruption and restoration. Such is also the case on the Shakespearean stage. As Robert Lublin points out, although many of these plays probe gender relations through cross-dressing, "they ultimately reassert the idea that 'male' and 'female' are concrete and unambiguous categories by establishing the 'rightness' of particular clothes for particular characters."[30] During the Ming–Qing transition, however, Chinese men had to abandon their original hairstyle and clothing and submit to a new sartorial system. As illustrated in *Lovebirds*, when a story of cross-dressing spans the dynastic transition, the characters are no longer able to return to their original clothing and identity, as they would have in traditional dramas. Just as literati scholars in early Qing China experienced an unprecedented identity crisis caused and marked by the infliction of Manchu hairstyle and clothing, early Qing dramas of cross-dressing encountered a crisis in representing the experience of dressing across ethnicities.

The Manchu hair and dress regulations not only disrupted the gender balance in the text of *Lovebirds* but also posed particular challenges to the stage performance of cross-dressing. Scholars of Chinese theater have discovered recorded practices of cross-dressing in drama performance dating back to the Han dynasty.[31] Existing records show that many actresses in the Song and Yuan dynasties were expert at performing both male and female characters.[32] The late Ming period saw an increasing number of and interest in actors impersonating female characters onstage, leading to the prevalence of *qiandan* 乾旦 in *kun* and Beijing opera performances in the following centuries.[33] In the case of *Lovebirds*, the long-standing tradition of cross-dressing onstage faced challenges related to ethnic hairstyle and dress. As I discuss in the epilogue, it was not until the late Qing period in the nineteenth century that Manchu clothing became a particular type of stage costume. In early Qing China, Manchu clothing remained an alien subject, unable to be integrated into theatrical costumes.

Inasmuch as Manchu clothing was taboo on the early Qing stage, it was even more the case with the Manchu hairstyle. Even in contemporary performances of Beijing opera, a female actor dressed as a male scholar would still keep her long hair exposed (figure 2.1).[34] *Lovebirds* had no available trope for performing the couple's shaving their heads and changing into Manchu clothing on the early Qing stage and probably long thereafter. After all, *Lovebirds* provides only an imagined spectacle of cross-dressing involving Manchu clothing on public display.

YINYANG, NANNÜ, AND CATEGORY CRISIS

Lovebirds follows the structure found in traditional tales featuring cross-dressing to represent the scholar's story at a specific historical juncture. Although it concludes with a happy ending of grand reunion, some paradoxes remain. In addition to the identity crisis of Chinese scholars, the drama reflects a crisis in theatrical costuming and the existing categories of gender. In traditional China, binary terms like *yinyang* had long been part of a constitutive structure in discourses about gender. As pointed out by Maram Epstein, the Han-dynasty Confucian master Dong Zhongshu 董仲舒 proposed treating *yinyang* and *nannü* as equivalents, thereby "incorporat[ing] five-elements (*wuxing* 五行) correlative thinking into a *yingyang*-based moral order."[35] The symmetry and balance between these categories defined the understanding of gender relations in traditional China. As Epstein puts it, "In contrast to the European discursive emphasis on biology and the materiality of the individual body as the essential foundation of gendered identity, the Chinese emphasis was on demonstrating and maintaining the symmetrical relationship between male and female, a symmetry that came to be a defining feature of both the natural and social orders."[36]

It is based on the balance between the binaries of *yinyang* and *nannü* that Zhu Ying structures his dramas. In *Lovebirds*, Zhu attempts to promulgate a story of gender disruption and restoration. The play's title, *Dao yuanyang*, literally means "misplaced male and female mandarin ducks," and it indicates the existing dyad pertaining to male and female gender. In his preface Zhu Ying explains how he maintains a balance between yin and yang by assigning male and female characters to specific scenes in several of his dramas.[37] The opening scene of *Lovebirds* summarizes the plot: "The woman impersonates a man for fear of crazy villains; the man temporarily adopts a female form for fear of losing the hair. Yin and yang are later restored" (scene 1). As this aria indicates, yin and yang are to be conveniently and successfully restored, with the hero and heroine changing back into their original clothing. The *yinyang* binary encapsulates all the changes to the hero's and heroine's hair, body, and clothing, and the balance between yin and yang serves as an organizational principle for the entire drama. For that very reason, Zhu Ying deems it sufficient to explain gender and political changes through the categories of *yinyang*.

Following a comment on the balance between yin and yang, in his preface Zhu Ying uses the five elements to interpret the historical changes during the Ming–Qing transition. "A torch dies out while the real fire starts. The situation was such that metal was necessarily used in response. Metal means to kill. Wars spread in the Song and Liu area, and Yangzhou was trampled. Alas! The force of metal is great!" The references to "metal" (*jin* 金) and "real fire" (*zhenhuo* 真火) indirectly allude to the Manchus, who considered themselves descendants of the Jurchens (Nüzhen 女真) in the Jin 金 dynasty. The last line refers to the battles in Yangzhou, which constituted an emblematic event during the Ming–Qing transition. The categories of gender correspond with the categories of political transition. If temporary gender disorder can be corrected, so can temporary political disorder.

In traditional China, cross-dressing was usually regarded as a threat to political and social order based on *yinyang* and the five elements. Judith Zeitlin points out two traditions in regard to cross-dressing: whereas early Chinese historiography was generally hostile to male impersonation, cross-dressing was a recurrent theme in romantic literature.[38] Tensions between political order and gender disorder do not hinder the story in *Lovebirds*, since the drama itself is set in a time of radical upheaval. The disruption and rehabilitation of political order corresponds seamlessly with the disruption and rehabilitation of gender relations in a story of cross-dressing.

Zhu Ying further depicts a cosmos in the fashion of a well-orchestrated stage performance. In the opening scene of *Disturbance at the Wu River*, he writes,

TO THE TUNE "LINJIANG XIAN"

The motley cosmos masquerades
To gongs of wind and thunder drums;
With sun as *sheng* and moon as *dan*
Accompanied by yin and yang.

Heaven and earth act graybeard *wai,*
While rain and lightning play the clown.

Hodgepodge costumes hang in rows;
Pan Gu declaims his opening lines.
Daoist Chen Tuan's mesmerized,
He stares and rubs his aching eyes.
The days click by to clapper's beat;
Lord Yama whisks his costume on.

臨江仙：籠統乾坤大戲面，風鑼雷鼓開廂。
日生月旦配陰陽，天地為老外，雨電丑裝腔。
行頭混屯連排掛，盤古踱出沖場。
看得陳搏瞇眼傷，干支打板快，老閻紥扮忙。

This aria describes the entire universe as a lively drama. Based on the interaction between yin and yang, different elements in nature perform different role types in traditional Chinese theater. The balance between male and female gender, embodied in the *sheng* and *dan,* naturally accords with the balance of the entire universe. The stem and branch calendar (*ganzhi* 干支) mentioned in the aria (though not apparent in the English translation here) indicates historical time that passes both on- and offstage. By describing the mythological figures Pan Gu 盤古, Chen Tuan 陳搏, and Yama 老閻 as actors or audience members, the aria empowers drama to be an epistemological anchor that encompasses nature, history, and gender and that transcends the boundaries between different worlds. The opening scene of *Disturbance at the Wu River,* therefore, reinforces the basic categories of *yinyang* and *nannü* that Zhu Ying uses to structure his dramas.[39]

Scholars of gender studies, such as Judith Butler and Marjorie Garber, have challenged not only the binary definitions of men and women but also the preexisting categories of person and gender. Garber uses the phrase "category crisis" to refer to "a failure of definitional distinction, a borderline that becomes permeable, that permits of border crossings from one (apparently distinct) category to another: black/white, Jew/Christian, noble/bourgeois, master/servant, master/slave."[40] In *Lovebirds,* the categories of *yinyang* and *nannü* are in crisis precisely because of the disturbance caused by the dress regulations of the Manchu government. The traditional gender balance based on yin and yang fails to uphold a plotline concerning dressing across both genders and ethnicities. In other words, dressing across ethnicities cannot be readily represented using traditional tropes for representing dressing across genders.

If, as *Lovebirds* shows, changing one's clothing would alter one's cultural and gender identities, how much of a change would have occurred with literati scholars during the Ming–Qing transition? Whereas other writings remain reticent on the issue, *Lovebirds* allows us to see that it was impossible for a cross-dressed scholar to return to who he was before the Ming–Qing transition. The sartorial transition in seventeenth-century China not only challenged the masculinity of Han Chinese but also transformed women's bodies and clothing into political metaphors. Through costuming, *Lovebirds* mobilizes the ethnic and gender dimensions of body and clothing to create a space that allows us to probe the identity crisis caused by the Ming–Qing transition. Following from this story, the next two chapters explore in turn the experiences of men and women during the dynastic change.

CHAPTER THREE

Between Family and State

In *Lovebirds*, the hero's family comprises a father and two sons; the heroine's family includes a mother and two daughters. The marriages between the sons and daughters of the families symbolize the balance of yin and yang. In a farcical tone, the drama describes the Ming–Qing transition as a factor that creates united families. In early Qing society, however, the Manchu hair and dress regulations directly challenged the Confucian teaching regarding filial piety that one should not harm one's body, including the hair. The Manchu rulers demanded submission from Han Chinese at the expense of the existing order in Chinese families. How, then, did men in early Qing China remain filial while complying with the sartorial regulations? How do early Qing dramas represent their difficulties and struggles? Led by these questions, this chapter focuses on *A Ten-Thousand-Li Reunion* (*Wanli yuan* 萬里圓), a drama about a Chinese family separated and reunited during the dynastic transition.

The drama *Reunion* is based on real historical events. In the winter of 1643, a scholar named Huang Kongzhao 黃孔昭 (1589–1678) left his home in Suzhou, a city in the lower Yangzi area, to serve as a magistrate in the far southwestern county of Dayao 大姚 in Yunnan province. By the time he arrived at his post, the Ming capital of Beijing had fallen to the peasant rebellion and, later, the Manchu army. The constant skirmishes in the Yunnan–Guizhou district led the magistrate to resign from office and live in seclusion until 1652, when his son, Huang Xiangjian 黃向堅

(1611/1613–1679), traveled from Suzhou to find his parents and bring them back home. Huang Kongzhao passed away in Suzhou twenty-five years later, and soon after his son died.[1] The tale of the filial Huang Xiangjian circulated widely in the Suzhou area both orally and through writings. A few years after the Huang family reunited in Suzhou, the *chuanqi* drama *Reunion*, commonly attributed to Li Yu 李玉, appeared. Among existing early Qing dramas, *Reunion* is the only one that directly represents the Manchu government's suppression of Han Chinese at the time of transition. Although *Reunion* was composed in the early Qing period, it circulated widely in manuscript and stage performances throughout the Qing dynasty, reaching audiences that included local Suzhou residents and even the Manchu royal family.

The changing of dress codes in early Qing society posed particular challenges for the Huang family. Traveling between Suzhou and Yunnan, Huang Xiangjian had to alternate between Manchu and non-Manchu ways of dressing and, ultimately, persuade his father and cousin to follow him in changing their hairstyle and clothing. The dialectic between clothing and body in the drama illustrates the identity conundrum faced by one Chinese family during the Ming–Qing transition. Starting from a surprising absence of costume instructions in *Reunion*, this chapter examines textual fragments, woodblock illustrations, and performance records to explore how the drama dresses its characters as members of a Chinese family and as subjects of changing states. I suggest that *Reunion* reveals a major consequence of the dynastic change—the fragmentation of costuming and personal identities.

THE ABSENCE OF COSTUME INSTRUCTIONS IN *REUNION*

As a professional playwright and virtuoso of *kunqu* performance, Li Yu is credited with the composition of more than thirty plays.[2] In the late Ming period, Li Yu's dramas circulated widely in print and through performances. Four of them were especially well received, collectively known as *Yi-Ren-Yong-Zhan* 一人永占, all of which were printed during the Chongzhen reign (1610–1644).[3] A large majority of Li Yu's dramas contain detailed instructions related to costumes and stage action, a result of as well as evidence of the dramas' close connection with stage

TABLE 3.1

Costume instructions in Li Yu's dramas on dynastic transition

Title	Flower Queen (Zhan huakui) 占花魁	Thousand Loyal Ones (Qianzhong lu) 千忠錄	Mount Ox Head (Niutou shan) 牛頭山	Two Manly Heroes (Liang xumei) 兩鬚眉	A Ten-Thousand-Li Reunion (Wanli yuan) 萬里圓
Number of scenes	28	18	25	30	24
Number of character entrances	102	114	128	109	63+
Costume instructions	23	24	21	52	1
Percentage (%) (number of costume instructions by number of entrances)	22.5	21.5	16.4	47.7	ca. 1

performance.[4] His dramas concerning dynastic change, in particular, frequently use clothing to symbolize the transition in political order.[5] To examine the usage and representation of clothing in *Reunion*, one would naturally turn to see what the drama offers in the form of costume instruction. When a character comes onto the stage, Li Yu's dramas almost always indicate "a certain role type enters [*shang* 上]," especially when a character first appears onstage or reenters with an altered identity.

As shown in table 3.1, about 20 to 50 percent of the time when a character enters the stage, Li Yu's dramas provide a description of the character's costumes.[6] These instructions prescribe the dramas' main costumes, providing sufficiently detailed references for their stage execution. *Reunion* differs from the other dramas by Li Yu in that almost none of its existing editions carries any explicit costume instruction. *Reunion* is not a closet play far removed from stage performance. Rather, the drama's existing editions include detailed musical notations, instructions for movements onstage, and textual variations derived from different performances, all of which attest to the popularity of the drama onstage (figure 3.1). In the continuous staging of *Reunion*'s popular scenes, it is likely that different directors, performers, scribes, and collectors participated in shaping the drama in both stage and textual appearances. When the drama's author and editors added stage directions throughout the Qing dynasty, why did they consistently omit costume instruction?

The puzzle deepens in the face of the inadequate information about the author or an original edition of the drama. Li Yu did not leave behind any writing other than his theatrical works.[7] After its composition in the 1650s, *Reunion* never circulated in a complete print edition before the twentieth century. There is no edition of the drama definitively produced in the early Qing period immediately after its completion. Nor are scholars certain of what proportion of the text was originally composed by Li Yu and what proportion was the result of continuous editing and rewriting. What we have is a rich body of texts including two relatively complete editions and a series of individual scenes. Although not all the editions of the drama can be dated, we can discern that some of the materials were produced in the early period of the Qing dynasty and others in the late Qing period. A biweekly newspaper devoted to theater performance, *The Player's Press* (*Liyuan gongbao* 梨園公報), published an edition

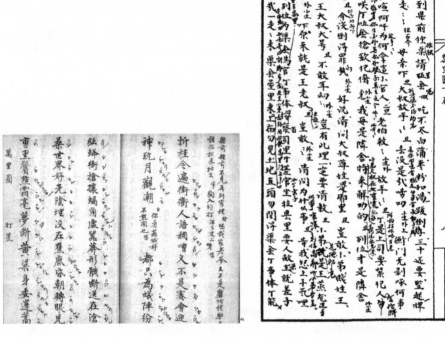

FIGURE 3.1 Pages from two manuscript editions of *Reunion*: *left*, National Library of China edition; *right*, *Guben xiqu congkan* edition.

of *Reunion* in a series of 121 issues from 1929 to 1930.[8] The editor of *The Player's Press* claimed that the edition was based on a manuscript produced in 1716.[9] If his words are true, that edition would be the earliest one available. After several decades of circulation, three scenes from *Reunion* had been printed in *Patched White Fur* (*Zhui baiqiu* 綴白裘) by the mid-eighteenth century. The frequent staging of these three scenes also led to the production of a number of manuscripts preserving performance notes. A largely intact manuscript of *Reunion* was collected by the former Beijing opera actor Cheng Yanqiu 程硯秋 and reproduced in *Guben xiqu congkan* 古本戲曲叢刊 (hereafter *GBXQ*).[10]

Regardless of whether the absence of costume instructions in the drama resulted from the sensitivity surrounding clothing and hairstyle, we still face the question of how the drama dresses its characters. As shown in table 3.2, scenes concerning the two themes of family and the

TABLE 3.2

Themes and dress codes in *Reunion*

Themes	Primary scenes	Main characters	Setting	Corresponding dress codes in early Qing society
Family	11, 12, 14, 16, 17, 24	Huang Xiangjian	On the way to Yunnan	Manchu, Han, and other
State	5–7, 10, 15	Huang Kongzhao	Yunnan	Han and other
	21, 22	Huang family vs. Manchu officers	Suzhou	Manchu

state are set in different spaces, feature different characters, and correspond to different dress codes in early Qing society. The Manchu hair regulations triggered rampant upheavals during the Shunzhi reign, precisely the time when Huang Xiangjian left for Yunnan in search of his parents. Suzhou, under Manchu rule, was in the process of adjusting to Manchu hairstyle and clothing. Yunnan, yet to be captured by the Manchu government, maintained its original dress codes.[11]

On the surface, the drama recounts a familial story. A series of scenes in the drama feature the filial son Huang Xiangjian's journey to Yunnan. Another group of scenes focus on the negotiation between the state and individual Han Chinese: Huang Kongzhao abandons his office in the Ming dynasty and later transforms into a subject in the Qing dynasty; two officers from the Manchu government harass the Huang family in Suzhou, only to be beaten by a heroic young man named Huang Chengyou.[12] A study of these represented characters not only reveals the personal experiences mediated by body and clothing in early Qing China but also shows how the dynastic transition influenced theatrical costuming as practice as well as representation. The rest of this chapter discusses different characters in the drama to show how the dynastic and sartorial changes influenced the relationship between body, clothing, and identities in seventeenth-century China and beyond.

As a filial son who traveled nearly three thousand miles to find his parents, Huang Xiangjian traversed areas controlled by different military powers.[13] Extant editions of *Reunion* feature a variety of depictions of Huang, including disparate styles of his clothing. In scenes 8 and 9 Huang Xiangjian, living in Suzhou under Manchu control, prepares for his journey to Yunnan. According to the historical context, men in early Qing Suzhou were required to wear Manchu clothing. Yet these scenes do not carry costume instructions, nor do the characters in the drama mention clothing in their dialogues.

Despite the general absence of costume instructions, the drama emphasizes Huang Xiangjian's travel pack and umbrella. Scene 12, titled "Stumbling in Snow" (Diexue 跌雪), depicts Huang traveling on a snowy day and being robbed by a bandit dressed as a tiger. Upon Huang's entrance, the stage direction reads, "[Enter] *sheng* with a bag and an umbrella" (生包傘). A late nineteenth-century illustration of the scene depicts Huang holding an open umbrella and trying to escape from the bandit (figure 3.2).[14] In the picture, Huang's scholarly hat is missing, revealing something like a hairnet used to bind his hair. A common piece of equipment for travelers, Huang Xiangjian's umbrella serves as an important symbol of his identity as a filial son on a painstaking journey. The textual descriptions of his clothing serve a similar purpose. For example, when Huang Xiangjian walks on narrow bridges in scene 14, "Three Rivers" (Sanxi 三溪), he sings, "I steadily fasten my tattered clothes." The umbrella, travel pack, and ragged clothes together illustrate Huang as a rugged traveler who withstands all kinds of difficulties.[15]

In addition to describing these exterior articles, the drama foregrounds Huang Xiangjian's naked body, which fundamentally provides a person with corporeality. In "Stumbling in Snow," the stage instructions describe the bandit robbing and undressing Huang. After being undressed, Huang sings a series of arias about his nudity, and says, "[The bandit] robbed me of all my baggage and clothes, leaving my body stark naked" (scene 12). The reference to Huang's naked body exists in almost all the editions of the scene. The frequent references to a nude body recall the term "a newborn infant" (*chizi* 赤子) that appeared frequently in early Confucian classics. Scholars have long pointed out the importance of

FIGURE 3.2 Illustration of the scene "Stumbling in Snow" of *Reunion*. Wanhua Zhuren 玩花主人 and Qian Decang 錢德蒼, eds., *Huitu zhuibaiqiu* 繪圖綴白裘 (Shanghai: Shanghai shuju, 1895), vol. 9, 10a. Image courtesy of the East Asian Library, Washington University in St. Louis.

clothing in defining one's identity.[16] During the Ming–Qing transition, clothing became a mobilized indicator of one's political identity. The naked body, in contrast, is the most basic component bestowed by one's parents. In the case of the character Huang Xiangjian, it is not his clothing but his bare body that comes to define his identity as a filial son. In actual performances, Huang probably would not appear unclothed, yet the metaphorical naked body signifies his identity removed of political connections.[17]

Starting from that naked body, Huang later dons other items of clothing. Soon after the robbery, an old monk discovers Huang lying in the snow and provides him with Buddhist clothes. The added notes in the *GBXQ* edition read, "Buddhist robe covers from head" (連頭僧衣遮; scene 12). The Buddhist robe Huang temporarily dons is reminiscent of early Qing Chinese who "took refuge in Buddhism" (*taochan* 逃禪) to avoid changing into Manchu hairstyle and clothing. When Huang Xiangjian later resumes his journey, he recalls the help he received from the monk, mentioning the "scholarly garments" (*jinfu* 巾服) bequeathed to him (scene 14). This is the first time in the drama when Huang Xiangjian explicitly mentions his Han-style scholarly dress. The travelogue of the historical Huang Xiangjian records one occasion when he was rescued from exhaustion by a Buddhist monk and another when he was robbed of his clothes and shoes.[18] It is the drama that combines these events into a story of undressing and reclothing the protagonist. From unspecified clothing to a naked body then to a Buddhist robe and finally to scholarly garments, the drama script includes a series of plot segments of changing clothes, which together highlight Huang's image as a dogged traveler.

Compared with his clothes, Huang's Manchu hairstyle would have more easily betrayed his origins. By the time of Huang Xiangjian's arrival, the Manchu army and the remaining Ming army were at war in southern and southwestern China. In his travelogue, Huang records multiple occasions on which he was questioned and even detained because of his altered hair. He writes, "Some noticed that my hair was not lustrous and hence they were waiting to arrest me. . . . There was a large number of soldiers and war horses in the provincial capital. Seeing my unbound hair, they surrounded and questioned me."[19] In the widely circulating "Biography of Huang the Filial Son" (Huang Xiaozi zhuan 黃孝子傳), the author, Gui Zhuang 歸莊 (1613–1673), provides information about Huang

Xiangjian's experience when caught by the military general in Yunnan: "Because of the Filial Son's short hair and Wu dialect, they suspected that he was a spy."[20] These records clearly indicate that Huang's hairstyle incurred local people's suspicions. They document Huang's experiences when crossing the boundaries between different political and cultural milieus.

The drama, however, does not highlight the ethnic connotation of Huang's clothing and hair. By scene 16, Huang Xiangjian has finally entered the area controlled by non-Manchu armies. When the general of Yunnan captures Huang, he comments on Huang's appearance and speech: "Look! Your appearance is anomalous, and your words incoherent. You must be a spy." Compared with Huang's travelogue and Gui's account, the drama makes only a cursory reference to Huang's appearance without pinpointing his hair.

Another incident further demonstrates the differences in the writing in Huang Xiangjian's travelogue and in the drama *Reunion*. Huang's travelogue provides details about his clothing and hair upon the family reunion in Yunnan: "My hair was robust and temples tousled, my face sun-blackened, eyes swollen, beard hoary. In short clothes and straw sandals, I looked far different from the past. At this, my parents once more lamented facing each other."[21] Long hair, which is the scholarly style in the Ming dynasty, would not look robust and tousled even after painstaking travels. This description indicates how Huang Xiangjian's shorn hair surprised his parents and caused them pain. The drama, by contrast, stresses Huang's chapped body and tattered clothes. In the drama, upon seeing his son Huang Kongzhao laments, "How bitter, when I see you languishing with gaunt complexion! My tears stream down when I look upon your tattered clothes." This line touches only on Huang Xiangjian's complexion and clothing. Whereas Huang Xiangjian underwent a series of clothing changes between Manchu and Han styles in early Qing society, what we see in the drama is merely ragged Han-style clothes appended to a suffering body.

A woodblock illustration of scene 14, "Three Rivers," depicts Huang Xiangjian wearing traditional scholar's clothes in the Han style (figure 3.3). The details of landscape in the picture exceeds the level of verisimilitude in a stage performance of the scene, but the character's clothes depicted here would be consistent with the actual

FIGURE 3.3 Illustration of the scene "Three Rivers" of *Reunion*. Wanhua Zhuren 玩花主人 and Qian Decang 錢德蒼, eds., *Huitu zhuibaiqiu* 繪圖綴白裘 (Shanghai: Shanghai shuju, 1895), vol. 6, 9a. Image courtesy of the East Asian Library, Washington University in St. Louis.

costumes employed for performing Huang Xiangjian on the early Qing stage, which would have constituted a stark contrast to the Manchu-style clothes Huang wore in early Qing Suzhou.[22] The contrast, however, did not hinder early Qing audiences from associating the theatrical character with the real person. A record produced not long after the drama's completion demonstrates the far-reaching influence of *Reunion* in spreading the story. "Duanmu [Huang Xiangjian] traveled by foot to the southernmost point under heaven. . . . Those who heard of his deeds were greatly shocked and spread the story as something worthy of praise. Performers in the Pear Garden produced a drama based on the event and performed it with music. There wasn't anyone among the audience who did not shed streams of tears and try to meet [Huang] in person to pay respect."[23] This record indicates a striking equivalence between the theatrical representation of Huang the filial son and the historical person Huang Xiangjian. The discrepancy between Han-style costumes and Manchu-style clothes did not obstruct the audience from translating filial piety onstage into filial piety in society.

Some historical records enable us to understand the specific contexts in which *Reunion* was staged in the Qing dynasty. In a chronicle biography (*nianpu* 年譜) Wang Bian 王忭 (1628–1702) edited for his father, Wang wrote,

> That year, the Venerable was seventy years old. In the middle of the first month, we celebrated this by inviting the intermediate troupe of the Shen family to stage a performance at our household for a few days. The first script staged was *Reunion*, representing the contemporary story of the Filial Son Huang. All who watched the performance felt amused in their hearts and entertained by the scenes. This is indeed a nonpareil piece throughout history.[24]

The year mentioned in this record was the eighteenth year of the Shun-zhi reign (1661), only a few years after the composition of *Reunion*. The record indicates that the performance of *Reunion* took place in the middle of the first month—the Lantern Festival—as a celebration of the father's longevity. Conceivably, the highlight of that performance would be Huang Xiangjian's filial deeds.

In its opening chapter, the *Classic of Filial Piety* (*Xiaojing* 孝經) defines filial piety based upon body, hair, and skin: "Our bodies—to every hair and bit of skin—are received by us from our parents, and we must not presume to injure or wound them—this is the beginning of filial piety."[25] These lines highlight the intact condition of the human body, including hair, as the basis of filial piety. Shaving the head clearly violated that principle, which was one of the main reasons that Han Chinese people resisted the Manchu hair regulation. As seen in the drama, even though his clothing and hairstyle are altered, Huang Xiangjian's bodily sufferings still suffice to define him as a filial son. While Manchu rulers claimed dominance over one's exterior appearance, the drama reserves the body proper for Huang to perform his acts of filial piety. In theatrical representations of the story, Huang's physical suffering on a filial pilgrimage redeems his loss of hair and his change of clothing in submission to the Manchus.

CHANGING STATES AND CHANGING CLOTHES

Whereas *Reunion*'s story of the son, Huang Xiangjian, revolves around filial piety, the part about the father, Huang Kongzhao, necessarily involves his political allegiance. Li Yu's historical dramas composed in the early Qing period portray loyal subjects defending the country as well as turncoat officers changing their political allegiance. In all the dramas, changing clothes is a convenient trope to signify a character's change of political affiliation. As a salient example, Li Yu exploits the symbolic meaning of clothing and hair in *The Slaughter of the Thousand Loyal Ones* (*Qianzhong lu* 千忠錄).[26] Also featuring dynastic transition, the *Thousand Loyal Ones* constitutes a contrasting case with *Reunion* to illuminate the characteristics of costuming.

The *Thousand Loyal Ones* is a drama about a political coup within the early Ming royal family. After the death of Zhu Yuanzhang 朱元璋, the founding emperor of the Ming dynasty, his grandson, the Jianwen emperor 建文, ascended the throne. As the new emperor attempted to curtail the power of provincial princes, his uncle Zhu Di 朱棣, Prince of Yan, rebelled against him and laid siege to the capital, Nanjing. Scene 6 of the *Thousand Loyal Ones* features Jianwen escaping from the palace. In the GBXQ edition, upon the characters' appearances in the scene, the main text introduces their costumes, which are further elaborated on in the interlinear notes. When Jianwen shaves his head and changes his clothes to become a monk, the interlinear notes instruct the actor on how to perform it onstage: "*Sheng* [Jianwen] sits properly; *wai* removes the hat and carries it offstage and then holds a coat to cover [*sheng*]; *mo* and *fu*, on both sides [of *sheng*], cover up the knife with their hands and put the beard in sleeves. . . . Remove the boots and dress [*sheng*] again" (scene 6). Immediately afterward, an official changes into a Daoist robe so that he can accompany Jianwen on his flight, for which the drama also provides stage instructions. The series of actions of changing hairstyle and clothes resemble a rite of passage, after which Jianwen begins to be addressed as a Buddhist master (*dashi* 大師) by his followers. As Jianwen changes his clothes, his empire is surrendered to the usurper.

Clothing continues to demonstrate highly symbolic meanings in the rest of the drama. When Jianwen finally returns to the imperial court after the death of the former usurper, the current emperor provides him "a Vairocana cap with a golden crest and a *kāṣāya* robe decorated with nine dragons" (scene 24). The stage instruction indicates that Jianwen is to "put on the robe and cap at the accompaniment of pipe and percussion instruments" (scene 24). At this moment, Jianwen is performed by an actor in the supporting role *xiaosheng* (second male lead), while the *sheng* is assigned to the actor performing the new emperor, a change of role types rarely seen in traditional Chinese drama. Jianwen's acceptance of the Buddhist robe symbolizes his recognition of the new political order and his own resignation from the historical stage. Throughout the drama, the deprivation, changing, and loss of clothing and the reinvestiture mark different stages of political transition.[27]

In contrast to the detailed costume instructions in the *Thousand Loyal Ones*, *Reunion* adopts an oblique tone when describing Huang Kongzhao changing his clothes, once as a loyal subject of the Ming dynasty and another time submitting to the Qing dynasty. Upon his resignation from the Ming government, Huang Kongzhao delivers the official seal to his successor and laments, "Alas! My Lord! I bid farewell to the appointment conferred by imperial favor; I bid farewell to the destiny of the bronze seal. I remove the blue robe worn on my body; I unfasten the black silk cap" (scene 7). A blue robe and a black silk cap were part of the official uniform of a low-ranking official in the Ming government. This moment is one of the few places in the drama where Huang Kongzhao expresses his loyalty to the Ming court. By choosing the life of a recluse, Huang Kongzhao abandons his duties as a Ming official. The interlinear commentary in the *GBXQ* edition adds a performance instruction, "*Wai* removes his clothes," but does not indicate into what kind of clothes he changes.

Toward the end of *Reunion*, Huang Kongzhao will have to confront the requirement of shaving his head and changing into Manchu clothing. After leaving Yunnan, the family soon arrives at a border pass. Huang Xiangjian says, "Father, this is where the border lies. Further ahead will be the territory of the Qing dynasty. I'm afraid you and my cousin will need to shave your heads and change your dress [*tifa gaizhuang* 剃髮改妝]" (scene 26). This is a rare occasion in early Qing drama of a clear indication of the territory of the Qing dynasty. Huang Xiangjian points out not only the geographical boundary but also a boundary between different dress codes. The statement also affirms that the stage represents a space outside Manchu rule, where the characters wear Ming clothing.

At this point, Huang Kongzhao, a former official of the Ming dynasty, willingly agrees with his son's suggestion and says, "Certainly so." Then with the other characters he sings, "With an empty bag, why must I solitarily stay afar? Years and months press while my tattered cassock floats and flutters. (Together) Ten thousand *li* away, where is our home? Cloudy mountains fill our eyes till our tears start to stream" (空囊寂寞何須遠, 破衲飄颺歲月侵. [合] 迢迢万里家何在, 一望雲山几泪淋; scene 26). *Na* 衲 refers to the Buddhist cassock. When Huang Kongzhao uses "tattered cassock" in reference to his clothing, he indirectly compares himself to a monk who remains outside worldly conflicts. In the following line, he laments the long distance he must travel before returning home. Whether "home" refers to his hometown of Suzhou or his home country of the fallen Ming dynasty remains open to interpretation. Since this conversation takes place near the end of the scene, there is no more time or space for the changing of clothes to take place onstage. Thus, the drama avoids directly representing Huang Kongzhao's change to the Manchu hairstyle and clothing, a sensitive topic in society and onstage.

Most of the scenes with Huang Kongzhao in the drama do not include stage instructions or interlinear comments, with the exception of the aforementioned note about his departure from Yunnan. In the *GBXQ* edition, an unknown editor crossed out Huang's aria quoted in the preceding, replacing it with a single line grafted from the previous aria, reading, "Our smooth journey back to our hometown relies upon the favor of Heaven" (早歸故里仗穹蒼). The revision might have been for musical purposes since the revised ending maintains the same rhyme category from the previous aria, while the original ending does not. It is also possible that the editor tried to keep the entire aria more concise, making it easier for stage performance. In either case, replacing the word "home" (*jia* 家) with "hometown" (*guli* 故里) eliminates the potential reference to home country—the deceased Ming dynasty. After the family's departure from Yunnan, the drama quickly ends with a final scene about the Huang family's grand reunion in Suzhou.[28] One would expect that all the male members would have changed into Manchu clothing, yet this brief scene does not mention clothing at all. Given the similar plots in other dramas by Li Yu, such as the *Thousand Loyal Ones*, *Reunion* could have elaborated on Huang Kongzhao's costuming. At both moments, however, the drama makes only oblique references to his hairstyle and clothing.

In the final scene, the entire Huang family pay their respects to their ancestors in the ancestral hall, and together they sing,

To the Tune "Yellow Bean Leaf": Thanks to our ancestors' blessing and shielding, we have safely returned to the familial quarters. I am ashamed for not wearing a jade plate or a goldfish sash, not wearing a jade plate or a goldfish sash to honor generations of forefathers. Integrity has been our family heirloom, which I humbly claim to have preserved intact. How admirable that our child can follow the filial way, follow the filial way, to look for his parents ten thousand *li* afar, and eventually we have the good fortune of this remarkable family reunion.

At this ceremony in the ancestral hall, all the participants are descendants of the Huang family. The aria is sung in the voice of Huang Kongzhao. Again, it deals with the multifaceted meanings of filial piety. In the first sentence, Huang expresses gratitude for ancestral protection during their journey home, which is immediately followed by a repeated expression of "shame" (*kui* 愧). The opening chapter in the *Classic of Filial Piety* dictates, "Filial piety commences with service of parents; it proceeds to service of the ruler; it is completed by the establishment of character."[29] In Confucian ethics, one's political allegiance naturally follows one's filial piety. To be filial includes two inherent requirements: serving one's ruler as well as serving one's parents. Since filial piety requires one's success in serving the ruler, Huang Kongzhao indeed bears the blame of not holding high official titles. Right after this line, however, Huang excuses himself by announcing his "integrity," which refers to the fact that he did not comply with the Manchu government by taking office in the new dynasty. The aria illustrates Huang Kongzhao's paradoxical mentality of being filial and unfilial at the same time.

The drama's concluding line once again stresses its bipartite theme, "Composing the script to musical tunes is not a game, but to spread loyalty and filial piety among the public. Do not treat this as colorful words trumpeting romance" (scene 27). The two-element phrase *gongshang* (musical tunes) in the first line ties to the phrase *zhongxiao* (political loyalty and filial piety) in the second line. The juxtaposition of political loyalty and filial piety demonstrates the essential role of these two virtues for an ideal person. Instead of showcasing the simultaneous fulfillment of these virtues, however, the drama illustrates a tension between serving one's parents and serving the ruler. Political loyalty and filial piety become separated virtues for the characters Huang Kongzhao and Huang Xiangjian.

Borne out by the clothes-changing plot juncture, the ambiguity in Huang Kongzhao's political identity poses a particular challenge for the drama. To represent Huang Kongzhao as a Ming loyalist, the drama should have avoided mentioning his changing clothing and hairstyle toward its end. To represent him as a traitor, the drama should not have included his lament over the death of the Chongzhen emperor in scene 7. For Huang Kongzhao, it was a difficult choice whether to be a Ming loyalist, a recluse, or a subject of the Manchu regime. It was equally difficult for an early Qing drama to represent a Han Chinese changing to Manchu clothing. The awkwardness of representing clothing provides a possible explanation for the subdued approach to Huang's dress in *Reunion*.

In early Qing society, both Huang Kongzhao and Huang Xiangjian survived the transition and lived under Manchu rule. At the same time, resistance against the Manchus continued in multiple areas of China. *Reunion* directly represents the confrontation between the Manchu government and Huang's family in the drama's latter half with a significant number of scenes set in Suzhou. The scenes constitute a rare body of materials for exploring how early Qing drama represented the Manchu government and Manchu clothing. Political conflicts between the Huang family and the Manchu government reach a climax in scene 21, "Harassed by Officers" (Chairao 差擾), and scene 22, "Beating the Officers" (Dachai 打差).[30] Unlike the scenes extolling filial piety, these scenes portray ethnic conflict under the camouflage of humor and farce. In "Beating the Officers," two Nanjing officers, accompanied by the clownish character Wang Zhenglong, arrive at the Huang family's home to harass them and exact bribery under the pretext of investigating Huang Kongzhao's service in the previous Ming dynasty. When they try to arrest Huang Xiangjian's son, Huang's cousin Huang Chengyou, performed as the *mo* role, fights back and beats the officers, hence the title of the scene.

To understand how such a representation of insubordination was possible in the formidable political climate of early Qing China, we have to place the scene in China's theatrical tradition. Acting out a beating onstage was a time-honored tradition in Chinese theater. In adjutant plays (*canjun xi* 參軍戲) of the Tang dynasty, the two roles of gray hawk (*canghu* 蒼鶻) and adjutant (*canju* 參軍) would be used in performing physical assault onstage.[31] Ming–Qing drama performances also include scenes featuring acts of beating, which provide an opportunity for performers to display their martial skills, adding to the performance's buoyancy. Very often, such scenes feature the resistance of the disadvantaged against the powerful. Li Yu frequently used this trope in his dramas. For instance, in the scene "Beating the Officers" (Dawei 打尉) in *Qingzhong pu* 清忠譜, local Suzhou people wage a public fight against the officers sent by the corrupt eunuch Wei Zhongxian. In "Attacking the Carriage" (Dache 打車) in the *Thousand Loyal Ones*, a loyal official single-handedly confronts the usurping army and rescues the Jianwen emperor from a prisoner carriage. It is in this tradition that "Beating the Officers" in

Reunion enacts the confrontation between the Huang family and the officers from the Manchu government.

In "Beating the Officers," the heroic Huang Chengyou wears headgear *jinzi* 巾子. Upon seeing Huang Chengyou, the two officers comment on his clothing: "A slave pretending to be an idiot! What gall of the fool to wear a fucking *jinzi* on his head." Later in the scene, they again speak with anger: "What Master Huang, Master Huang? He has such atrocious manners, wearing a fucking *jinzi*."[32] The *jinzi* would have been worn only in the Ming dynasty, since men in the Qing, with their heads shaved and hair in queues, would not have required a headpiece to hold their hair together. In fact, as a representative piece of Ming attire, the hairnet (*wangjin* 網巾) was strictly prohibited by the Manchu government from being used in everyday life.[33] In the drama, we are led to believe that the upright Huang Chengyou wears Han-style clothes in accordance with the traditions of *kunqu* performance.

Few dramas in early Qing China include references to the Manchu state, much less to Qing attire in the Manchu style. In "Harassed by Officers," Wang Zhenglong explains that two Nanjing officers have arrived at the county office to look into the matter involving the Huang family. The main text of the *GBXQ* edition refers to the two characters as "officers from Nanjing" (*Nanjing chaiguan* 南京差官), while the interlinear materials render it "two barbarians" (*liangge manzi* 兩個蠻子). The term *manzi* appears at least three times in the scene and once in the following scene.[34] The two words *chaiguan* and *manzi* indicate two ways of categorizing the Qing political regime. On the one hand, the two officers represent the Qing state, and on the other they represent the Manchus as a ruling ethnic group. The term *manzi*, used in reference to the two characters, potentially translates the antiauthority trope in Chinese theater into an anti-Manchu reference. Clothing serves as an important venue enabling such a translation.

Li Yu would not have run short of tropes for dressing the officers as "barbarians." His other dramas include ample descriptions of northern minorities, including the Jurchens, whom the Manchu people considered to be their ancestors. *Mount Ox Head*, another early Qing drama by Li Yu, includes frequent appearances of such words as *fan* 番 and *hu* 胡 referring to the Jurchen regime. The drama also includes clear indications of particular ways of dressing these "barbarian" characters.[35] *Flower Queen*, a late Ming drama by Li Yu, includes an explicit note on cultural and ethnic differences—when a general of the Song court successfully escapes from the Jurchen land in the north, he says, "Finally I have become a person of the Central Plain [*zhongguo*], no longer a ghost in the barbarian land."[36] An illustration to that scene (figure 3.4) depicts two Jurchen soldiers, one of whom features the Jurchen hairstyle with the majority of the head shaved and the remaining hair hanging from the temples; his hairstyle is similar to that of the Manchus. The soldier's hairstyle clearly contrasts with the apparently unfastened long hair of the Song general also depicted in the picture.[37] These materials show that Li Yu was unequivocal about ethnic distinctions and that there were specific ways of representing ethnicity by means of costuming.

Compared with other characters in Li Yu's dramas, the costuming of the two officers from the Manchu government in *Reunion* would have been particularly sensitive. As a consequence of Huang Chengyou's beating, the officers flee the scene, leaving behind pieces of their garments. Having previously sided with the officers, Wang Zhenglong now takes pride in Huang Chengyou's heroic deeds and makes a long speech ridiculing the officers.

As shown in table 3.3, despite textual variations in Wang Zhenglong's words, every rendition of "Beating the Officers" includes information about one officer's cap. The *GBXQ* edition refers to the cap as a *saozi* hat (*saozi mao* 騷子帽). A *saozi* hat, also known as a *shaozi* 哨子 hat or *shaozi* 梢子 hat, was the official cap for government runners in the Ming dynasty, whose uniform remained largely unchanged during the Ming–Qing transition.[38] It is probable that the early Qing performances of "Beating the Officers" showed the two officers dressed in the traditional uniform for government runners in order to avoid presenting clothing with Manchu ethnic features.

In several editions, Wang Zhenglong expresses his surprise at seeing a belt as part of the officers' apparel. In the *Patched White Fur* edition, Wang makes an explicit comment: "Oh? There is even a piece of rope at the neck."[39] Here the strap is referred to as a rope (*sheng* 繩) attached between the head and the neck. This piece of information hints that the two runners wear queues following the Manchu hairstyle. More specifically, since the rope is beaten off the neck, it is probable that the runners, eager to show their submission to the Manchus, are wearing fake

FIGURE 3.4 Illustration of the scene "Returning from the North" of *Flower Queen*.
Guben xiqu congkan 古本戲曲叢刊 (Shanghai: Wenxue guji kanxingshe, 1957), ser. 3,
front matter.

TABLE 3.3

Textual variations relating to hairstyle and clothing in "Beating the Officers"

No.	Edition	Time of production	Text
1	*The Player's Press*	1929–1930 (allegedly based on a 1716 manuscript)	A hat suddenly fell off the head of the number-two guy. Lucky that I'm nimble-handed. Now it's already in my hand.
2	*Patched White Fur*	1777	I have picked up a hat that fell off the head of the number-two guy. . . . Oh? There is even a piece of rope at the neck.
3	Chinese National Academy of Arts	1866	There is a hat off the head of the number-two guy. Ba! How filthy is the head of the old lazy guy! There is also a belt.
4	Youguxuan	1890s	A hat and a belt—not a bad idea to trade them for some drink.
5	National Library of China	Undated	A hat and a waist belt from the number-two guy—not a bad idea to trade them for some drink.
6	*GBXQ*	Undated, possibly nineteenth century	Now a belt is left with me. . . . What is the use of a belt and a hat for me?

queues. Another edition of the scene corroborates this hypothesis. At the end of the Chinese National Academy of Arts edition of the scene, Wang Zhenglong says, "I had thought they were real Manchus, but actually they are only fake Tiger Hills."[40] This line clearly differentiates between real Manchus and Han Chinese pretending to be Manchus. It is possible that editions of "Beating the Officers" with more explicit information on hairstyle circulated in early Qing society when Han Chinese were still adjusting to the Manchu hairstyle. It is also conceivable that

FIGURE 3.5 Illustration of the scene "Beating the Officers". Wanhua Zhuren 玩花主人 and Qian Decang 錢德蒼, eds., *Huitu zhuibaiqiu* 繪圖綴白裘 (Shanghai: Shanghai shuju, 1895), vol. 8, 7b. Image courtesy of the East Asian Library, Washington University in St. Louis.

the reference to the fake queues on the early Qing stage could have served to ridicule those who surrendered to the Manchus. In later editions of the scene, the rope became a belt, more explicitly a waist belt. The oblique indication of a Manchu queue gradually faded away.

A late-Qing woodblock illustration provides a visual representation of a possible stage performance of "Beating the Officers" (figure 3.5). In the illustration, Huang Xiangjian's son (*right-hand corner*) wears Han-style scholarly attire. The heroic Huang Chengyou wears the typical dress of a martial figure, with headgear binding his hair. The two officers (*on the ground*) and the clownish Wang Zhenglong (*bottom*) wear the same style of caps that are part of government runners' uniforms. One officer's hat has been knocked off, revealing his hair in a bun. The officers' clothes and hairstyle do not carry any indication of Manchu ethnicity. If this illustration reflects the actual performance onstage, then before the late Qing period, the performance of "Beating the Officers" employed primarily traditional Han-style costumes. Occasionally, the performance might insinuate the use of Manchu clothing and hairstyle through conversation or by using metaphorical props such as a rope or a belt. The absence of costume instructions in the scripts of "Beating the Officers" enabled performers to improvise with different props, at times encouraging expression of ethnic sentiments against the Manchus.

From this scene we can see that clothing, or the allusions to clothing, enabled the expression of discontent on the early Qing stage, which was the only space where Manchu clothing could become a subject of ridicule. Differentiating practice and representation as two ways to understand the state, anthropologists Aradhana Sharma and Akhil Gupta write, "The dialectic between practices and representations also opens up the possibility of *dissonance* between ideas of the state gleaned from representations and those arising from encounters with particular officials."[41] *Reunion* illustrates these two ways of understanding state power. Whereas the Manchu state exercised authoritative power to standardize sartorial practices in early Qing society, theatrical scenes like "Beating the Officers" provide an opportunity in which local Chinese encounter and contest the state through daily bureaucratic practices—although imaginatively. What the drama stages is not a celebration of state power but instead a spectacle of Manchu clothing and Manchu lackeys being repudiated.

The representation of clothing and identity in *Reunion* suggests issues beyond the drama proper. After returning to Suzhou, Huang Xiangjian produced a series of landscape paintings to record his journey to Yunnan. In accordance with a common practice in landscape painting, almost all the characters depicted appear to be wearing traditional Han-style clothing, with their hair in a bun. One of these paintings represents Huang and his father visiting Mount Jizu. In all five locations where they appear, both father and son are depicted in Han-style scholarly robes and Chinese hairstyles. In a few places, the father appears wearing a red scholarly robe, a possible indication of his being a Ming subject since the Ming royal family was surnamed Zhu 朱, which also refers to the color red (figure 3.6, *far left*). Discussing what she refers to as geo-narrative painting, Elizabeth Kindall writes, "The personalized experiences depicted in these types of paintings and the functions they served present an alternate lineage of artistic expression in which place and person

FIGURE 3.6 Huang Xiangjian and his father visiting Mount Jizu. Huang Xiangjian 黃向堅, *Searching for My Parents* (*Xunqin tujuan* 尋親圖卷), 1656 (ink and color on paper, handscroll, 31 x 561 cm; detail); no. 1995.0563, gift of Bei Shan Tang, collection of the Art Museum of the Chinese University of Hong Kong. Image courtesy of the Art Museum.

merge."[42] Clothing, as shown in such paintings, constitutes an important aspect of experience and contributes to the expression and representation of "various elements of personhood."[43] Similar to drama, the genre of landscape painting provides an artistic space for Huang Xiangjian and his father to perform as traditional scholars wearing Han-style clothing and retaining their original hairstyle.[44]

The artistic freedom in representing clothing and hairstyle enjoyed by Huang Xiangjian disappears when it comes to portrait painting in a historical setting. In the 1820s, Gu Yuan 顧沅 (1799–1851) and several other scholars collected the portraits of 570 former worthies (*xian* 賢) from the Suzhou area, engraved them in a newly built shrine, and reproduced these portraits in a printed book.[45] The collection includes portraits of local celebrities starting from Ji Zha 季札 in the Spring and Autumn period to the early nineteenth century, including Huang Kongzhao and Huang Xiangjian. In the prefatory pieces of the collection, the editors write of their special attention to clothing according to the character's time of life.[46] In the collection's "Editorial Principles" (Liyan 例言), Gu Yuan emphasizes, "Occasionally when a cap or attire contradicted ancient styles, [we] examined [documents of] the Ming dynasty to rectify it."[47]

In the collection, Huang Kongzhao's portrait carries the name of Huang Dayao, after the county in Yunnan where he served in his post. Huang Xiangjian's name is shown as Huang Xiaozi (Filial Son Huang). The poetic encomium for the father ends with the line "[his son] sought him from ten thousand *li* away" (萬里相尋), whereas the opening line for his son reads, "Seeking his parents ten thousand *li* away" (萬里尋親). The short biographies accompanying each portrait highlight the story of Huang Xiangjian's journey to Yunnan in search of his parents. The familial theme of filial piety connects the two portraits. Despite their familial connection, the father and son are separated by the states to which they belonged. The two portraits of Huang father and son are located, respectively, in volumes 14 and 16 of the collection among those categorized as either Ming subjects or Qing subjects (figure 3.7).[48] In accordance with their different political affiliations, the father is illustrated wearing Han clothing typical of the Ming dynasty, whereas his son wears Manchu clothing of the Qing dynasty. Gu Yuan and his collaborators dictated that each person could belong to only one dynasty, and accordingly could be portrayed in only one particular type of dress. The two portraits of Huang

FIGURE 3.7 Portraits of Huang Kongzhao (*left*) and Huang Xiangjian (*right*). Gu Yuan 顧沅 et al., eds., *Wujun wubai mingxian tuzhuanzan* 吳郡五百名賢圖傳贊, 1829 (repr., Taipei: Guangwen shuju, 1978), *juan* 14, 17a, *juan* 16, 30a.

Kongzhao and Huang Xiangjian reveal a tension between their familial and political identities. Whereas family relation bonds them together, their respective political affiliations separate them.

In between the portraits of the father and son, the collection includes sixty-eight other figures. Most of them went through the Ming–Qing transition, including famous scholars such as Gu Yanwu 顧炎武 (1613–1682) and Gui Zhuang, who once participated in military activities against the Manchu invasion. All sixty-eight figures are portrayed in Han-style clothes. Starting from Huang Xiangjian, the collection intermittently depicts characters in Han, Manchu, and Buddhist dress, until Manchu dress dominates the pictures from *juan* 17. The portraits of the father and son, two main figures in the story of a Chinese family, mark an important phase of the radical Ming–Qing transition.

Compared with portrait painting, the drama *Reunion* provides a more complicated space to represent personal experiences during the dynastic change. Echoing the disparity between the father's and son's clothes in their portraits, the divergent themes in *Reunion* stretch the use of costuming in two opposite directions: while the promotion of filial piety allows the drama to obscure the disparity between Manchu and Han clothing, the ethnic-political theme demands otherwise. As a drama based on a contemporary event, *Reunion* uses a group of techniques to create a sense of "the present day."[49] It runs against the drama's realistic orientation to use Han-style clothes throughout. At the same time, the political context relating to the Manchu government's dress regulations rendered it impossible to explicitly employ Manchu clothing onstage. This dilemma partly explains why, through more than two centuries of circulation, none of the drama's extant editions includes detailed costume instructions.

MANCHU ATTIRE IN LATE QING PERFORMANCES OF *REUNION*

In contrast to the situation in the early Qing period, Manchu-style costumes increasingly appeared onstage in the mid to late Qing period, which indicates changing relations between theatrical costuming and ethnicity.[50] Among all the scenes of *Reunion*, "Beating the Officers" was the first to be included in *Patched White Fur*, and the only scene that continued to be performed in the twentieth century.[51] Departing from *Patched White Fur*, later editions of the scene increasingly incorporated Suzhou dialect into the dialogue. The Youguxuan manuscript edition was produced in the late nineteenth century by a circle of literati *kunqu* aficionados who frequented the Bu Garden 補園 in Suzhou for musical gatherings.[52] Literati scholars' participation in the production of these editions shows that "Beating the Officers" was popular with the elites in southern China.[53] In 1827, the department of musical performance for the Manchu royal palace changed its name from Nanfu 南府 to Shengping Shu 昇平署. A copy of "Three Rivers" with arias and musical notation was used for performance by the Shengping Shu, and a copy of "Stumbling in Snow" was collected by the Shengping Shu under the title "Encountering a Tiger" (Yuhu 遇虎). Accordingly, these scenes were possibly performed in the Manchu palace in the nineteenth century, although it is not clear when the manuscripts were produced.

Whereas it is not surprising that the scenes of *Reunion* featuring filial piety were performed in the Manchu court, the performance of

FIGURE 3.8 Hu Sanqiao 胡三橋, drama painting of "Beating the Officers," 1879. Lu Eting 陸萼庭, *Kunju yanchu shigao* 崑劇演出史稿 (Shanghai: Shanghai jiaoyu chubanshe, 2005), front matter.

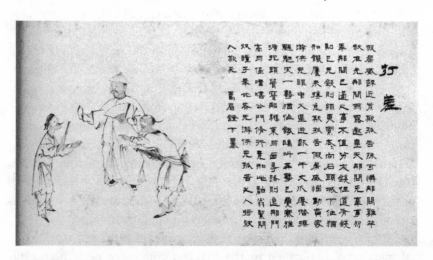

FIGURE 3.9 Xuan Ding 宣鼎, drama painting of "Beating the Officers," 1873. Wang Wenzhang 王文章 et al., eds., *Kunqu yishu dadian* 崑曲藝術大典 (Hefei: Anhui wenyi chubanshe, 2016), 146:2164.

"Beating the Officers" invites special deliberation. *A Register of Costumes* (*Chuandai tigang* 穿戴題綱), a document dated to the Daoguang reign (1782–1850), records performances of "Beating the Officers" in the Manchu court.[54] The *mo* (Huang Chengyou) and *xiaodan* (Huang Xiangjian's son) roles feature Han-style clothing such as high, square headgear (*gaofang jin* 高方巾) and Daoist robes (*daopao* 道袍). The text uses the term "contemporary costuming" (*shiban* 時扮) to describe the costumes for the *jing* and *fu* roles (Manchu officers) without listing specific items. The costumes for the *chou* role (Wang Zhenglong) indicate what "contemporary costuming" would involve. The term *youying mao* 有英帽 (homophonous with *youying mao* 有纓帽) possibly refers to the Manchu official cap with red tassels, and the term *lan jianxiu* 藍剪袖 possibly refers to the typically Manchu-style jacket with horseshoe-shaped cuffs (*jianxiu* 箭袖). "Contemporary costuming" in this record thus refers to Manchu-style attire for officers in the Qing dynasty.

The information in *A Register of Costumes* is congruent with textual and visual records beyond the Manchu court. In the manuscript edition of "Beating the Officers" collected in the National Library of China, one officer—referring to the other's clothing—tells Huang Chengyou, "Our Master only has this one horse jacket, which is borrowed from someone else. You will have to compensate him if you tear it apart."[55] Judging from this text, some performances of "Beating the Officers" (presumably in the late Qing period) explicitly adopted the Manchu horse jacket as a costume for the Manchu characters. Visual materials in the late nineteenth century further corroborate the change from government runner's uniform to Manchu-style uniform in staging "Beating the Officers." In a drama painting (*xihua* 戲畫) about the performance of the scene in late Qing China, one officer is wearing a horse jacket and a cap with red tassels, a typical Manchu uniform (figure 3.8).[56] Figure 3.9, another drama painting clearly shows the Manchu-style queue of one officer in addition to the tasseled cap, horse jacket, and horseshoe-shaped sleeves of the other officer.[57]

A document concerning the performance of "Beating the Officers" in the twentieth century lists in great detail the costumes used to dress the government officers from Nanjing: "White face, red-top summer hat, full black beard, black archer's jacket, black horse jacket with round flowers, white sash on waist, red pants, thick-soled boots, holding a fan."[58]

Many of these items, such as the red-top summer hat and horse jacket, are typical Manchu clothing articles. *A Chronicle of Kun Opera in Shanghai* (*Shanghai kunju zhi* 上海崑劇志) records the most recent performance of "Beating the Officers" in 1986. The book notes that the late Qing performance of the scene used Qing-dynasty costumes (*qingzhuang* 清裝) for the two officers, which were considered contemporary costumes (*shizhuang* 時裝) at the time of the performance.[59] These records lead us to the conclusion that different types of Manchu clothing gradually entered performances of *Reunion*, especially "Beating the Officers." Furthermore, the onstage employment of Manchu clothing was considered an invention of the late Qing period.

The use of Manchu clothing in late Qing performances of *Reunion* forms a clear contrast to the absence of Manchu clothing in earlier renditions of the drama. Catherine Swatek points out that the use of local dialect, in particular the Suzhou dialect, allows *Reunion* to smuggle in expressions of "anti-Manchu bias."[60] Whereas it is highly possible that "anti-Manchu digs" appeared in the drama's early Qing performances, the stage use of Manchu clothing in the late Qing period indicates a more complicated relationship between theater and the state, which I discuss further in the epilogue.[61] As far as *Reunion* is concerned, it is the absence of early Qing editions of *Reunion* and the absence of Manchu clothing therein that more accurately reveal the sensitive nature of costuming in the drama.

The dramatization of the Huang family's experiences allows us to see that clothing in mid-seventeenth-century China was a problematic issue both off- and onstage. In society, it was difficult for the actual father and son in the Huang family to maintain their Han clothing or to change to Manchu clothing. Onstage, it was equally difficult to represent sartorial changes during the Ming–Qing transition without using Manchu clothing proper. Early Qing history challenged the identities of the Huang family as Ming loyalists, Qing subjects, or unruly Chinese under Manchu rule as much as it challenged *Reunion* to represent these rival identities. This case study of *Reunion* has shown different modalities of dressing in the drama. We see the absence of costume instructions and only sporadic traces regarding clothing in the scripts and performances. But it is only through the silence, the absence, and the sporadic textual traces that we can adequately understand clothing as a strategy of state control and as a special realm of experience for early Qing individuals. In a word, the fragmentation of *Reunion* reflects the fragmentation of individual identities in early Qing China.

Explaining the productive effect of discipline, Timothy Mitchell writes, "Discipline, by contrast, works not from the outside but from within, not at the level of an entire society but at the level of detail, and not by constraining individuals and their actions but by producing them."[62] Both dress regulation and drama censorship in early Qing China were aimed at standardizing certain practices (ritual and theatrical), yet *Reunion* illustrates the twofold consequences of state control: the Manchu regulations on clothing and costuming resulted in the absence of certain types of costumes in the scripts of *Reunion* and simultaneously shaped the representation of the Manchu government in performances of the drama.[63]

CHAPTER FOUR

The Chaste Lady Immortal of Seamless Stitching

The Ming–Qing transition influenced both ethnic relations and gender relations. As chapter 2 illustrated, a woman could serve as a surrogate for the Chinese scholar to undergo ethnic and sartorial changes during the transition. Whereas chapter 3 featured men from a Chinese family crossing geographical and sartorial borderlines, this chapter discusses a woman crossing the boundaries separating the household, the local community, and the state. It takes up two dramas based on the story of a chaste lady who committed suicide after being sexually harassed and shows how costuming allowed the dramas to represent disparate and even competing themes around an event of chastity suicide.

In the sixth year of the Kangxi reign (1667), an impoverished scholar, Chen Youliang 陳有量, and his wife, née Hai 海, were traveling far from home in Changzhou, Jiangsu province.[1] Lin Xianrui 林顯瑞, a head soldier for canal transport in the Fengyang 鳳陽 garrison, with his accomplice, Yang Er 楊二, set a trap and hired Chen to work on Lin's boat.[2] After sending Chen off to manage some business, Lin made sexual advances toward Lady Hai. Having sensed the imminent threat, Lady Hai stitched together her entire outfit—from shoes to collar—in defense of her body. Lady Hai's unusual strategy successfully prevented her from being physically violated when the villain Lin approached her at night. Feeling humiliated, however, Lady Hai committed suicide after the harassment. The incident was later investigated by local authorities and Lin was executed. The local community raised funds to build a shrine for Lady Hai, who also received official commendation from the Manchu state.

The incident, especially Lady Hai's suicide, was intricately interwoven with the political and ethnic conflicts during the Ming–Qing transition. The early Qing era saw paradoxical attitudes and policies toward female chastity. On the one hand, early Manchu emperors discouraged some mutilating forms of female virtues such as filial mutilation (*gegu* 割股). Widow suicide, as an extreme statement of loyalty to one's husband, was considered to represent Ming loyalism. As historian Susan Mann points out, "During the early Qing period, the Manchus were reluctant to embrace dramatic images of female suicide as emblems of fidelity."[3] On the other hand, the cult of chastity became increasingly intense, and even "religionized," in the Qing dynasty.[4] Committing suicide in resistance to sexual assault started to qualify for official commemoration largely after the beginning of the Qing dynasty.[5] The story of Lady Hai was thus simultaneously interwoven with Ming loyalism and the Manchu regime's project of shaping its male and female subjects.

Lady Hai's body and clothing lie at the very center of the incident. It was through stitching up her clothing and shaping her body that Lady Hai claimed her identity as a chaste lady; it was also by means of viewing her body and the stitched clothing that the local community and Manchu government recognized her as a chaste lady. A large number of writings appeared recording and spreading Lady Hai's story in the early Qing period, including biographies, novels, and dramas. Local gazetteers in the following centuries also included entries on Lady Hai. Yet it remains to be seen how she stitched her clothing and how her body as covered by the stitched clothing was interpreted by different audiences. Historical records such as her biographies do not provide a ready answer to these questions. Some records indicate that portraits—and even a statue—of Lady Hai were produced immediately following her death.[6] An early Qing poem makes an explicit remark on the clothing on Lady Hai's statue: "In plain white silk enthroned on high, she sits in the flowery shrine / Her gown recalls her dress of old, with stitches dense and fine" (花龕高坐素羅裳, 密密針縫舊樣裝).[7] This poem on Lady Hai's statue specifically mentions that Lady Hai's stitched clothing is replicated as the most salient marker of her heroic suicide and her female chastity. Another record describes the face and clothes of Lady Hai's portrait: "A portrait of her was placed on the left side of her tomb shrine. I entered [the shrine] and paid my respects to her. She was looking down slightly and to the side, and she was brightly and majestically dressed."[8] This record briefly describes the lady's face, yet it provides little information about Lady Hai's stitched clothes. Other biographical writings, though highlighting the lady's activity of stitching her clothing, do not provide enough detail to reveal the social meanings associated with her clothing.[9] A full-length novel based on the story, *Bailianzhen Hai Liefu* 百煉真海烈婦, includes only a few pages concerning the lady's stitching of her clothes.[10] In these records, Lady Hai's clothes, either as actual garments or in textual representations, are merely static objects. The aforementioned writings interpret the clothes as a testimony to the lady's chastity, but the interpretation does not do justice to the rich connotations of her clothing.

Since costuming is a primary method for theatrical works to portray characters, Lady Hai's stitching of her clothing provides an opportunity for early Qing dramas to explore the meaning of clothes in her sensational story. Four months after the incident took place, a young scholar, Shen Shouhong 沈受宏 (1645–1722), started to compose *Chuanqi Drama on Chaste Lady Hai* (*Hai Liefu chuanqi* 海烈婦傳奇). He completed the drama early the next year.[11] The years following the incident saw the publication of another drama based on Lady Hai, *An Immortal of Chastity and Righteousness at the Piling Post* (*Piling yi jieyi xian ji* 毗陵驛節義仙記), by Monk Hui Mu from Chu 楚僧灰木.[12] In these dramas, Lady Hai's clothes conceal some parts of her body, such as her feet, and highlight others, such as her face. Costuming in the dramas about Lady Hai not only involves different types of dress for the male and female characters but also encompasses Lady Hai's actions in stitching her outfit, as well as different ways of embellishing her dead body with a coffin, architecture, and writings.

Theatrical costuming in these dramas faces two challenges. The first has to do with the central conundrum this book addresses—that is, how theatrical works represent early Qing events and early Qing people given the political sensitivity of such representations in early Qing China. Although the story was not directly related to the Manchu–Han conflicts, it nonetheless involved different parties in early Qing society. The naked body of a chaste lady would easily have invoked Chinese people's traumatic memories of the sexual violence rampant in the Ming–Qing transition.[13] If the authors meant to represent the story as a real event in early Qing society, they needed to confront the question of how to dress the chaste lady and the male villains. The second challenge involves the literary representation of sex and violence. Many dramas before the Qing dynasty address sexual harassment, such as *Yuanyang zhong* 鴛鴦冢, *Bao-jian ji* 寶劍記, and *Zhenwen ji* 貞文記, but seldom does any drama explicitly depict sexual assault. The theatrical tradition and the historical context together conditioned the nuanced costuming in the dramas about Lady Hai. Thus, this case study shows the intricate connections between costuming, chastity, and early Qing history.

THE IMMORTAL OF SEAMLESS STITCHING

That Lady Hai stitched up her clothing to protect herself from sexual harassment was itself an unusual activity within Chinese history.[14] Yet such a story does not necessarily serve the purpose of promoting chastity. *Immortal* tells the story of four deities exiled to the human world who return to the celestial world after a process of cultivation and enlightenment. Among them, the Chaste Lady of Crimson Snow (絳雪貞姑) is banished to the human world because of her indulgence in literary writings. Reborn as Lady Hai, she is destined to suffer from an attempted rape and to commit suicide. Her noble suicide would allow her to redeem her original identity and return to the heavenly world. The existing copy of *Immortal* includes twenty-seven scenes, with sixteen and eleven, respectively, in the first and second volumes.[15] Scenes 2 to 15 feature the sexual harassment and suicide of Lady Hai. The rest are devoted to two themes: the investigation of the case and the proclamation and divination of the heroine. Although based on Lady Hai's story, the drama introduces a few themes that overshadow female chastity.

Given how the story is framed as one of religious transcendence, the drama dehistoricizes the plot and characters. The extant edition of the drama includes no paratextual material and includes only sobriquets of the author and editors instead of their real names. Nor does the drama include any costume instructions. Little information about the play being based on an incident in the Qing dynasty is included. Toward the end of the drama, an imperial messenger (*tianshi* 天使) announces an imperial edict, appointing the characters involved in investigating the crime case as Military Commissioner of Huainan (淮南節度使), Transport Commissioner of Jiangnan (江南轉運使), and Prefect of Xiangzhou (襄州刺史), all of which are fictional titles without corresponding official positions in Qing society.[16] The fictional rather than historical setting allows the drama to avoid the topic of the Ming–Qing transition and, consequently, eschew the challenge of representing people and politically sensitive events in early Qing society.

Not only removed from early Qing history, the drama also introduces descriptions of erotica and violence that potentially undermine the theme of female chastity. In scene 15, Lady Hai senses the imminent threat from the villain Lin Xianrui and sings while stitching up her clothes: "Living in seclusion in Wuling, my family was engaged in spinning and weaving for generations. Our bedding and clothing are as beautiful as caltrop and lotus blossoms. Today, I request the Needle God's patterns and learn from the Weaving Lady's craft, and so I, too, may become a seamless goddess [*wufeng xianshu* 無縫仙姝]."[17] Wuling alludes to a gentleman of self-denying purity as recorded in the Confucian classic *Mengzi*.[18] Caltrop and lotus blossoms (*jihe* 芰荷) immediately remind readers of Qu Yuan, the loyalist in the Warring States period, who committed suicide in fragrant clothes after the fall of his country.[19] These allusions, together with many more in this style, depict the heroine as a noble lady of elegance and purity.

The expression "seamless goddess," however, contains divergent connotations. The line invokes the Needle God and the Weaving Lady, known for their ability to produce clothes without seams. Lady Hai would soon join both celestial beings because of her chaste action of stitching her clothes together before committing suicide. In that sense, the identity of "seamless goddess" is a result and continuation of her being a chaste lady. At the same time, the word "seamless" (*wufeng*) suggests her body is protected by the seamless stitching from sexual penetration. Thus interpreted, the phrase necessarily encourages one to imagine Lady Hai's body as impenetrable.

The detailed description of Lady Hai stitching her clothing further corroborates the second reading. Before Lady Hai starts sewing up her clothing, she thinks aloud, "I shall start to stitch together the garments close to my body." The stage instruction immediately following that line reads, "[She] takes up the needle and thread, unties her belt, and stitches."

The expression "close to my body" invites voyeurism upon the pure body of Lady Hai. She continues to sing, "The shuttling threads and tight golden needle soundly safeguard my fragrant flesh . . . (stitching breast area) Stitching a beaded vest to cover my ivory breast. (Stitching waist area) Stitching the tattered pants to densely protect my slender waist. (Pause sewing, watch, and stitch again) The critical part I stitch once more, lest it be still loose" (*juan* a, 42a). Such expressions as "fragrant flesh" and "ivory breast" were pervasive in traditional dramas featuring illicit love. These dramas would describe the female body only in metaphorical terms, whereas *Immortal* directly refers to the body and clothes such as breast, waist, and pants. The mentioning of "the critical part" (*guan'ai chu* 關隘處) in the last line all too easily stimulates a reader's imagination of Lady Hai's genitalia.

The voyeuristic depiction of the lady's body is immediately followed by descriptions of sexual violence. In describing the rape scene, the drama instructs, "The *jing* [Lin] clutches the *dan*." When the villain is obstructed by some deities, the text instructs, "The ghosts pull the *jing*, who stumbles and bumps his head when struggling to get up, and again he advances to clutch the *dan* as before." After the assault, Lady Hai decides to commit suicide by hanging herself, at which the stage instruction reads, "She performs the act of self-strangulation and falls to the ground."[20]

Lady Hai still faces the danger of her body being exposed after her suicide. At the end of scene 15, the text instructs that the *fujing* and *laodan* together carry away the heroine's dead body. In scene 19, "Initial Investigation" (Chukan 初勘), the instruction reads, "The *laodan* and *fujing* carry the *dan* on their shoulders and put her down on the ground as though she were a corpse." The expression "as though she were a corpse" indicates that the actor in the female leading role would perform the dead body onstage. The coroner examines her body and reports traces of strangulation on the neck. Suspecting there might be knife wounds on the body, the official orders the coroner to undress her, at which the text instructs, "The coroner finds it difficult to undress her and reports the situation." The official praises the lady's chastity and stops the physical examination, after which the heroine's body is carried offstage. During the process of forensic examination, the drama emphasizes Lady Hai's dead body as an object for public view. The instructions highlight the activity of viewing: "A miscellaneous role represents the coroner who examines and reports; the crowd watch and are startled; the actor in the *xiaosheng* role steps out of position and watches." Whereas the description of Lady Hai's stitching invites readers to view her body only voyeuristically, the forensic examination provides an opportunity for the drama to openly display the lady's body and clothes for public appreciation. The act of undressing and the physical examination onstage, though unfulfilled, produce a startling experience for audiences.

The details related to forensics and public execution resemble the descriptions in court-case novels of the Ming–Qing period. As Huang Yishu points out, the descriptions of prosecution, forensic examination, and the final sentence in the drama appear very "professional," which might be connected with the author's identity as a local official personally involved in investigating the crime.[21] The novel *Bailianzhen Hai liefu*, published the year after Lady Hai's death, includes details that are quite similar to those in *Immortal*. Robert Hegel has found significant similarities between the graphic descriptions of crime scenes in legal reports and those in fictional writings of Qing China.[22] A manual on forensic examination for Qing-dynasty magistrates, as Hegel points out, emphasizes "seeing"—the visual observation of the injured body.[23] Graphic depictions of violence also abound in writings about chaste ladies in *Ming History* (*Mingshi* 明史) and other historical texts. Behind such writings on female chastity, scholars have discovered a strong interest in erotica coupled with sexual violence.[24] The details about Lady Hai's body and clothes, as well as the detailed description of violence, correspond with the existing tradition of writing about exemplary women. Such writings satisfy an audience's desire for erotic and brutal spectacle. According to the "chastity and righteousness" of the title, the drama ostensibly lauds the lady's chastity, yet the display of a female body and the tentative undressing make the scene sexually evocative. As Katherine Carlitz's study of *Lienü zhuan* shows, the late Ming representation of female virtue was incorrigibly intermingled with representations of romantic love or death—women appeared simultaneously as icons of virtue and as objects of conspicuous consumption.[25] Specifically concerning the female body in these representations, Carlitz argues, "No one is supposed to desire the young widow's body, but the focus is unremittingly *on* her body."[26] Inheriting the literary tradition of mixing female chastity with erotica, *Immortal* turns Lady Hai's body into an object of sexual fantasy by describing her activities of stitching her suicide dress.

Immortal's story comprises two parts: one in the human world and the other in the celestial world. In addition to the erotic connotations and the display of violence, another theme of the drama—celestial transcendence—further undermines the theme of chastity. Before Lady Hai's suicide, the stage instruction indicates that the performer in the *xiaodan* role enters with a kerchief (*pa*) covering her head and hides under a table (scene 15). At the moment of the heroine's death, the *xiaodan* performer, as the soul of the heroine, follows a heavenly official off-stage while holding on to a whip offered by the official.[27] A moment before, Lady Hai had stitched up her clothes to protect her body and sense of self. That symbolic death, however, separates Lady Hai's soul from the body enwrapped in the stitched clothes. The *xiaodan* role represents the true heroine, whereas the *dan* role is reduced to a dead body.

Following Lady Hai's suicide, the drama maintains a clear contrast between the lifeless body in worldly dress and the celestial being in celestial dress. The restoration of Lady Hai's celestial identity requires her denial of her worldly experiences. In scene 16, "Guizhen" 歸真, the *dan*, supported by the *mo*, enters the stage wearing celestial dress with a scarf covering the head (*juan* a, 45a). Her celestial dress indicates her true identity as an immortal, whereas the headscarf indicates her current identity as a ghost, corresponding with the *xiaodan* in her death scene. The heroine, still deluded by her worldly experiences, accuses the villain Lin of rape and laments her miserable experience, whereas Lord Guan 關帝, performed by the *wai*, raises a series of questions to awaken her. The questions include, "Who are you?... I am asking the undead. Who cares about the dead?... Since you have abandoned your body, who is the one now reporting being wronged?... Since you are already dead, is the one being wronged not yet dead?" (scene 16). The conversation follows the convention in deliverance plays from the time of the Yuan dynasty, where a Daoist or Buddhist master would enlighten another immortal lost in the human world by pointing out the ephemerality of mundane affairs.[28] Thus enlightened, the heroine "rolls on the ground, removes her headscarf, reveals her celestial dress, and pays her respects to the *wai*."

Having resolved her mundane entanglements, the heroine recognizes her previous experiences as untrue and even requests pardoning the criminal Lin who caused her suicide. The lady's change of identity in turn triggers a change in the meaning of her clothes. When Lady Hai adopts the sacred celestial dress as an immortal, her earlier suicide dress becomes a profane object. In the latter half of the drama, the heroine appears as a celestial figure to assist enlightening her banished fellows. In scene 26, "Yuzhen" 遇真, the heroine enters in a bright celestial dress (*xianzhuang yanfu* 仙裝豔服), accompanied by maid fairies and dragon and tiger generals. Although the hero recognizes her from her appearance as his former wife, the heroine discourages him from approaching her.

In scene 27, "Erdan" 餌丹, the actor in the *dan* role performs a flower spirit impersonating Lady Hai by wearing her original dress to test the hero's determination for Daoist cultivation. When the hero is standing guard at the furnace of immortality pills, the flower spirit pretends to be his deceased wife and requests immortality pills to bring herself back to life. "I am your wife. I sacrificed my body to preserve my chastity for you. . . . For you, I strangled myself with a length of my sash and turned into a lonely wandering ghost." The flower spirit recounts the fact that Lady Hai committed suicide out of loyalty to her husband. However, the hero rejects the request, denouncing the scene as karmic illusion (*yejing* 葉境). The familial relationship between Lady Hai and Chen Youliang is ultimately rescinded in favor of the quest for immortality. While Lady Hai's stitched clothes symbolized that loyalty earlier in the drama, after her suicide the attachment to the mundane clothes would become a hindrance to the hero's return to heaven.

Although *Immortal* alludes to chastity and righteousness in its title, it draws from a diversified theatrical tradition that ultimately dilutes and even undermines an ethical tone. First, following the tradition of talented scholars and beautiful ladies, *Immortal* depicts the heroine as a well-versed lady from a noble family. Blended into romance is the tradition of the crime play, a primary theme in Yuan dramas. The latter half of *Immortal* is devoted to solving the crime and bringing the culpable parties to justice. The propensity to twist the moral voice turns the drama into a display of sensual and violent spectacles. Finally, the overarching theme of immortality undermines the ethical theme of female chastity. As the word *xian* 仙 in the title indicates, the drama features Lady Hai as a goddess in her exile in the mundane world. Her tragic experience is but part of her cultivation through which she returns to the heavenly realm. Although the drama is based on a historical event, the emphasis upon immortality jeopardizes the theme of female chastity.

These different themes in the drama, in turn, place different clothing types in tension—Lady Hai's clothing before her suicide, her stitched dress, and the celestial dress. Although the stitched dress symbolizes Lady Hai's chastity, once enlightened the heroine readily abandons the garment in favor of the celestial one. The stitched dress is to be studied in public as part of the crime scene, and Lady Hai's clothing before her suicide will be used by a flower spirit to test her husband's commitment to Daoist cultivation. Lady Hai's body and stitched clothes are merely an expedient means through which she transcends the mundane world. Theatrical costuming allows the drama to completely change the meaning of Lady Hai's suicide and the chaste activity of stitching up her clothes.

THE DIALECTIC BETWEEN NEEDLEWORK AND WOMANLY VIRTUE

Compared with *Immortal*, *Chaste Lady Hai* follows a completely different trajectory in representing the virtuous lady. Instead of the fictional setting of the former, *Chaste Lady Hai* bears an explicitly historical setting. A large number of the characters in the drama are based on actual historical persons. Frequently, the drama refers to the time of the story as the Great Qing dynasty. The fact that the author completed the drama a year after the incident attests to the authorial intention for the drama to be a commentary on a contemporary event.

The historical setting immediately begs the question of whether the drama uses Manchu clothing to represent the male characters, especially the villains. In contrast to *Immortal*, where there is almost no costume instructions, *Chaste Lady Hai* includes detailed stage directions and costume instructions. When Lin Xianrui first appears in the drama, the costume instruction reads, "Enter [Lin] wearing a brocade archer's jacket [*duanzi jianyi* 緞子箭衣]." As noted in chapter 1, the term *jianyi* already appeared in late Ming dramas and thus can refer to either the military uniform of Han Chinese soldiers or the Manchu uniform with its characteristic horseshoe-shaped cuffs. In scene 3, the righteous boatman, Lan

Ting, appears wearing a black jacket and a capital-style hat (*qingyi jing-mao* 青衣京帽). *Jingmao* was a term referring to the Manchu-style hat in the Qing dynasty.[29] These two possible references to Manchu-style clothing serve as indicators that the setting of the drama is in the Qing dynasty and that Manchu-style clothes could possibly be employed in it. An aficionado of Beijing opera, Qi Rushan notes that when performing some dramas based on real events in Qing society, the Beijing opera troupes would have one of the characters dressed in the Manchu style to indicate the realistic nature of the story, with the rest of the characters still dressed in traditional costumes.[30] Qi's comment sheds light on the fleeting references to Manchu clothing in *Chaste Lady Hai*—the drama indicates its historical nature with only a few possible references to Manchu clothes.

Except for these cursory references, the drama does not provide further information about Manchu clothing. Instead, it places predominant emphasis on the lady's chastity. The fact that Lady Hai stitched up her clothing lies at the very center of the drama. A marginal commentary in *Chaste Lady Hai* reads, "Stitching clothing [to resist rape] is a spectacular event unprecedented in a thousand ages. When there is a great story, such a great piece of work naturally follows."[31] We usually understand costuming as a theatrical trope used by a drama's author or performers to represent certain characters. In *Chaste Lady Hai*, however, it is Lady Hai herself who produces the very costume that covers her body and defines her identity. The production and valorization of the stitched clothing involves Lady Hai's activity of stitching, the forensic investigation of her dead body, and the government proclamation. The entire process of crafting Lady Hai's image as a chaste lady by means of depicting her clothing constitutes a unique example of costuming in early Qing drama. The rest of this chapter focuses on the different steps of representing the heroine of *Chaste Lady Hai*.

Whereas male scholars in early Qing China used their pens to spread Lady Hai's story, the lady in the drama takes up her needle to produce her own costume. The meticulous preparation of the needle and the process of stitching are inherent steps of producing Lady Hai's costume. The production of the suicide dress first requires Lady Hai's needlework, which involved ambiguous connotations in late imperial China. According to studies by Francesca Bray and Angela Sheng, "womanly work," a general reference to *nügong* 女紅, *nügong* 女工, or *fugong* 婦功, had been a metaphor for women's virtues ever since predynastic China.[32] "Womanly work" refers mainly to spinning and weaving, the production of cloth and clothes. As dictated in Confucian classics for women, education in needlework constitutes a large part of a woman's adolescent life.[33]

Economic developments beginning in the Song dynasty resulted in a division of labor between the sexes that marginalized women in textile production. By the late imperial period, the specific definition of womanly work was an issue of heated debate. As women of different classes engaged in many different types of work, a hierarchy of womanly work appeared: at the top was silk embroidery for genteel ladies, next came spinning and weaving cotton, and at the bottom were the lowly tasks of sewing and mending.[34] Although textile production had become largely a profession dominated by male workers, in ideological discourses moralist officials and scholars still imagined virtuous women to be spinning and weaving. The Manchu government placed ever-stronger emphasis upon womanly work and female chastity to remedy what it perceived as the degeneracy of the late Ming. The Qing government highlighted needlework as a prominent symbol of womanly virtue. As Susan Mann suggests, this prescription reflected the Qing government's efforts to promote a "familistic moralism" in the eighteenth century: "But all women, regardless of class, were expected to work with their hands."[35]

Chaste Lady Hai complicates the meaning of needlework by employing embroidery as a symbol of Lady Hai's womanly work, which is open to diverse interpretations. Literati scholars in late imperial China debated among themselves whether embroidery counted as womanly work in the traditional sense. Francesca Bray points out that "in the Ming and early Qing, embroidery had a rather ambivalent status in the eyes of elite men," and that it was at the same time a frivolity that distracted from proper work and the symbol of leisure in a well-off family.[36] Whereas popular literature in late imperial China frequently highlights literary talent and embroidery as symbols of the ideal woman, moralist scholars renounced embroidery as a frivolous undertaking.

To rescue embroidery from these negative connotations, the drama represents Lady Hai's embroidery as defined by marital life and confined within the inner space of the household. Needlework itself is a skill practiced by almost every woman in traditional China. Lady Hai recalls practicing embroidery when she was young: "In those days when I was not yet married, my mother asked me to embroider. How happy I was at that time! How have I come to this situation today?" (scene 9). During Lady Hai's innocent youth, embroidery was an enjoyable pastime. It is her marital life that turns embroidery from a hobby into womanly work. When embroidery is practiced by a noble lady in support of her family, it counts as womanly work instead of frivolous entertainment.

The drama continues to elaborate on Lady Hai's diligent embroidery as a symbol of her womanly virtue. At the beginning of scene 9, Lady Hai reads a lyric that ends with, "I pause the needle, wordless." While working with the needle she sings, "Stopping the needle I look around." Still, upon Chen's return in scene 11, Lady Hai says to herself, "I just stopped my needlework and am sitting alone." These descriptions reveal another dimension to the virtue embodied in womanly work: it must take place within the household, apart from public life. This is particularly difficult for the couple, since they are traveling far from their hometown, without a household of their own. To solve this problem, the drama arranges for the couple to borrow a household from Lady Hai's relative, so as to set up a boundary between inside and outside. This boundary produces a space for Lady Hai's needlework to symbolize the virtue belonging to the inner chamber.[37]

Although embroidery allows the drama to represent Lady Hai as a virtuous lady from a noble family, it also brings with it potential perils, the first being the transgression of the inner-outer boundary, and the second its erotic implication. Rather than producing cloth and making clothing for the family to use, Lady Hai produces commodities that travel out of the interior space. The usual way for women to enter the public sphere in late imperial China was through literary composition.[38] Instead of literature, in this drama embroidery serves as Lady Hai's sole language to communicate with the outside world. In scene 9, while Lady Hai is embroidering at home alone, Yang Er arrives. Lady Hai first refuses to open the door since her husband is absent. Only when Yang Er entreats her help with the excuse of embroidery does she allow him in. Embroidery becomes the only means by which Lady Hai would interact with a man.

In addition to breaching the private space for women, embroidery also evokes sexual connotations that were typical in late Ming popular literature. Embroidery was a common theme in romantic plays and in particular those about illicit love. After entering the household, Yang Er soon invokes the romantic allusions related to needlework: "A heavenly lady like the Weaving Girl, how can you engage in work on the Milky Way loom? Broken silks and tangled threads, how can they be worthy of your jade fingers and golden body." Utilizing references to the Milky Way and jade fingers, Yang Er compares Lady Hai to the goddess of weaving. It is also through the allusion to the Weaving Lady that *Immortal* introduces Lady Hai as a goddess with inherent sexual connotations. The allusion to the Weaving Lady in *Chaste Lady Hai* soon lapses into an explicit sexual allusion to the Goddess of Mount Wu, "a renowned lady, with long sleeves fluttering behind and light skirt trailing, outshines the clouds of Chu and rain on Mount Wu" (scene 9).

To dissociate embroidery from these illicit connotations, *Chaste Lady Hai* repeatedly emphasizes embroidery as womanly work. When Yang Er asks about Lady Hai's work, she replies, "I am embroidering a couple of flowers to eke out a living." When Lady Hai adds "eke out a living" to her reply as the purpose of her embroidery, it defines her actions as womanly work and prevents it from the contamination of romantic allusions. In response to Yang Er's further seduction, Lady Hai replies, "Needle and thread are the constancy of the womanly way." Lady Hai further reduces embroidery to its most basic components, *zhenxian* 針線 (needle and thread), a term that refers to the household needlework of a married woman. The arias that follow employ the tune "Pounding White Silk" (Dao bailian 搗白練), a textile metaphor clearly alluding to her moral purity.

The conversation between Lady Hai and Yang Er reflects the tension between the two connotations of embroidery. Countering Yang Er's seduction, Lady Hai vindicates her character by defending needlework as a symbol of womanly virtue. Studying European women's embroidery, Christopher Breward discusses how women embroidered their political comments into their textile work.[39] For women in both Europe and Asia, needlework served as a means of self-expression. In the case of Lady Hai, what she expresses is not personal talent or political comment but a statement of moral credo.

Stipulations about womanly virtues simultaneously dictate male responsibilities. Whereas women were supposed to manage the interior business of the household, men were supposed to maintain its exterior business. Her husband's inability to support the couple forces Lady Hai to engage in needlework, allowing villains like Yang Er to intrude into the interior space of the household. Chinese dramas usually rescue a scholar's masculinity by granting him an official title based on his literary or military achievements. In contrast, *Chaste Lady Hai* describes Chen Youliang as "cowardly" (*nuo* 懦) to summarize his character; as the introduction to Chen in the opening scene reads, "Cowardly husband Chen puts up with poverty" (scene 1). When Chen sighs over their poverty, Lady Hai encourages him: "Do not be sad. A man [*zhangfu* 丈夫] should bear a heroic spirit" (scene 4). In this context, the term *zhangfu* has two references. On the one hand, it is an appellation Lady Hai uses to address her husband; on the other, it is a descriptive noun, meaning "a heroic man." Lady Hai makes a normative statement that a *zhangfu* (husband) should be a *zhangfu* (heroic man).

As the exterior threat encroaches, Chen Youliang appears to be further subject to manipulation by the villains. The drama's first volume depicts Chen's lack of masculinity by detailing his suspiciousness, hesitancy, and indecisiveness. The villains take advantage of his impotence and trick the couple onto a cargo boat. When Lady Hai tries to stop Chen from falling into the trap, the villains say, "Brother Chen, you are a man [*nanzi han* 男子漢]. Can it be your wife who is in charge?" (scene 11). That Chen Youliang is the automatic head of his household is predetermined by the nature of the patriarchal family. In this case, then, masculinity is not an innate quality of Chen's but an attribute that the villains use to manipulate him.

The first few scenes of *Chaste Lady Hai* represent Lady Hai as a virtuous wife who withstands poverty and supports the couple with her needlework. Her frugality and diligence in needlework are both based on her identity as a wife. The insufficient agency of the husband undermines the family and problematizes Lady Hai's womanly virtues based on womanly work. Female chastity is then brought under the spotlight and problematizes the couple's marital and gender relations. It is the emasculated husband who pushes Lady Hai from the inner quarter of the household to the front stage of confrontation against the villains. On that newly fabricated stage, we witness Lady Hai turning her needle from an instrument for womanly work into a pen for writing her chastity.

Scenes 15 through 18 of *Chaste Lady Hai* represent Lin's seduction and assault and Lady Hai's tragic suicide. Trapped in Lin's boat, Lady Hai refuses to watch a sexually provocative drama performance that Lin arranges to seduce her and rebukes the two women serving as Lin's messengers. The drama devotes an entire scene to representing Lady Hai's suicide when her tattered death dress becomes a symbol of her new identity as a martyr for chastity. In the very beginning of her monologue in scene 18, she says, "These few pieces of clothing have been patched hundreds of times but have accompanied me for years." Her ragged clothes, formerly a symbol of her frugality, now serve a different purpose: to protect the body of a chaste lady. The process of stitching changes the meaning of needlework. While stitching, Lady Hai sings, "I used to hold a needle and vie with the very spring in prowess—but it was all vain bluster before the east wind. At this moment I stitch my clothes and face the death and burial of my flowerlike countenance—transformed into merely a dream of return back into the vast sky" (scene 18). These few lines recapitulate her life from a young girl to a suicidal lady. As a girl, she played with the needle only to show off her skill. As shown in the previous scenes, her married life turns her needlework into womanly work.

The last line about stitching underscores the sacred nature of needlework: "The dripping blood on my finger comes bursting out from my very heart. My whole life I have practiced the needlework [*zhenzhi* 針指] to be used tonight" (scene 18). *Zhenzhi* is a reference to needlework that applies to both young girls and married women, like the expression *zhenxian* 針線, which Lady Hai used earlier in response to Yang Er's seduction. As described in this line, all her previous practice with the needle serves the ultimate purpose of suicide. Lady Hai uses "dripping blood" (指血淋漓) to describe her finger pricked by the needle. Such a tragic scene immediately brings to mind the classic scene in *The Lute* (*Pipa ji* 琵琶記) when the filial daughter-in-law Zhao Wuniang uses her bare fingers to dig a tomb to bury the dead bodies of her parents-in-law. One edition of the scene reads, "With ten bare fingers, how can I build a high tomb? (Action) See, my dripping blood wets my jacket. How bitter!"[40] The scene in *The Lute* is a symbolic moment of Zhao Wuniang's virtue of filial piety. *Chaste Lady Hai* invokes the allusion to highlight Lady Hai's chastity.[41] The sacred purpose of suicide for the protection of chastity subsumes all the previous meanings applied to her needlework.

Lady Hai's activity of stitching not only transforms the very meaning of needlework but also redefines her clothing and body as a medium of self-expression. Lady Hai perceives herself as a physical person and, simultaneously, as a person in social relationship. The two groups of arias in scene 18 address, respectively, these two dimensions of her personal self. In the fourth aria of the first set, Lady Hai emphasizes that she relies upon her clothes to cover up her "entire body," "leaving no space exposed from top to bottom." Then she specifically refers to two parts of her body: her feet and face. She states that to cover up her feet, she sews together the shoes, knee coverings, and the lower garments (*xiayi* 下衣). Women's feet were one of the most sexually provocative objects in Chinese literature of the Ming–Qing period. While stitching her clothes to cover her feet, Lady Hai sings, "I am afraid my golden lotuses [bound feet] will suffer from treading the road to the Yellow Springs." As historian Dorothy Ko points out, "In the late sixteenth and early seventeenth centuries, footbinding was considered part of female attire, an adornment to be exact, not a form of bodily mutilation."[42] When the drama describes the feet as walking on the road toward the netherworld, though, it eliminates any erotic connotation.

While covering her feet, Lady Hai points out that the only part left exposed from the stitched clothes is her head and face. As she sings, "Even if my face is exposed, it will shine out jadelike with a righteous air." By stitching up her clothing, Lady Hai reconfigures her body. In Lady Hai's aria, sexually evocative parts like the feet become profane objects to be covered. Her words forestall any illicit imagining of those objects. Her face, instead, becomes the only place where she publicly discloses her personhood. The covered and exposed parts of her body as well as her attire together shape the meaning of Lady Hai's suicide.

Whereas in the first group of arias Lady Hai reconfigures her physical body, in the eleven arias following she unties herself from social bonds and ultimately claims her identity as a chaste woman. As a social person, Lady Hai is a wife, a daughter, and a daughter-in-law. Right after she finishes stitching up her clothing, Lin Xianrui executes his premeditated assault and is defeated only by Lady Hai's fierce resistance. Her well-wrought clothing successfully protects her physical body. However, Lady Hai still feels herself contaminated: "Although my body is not tarnished, what face do I still possess to continue living in the world?" While body (*shen* 身) refers to her physical self, face (*mianmu* 面目) refers to her social self. It is the destruction of the latter that forces Lady Hai to give up her life.

After reconfiguring her physical body and reshaping her imagined social self, Lady Hai's new identity emerges from her suicide. She says, "I, Lady Hai from Xuzhou, am only twenty-one years of age. I have never expected that at the third watch of tonight, on the twenty-seventh day of the first month in the sixth year of the Kangxi reign, I am to die in the boat of banner laborer Lin Xianrui, in Fengyang garrison, Piling post, Changzhou prefecture" (scene 18). The marginal comment on this line says, "Writing the place, writing the year, writing the month, writing the day, writing the surname, writing the first name—this is excellent writing like the technique in *The Spring and Autumn Annals*." The commentary draws attention to the fact that the line specifically states the details of the event in the style of historical writing. Lady Hai describes herself as an individual person from Xuzhou with the surname Hai—her maiden name. Her last words in the scene read, "This time, the disaster with knifelike wind is resolved. The name of Chaste Lady Hai will be passed on for all eternity" (scene 18). In previous scenes, Lady Hai had defined her own identity in relation to her husband. Rebuking the villains, she pronounced, "He is surnamed Lin and I am surnamed Chen" (scene 17), in which she recognizes the husband's surname, Chen, as hers. Upon committing suicide, she explicitly describes herself as Chaste Lady Hai, a female subject with agency and an independent identity. Her newly produced suicide dress integrates her tattered clothing, her needlework, and her physical and social bodies.

Early Qing scholar Jiang Cai 姜埰 (1608–1673) succinctly summarized the process of transforming Lady Hai's old dress into a suicide costume:

These threadbare socks and dress on my body
Were part of my wedding dowry.

As they are densely stitched with needle and thread,
So on the road to the Yellow Springs, [the marriage] will forever be
　　remembered.

身上舊袜服，是我嫁衣裳。
鍼線密密縫，泉路永不忘。[43]

Echoing the drama, the poem indicates that Lady Hai's old clothes bound her to the marital family, and her suicide dress accompanies her to the netherworld, potentially altering the lady's relation with her husband.

As *Chaste Lady Hai* indicates, womanly virtue, signified by womanly work, belongs to the inner space of the household. Up to scene 18, most of the stories about Lady Hai take place in private spaces: first in the couple's borrowed house in Piling and second in the villain Lin Xianrui's enclosed boat. The suicide scene consists largely of Lady Hai's monologue. In the scene, Lady Hai integrates different factors—her physical body, personhood, and clothing—via the activity of stitching. After her suicide, these factors collapse into discrete and even conflicting elements to be circulated and embellished in the public realm.

Upon Lady Hai's suicide, a group of deities are already awaiting her. The stage instruction reads, "Two miscellaneous actors perform the roles of black-jacket servants holding pennants; two followers, carrying a set of cap and gown, slyly enter, stand, and wait" (scene 18). When Lady Hai commits suicide, the stage instruction clearly indicates how it is to be performed: "[She] hangs herself and dies; the *wai* and *fujing* wave over the *dan*; the *xiaodan* performs Lady Hai's soul and enters from backstage wearing cap and gown; the *wai*, *fujing*, and *za* guide [*xiaodan*] to walk in circles onstage and then exit" (scene 18). This description indicates a separation between Lady Hai's body and her soul. Whereas her soul will reappear as a celestial figure in celestial dress, her body in the stitched clothing will remain onstage to be hidden, discovered, examined, and ultimately worshipped. The separation between Lady Hai's body and soul in *Chaste Lady Hai* is similar to that in *Immortal*. In contrast to the latter, which relegates the lady's body to a prop onstage, *Chaste Lady Hai* sends the lady's dead body onto a journey of public worship.

The remaining part of the drama recounts the investigation of the case, the punishment of the perpetrators, and the commendation and divination of Lady Hai. Scene 18 continues to represent Lin Xianrui and his fellows trying to hide Lady Hai's dead body: "[They] put down the *dan* looking fearful and support her looking fearful. The *jing* performer helps to support her, appears fearful, and supports her offstage." Here, Lady Hai's body has not yet become a sacred object and still functions as a prop on stage. While the group examines Lady Hai, they contrast her body with her face: "Her body is dead, yet the face is alive." This is reminiscent of the moment of her suicide when Lady Hai contrasts her covered body and exposed face. Her face, full of valor, has indeed become a carrier of her righteousness and chastity.

A dead body could be subject to multiple interpretations. Lady Hai's suicide itself is not sufficient to prove her chastity in defense against the attempted rape. To turn the body into a symbol of chastity, the stitched clothing is a critical component. *Chaste Lady Hai* refrains from illustrating the forensic examination of Lady Hai's body. In scene 20, "Uncovering the Villainous" (Fajian 發姦), county government officials arrive at the boat to arrest Lin Xianrui. When the officials recover Lady Hai's body, two of them enter the boat to examine it. Later, the coroner, Miao Ming, reports the results: "I see that her face is as if living and her clothing is stitched from top to bottom. It is clear that she died under duress." It is the stitched dress that proves Lady Hai's suicide under the coercion of Lin Xianrui. The officials once more invoke Lady Hai's face and clothing as proof of her chastity. Again, the plot aspect of forensic investigation itself echoes that in *Immortal*. Rather than manipulating the lady's body onstage and inviting various parties to view the body—as we see in *Immortal*—*Chaste Lady Hai* simply emphasizes the stitched clothing as sufficient evidence of the lady's chastity.

Her stitched clothing not only prevents the exposure of her body but also saves her reputation from being corrupted by Lin's slander. A biography of Lady Hai recounts, "[Lin] alleged that he had indeed committed adultery with the woman. Her death resulted from the humiliation by the wife of a boatman. He was hoping to avoid the death penalty with the excuse of adultery, and he requested lessening the punishment."[44] According to Qing law, adultery was a much lesser crime than rape and thus would exempt Lin from capital punishment. As Matthew Sommer writes about chastity commemoration in the Qing dynasty, "If the boundary of consummation had been crossed during rape, then the victim had been polluted irrevocably, regardless of her previous record of chastity, the intensity of her resistance, or the violence or numbers of men by which she had been subdued."[45] Had Lin's story been accepted, not only would Lady Hai have died in vain but her reputation would have been ruined as well.

Scholars have stressed the increasingly rigorous stipulations regarding the criteria for commending chastity in early Qing society. In the evaluation of a rape case, clothing served as significant evidence. A 1646 commentary to the Ming code reads, "In prosecution for rape, there must be evidence of violent coercion (*qiang bao*), and the situation must have been such that the woman could not struggle free; there must also be persons who heard what happened, as well as evidence such as physical injury or torn clothing. Only then shall the offender be sentenced to strangulation."[46] In the drama, Lady Hai's stitched clothing simultaneously demonstrates both her fierce resistance and her success in preserving her chastity. The drama also depicts people in neighboring boats witnessing Lady Hai's struggle. All these details satisfy the early Qing legal demands for proving that she successfully resisted rape.

For the dead Lady Hai, her clothing, face, and body proper bear different relations to her identity. The private body of a chaste lady must be kept out of public view. Her clothing serves as the sole evidence of her purity and the interface between her physical body and the social environment. Her face remains visible throughout the process and functions as a signifier of her personhood. In the public journey of her commemoration, her face and clothing together attest to her chastity and eventually turn her into a figure for public worship.

WRITING ON HER COFFIN AND SHRINE

The drama represents three bodies of Lady Hai: her physical body in stitched dress and buried in a coffin, her statue with a replica of her face and stitched dress, and her celestial body in celestial garb. After her suicide, Lady Hai leaves the familial confines and enters the public space. The drama associates the multivalent bodies of Lady Hai with different coverings—clothing, coffin, and shrine. Her coffin and shrine constitute two new layers of her clothing upon which different parties will write about Lady Hai in different tones. Her commemoration also incorporates other characters—her husband, local Chinese scholars, and Manchu government officials—into the social spaces that contain her bodies. Costuming in *Chaste Lady Hai*, therefore, involves the construction of social spaces to juxtapose a variety of bodies, clothes, and words.

As narrated in the drama, after Lady Hai's chastity is verified through forensic investigation, the local community erects a statue to commemorate her. On her statue, what represents her social self will be her stitched clothing and her face. These two elements last appear in the discourse of Zhou Yiduan, a local doctor in Changzhou. Zhou describes the making of a statue for Lady Hai: "Yesterday the venerable elderly Zhou Shinan and his fellows had opened her coffin and made a statue of her. After more than seventy days, her chaste complexion had not withered or altered" (scene 26). The drama once again emphasizes that her face remains alive and unchanged as evidenced by the craftsmen who opened her coffin to make a statue resembling her. A female scholar in the early Qing period explicitly pointed out the importance of Lady Hai's stitched clothing in transmitting her reputation of chastity. Describing Lady Hai's statue, she wrote, "Had she then not stitched her clothing with thread, how could her pure name echo ancient fragrance?" (當時若不縫裳線，怎得清名效古香?).[47] Together, Lady Hai's face and clothing allow her chastity to be transposed from the dead body onto the statue.

Lady Hai's physical body remains unseen by the general public. With her body enclosed within, the coffin becomes a new piece of clothing, on which male literati write their words of eulogy. As the local community contributes to the making of Lady Hai's statue and the building of her shrine, they simultaneously become witnesses to a moral event. *Chaste Lady Hai* records a group of local literati attending the public worship. Three licentiates (*xiucai* 秀才) from Changzhou prefecture arrive at the site. Belonging to a younger generation, the scholars were possibly born in the early years of the Qing dynasty and received degrees from the Manchu state.[48] As scholars continue to gather, they create more and more poetic odes to Lady Hai. One scholar writes, "We, who are celebrated in the garden of letters, generals amid the ranks of elegists, pay our obeisance to you, an illiterate gentlewoman and a true sage" (scene 26). The marginal comment reads, "It is fantastic that she is illiterate. If she were one of those lettered ladies, she would most likely fall into the company of Cui Yingying and Zhuo Wenjun." There is a conspicuous contrast between the two dramas' rendering of Lady Hai's literacy. In *Immortal*, Lady Hai is banished to the human world because of her indulgence in literary writing, and the drama itself is replete with iridescent literary diction in the arias she sings. In contrast, *Chaste Lady Hai* depicts Lady Hai as illiterate, a fact not recorded elsewhere. When rendered illiterate, Lady Hai has no recourse but to resort to the needle to write a vow across her body. Instead, equipped with real pens, the scholars write on the coffin their interpretation of the story.

The scholars further attempt to connect Lady Hai's chastity with their literary talent. One of them remarks on another's writing, "Brother, your works like pearl and jade, and the lady's chastity like ice and frost—will both endure forever" (scene 26). After their poetic conversation, the scholars paste their poems onto Lady Hai's coffin. The marginal comment reads, "There had been no coffin like this before this chaste lady." It was not unusual for a traditional Chinese scholar to claim a lasting name based on his literary talents. What is surprising about the scholars' words is that they compare their literary writing to the chastity of an illiterate lady.

Besides the degree holders of the Qing dynasty, the audience at Lady Hai's shrine also includes remnant subjects of the Ming dynasty. As described in the drama, both the statue and the coffin of Lady Hai are located on the site of her shrine. The sacred figure of Lady Hai, worshipped at her own shrine, reconciles the conflicts among different parties. In the same scene, an old gentleman, Zhao Jiding 趙繼鼎 (1606–1673), laments his moral inferiority to the lady: "Ever since I learned about the recent event, I have been so stricken as to keep lamenting. No difference exists between a loyal subject and a chaste wife. See, we fellows wear caps and gowns and drag on in life. I admire ladies like her who can sacrifice her life. How can daylight compare with everlasting night?" (scene 26). As a real person in history, Zhao Jiding received a *jinshi* degree in the late Ming (1640) and served as a secretary in the Ministry of War. Following the dynastic transition, he no longer served in the government and named himself an "old schoolman of the south" (江南老教書).[49] As a person who lived through the Ming–Qing transition, Zhao Jiding expresses his feeling of shame and guilt in comparison with the chaste lady.

Zhao's betrayal of his responsibilities is best reflected in his clothing. The drama describes the costumes of the literati scholars: "*Mo*: three-part beard, square headgear, unofficial dress; *wai*: beard, square headgear, broad robe; *xiaodan*: fluttering headgear, colorful dress; *sheng, dan, laodan*: fluttering headgear, colorful dress" (scene 26). These costumes are based on typical dress for literati scholars in the Ming dynasty. Whereas this type of apparel was banned as regular clothing in the Qing dynasty, it remained in use onstage. The theatrical nature of *chuanqi* drama allows characters to appear in Han-style clothing when in reality they should have been wearing Manchu-style clothing. Wearing the very clothing he could not wear in real life, Zhao comments on his betrayal of his political responsibilities as one of the *yiguan* group. In the biographies of his grandfather and teacher, the playwright Shen Shouhong recorded their resistance to Manchu hair and dress regulations: the former became a monk and the latter gave up his hair only with tears.[50] In the drama, Zhao Jiding's lament epitomizes the experiences of Ming loyalists at the time of dynastic change.

A preface to an early Qing novel based on Lady Hai's story inadvertently reflects the dilemma of costuming inherent in the drama: "When men wearing caps and gowns act as wives and concubines, how can we expect wives and concubines to act like heroic men?"[51] This line describes the mentality of Zhao Jiding in his commenting on the *yiguan* community. As Martin Huang notes, "Deploring men's moral deficiencies was a common topic in literati writings on chaste women. However, by the mid-seventeenth century, the moral superiority of a chaste woman began to provoke a different kind of uneasiness in some literati."[52] In this drama, Lady Hai's tragic suicide arouses Zhao Jiding's sense of guilt for maintaining an ignoble life.

Worshipping Lady Hai's heroic activities in defending her chastity provides the literati group an opportunity to mitigate their frustrations. Immediately after Zhao Jiding's lament, his son says, "When her shrine and statue are completed, sacrificial dishes and platters will be offered forever" (scene 26). His comment on the shrine and sacrificial vessels for Lady Hai reminds readers of Chinese scholars' worship of Confucius and their former political rulers. Lady Hai's heroic suicide poses a challenge to scholars, who have failed to become martyrs for the deceased Ming dynasty. When worshipping the defeated Ming dynasty becomes impossible, Lady Hai serves as a redemptive figure for Ming loyalists to worship.

It is all the more surprising that among those worshipping Lady Hai is her former husband, Chen Youliang. The drama makes it explicit in the prologue that her widower, scholar Chen Youliang, becomes a monk at Lady Hai's shrine in order to maintain sacrifices to the female immortal. According to existing records in gazetteers and biographical writings, Lady Hai's shrine was established the year after her death. The record in *Changzhou fuzhi* 常州府志 reads, "Chaste Lady Hai's shrine is located at Longshejian, Longxing Temple, on the other side of the canal; it was constructed in the seventh year of the Kangxi reign."[53] In addition to Lady Hai's shrine, the record names Longxing Temple 龍興禪院, whose relation with the shrine is ambiguous—the shrine could be adjacent to, part of, or simply another name for the Buddhist temple.

By the last scene, "Honorable Commendation" (Rongjing 榮旌), Lady Hai's shrine has been completed. Chen enters the stage as a monk wearing Buddhist dress and sings, "The husband and wife with bound hair are separated through the cutting of hair. I discard my Confucian dress and change into the garb of a monk." Recounting Chen Youliang's whereabouts, a biography of Lady Hai reads, "Filled with regret and remorse, Youliang cut off his hair to become a monk."[54] Both the drama and the biography refer to the cutting of hair to indicate Chen's becoming a monk. In the drama, however, "the cutting of hair" is juxtaposed with "bound hair"—a term referring to a conjugal relationship. In addition to cutting his hair, Chen Youliang changes his clothing from that in the Confucian style to Buddhist garb, which camouflages the possible course of altering his clothing in society—from Han Chinese style to Manchu style. In the 1660s, shaving one's head and changing one's clothing would naturally have complied with the Manchu government's dress regulations. Chen's words in the drama weaken the ethnic and political connotations of hair and clothing. Thus, the drama's audience sees an emasculated scholar shaving his head and abandoning his scholarly dress in service not to the Manchu government but to the chaste lady. Chen Youliang becomes a loyal subject not to the Ming or Qing dynasties but to his chaste wife. At this point, we see a complete reversal in the relation between husband

and wife. In the beginning of the drama, Lady Hai was dependent upon her husband to claim her identity as a virtuous wife. Lady Hai's suicide not only severs her relationship with her husband but also creates a new relationship between the worshipper and the worshipped.

In early Qing society, the local people in Changzhou built a shrine for the living vice-commander of Changzhou prefecture, Miao Ming, annexed to Lady Hai's shrine.[55] Lady Hai's shrine thus possessed the power to subjugate her former husband and officials of the Manchu government. Lady Hai's husband, local scholars, and Qing officials were all rendered subordinate to the chaste lady.

Meanwhile, the drama describes the Manchu state's interpretation of Lady Hai's story. In the last scene, Chen Youliang comments on the government proclamations hanging in the shrine: "Behold, ever since the shrine was established, different levels of officials have offered their proclamations. The hall of the shrine is resplendent with honorary plaques lined up" (scene 28). The drama then lists the plaques commissioned by the central and local governments to praise Lady Hai's chastity. In the drama, two officials from the Manchu government arrive at the site and sing, "The hall full of plaques and tablets make no mistake: the deeds of a chaste and heroic beauty last for a thousand ages, just like loyalty and filial piety" (scene 28). Earlier, Zhao Jiding invokes a similar comparison between chaste women and loyal men. In comparison with Lady Hai, Zhao criticizes himself for not being as loyal to the Ming dynasty as Lady Hai is to her husband. In the words of the two Qing officials, however, chastity becomes an ethical norm parallel to loyalty and filial piety, all of which are part of the ideology in the newly established Qing dynasty.

The description of state discourse at the end of the drama corresponds with the actual situation in early Qing history. Qing rape law was focused on protecting the patriarchal family from intrusion by outside scoundrels. While local literati families in the Ming dynasty took the initiative in promoting the cult of chastity, the Qing government directly concerned itself with promoting chastity as a way to bypass local communities and reach into patriarchal families. Based on her study of local documents in southwestern China, Janet Theiss identifies the 1660s as an important moment in the Manchu state's assertion of control of female chastity: "The state was intervening for the first time in the negotiation over the cultural and political meanings of chastity suicide that had until then been structured by the physical gestures of individual women and the empathetic encomia of the male literati who revealed their deaths to history."[56] Matthew Sommer's study shows that "beginning in 1672, the Qing state also canonized martyred victims of attempted rape."[57] These studies of law in early Qing China corroborate the state discourses seen in *Chaste Lady Hai*, which conflate female chastity, filial piety, and political loyalty.

It is not the dead body or the statue of Lady Hai but the third body, the celestial one, that concludes the drama. In the last scene, Lady Hai, now an immortal wearing a set of celestial robes, descends upon her shrine and remarks upon her struggles in the drama. She introduces herself as Master Red Talisman (Chifu Zi 赤符子) and Lady Hai in her former human life. Although it is only a few years after her death, she sings of the changes of the landscape as a way of lamenting the dynastic change: "Look how much moss has grown on deep wells, how much grass covers the abandoned palaces, and how many trees overshadow the former towers. Green mountains suffer no misfortune, and rivers flow in vain. Have crying partridges flown over the Xiang River?" (scene 28). Lady Hai's lines demonstrate her omniscient perspective on history. By the end of the drama, she has transcended the specific time and place of her suicide as well as the dynastic change the local literati have suffered. Ellen Widmer suggests that after the dynastic change, "ghosts and their poems built on all too familiar memories of slaughter and suicide, the hallmarks of those transitional years."[58] In contrast to those ghost poems, the lady immortal calls for reconciliation among all parties. She sings, "In vain you turn your eyes upon the former state in a foreign land. Do not cling to gratitude or vengeance." For Lady Hai and her husband, they have encountered radical changes in a foreign land (*taxiang* 他鄉). For early Qing Chinese, the Ming dynasty had already become a former state (*guguo* 故國). As a celestial figure, Lady Hai urges people to abandon all the emotional entanglements with both their homeland and home country. Early on, Zhao Jiding referred to Lady Hai's suicide as "news/a recent event" (*xinwen shi* 新聞事). Although *Chaste Lady Hai* represents an event that took place only months earlier, by the end of the drama it relegates the event to the historical past and urges the past be forgotten.

Traditional Chinese books, like clothed bodies, reveal meaning through the practice of turning the pages. This last section treats the printed book as a medium containing the story of Lady Hai. *Immortal* and *Chaste Lady Hai* circulated in contrasting ways and exist in sharply different forms. The single existing copy of *Immortal* printed before 1670 (incomplete) does not have any preface, marginal commentary, or other types of paratextual material.[59] In a group of poems about Lady Hai, the early Qing scholar He Qie wrote, "Green, green the lonely tomb stands beside the shrine / passersby all vie to spread the Chaste Immortal's fame" (青青孤塚傍祠邊, 來往爭傳節義仙).[60] If he was referring to the drama *Immortal*, then we know that the play was already well known in the early Qing period. Other than that, however, we have little evidence of the play's circulation in the following centuries.

The circulation of *Chaste Lady Hai* was completely different. According to its author, Shen Shouhong, *Chaste Lady Hai* was performed after its completion.[61] But we do not have any record of the drama in the popular repertoire of drama performances before the late Qing period. *Chaste Lady Hai* circulated as a manuscript in the early Qing period. In 1841, Jiang Wenxun 蔣文勳, together with other literati scholars, saw to the printing of the drama. As Jiang's postscript indicates, he printed the drama based on a manuscript edition passed down from his former teacher. Both the drama and the historical site of Lady Hai's shrine had faded out of people's memory toward the late Qing period. By publishing *Chaste Lady Hai*, Jiang brought the drama back to the attention of the reading public and promoted it as a didactic textbook. The drama's printed format gave final shape to the story of the chaste lady. For that reason, I consider the woodblock print produced in the 1840s as Lady Hai's last layer of costuming, including the binding, title page, prefaces, commentaries, and other dimensions of the material book.

The existing copies of *Chaste Lady Hai* are bound in the traditional way of stitching with threads (*xianzhuang* 線裝). Much like the stitching of Lady Hai's clothing, where only the heroine's face was left exposed for appreciation, the stitching of the drama also is a process of hiding and revelation. In the process of binding the book, the editors participated

FIGURE 4.1 Title page of *Chaste Lady Hai*. Shen Shouhong 沈受宏, *Hai Liefu chuanqi* 海烈婦傳奇, 1841, in *Guben xiqu congkan* 古本戲曲叢刊, ser. 7 (Beijing: Guojia tushuguan chubanshe, 2018).

in reshaping the drama's message by deleting morally inappropriate parts. The original prints included all twenty-eight scenes of the drama. In some later prints, however, all of scene 7 is missing. There is a printed note at the end of scene 6, reading, "Scene 7, 'Chouni,' comprises transitional scripts where the boatman's wife appears, and in it there are lewd words. Therefore, we removed and destroyed those woodblocks." The note uses the word *hui* 燬 to indicate the destruction of the woodblocks by fire. The remaining parts of the drama would be bound together using thread to realize the producers' intention of promoting female chastity.

Opening the book, a reader first encounters the page showing the title of the drama, the time of printing, and the owner of the woodblock plates (figure 4.1). As the author's preface to the drama indicates, the drama was originally named *Record of Three Exceptionals* (*Sanyi ji* 三異記). The first title emphasizes three characters of low social status in the drama: Lady Hai, boatman Lan Ting, and Miao Ming, the vice-commander of Changzhou prefecture who uncovered the crime.[62] Later, Mr. Wang, the chamberlain for ceremonies (王太常), changed the title to *This, a Real Hero* (*Ci zhangfu* 此丈夫). This title corresponds with scene 28, where the last plaque for Lady Hai reads, "This shall be called a real hero" (此謂丈夫). Characters in the scene refer to the tribute as "the laureate among all the encomia" (諸語之冠). The term *zhangfu* in the title and the tribute allowed early Qing literati to voice their lament over the failure of masculinity during the dynastic transition. The second title, accordingly, deeply embeds the drama into the immediate history of the Ming–Qing transition. By the time of the drama's printing in the 1840s, the editor had changed the title to *Chuanqi Drama on Chaste Lady Hai* (*Hai Liefu chuanqi* 海烈婦傳奇). In contrast to the first two titles, the new title stresses not Lady Hai's courageous conduct but instead her chastity.

Following the title page, the woodblock print of *Chaste Lady Hai* includes replicas of the plaques inside and steles outside Lady Hai's shrine, listing them page by page, as if reproducing rubbings from the steles and plaques (figure 4.2). As discussed earlier, most of the plaques were issued by the Manchu government to commend Lady Hai's chastity. The textual space of the woodblock print thus reproduces the architectural space of the Manchu state's writing regarding Lady Hai.

Following the plaques and steles, the drama includes a series of prefaces and biographical materials on Lady Hai. These materials

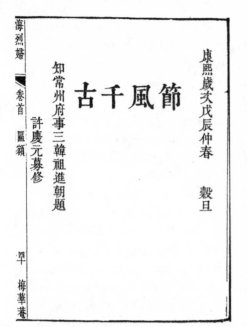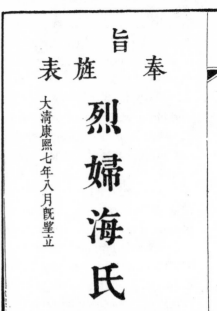

FIGURE 4.2 Printed pages from *Chaste Lady Hai*, in imitation of a stele (*right*) and a plaque (*left*), both produced in the Kangxi reign. Shen Shouhong 沈受宏, *Hai Liefu chuanqi* 海烈婦傳奇, 1841, in *Guben xiqu congkan* 古本戲曲叢刊, ser. 7 (Beijing: Guojia tushuguan chubanshe, 2018), *juanshou*, 36b, 40a.

demonstrate a similar change of message as in the changing titles. One of the prefaces to *Chaste Lady Hai* composed in the early Qing period states, "A woman dying for the sake of her chastity resembles a gentleman dying for the sake of state affairs."[63] The remark expresses the same lament as Zhao Jiding's comparing the chaste lady to loyal officials. Other prefaces repeatedly describe Lady Hai as a true hero (*zhangfu* 丈夫): "Can a woman be a man? If heroic [*lie* 烈], a woman is a man; if not, a man is a woman."[64] The word *lie* bears the double meaning of "chaste" for women and "heroic" for men. These lines obscure the gender division, turning *lie* from a description of female chastity to a criticism of the lack of masculinity. The prefatory materials after the early Qing period, however, downplay the criticism of foiled men in favor of a didactic tone praising Lady Hai as a model subject of the Qing dynasty. Among them, only the biography of Lady Hai written in 1698 by Wang Yuanxuan 王元 烜 includes a direct comment on her being a *zhangfu* (man) in reference to Mengzi's definition of *da zhangfu*. The comment, however, is quickly followed by a eulogy of the Manchu emperor and a claim that the lady's story was proclaimed to "establish the principles and constancies [for women] and to maintain moral customs" (立綱常維風教).[65]

The editorial materials added to the drama upon its publication further strengthen that didactic tone. The opening preface written by Ge Zai 戈載 in 1841 refers to the drama as a morality book (*shanshu* 善書) and explicitly states that the drama was printed in order to "maintain principles and constancies" (維持乎綱常).[66] The editor Jiang Wenxun's postscript starts with a description of Lady Hai's tomb and shrine in Changzhou and then comments on the popularity of *kunqu* in Suzhou, in which city drama performances were offered in more than ten wineshops. Denouncing the popular enthusiasm for obscene and erotic (*yinyan* 淫艷) dramas, Jiang points out the purpose of reproducing *Chaste Lady Hai*: "Since custom has been corrupted by illicit dramas, we should rescue and correct it with dramas of chastity."[67] The published drama, in the editors' eyes, was meant to be a moral lesson for the Suzhou public in the nineteenth century and was far removed from Han Chinese people's struggles during the Ming–Qing transition. As Susan Mann succinctly points out, by the High Qing era—especially the long eighteenth century—"Female suicide was no longer associated with Ming loyalism, and Qing rulers continued to honor female martyrs who died resisting rape, but they declared themselves in firm opposition to widow suicide."[68] The editorial tone of Jiang's postscript echoes well the state's appropriation of female chastity.

Later folk literature based on the same event increasingly depicts Lady Hai as a virtuous woman. Such writings not only eschew critiques of the failure of masculinity during the dynastic transition but also change the theme of embroidery to spinning and weaving—the orthodox definition of needlework and womanly work.[69] Lady Hai's story was included as part of *Biographies of Exemplary Women* (*Lienü zhuan* 列女傳) in the *Draft History of Qing* (*Qingshi gao* 清史稿), which completely leaves out her act of stitching up her clothing before her suicide.[70] The heroic Lady Hai in early Qing China was ultimately written into Qing history as an exemplary woman of the Manchu Qing dynasty. By the late Qing and early Republican periods, Lady Hai had become merely one of the numerous chaste ladies in Chinese history who committed suicide to preserve their chastity. Her stitching together her clothing no longer seemed marvelous enough to be mentioned by the editors of the *Draft History of Qing*. The ethnic and gender tensions in the story and in the drama *Chaste Lady Hai* were no longer easily decipherable to their late Qing audiences.

In the two early Qing dramas about Lady Hai, Lady Hai's socially constructed body opens up spaces for competing ways of dressing enabled by literary traditions, literati experiences, and the nascent Manchu state. Although both dramas highlight the remarkable fact that Lady Hai completely stitched up her clothing before her suicide, they depict her body and clothes in contrasting ways. *Immortal* depicts Lady Hai's body as an object for voyeuristic view and her stitched dress as an expedient means to immortality—a profane object to be abandoned after her suicide. In contrast, *Chaste Lady Hai* turns the lady into a heroic woman with agency, a reconciling goddess for rival parties during the Ming–Qing transition, and a model subject of the Manchu regime. In both dramas, it is theatrical costuming that moves the lady across boundaries—those between the human and the celestial, familial and societal, and genders and ethnicities. Lady Hai's costuming makes visible the competing and occasionally conflicting efforts that produce multiple facets of the Lady Hai character in the two dramas.

The contrast between the two dramas epitomizes the prolonged transition from the late Ming to the mid-Qing dynasties. *Immortal* incorporates various elements prevalent in late Ming literature and theater. Based on the same story, *Chaste Lady Hai* reflects political, legal, ethnic, and gender issues specific to early Qing China. The disappearance of *Immortal* after the early Qing period and the wide circulation of *Chaste Lady Hai* by the mid-Qing period indicate a continuous shaping of the chaste lady as a fictional figure, a heroic woman during the Ming–Qing transition, and a model subject of the Qing state.

CHAPTER FIVE

From State Attire to Stage Prop

Figure 5.1 is from the "Stage Items" (Qiemo 砌抹) section appended to an early Qing edition of *Peach Blossom Fan* (*Taohua shan* 桃花扇), in which the author, Kong Shangren 孔尚任 (1648–1718), lists role types and stage properties for each scene.[1] For scene 16, which represents the first meeting of the Southern Ming court immediately after the fall of the Ming capital, Beijing, in 1644, Kong lists items of gowns and tablets (*paohu* 袍笏).[2] Writing about the drama's performance in Ji Garden in early Qing Beijing, Kong Shangren refers to the pieces listed in "Stage Items" as "various objects" (*zhuwu* 諸物).[3] I turn attention here first to the meaning of the gowns and tablets in the drama and in early Qing China.

When used onstage, the gowns and tablets symbolize the solemn attire of the Ming state worn by civilians and officials throughout the Ming dynasty. When not in use onstage, they are stored in theater trunks with other stage items. Within the trunks, the gowns and tablets are a group of marginal objects because the Ming garments listed are not the costumes in the regular collection of a drama troupe but items temporarily employed for a performance. As costume items for an early Qing drama performance, the gowns and tablets representing the fallen Ming dynasty are nonessential accessories.

As objects, are the costumes of the same level as the teacups and knives listed on the same page? The teacups and knives on the list suggest the teacups and knives used in early Qing society, creating a

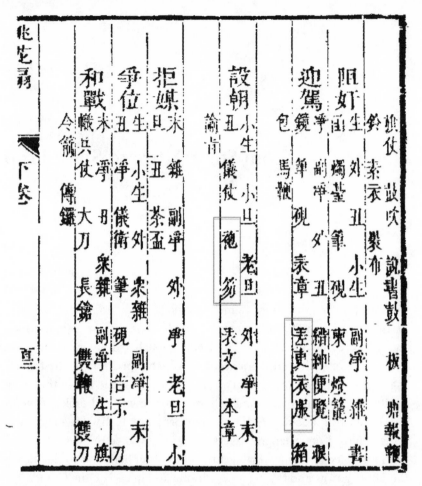

FIGURE 5.1 A woodblock page from the "Stage Items" section in *Peach Blossom Fan*. Kong Shangren 孔尚任, *Taohua shan* 桃花扇, Kangxi edition, in *Guben xiqu congkan* 古本戲曲叢刊, ser. 5 (Shanghai: Shanghai guji chubanshe, 1986), *juan* b, 138a.

potential connection between things in the drama performance and things in society. This connection does not hold for Ming official gowns and tablets since Ming state attire ceased to be used in daily life after the dynastic transition. Can we refer to the gowns and tablets as props or signs? The Prague school of theatrical semiotics proposes that everything onstage is a sign.[4] Revising this proposition, Andrew Sofer suggests that "motion is the prop's defining feature" and that "a prop is an object that goes on a journey."[5] Read against these propositions, the items on the "Stage Items" list are neither props nor signs since they are not placed into the specific scenes of the drama. They remain silent, static, and dead—as actual things stored in theater trunks and as names of things on the "Stage Items" list. Such is the destiny of Ming state attire in early Qing China: only onstage could people experience the display of Ming state attire; offstage, such garments existed as mere things, unnoticed and meaningless.

The previous three case studies in this book address the sartorial experiences of individual persons in society and represented characters in drama. This chapter takes a macrolevel perspective and discusses the fate of Ming state attire in early Qing China. By "Ming state attire," I refer to the material and social modes of dressing that integrate individual persons with the Ming state, not merely the apparel fabricated during the Ming dynasty. Ming state attire as material objects disappeared in early Qing society and could be represented onstage only through the performance of historical dramas such as *Peach Blossom Fan*, resulting in its reduction to theatrical props. Thus by "theatricalizing Ming state attire," I do not mean a nascent theatrical appropriation of something that had never before been dramatized. Instead, my usage of the term refers to the governance of clothing during the regime change, with Ming clothing being assigned to the subordinate and profane space of the theatrical.

Peach Blossom Fan is not only one of the few early Qing dramas that elaborately represent the Ming–Qing transition but also the single Chinese drama that captures the changing meaning of Ming state attire through the dynastic transition.[6] Kong Shangren kept revising the drama for more than a decade, successively adding seven prefaces and postscripts and paying particular attention to the material dimensions of the drama, including clothing.[7] The drama uses Ming uniforms to signify the collapse of the Ming state and includes a series of plot actions of clothes changing onstage as indicators of identity transformation. In addition, the framing scenes comment on the performance of the drama itself, showcasing the sartorial spectacle in early Qing theater. The fact that *Peach Blossom Fan* uses clothing as a metalanguage to represent the sartorial transition renders the drama a unique case for studying the interaction between theater and society during the Ming–Qing transition.

Readers of *Peach Blossom Fan* in past centuries, however, have failed to realize the significance of the "Stage Items" section. Editors of several woodblock-print editions of *Peach Blossom Fan* produced in the Qing dynasty chose to delete the "Stage Items" list, deeming it extraneous for the purpose of reading. The list is also missing in several editions of *Peach Blossom Fan* edited by modern scholars.[8] This neglected list of stage items, however, promises to yield a fresh understanding of the drama as a critical representation of the dynastic transition. This chapter examines the journey of Ming state attire through space and time and in relation to the human body. It answers two questions: How does *Peach Blossom Fan* represent state attire in the Southern Ming capital, Nanjing, being transformed into stage props in the Qing capital, Beijing? How does this transformation influence clothing as a connection between the theatrical and social realms?

THE DISLOCATION OF MING STATE ATTIRE

The main story of *Peach Blossom Fan* spans the Ming–Qing transition from 1643 to 1645 and includes events taking place mainly around Nanjing, the capital of the Southern Ming dynasty.[9] The function of Ming state attire is best exemplified by occasions of state ritual when participants' ceremonial costumes integrate their bodies into the ritual environment. Scholars have used the terms "ritual" and "theater" to describe two very different types of performance.[10] Authenticity and spectatorship separate the two types of practices from each other. On the one hand, antitheatrical traditions have associated the theatrical with the artificial and the insincere.[11] In contrast, a successful ritual involves all participants' sincere participation. On the other hand, some scholars have defined theatricality as a viewing-viewed relationship built on spatial distance. Accordingly, an observing audience is always present in theater but is not necessary for ritual performances.[12] In this section, I use the criteria of authenticity and spectatorship to discuss how *Peach Blossom Fan* represents the transformation of Ming state attire from a ritual language to a theatrical language.

The ritual performances in *Peach Blossom Fan* take place in different locations ranging from the political center to the apolitical periphery. A map of Nanjing, produced in Qing China, includes the major locations of the ritual performances depicted in the drama (figure 5.2).[13] At different moments of the performances, Ming state attire is gradually disengaged from the Ming state. The first group of Ming state rituals take place within the inner city of Nanjing (location A in figure 5.2). At these state ritual performances, the Ming state attire provides a language that signifies state power. Scene 16, set in 1643, features the first court meeting of the Southern Ming dynasty. The newly enthroned Hongguang emperor appears wearing a set of imperial cap and robe (*gunmian* 衮冕) and recites, "No sooner is the dust washed from my face than I don my imperial robes." The court officials, wearing gowns and carrying tablets, read in unison, "Day dawns again on royal pageantry [*guanshang*]; regard anew the palace's splendor." The establishment of the Southern Ming dynasty accompanies the investiture of the new emperor and reattiring of the state. Following millennia-long tradition, Ming state attire proclaims the legitimacy of the new ruler and the new order.

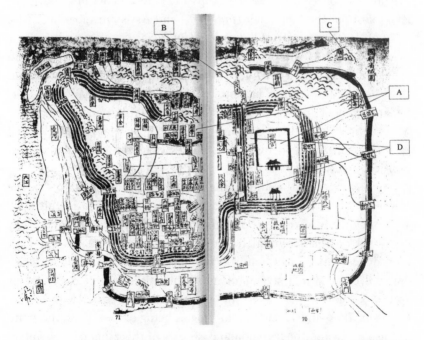

FIGURE 5.2 A map of Nanjing in the Qing dynasty. *Jinling dizhi tukao* 金陵地志圖考, in *Zhongguo fangzhi congshu* 中國方志叢書 (Taipei: Chengwen chubanshe youxian gongsi, 1983), Huazhong district, Jiangsu province, 437:70–71.

In addition to instating the Southern Ming court, Ming state attire also defines individual persons as Ming subjects. Scene 3 features a Confucian ritual ceremony that involves scholars in the Restoration Society (复社) and the corrupt official Ruan Dacheng. The scene, "The Disrupted Ceremony" (Hongding 哄丁), is set on the *ding* day of the stem-and-branch calendar, one of the two most important dates for the worship of Confucius.[14] In the "Stage Items" section, the drama lists a sacrificial table, an incense burner, and a candleholder. In a conversation between two servants in the Confucian temple, they read out a list of ritual paraphernalia, including chestnuts, dates, freshwater roots; ox, sheep, pigs, rabbits, and deer; fish spinach, celery, bamboo shoots, and garlic; salt, wine, incense, silk, and candles. These categorized items of sacrifice (nuts, meat, vegetables, and objects) help establish the environment of a ritual performance. The sacrifices are offered to Confucius and his disciples, and the costumes depicted in the scene indicate the participants' identity. The drama depicts the participants' ceremonial costumes: the *wai* and *mo* roles, both dressed in caps and belts and holding court tablets, represent the Libationer (*jijiu* 祭酒) and Assistant Libationer (*siye* 司業) of the Directorate of Education; Confucian scholars and students who hold degrees without official titles attend the ritual ceremony in scholarly dress with a headpiece (*yijin* 衣巾). Scholars have pointed out that the sacrificial paraphernalia, the ritual music and dance, and the personnel in the drama all correspond to ritual performances in the Ming dynasty.[15] At this assembly of Confucian scholars, one's clothing most conspicuously demonstrates one's position in academic and political institutions.

As indicated in the drama, the participants line up in front of the statues of Confucius and his disciples, who are dressed in the same style of clothing as the participants themselves. In their singing, they comment on the ceremonial costumes on display: "Behold our Sage enthroned in majesty; his four supreme disciples sit beside him with ceremonial caps. While strains of music bid his spirit welcome, let us spread our gowns and tablets and prostrate ourselves below the steps" (scene 3). These lines mention clothing as being of two types: the attire of the statues and the ceremonial costumes of the ritual participants.[16] The costumes of the participants correspond to those on the statues they worship, confirming the participants' linkage with the Confucian tradition. The sartorial spectacle depicted here mirrors ritual scenes in Ming society, where clothing constitutes one of the major dimensions of ceremonies.

The participants' bodily performance further integrates them into the ritual environment. In scene 3, the Ceremonial Assistant declares, "Kneel, rise" four times, at which the participants perform the ritual of kneeling. Arguing that "ritualization" is a process of producing a ritualized agent through the interaction between the human body and the environment, Catherine Bell writes, "Hence, through a series of physical movements ritual practices spatially and temporally construct an environment organized according to schemes of privileged opposition."[17] A ritual environment is constituted in *Peach Blossom Fan* by means of the Confucian ritual performance in the way the objects are laid out and referenced and through the physical movements of the participants. In the scholars' ritual performance, clothing serves as an immediate expression of their authentic selves as well as of their collective identity. Their inner selves, their bodies, and their exterior clothing are seamlessly integrated into the ritual environment.

This successful ritual performance is disturbed by the presence of a corrupt official—more specifically, by the theatrical nature of his performance. In *Peach Blossom Fan*, the character Ruan Dacheng embodies the negative connotations of theatricality. On the one hand, he is a playwright, a drama director, the owner of a private troupe, and occasionally an actor himself. On the other, he is considered a partisan of the corrupt eunuch Wei Zhongxian and thus is an enemy of the upright officials in the Restoration Society. Whereas scene 3 depicts Ming state attire as a sacred ritual language, the arrival of Ruan Dacheng introduces the peril of theatrical performance. Theatricality, defined by inauthenticity and spectatorship, challenges the purity and validity of Ming state ritual.

Ruan enters the stage with a full beard and wearing a uniform with a cap and a belt in accordance with his former official title. The way he is depicted in the scene, however, conjures up the negative connotations of theatricality. He introduces himself to the audience as follows: "I have come to watch this grand ceremony." Placing himself in an ambiguous position as both participant and spectator, Ruan's words imperil the ritual ceremony, potentially turning a solemn ritual into a theatrical spectacle. The entire struggle between Ruan and the literati group in scene 3 revolves around his body and clothing. In an aria sung by the crowd, Ruan slyly inserts his own line: "I have washed shame off my face to sneak into this solemn gathering." The reference to the washing of his face echoes the comment made elsewhere in the play about the corrupting power of theatrical paint that cannot be washed off.[18] Washing his face proves inadequate, however, since he must cover his face (*yanmian* 掩面) while he sneaks into the ceremonial line. His face would betray his true identity, but his clothing gains him access to the gathering of Confucian scholars. For all the other participants at the ceremony, clothing immediately signifies and confirms their literati identity. For Ruan Dacheng, clothing serves as camouflage, as does a theatrical costume.

Whereas clothing as an element of ritual language solidifies one's social identity, clothing as theatrical language destabilizes it. Although Ruan wears the uniform of literati scholars, the public refers to his attire in profane terms. When the scholars of the Restoration Society wage a fight against Ruan, they refer to him as the "spawn of a eunuch" (*yan'er dangzi* 閹兒璫子). The word *dang* 璫 refers to an ornament on the official cap of eunuchs, and the insult targets the eunuch Wei Zhongxian, whom Ruan Dacheng has recognized as his father. Using the cap as synecdoche, the scholars distinguish the sacred clothing of Confucian scholars from the profane clothing of Ruan Dacheng and the eunuch clique. To protect the purity of the former, they separate Ruan's body from his Confucian dress. The scene ends as they sing, "His scholarly hat has been beaten flat; it is time for him to burn his ink and brushes." The scholarly hat contrasts with the eunuch's hat mentioned earlier in the play. The destruction of Ruan's scholarly identity first involves attacking his scholarly dress.

Ruan's gradual appropriation of Ming state attire signifies its corruption from the interior of the Southern Ming court. Tina Lu has discussed in detail Ruan's rise to an official position and the associated constant changes of his clothing. She writes, "All it takes for him [Ruan] to transform himself from shamed, exiled partisan of Wei Zhongxian to honored official is a simple change of costume."[19] With Ruan taking power in the Southern Ming court, the separation between ritual and theater in place at the beginning of the play is gradually relinquished.

Both the court ritual and the worship of Confucius take place within the inner city of Nanjing. Contaminated by theatricality, the next state ritual of the Ming court takes place at the boundary between the inner and outer cities of Nanjing. In scene 32, the Southern Ming court stages a ritual of sacrifice for the deceased Chongzhen emperor outside the Taiping Gate on the first anniversary of his death (location B in figure 5.2). The "Stage Items" list mentions a sacrificial table, an incense burner, silk, wine cups, court tablets, and a sacrificial elegy to be read out loud. *The History of the Southern Ming* (*Nanming shi* 南明史) records this sacrifice: "On the anniversary of our former emperor in the first year of the Hongguang reign, [the Hongguang emperor] mourned by wailing in the Hall of Ancestral Worship. An altar was set up outside the Taiping Gate for hundreds of officials to offer their respect and devotion from afar."[20] This record corroborates that *Peach Blossom Fan* represents the ritual performance according to the actual time and place in history. In the scene, the Ceremonial Assistant again presides over the ceremony, wearing a cap and a belt and sporting a long white beard. Ma Shiying, Shi Kefa, and other officials attend the ceremony wearing white clothing (*sufu* 素服).[21] The *Ming History* stipulates mourning dress for Ming officials following the death of an emperor: "Military and civil officials . . . should wear mourning dress for twenty-seven days. . . . Beyond that, they should wear white dress, black silk hats, and black leather for twenty-seven months before removing them."[22] The description of mourning robes and the wailing ritual in the drama also corresponds to that found in historical records. Just like "The Disrupted Ceremony," the scene describes the ritual as taking place in the right time and place, with adequate ritual paraphernalia, and with all the participants wearing appropriate dress. At the ritual performances in the Confucian Temple and Southern Ming court earlier in the drama, the ritual costumes signify Confucian tradition, the political order, and the scholar-officials' literati identities. At this ritual performance, the same ritual costumes fail to serve the same purpose.

Some details reveal that the ritual performance fails to be an authentic memorialization of the deceased Chongzhen emperor. In the scene, the Ceremonial Assistant announces each step of the ritual, including "wailing" (*juai* 舉哀), as everyone present cries three times and kneels down four times as prescribed by the ritual code. After the Ceremonial Assistant announces the completion of the ceremony, he comments, "None of the other officials is weeping bitterly. I, the Ceremonial

Assistant, cannot help but cry my heart out." By criticizing other officials for not crying bitterly enough, he delivers the message that the worship ceremony's purpose has not been fulfilled. Although the participants wear appropriate ritual attire and follow prescribed procedures, because sincerity is lacking the ritual fails. Ruan Dacheng's arrival and his ostentatious crying further augment the hypocritical nature of the ritual performance. After Ruan joins the group, the characters all sing together, "All libations poured and voices having wailed, none can tell true grief from false." Here we see three types of crying: the first by the ritual participants in accordance with the ritual code, the second by the Ceremonial Assistant after the ritual performance proper, and finally that by Ruan Dacheng feigning mourning. The theatrical nature of Ruan's performance threatens the legitimacy of Confucian ritual, which is the very reason he is excluded from the literati community in scene 3. At the sacrifice to the Chongzhen emperor, it is ultimately the theatrical nature of the officials' performance that undermines the state ritual.

At a third ritual performance, Ming state attire arrives at the end of its journey. After the fall of Nanjing, a group of characters flee to the mountains. Among them is Zhang Wei 張薇, a former Embroidered-Uniform Guard (Jinyiwei 錦衣衛) in the Chongzhen court and now a Daoist master living in White Cloud Temple 白雲庵 on Rose-Cloud-Dwelling Mountain 棲霞山.[23] As shown in figure 5.2, the mountain, also named Sheshan 攝山, is located to the northeast of Nanjing (location C), on the very periphery of the city, separated from the city proper by walls painted in dark lines.[24] It is also noticeable that neither the map nor *Peach Blossom Fan* includes any indication of Ming Xiaoling Mausoleum, the tomb of the founding emperor of the Ming dynasty located outside Nanjing. It is in the liminal space of Rose-Cloud Mountain that the Daoist master Zhang Wei performs a ritual of passage for Ming state attire.

In scene 40, "Entering the Way" (Rudao 入道), the Daoist Zhang presides over a group of rituals that transcend political disputes, individual entanglements, and sartorial turbulence. At the beginning of the scene, Zhang Wei explains that that day is the Middle Primordial Festival in the *yiyou* year (1645) and that he is conducting a Daoist *jiao* ritual (*huanglu keyi* 黃籙科儀) and offering sacrifices to the Chongzhen emperor. The stage instruction specifies that he should wear a broad-sleeved robe and gourd-shaped hat (*piaoguan nayi* 瓢冠衲衣) and carry a whisk. Later he changes into Daoist ritual costume (*fayi* 法衣) to circumambulate the altar, turning the setting into a ritualistic space. By the end of the scene, he wears a golden Daoist hat, a *huayang* headpiece (*huayang jin* 華陽巾), and a crane cloak (*hechang* 鶴氅) to preside over a food-offering ritual (*shishi gongde* 施食功德). Dressed in religious costumes, the Daoist Zhang witnesses the destinies of all the characters, who either are deprived of Ming uniforms, like Ruan Dacheng, or willingly give them up in favor of Daoist robes, like the hero and heroine, Hou Fangyu and Li Xiangjun. The religious setting provides a space where Ming state attire undergoes its final transformation.

In between these two religious ceremonies, Zhang performs a grand Ming court ritual (*chaoqing dali* 朝請大禮). Sandwiched between two religious rites, the Confucian court ritual loses its independence, subdued and thus transcended by the religious rituals. At the same time, the meaning of Ming state attire is transformed. Zhang carries an ivory tablet and wears a nine-ridged cap (*jiuliang chaoguan* 九梁朝冠), an official robe with a crane badge (*hebu chaofu* 鶴補朝服), a golden girdle, and thick-soled court boots. The specific cap and robe can be worn only by the highest-ranking officials in the Ming court, yet Zhang Wei served only as director of the Embroidered-Uniform Guard and is undeserving of the official robe employed in the scene. Wearing clothes that do not befit his identity as a Ming official, Zhang Wei "performs" the role of a loyal subject of the Ming dynasty. In the scene's "Stage Items" section, Kong Shangren specifically lists the nine-ridged cap and the robe with crane badge for the very reason that they are not part of a troupe's regular costumes and have not appeared earlier in the play.[25] Rather than part of a real Ming uniform, these two pieces of clothing are theatrical costumes that "represent" Ming state attire.

Paratextual commentary further points to the theatrical nature of this performance. Alongside the detailed descriptions of the ritual, marginal comments in the drama's Kangxi print edition repeatedly heap praise on the costuming: "Such dressing up is indeed magnificent for watching." . . . "The three attires of the three loyal officials are magnificent for watching." The comments underscore how the clothing contributes to a successful spectacle for visual appreciation. In "The Disrupted Ceremony," Ruan Dacheng's spectatorship potentially turns the

Confucian ritual into a theatrical performance. Here at the end of the drama, we are reminded that we are "watching" an ensemble of costumes—those for officials and Daoists, both the living and the dead. Whereas Ruan's spectatorship threatens the ritual performance, the conscious watching in the last scene transforms Ming state attire into a visual spectacle similar to that found in a theatrical performance.

SEVERING THE BODY AND CLOTHING OF A MING MARTYR

Peach Blossom Fan represents the undoing of Ming state attire through state rituals as well as via personal experiences. After the attire is detached from the Ming state, it is further disengaged from the bodies of Ming subjects, as seen through a special anecdote regarding the suicide of the upright official Shi Kefa. In earlier scenes, Shi Kefa appears in an official cap and belt to welcome the Prince of Fu—the future Hongguang emperor. At the sacrificial ritual for the Chongzhen emperor, he wears white mourning dress. In scene 35, when the Manchu army approaches Yangzhou, Shi Kefa appears in unofficial clothing and wears a white felt cap as a defense general. On most of these occasions, he dresses according to his identity as a Ming official, his clothing representing the Ming state.

After the loss of Yangzhou, he travels to Nanjing wearing a felt hat and encounters the Ceremonial Assistant, from whom he learns of the fall of Nanjing (scene 38). With no emperor to serve, he commits suicide by throwing himself into the river but not before he removes his official apparel. The drama reads, "(Looking down at his body) But it is not fitting that the cap and gown [*guanshang*] should adorn Shi Kefa, culpable for the fall of the state. (Removing hat, robe, and boots, he sings) I strip myself of robe, boots, and ceremonial hat [*guanmian*]." In the aria before these lines, he refers to the white waves in the river as the misgivings of Qu Yuan, the scholar-official in the Warring States period who threw himself into a river following the defeat of his country.[26] Historical and literary writings by and about Qu Yuan often feature his prominent self-made apparel, especially the high cap. To Qu Yuan, his unmistakable clothing and fragrant accessories serve as an exterior representation of his inner virtues. In contrast, Shi Kefa deems it necessary to sever his clothing from his body. His official clothing is a symbol of the Ming state, and he is culpable for having undone the state and thus unfit to wear state attire. A stage instruction indicates that the items Shi removes from his body include a felt hat, a gown, and boots. In Shi's own words, they are collectively referred to as *guanshang* (cap and gown) and *guanmian* (ceremonial cap). Throughout the play, *guanshang* and *guanmian* are used to represent the splendor of the Ming political regime. These two terms would not befit the felt hat Shi Kefa wears during his travels. With these highly symbolic words, Shi Kefa not only describes his own clothing but also makes a comment on Ming state attire in general.

After undressing himself, Shi Kefa "regards his body and then throws himself into the river" (scene 35). Severed from his uniform, Shi Kefa's body becomes the sole carrier of his person as a criminal. As he indicates in an aria, his body will be consumed by fish, and, consequently, he will completely disappear in material form. Since Shi Kefa has destroyed his own body after stripping off his clothing, what will become of him as a person? What will happen to his clothing after his death?

The very action of undressing himself dissociates the clothing from his body and initiates a journey whereby the clothing circulates in public. As the Ceremonial Assistant kneels down by the discarded clothing and wails over Shi Kefa's suicide, Hou Fangyu and his fellows in the Restoration Society arrive at the site. They examine the clothing, referring to the pieces as *yishang* 衣裳, *yifu* 衣服, and "boots and hat" (*xuemao*)— terms used for ordinary clothing. When inspecting the clothes more closely, they realize that "the inside of the clothing [*yishang*] is full of vermilion seal stamps" (衣裳裡面, 渾身朱印),[27] a detail that reveals the complicated relation between Shi Kefa, his body, his clothing, and the Ming state even after his death. The line includes an ambiguous phrase, "full body" (*hunshen* 渾身), to describe the seal stamps in Shi's clothing. To the witnesses Shi's clothing and body are not completely dissociated; the absent body still ties the abandoned clothing with Shi Kefa. It is ultimately the official seal that integrates the clothing with Shi the person, as they read out the words on the seal: "Seal of the president of the Board of War and grand officer entrusted with the defense of the region north of the river." These words confirm the political identity of the clothes' owner. The word (*zhu*) describing the red color of the seal stamps is homophonous with the last name of the Ming imperial family, a correlation widely invoked in memory of the fallen regime during the dynastic change.[28] Shi Kefa has removed his clothing in the hope that he can keep distance from the political responsibilities his clothing carries, but the official seal stamps, symbols of the Ming state, claim both his body and his person as belonging to the state. In other words, after the disappearance of Shi Kefa's corporeal body, his clothing has encompassed the physical body and has become the embodiment of Shi Kefa's person.

Equipped with the crimson seals and invoking the absent body, Shi Kefa's clothing ceases being Ming state attire. After their inspection, one of the scholars suggests performing a ritual of worship in front of the clothing, which he refers to as cap and gown (*yiguan*). The stage instruction reads, "The *fumo* sets up cap and gown." This is the only place in the drama's stage instructions that employs *yiguan* instead of *guandai* or *guanshang* to describe a Ming official uniform, signaling a major change in the meaning of Ming state attire. In the historical context of early Qing China, *yiguan* became a politically and ethnically charged term, closely connected with the Han-style clothing of the Ming dynasty. The public worship transforms Shi Kefa's clothing from a set of Ming state attire to a symbol of Ming loyalism.

Later on, the Ceremonial Assistant will collect Shi Kefa's clothes and bury them in Shi's *yiguan* tomb (衣冠冢) by Plum Blossom Ridge in Yangzhou. In a conversation in the last scene, the Ceremonial Assistant and his friends again refer to Shi Kefa's *yiguan*: "I recall that three years ago you were intending to bury the *yiguan* of Marshal Shi Kefa below Plum Blossom Ridge. What came of that?" ("Sequel to Scene 40"). By play's end, Shi Kefa's attire has become a memory revisited in conversation. In his reply to the question, the Ceremonial Assistant points out that "we did not set up any tablet for him." A tablet would usually carry an epitaph summarizing the life of the interred person. Shi Kefa's tomb does not have such a tablet in part because providing one would have been too politically sensitive. Consequently, the only words inside and outside the tomb are the seal scripts with Shi Kefa's official title in the Southern Ming government. With the collapse of the sartorial order, Shi Kefa's *guanshang* uniform ceases to exist in society and changes into *yiguan*. It stops being clothing proper and instead becomes a symbol of the past.

Peach Blossom Fan does not, and cannot, provide an exact answer to the Ceremonial Assistant's question about the *yiguan* tomb because it is impossible for a theatrical performance to represent the changes of clothing buried in a tomb. When Kong Shangren personally paid a visit to Shi Kefa's tomb in 1689, he wrote a disconcerting poem about Shi's *yiguan*:

PLUM BLOSSOM RIDGE

> Plum flowers withered, the ridge collapsed.
> A person comes and stands there, sighing.
> The river keeps streaming down from the ridge;
> The general's cap and gown [*yiguan*] have rotted away.

梅花嶺
梅枯嶺亦傾，人來立腳歎。
嶺下水滔滔，將軍衣冠爛。[29]

He added a note to the poem: "Cabinet minister Shi Daolin; his cap and gown are buried here." As the poem has it, only the flowing water remains after the historical changes, while the plum trees, ridge, and clothing have all decayed. The disturbing mention of "rotted away" conveys the unfortunate reality that Shi Kefa's clothing is nothing but a set of boots and garments destined to decompose. After having been contaminated by theatricality defined through inauthenticity and spectatorship, Ming state attire is severed from the bodies of Ming subjects.

OLD BODY, NEW CLOTHING, AND DYNASTIC TIME

Discussing "performance illustrations," Li-ling Hsiao has suggested close connections between Chinese history and Chinese drama. She identifies three categories in which drama and history can be connected: drama as historical record, as commentary on historical events, and as a vehicle for transmitting exemplary names from past times.[30] Hsiao suggests that Chinese drama creates a space of historical memory, just as Ann Jones and Peter Stallybrass have explicitly viewed clothing as "materials of memory."[31] In the preceding analysis of *Peach Blossom Fan*, I have discussed how Ming state attire, as a ritual language, is corrupted by theatricality, how it moves from the center to the periphery, and how it is severed from the bodies of Ming subjects. Yet how does the drama represent Ming state attire as clothing of the historical past? More specifically, how is clothing associated with dynastic time—that of the Ming and that of the Qing?

Not every Ming subject sacrificed him- or herself for the Ming state. Some became recluses living in the mountains, and others became subjects of the nascent Manchu Qing dynasty. The play ends with an epilogue, or "Sequel to Scene 40," which depicts the life of some former Ming subjects living as recluses in a utopian mountain community apparently outside the new dynastic time. Titled "Remaining Trace" (Yuyun 餘韻), the scene is set in the ninth month in the fifth year of the Shunzhi reign (1648), bringing the audience back to the reality of the newly established Manchu dynasty. The scene involves only three supporting characters: musician Su Kunsheng, storyteller Liu Jingting, and the Ceremonial Assistant.[32] After all the previous ritual occasions, this last scene includes a local festival set in the mountains in worship of the god of wealth. Through the words of the characters, the drama reaffirms the extrasocietal nature of the mountainous space. Su Kunsheng starts his soliloquy as follows: "Three years have passed since I accompanied Xiangjun into these hills in the year *yiyou*. Rather than return home, I have lingered here on Bull's-Head Mountain and Rose-Cloud-Dwelling Mountain, earning my keep by gathering wood." These words describe his life as if he were living in a utopia outside political reality. Su Kunsheng uses the stem-and-branch calendar instead of dynastic time to refer to the year when Nanjing fell to the Manchus. In a similar way, the Ceremonial Assistant introduces the current time: "Today is the tenth day of the ninth month in the year *wuzi*, the birthday of the god of wealth."[33] Not only is this mountainous space far from the political center of Nanjing but also time is undisturbed by the changing regimes.

In this nearly timeless utopian space, what kind of clothes do the three characters wear? Upon their entrance, the stage instruction indicates that Sun Kunsheng carries a load of firewood, Liu Jingting rows a boat, and the Ceremonial Assistant brings an instrument as well as a wine bottle, without specifying their costumes. By the end of the scene, the three characters are collectively referred to as "mountain dwellers in plain clothes" (白衣山人). This expression is a metaphor for hermits without official titles, an appellation that reveals little about the specific costumes the three characters wear. Studies by historian Lin Li-yueh show that in early Qing China, many remnant subjects managed to retain Han-style clothing—and even their hair—by living in remote areas as recluses.[34] During his visit to southern China, Kong Shangren visited a number of these Ming loyalists. His poems about his visits frequently describe the Ming loyalists as wearing traditional Chinese clothing such as kudzu headcloth (葛巾), pleated headpiece (折角巾), gauze cap (紗帽), broad sleeves (大袖), and so on.[35] Although we might not necessarily read those poems as realistic records, we can safely assume that in the last scene of *Peach Blossom Fan*, the three characters still wear the clothing they have been wearing throughout the drama.

This utopian space, untarnished by political time, serves as a unique sartorial space where Ming clothing remains. The utopian picture is gradually undermined by the introduction of Qing time followed by Manchu hairstyle and clothing. At the request of the other fellows, the Ceremonial Assistant sings the tune "Questions to Heaven" (Wen cangtian 問蒼天), which he had previously performed at the local festival. The tune begins, "Fifth year of the new calendar, the era of Shunzhi, the year of *wuzi*, in autumn, the ninth month, the seventeenth day—fit time for celebration!. . . The aging recluse, white hair properly shorn, comes to the deity temple in the mountains."[36] Besides the stem-and-branch calendar, the song introduces a new calendar marked by the dynastic time—the fifth year of the Shunzhi reign. This way of introducing time breaks with the previous extrapolitical setting and discloses the message of Manchu rule. The introduction of dynastic time is immediately followed by a mention of hair. "White hair" indicates advanced age—the Ceremonial Assistant describes himself as "both temples grizzled" upon his entrance in the scene. Shaving the head would all too easily remind an early Qing audience of the Manchu government's regulations regarding clothing and hairstyle, potentially turning the Ceremonial Assistant from a recluse into a submissive subject. Following the mention of hair, the song brings up the hat: "Under the straw rain hat, here I stand, tug my beard and sigh." The bamboo or straw hat is a typical prop for Buddhist and Daoist monks in traditional *kunqu* performances.[37] Such a hat obviously differs from the Ming uniform the Ceremonial Assistant has donned earlier in the drama, and at the same time it covers up his shaved head.

If the Ceremonial Assistant's hair only obliquely indicates his para-doxical identity as a recluse or a Qing subject, the government clerk's uni-form directly ties the sartorial system with the time of the Qing dynasty. As the three old friends engage in a conversation, the stage instruction indicates that a government runner slyly enters in "clothing of the pres-ent" (*shifu* 時服). A comment in the Kangxi edition of the play immedi-ately points out the shocking effect of that plot detail: "Who would expect a runner with a red hat to arrive and conclude *Peach Blossom Fan*?"[38] The unexpectedness of the runner's appearance has much to do with his uni-form. *Shifu* is not the name of a particular costume but a general refer-ence to clothing of the early Qing period. Prior to the appearance of this term in the play, all the characters' costumes correspond to their spe-cific identities in the Ming dynasty. The differences in their clothing are determined by gender, social status, and the political occasion. Clothing remains synchronic without a temporal differentiation. The magical phrase "clothing of the present" immediately transforms all the previous garments into clothing of the past. In *Costume in the Theatre*, James Laver identifies "a sharp division between 'theatrical' and 'ordinary' clothes" and suggests the term "costume plays" for plays featuring dress in the styles of other times and places.[39] Laver's proposition is based on the temporal dimension of clothing. When the term *shifu* creates a divi-sion between past and present for clothing, it transforms the previous stories in the drama into a "costume play" about the past, and the rest of the drama into a play of the present.[40]

Given the sensitivity of staging Manchu clothing in the early Qing, the question of which costumes count as "clothing of the present" becomes important. The solution to this challenge lies in the government runner's special uniform. Some scholars have read the term *shifu* in *Peach Blossom Fan* as a reference to *qizhuang*, or Manchu-style costume, and consider the term as the earliest record of the stage use of Manchu cloth-ing.[41] In the "Stage Items" section, Kong Shangren lists only one item corresponding to *shifu*, a red hat. In this scene, the clerk's uniform with a red hat can be the same as the uniforms for the Ming government run-ners who appeared in the previous scenes of the drama, such as the one Ruan Dacheng dons upon receiving the Hongguang emperor (scene 15) or those of the runners when they set out to arrest scholars of the Restoration Society (scene 29). In figure 5.3, showing a Qing-dynasty

FIGURE 5.3 Illustration of the scene "Remaining Trace". Kong Shangren 孔尚任, *Qing caihuiben Taohua shan* 清彩繪本桃花扇, illustrated by Jianbai Daoren 堅白道人 (Beijing: Zuojia chubanshe, 2009), 181.

illustration of the scene, the runner's uniform does not show explicit Manchu features.[42] In another illustration (figure 5.4), the runner's uniform shows more Manchu features, especially the cap with tassels and the high position where the lapel joins the collar.[43] It is possible that the uniforms for government runners remained largely unchanged through the Ming–Qing transition. With the red hat symbolizing the Manchu uniform, Kong Shangren successfully conjures up a sense of the present, leaving the choice of costumes to individual performers of the scene.

Scholars have debated both the author's and the play's attitude toward the Manchu regime. They have uncovered criticism of late Ming corruption, eulogies of the Manchu emperor, and antagonism against Manchu rule. The description of the government runner best illustrates these

FIGURE 5.4 Illustration of "Remaining Trace". Kong Shangren 孔尚任, *Taohua shan* 桃花扇, in *Nuanhongshi huike chuanju* 暖紅室彙刻傳劇, ed. Liu Shiheng 劉世珩, Wu Mei 吳梅, and Li Xiang 李詳 (repr., Yangzhou: Jiangsu guangling guji keyinshe, 1979), 128a. Image courtesy of Harvard-Yenching Library.

ambivalent attitudes. In addition to his unique uniform, the runner also invokes the queue of the Manchu hairstyle, a potentially sarcastic nod to Manchu hair and dress regulations. Upon his entrance, the runner introduces himself as a direct descendant of Xu Da's, who received the title of Duke of Wei (魏國公) because of his military merit during the founding of the Ming dynasty. Now, after the dynastic transition, Xu's descendant can serve only as a low-level runner in Shangyuan county. To conclude his self-introduction, he says, "The meritocratic founders of a country leave/keep dog tails, and the reclusive elders in the new regime draw in their necks like turtles" (開國元勳留狗尾，換朝逸老縮龜頭). On the surface, the runner ridicules himself by calling himself a dog tail left (liu 留) by his meritorious ancestor. On a more oblique level, this line could be interpreted as a sarcastic insult of the turncoat officials in the early Qing who had to shave their heads and maintain (liu 留) a queue—that is, dog tail. In the latter reading, dynasty founders would not refer to the officials in the early Ming but rather to the Ming officials who surrendered to the Manchus and assisted them in establishing the Qing dynasty.[44] Read this way, the clerk's hair serves as a metaphor for the disgraceful service of the turncoat officials. This connotation of the tail/queue is indicated only through the runner's words; onstage, the runner's red hat could cover up whatever hairstyle he has.

At the very end of the scene, the government runner recognizes the three elderly men as talented recluses and tries to enlist them to serve the Manchu government. What we ultimately witness is a Manchu government runner in Qing clothing chasing three old men in Ming clothing offstage. The stage remains empty for a while as the backstage staff read a concluding poem. As Tina Lu argues, in the new world of the Qing dynasty there is no longer any space for these Ming loyalists, not even onstage.[45] Peach Blossom Fan creates a utopian space for some recluses to retain their Han-style clothing and at the same time introduces a Ming traitor intruding into that remnant space wearing clothing of the Qing dynasty. Through the lens of costuming, I have shown how the drama introduces dynastic time to clothing and simultaneously turns the stage into a space of the Qing regime. As my analysis shows, clothing in Peach Blossom Fan is not simply a vehicle of memory but rather a history-making device—a temporalized sign that immediately differentiates between past and present.

After the journey from the center to the periphery, and from the present to the past, Ming state attire is reduced to a group of garments ready to be adopted by theatrical performance. In this final section, I consider two modes of Ming state attire used as stage props, the first in the late Ming, the second in the early Qing. In these scenes, the shifting connections between costumes onstage and clothing offstage demonstrate the changing nature of theatrical costuming.

A special moment of a dramatic performance within *Peach Blossom Fan* illustrates the power of clothing to transgress the boundary between the social and the theatrical. In scene 4, "The Play Observed" (Zhenxi 偵 戲), the theatrical setting of Ruan Dacheng's private household features an obscure boundary of theatricality. In the scene, Yang Wencong, Ruan's colleague and friend, visits Ruan in his residence, Stone Nest Garden (石 巢園), designed by a celebrated garden designer. A plaque written by a famous calligrapher carries the name the Hall of Lyrics (詠懷堂), and in the innermost part of the household is a piece of red carpet, the stage of Ruan Dacheng's private theater. For this scene, Kong Shangren lists *bazi* 把子—a term for weapons used onstage—in the "Stage Items" section, although this term does not appear in the main text. It becomes unclear whether the private theater is part of the household décor, or the entire household is part of the theater's décor.

Within his theater-residence, Ruan Dacheng successfully "performs" a literati scholar wearing scholarly dress. From deep among the flowers, the visitor Yang Wencong hears Ruan reading. He will soon find out that Ruan is editing his drama *The Swallow Letter* (*Yanzi jian* 燕子箋) just before its publication. Yang describes Ruan as a reclusive playwright: "As if in the painting of a thatched hut, he wears a high black headpiece / and directs the players with silver lute and crimson clappers." "Thatched hut" alludes to Du Fu's humble residence, and "black headpiece" alludes to the dress of a recluse. The ensuing conversation between Ruan and Yang demonstrates the former's keen interest in and talent for playwriting.[46] Every detail attests to the lifestyle of an authentic literati scholar—or, more specifically, a literati playwright devoted to drama composition and performance. The drama does not specify how Ruan is costumed. It is possible that he indeed wears a black headpiece as a recluse, since in his theater-household, performing/being a scholar is completely legitimate, although such an identity has been denied him at the previous public gathering. The red carpet designating a performance space at the innermost part of his household problematizes the boundary between theater and reality in Ruan's private life.

A metatheatrical moment in the scene further illustrates the fluid boundary between onstage and offstage clothing in the late Ming. As Yang Wencong and Ruan Dacheng meet at Ruan's place, scholars from the Restoration Society send a messenger to borrow Ruan's private troupe to stage *The Swallow Letter* at their party. Only too eager to comply, Ruan sends his troupe over in the hope that he will be readmitted into the literati community based on his theatrical talents. He orders his servants to "run upstairs and fetch the best set of costumes; see that the troupe comb their hair, wash their faces, and hurry to follow the theater trunks." In "Stage Items," Kong Shangren lists "theater trunks" (*xixiang* 戲箱). It is readily conceivable that the theater trunks that the troupe used to store costumes and other articles outside the play would be temporarily used as props onstage. As a corollary, the choice costumes Ruan orders to be carried over in those trunks would be no different from those used in the ritual ceremony in the prior scenes. The same set of clothing as material objects can simultaneously be used as theatrical costumes and as Ming state attire as far as the performance of *Peach Blossom Fan* is concerned. This plot illustrates the permeability of the boundary between the theatrical and the social in the Ming dynasty.

Whereas the play demonstrates the collapse and dispersion of Ming state attire, a special anecdote indicates a different route for theatrical costumes to traverse. In scene 36, "Flight from Disaster" (Taonan 逃難), the Hongguang emperor and his officials flee Nanjing. Though they wear plain coats, the corrupt officials Ma Shiying and Ruan Dacheng are recognized by Nanjing urbanites, who angrily capture and undress both of them. Some of the actresses Ruan previously recruited are also fleeing the imperial palace. The stage instruction indicates that one performer runs onto the stage in tatters clutching his drum, and another performer, head uncovered, carries a silk hat and a beard. Within the drama, the silk hat and beard are objects from the imperial troupe's collection in the Southern Ming palace. The collapse of the Southern Ming court in the drama marks a critical moment when the symbolic meaning of clothing undergoes radical changes. Used as props by the Southern Ming palace troupe, the silk cap first signifies a Ming uniform in the court performance, and then the Ming political system. At the moment the Southern Ming court collapses, the Ming uniform loses its political legitimacy, and thus the silk hat no longer signifies the political splendor of the Ming regime but rather its undoing. As material items, these objects would be carried out of the Southern Ming court and become part of the props Kong Shangren lists in his "Stage Items." Their connection with the Ming regime as a political entity is forever severed.

The play's opening scenes, set in early Qing Beijing and depicting a performance of the play, introduce a new time and space in the Qing dynasty. In these scenes, costumes onstage, juxtaposed with clothing off-stage, constitute a unique sartorial spectacle in the early Qing performance of *Peach Blossom Fan*. The two opening scenes feature mainly the Ceremonial Assistant introducing the play's plotline through conversation with an invisible audience and the backstage staff. The historical story within *Peach Blossom Fan* ends in the year 1648, when the Ceremonial Assistant and his two fellows appear for the last time before retreating into the mountains. The opening scenes are set in the twenty-third year of the Kangxi reign (1684), thirty-six years after the time of the last scene. The twenty-third year of the Kangxi reign was the year of *jiazi* in the stem-and-branch calendar, the beginning of a sixty-year cycle. It was during that year that the Kangxi emperor visited Qufu, Confucius's hometown in Shandong province, when Kong Shangren served as the emperor's tour guide. Kong later received the title Erudite of the Directorate of Education because of his service to the emperor.[47] In the prologue that starts the drama, the Ceremonial Assistant sings for the peace and prosperity of Manchu rule, clearly connecting with the imperial visit in 1684.

The opening scenes introduce the performance of *Peach Blossom Fan* as taking place in the House of Great Serenity (太平園), a commercial theater in early Qing Beijing where Kong Shangren served in the Manchu government.[48] Far removed from Nanjing, where the stories in the drama take place, the setting creates a psychological distance for the audience, and with it a stronger sense of spectatorship. Just as *Peach Blossom Fan* negotiates the boundary between Ming and Qing clothing, its imagined performance in a commercial theater also lies at the border of Manchu and Han residential areas in early Qing Beijing. As I discussed in chapter 1, in Beijing in particular Manchu rulers reserved the inner city for those in the Eight Banners and designated the outer city as the residential area for Han Chinese.[49] Andrea Goldman's study shows that most theaters in early Qing Beijing were located outside the southern gate of the inner city, thus isolated from the Manchu residential area. Nevertheless, Manchu people keen for theater managed to trespass the boundary to watch dramatic performances.[50] The Manchus who sneaked out of the inner city to watch dramas not only mingled with Han Chinese but also became part of the sartorial spectacle in early Qing theaters.

In setting its opening scenes in a commercial theater in early Qing Beijing, the drama casts everyone present in the imagined performance space as a subject of the Manchu Qing dynasty. Since the government runner in the last scene of the drama introduced "clothing of the present," it can be assumed that all the male characters and the theater audience are dressed in the Manchu style as required by the government. An examination of the clothing for the Ceremonial Assistant, the actors, and the audience, however, reveals a rather complicated sartorial scene. For clarity, I refer to the Ceremonial Assistant by the role type, *fumo*, which is used in dramatizing the character. When the performer in the *fumo* role appears, the stage instruction indicates that he wears a felt hat and a Daoist robe (*zhanjin daopao* 氈巾道袍). This special set of apparel allows two interpretations. First, as the name implies, a Daoist robe could be the dress of a Daoist practitioner. Whereas the Manchu Qing dynasty required all male subjects to wear Manchu clothing, Daoists were allowed to continue wearing their Ming-style clothing.[51] Yet no textual evidence from earlier plot segments indicates that the Ceremonial Assistant has become a Daoist practitioner. On the other hand, the Daoist robe was an outfit in everyday life for literati scholars in the Ming dynasty and became one of the most common costumes onstage—known as *xuezi* 褶子—for a wide range of characters. Given these facts, it is unclear whether the felt hat and Daoist robe appear to the audience as "clothing of the present"—clothing of the Qing dynasty or of the former Ming dynasty. After the government runner demarcates different clothing with different dynastic time, the ambivalent costume of the *fumo* role in the opening scene only camouflages such a demarcation.

The *fumo* role's dress and words in the opening scene of the second half of the drama further complicate the relation between his clothes and the changing dynasties. The costume instruction indicates that the *fumo* role again features a felt hat and a Daoist robe. The *fumo* character describes himself as traveling to the same theater to watch the latter part of the performance: "Idly I stroll beside the stream, in flimsy garments clad and summer hat." A straw/bamboo summer hat contradicts the felt headgear specified in the stage instruction and corresponds instead with the Ceremonial Assistant's song in the last scene where he refers to his straw hat. Does this correspondence suggest any connection between the *fumo* in this opening scene and the Ceremonial Assistant in the last scene of the drama? If so, what connotations does a straw hat carry? Like the Daoist robe, the straw hat is, first, the ordinary headgear of early Qing people and, second, a typical garment of Han Chinese who refused to accept an official position in the early Qing government. In one of his poems, Kong Shangren writes, "A visiting guest presents his tribute in verses; a remnant subject's straw hat serves as a ceremonial cap" (使客詩 為贊，遺民笠是冠).[52] If the Daoist robe connects the *fumo* with late Ming literati, the straw hat associates him with literati living as recluses in the early Qing.[53]

Many scholars have observed the liminal identity of the *fumo* role in the theatrical setting. The *fumo* comments on his own liminal position at the performance site: "How amusing it was to recognize my decrepit self in a minor role! I was stirred so deeply that I laughed and wept, raged and cursed by turns. Needless to say, the audience had no idea that I was included in the drama." Different from the *fumo* who performs the Ceremonial Assistant in the drama proper, the *fumo* role opening the drama remains a spectator outside the performance. At the same time, he differs from the rest of the audience because he indeed is/ was one of the characters in the play. Dressed in politically neutral garments—a Daoist robe and a felt/straw hat—he can be either an actor in the drama or a spectator of the drama, and either a Qing subject or a remnant subject of the Ming dynasty. Just as his life spans the dynastic transition, his clothing bridges the staging of the drama and, in effect, the entire drama itself. From the Ming uniform of cap and belt to a set of mourning dress, from a plain coat to the Daoist robe, the Ceremonial

Assistant is the only person capable of transcending various sartorial boundaries. Sophie Volpp uses the phrase "ideological versatility" to describe Liu Jingting, a storyteller in *Peach Blossom Fan*.[54] In a similar way, the Ceremonial Assistant—or the *fumo* role—demonstrates the highest level of versatility in costuming.

At the drama's performance, the *fumo* maintains an ambiguous identity as mediator between Manchu and Han, Ming and Qing, and also between theater and reality. Situated on the border between theatricality and spectatorship, the *fumo* role makes oblique references to the clothes in both realms. In the opening scene of the second half he sings, "The spectacle of court gowns and tablets and the traces of powder and paint are rehearsed afresh time and again." I translate *yang* 樣 as "spectacle" because the *fumo* is commenting on the gowns and tablets neither as objects nor as theatrical props but as a comprehensive theatrical effect, one that temporarily resuscitates the Ming court. The gowns and tablets that enable this theatrical resurrection, however, are irrevocably consigned to the theatrical realm. They are meaningless objects offstage—or at most theatrical props onstage—and are clearly separated from the clothing of the *fumo* as a spectator and that of the other audience members.

It is not typical for a *chuanqi* drama to describe the clothing of its audience, but textual traces in *Peach Blossom Fan* incorporate the audience into the sartorial spectacle. In conversation with the *fumo*, the backstage staff say, "This very play will be performed at today's assembly of those wearing caps and gowns."[55] The phrase "cap and gown" (*guanshang* 冠裳) appears throughout *Peach Blossom Fan*. When the hero, Hou Fangyu, appears in the first scene, he introduces himself as follows: "I share the family name with Hou Ying the famous gatekeeper, and I belong to the gentlemen of caps and gowns like those frequenting the Liang Garden." Here, *guanshang* refers to his noble family lineage. At the Southern Ming court, the officials exclaim that they again see caps and gowns—that is, the political splendor of the Southern Ming court. Before Shi Kefa throws himself into the river, he removes his official attire, which he refers to as *guanshang*. When Ming state attire has been abandoned in society, *guanshang* remains in discourses and becomes a signifier of literati scholars' Manchu-style clothing in early Qing China. Early Qing

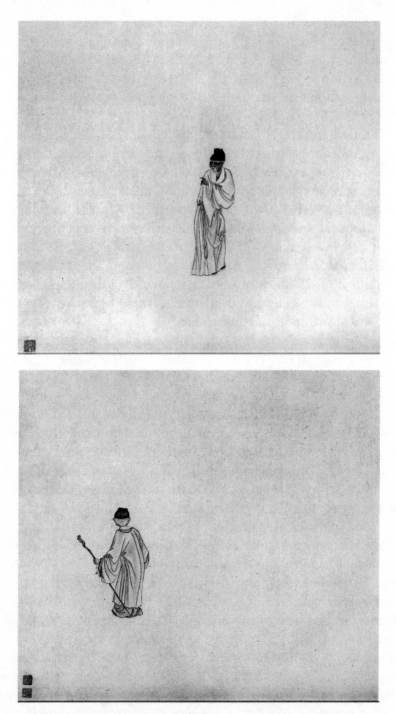

FIGURE 5.5 Illustrations of the opening scenes in *Peach Blossom Fan*. Kong Shangren 孔尚任, *Qing caihuiben Taohua shan* 清彩繪本桃花扇, illustrated by Jianbai Daoren 堅白道人 (Beijing: Zuojia chubanshe, 2009), 9, 97.

literati continued to address themselves as the *guanshang* community, a group defined by their Confucian learning and social status, regardless of the Manchu or Han clothing they wore.

In two illustrations to *Peach Blossom Fan* produced in the Qing dynasty (figure 5.5), the *fumo* role appears to be entering the stage in the opening scene of the first half and exiting the stage in the opening scene of the second half.[56] In both pictures, the *fumo* is the only character. Although he is talking to others in the first picture, both the audience and the troupe staff are absent. Conspicuously, the *fumo* is wearing traditional Chinese clothes without a Manchu-style queue, and the pictures provide no clue as to the dress of the absent audience. These pictures cast back onto the two opening scenes of the drama since in both of them we only hear the *fumo*'s soliloquy.[57]

Wai-yee Li has discussed how the elaborate framing device used in *Peach Blossom Fan* establishes a conjunction of two temporal sequences, linking a historical dimension to a metatheatrical consciousness.[58] In the same vein, Volpp notices a nascent separation between the space for performance and the space for spectatorship, which produces "a greater sense of an ontological division between worlds on- and offstage" in the drama.[59] The contrast between clothing onstage and offstage in the opening scenes of *Peach Blossom Fan* strengthens the spatial separation between performance and spectatorship. The space of theatrical performance would host the display of Han clothing alongside the advancement of the story. Within the space of spectatorship, the imagined audience would constitute part of the performance environment wearing Manchu clothing. Han clothing transfers its cultural meaning to Manchu clothing through such terms as *guanshang*, with Han clothing retreating to and remaining in the theatrical space. Through clothing, the separation between the space of performance and space of spectatorship produces a special effect of historical reflection. The juxtaposition of Ming (Han) and Qing (Manchu) clothing in different sectors of a performance site amplifies the disillusioning power of theatricality that features a distance between past and present and between spectacles and spectators.

Extant materials allow us to understand how early Qing audiences responded to play performances that actualized the sartorial spectacle introduced in the drama's metatheatrical framing. Around 1694, Kong Shangren composed a series of poems about current affairs during regular trips to his office in Beijing. One of the poems describes the House of Great Serenity, the setting of the drama's opening scenes:

Red dust a hundred feet high, one cave of ash;
High chariots, short fans, a thunderlike clamor.
Leisurely pipes and flutes in the House of Great Serenity,
Accompany a new set of lyrics up to the ninth scene.

十丈紅塵一洞灰，高車短扇呵如雷。
太平園裏閑簫管，演到新詞第九回。[60]

The phrase "red dust a hundred feet high" is a metaphor for the rise and fall of historical events, which have collapsed into a cave of ash. High chariots and short fans indicate the audience's noble status, which corresponds to the description of "an elegant assembly of those wearing caps and gowns" from the opening scene of *Peach Blossom Fan*. The phrase "new set of lyrics" indicates that the drama was a new production. Kong Shangren added a note to the poem: "The House of Great Serenity is today's Pear Garden. Whenever it learns about a new event, it produces a new tune based on it." The comment also corresponds with the *fumo*'s words in the prologue of *Peach Blossom Fan*: "The events it portrays took place in Nanjing not long ago, during the last years of the Ming dynasty. . . . Both plots and protagonists are drawn from life." Although those early Qing audiences craved "new" dramas on "current affairs," such performances were received as little more than entertainment, as Kong Shangren uses the word "leisurely" (*xian* 閑) to describe the music and performance. The theatrical costumes used in the House of Great Serenity would have resembled those from late Ming society, which had collapsed not long before.

Early Qing dramas were usually performed in either of two venues: private halls in noble and official residences and commercial theaters.[61] Although Kong Shangren imagined his drama as being staged in a public theater, extant evidence shows that it was performed only in government halls or private households in the early Qing period.[62] In Kong Shangren's notes about *Peach Blossom Fan*'s production and circulation, he recounted five incidents when he was invited to watch the performances, all of which were in private halls. He wrote, "There was not a single day when *Peach Blossom Fan* was not staged in the capital. The one at Ji Garden was most splendid. . . . All the props were amply prepared and ready at hand."[63] The handy props Kong Shangren mentioned would certainly include the pieces of clothing he listed in the "Stage Items" section. The performance events would actualize the juxtaposition of Manchu and Han clothing depicted in the opening scenes of the drama.

The sartorial spectacle in the performances of *Peach Blossom Fan* served two divergent purposes: political nostalgia and theatrical entertainment. At times, a performance of *Peach Blossom Fan* indeed stirred nostalgia for the previous dynasty among its audience. Describing one of those performances, Kong Shangren wrote, "However, under the resplendent music and songs, some people sat alone with sleeves covering their faces. They were the onetime officials and loyalists of the previous dynasty. After the lamps went out and the wine was emptied, they dispersed with sighs."[64] Although Kong Shangren did not state specifically what elements of the performance caused the emotional responses of the loyalists, hairstyle and clothing would easily be one of the reasons. Wu Mu 吳穆 provided a telling hint in the opening lines of a lengthy postscript to the drama's print edition in the Kangxi reign: "As if caps and gowns [*yiguan*] of passing sojourners reappear through the performers; as if post houses and imperial palaces resurface in the theater."[65] These lines stress the "caps and gowns of passing sojourners" as one of the most salient factors triggering historical sentiment. Once the Manchu government had prohibited the use of Han clothing in everyday life, the theatrical display of Han clothing in a drama of dynastic transition poignantly revived a visual experience of the past. As indicated by the phrase "passing sojourners," the characters portrayed in *Peach Blossom Fan*, together with their clothing, have become part of history and can resurface only in a drama.

Although not directly commenting on costuming, a Korean reader of *Peach Blossom Fan* immediately recognized the drama's political message. He wrote, "Isn't the so-called Yunting Shanren [Kong Shangren] apparently someone who shaved his head yet preserved a heart [for the Ming dynasty]?. . . I believe *Peach Blossom Fan* is aimed at stimulating the heart of sadness and anger among the loyalist subjects through the form of a play."[66] The Korean reader's response compares with the experiences of the drama's audiences in early Qing China. In 1700, the year after *Peach Blossom Fan* was completed, Kong Shangren was removed from his official position, which some scholars believe to be a consequence of his composing *Peach Blossom Fan*.[67] After completion, *Peach Blossom Fan* was not performed on a large scale throughout the rest of the Qing dynasty, a possible indicator of the sensitivity of the drama's theme.

At other times, however, early Qing audiences perceived the costumes onstage as mere props for the purpose of entertainment. Even Kong's own theater experiences confirm such a perception of Ming clothing. During his journey to southern China in 1686, he attended a performance with his colleagues at a hall in Yangzhou. He recorded his experience in a poem:

> Each tune sings the peaceful spring of the prosperous age,
> Accompanied by black silk hats, ivory tablets, swords, and official
>   boots.
> A dwarf full of humor entertains us all,
> By imitating a dignified manner with powder and paint.

曲曲盛世太平春，烏帽牙笏雜劍履。
亦有侏儒嬉諧多，粉墨威儀博眾喜。[68]

"Black silk hats, ivory tablets, swords, and official boots" all refer to theatrical costumes in the style of Ming official uniforms, which are used in the poem to extol the peaceful spring of the Manchu dynasty. *Weiyi* 威儀 refers to people's demeanor on official occasions, usually connected with Han-style clothing of the Ming dynasty, which in the poem is subjected to actors' imitation with powder and paint. Although Kong Shangren represented the complicated process of sartorial transition in *Peach Blossom Fan*, elsewhere he pointed out the fact that onstage, Ming attire was nothing but a prop for entertainment.

Over time, nostalgic responses to the performance of *Peach Blossom Fan* further faded away. *Opera of the Book-Storing Tower* (*Nashuying qupu* 納書楹曲譜), a selection of popular scenes in the late eighteenth century, includes three of the most popular scenes from *Peach Blossom Fan*: "A Visit to the Beauty" (Fangcui 訪翠), "The Message on the Fan" (Jishan 寄扇), and "The Painting Inscribed" (Tihua 題畫), all featuring

Li Xiangjun and Hou Fangyu's love affair instead of the dynastic transition.[69] It was not until the late Qing period that *Peach Blossom Fan* was again utilized to point to an imminent crisis, one no longer against the Manchus but against the intruding West.

In *Peach Blossom Fan*, Ming state attire undergoes a process of transformation through time and space. A Daoist ritual hosted by a former Ming official removes Ming clothing from reality. Loyalist officials such as Shi Kefa transform the Ming official uniform into an object of historical memory, dissociating Ming state attire from contemporary society. A clerk from the Manchu government wearing "clothing of the present" introduces the new calendar of the Manchu dynasty, associating the Qing dynasty and Qing clothing with the present and the Ming dynasty and Ming clothing with the past. At the same time, the drama represents theatrical costumes used in late Ming society being carried away to be used on the early Qing stage. As a result, the drama showcases the complicated process through which Ming state attire is transformed into a theatrical language.

Costuming also helps us understand the drama's complicated representation of theatricality. In *Worldly Stage*, Sophie Volpp identifies two opposite attitudes toward theatricality in late imperial China: the "negative charge of inauthenticity" and the "positive valuation of disillusion."[70] *Peach Blossom Fan* artfully weaves its plotlines alongside these understandings of theatricality. As represented in the drama, in late Ming society the connection between onstage and offstage clothing allows theatricality to corrupt Ming state attire as a ritual code. Costuming conflates the social and the theatrical. By the time of the Qing dynasty, costumes onstage and clothing offstage are clearly separated, fostering a new sense of theatricality, one of historical reflection and disillusion. The drama first associates theatrical practices with inauthenticity and represents them as a threat to society, and then associates theatrical practices with disillusion and represents them as a means of transcendence.

Most discussions on theatricality have focused on the spatial dimension, that is, the shifting boundary between theatrical performances and spectatorship. In *Peach Blossom Fan*, we indeed see theatrical costumes onstage in contrast to everyday clothing offstage: the spatial redistribution of Ming and Qing clothing around the stage. Theatricality as

reflected in the drama, however, is not a static or spatial essence of theatrical practices but a process of dialectical development through both
space and time. In early Qing China, Han-style costumes onstage were
associated with the historical past in contrast to Manchu clothing
offstage—clothing of the present. Theatrical costumes continually
reminded its audiences of a distance in time as well as in space. In early
Qing China, theatricality became a relational concept characteristic of
a new mode of human experience.[71]

Scholars have considered Kong Shangren's death in 1718 as symbolizing the end of a prosperous era in the history of Chinese drama.[72]
Through the case of *Peach Blossom Fan*, I have explored the systemic
change in the meaning of onstage and offstage clothing and its influence
on the connections between clothing, individuals, and the state. It is
against such a systemic change that I have probed the ramifications of
costuming in early Qing drama.

Dressing Other and Self

In the case studies explored in this book, Manchu clothing appears as an alien object intruding into the Chinese sartorial tradition. Except a few plays such as *Lovebirds Reversal* and *Unicorn Pavilion Awaiting*, which directly employ Manchu clothing, all the other plays in question either avoid mentioning Manchu clothing or reference it in oblique ways. *Peach Blossom Fan* does not directly describe the Manchu army. *A Ten-Thousand-Li Reunion* completely abandons costume instruction, allowing experimentation in its performances with different invocations of the Manchus. *Chaste Lady Hai* is based on a story about a villain's sexual harassment, yet it includes only a cursory mention of the villain's Manchu-style clothing. In this epilogue I explore the increasing use of Manchu clothing in drama texts and performances throughout the rest of the Qing dynasty and into the modern era. From its absence to its gradual appearance in dramas, Manchu clothing was associated with changing groups of people—Manchu conquerors, Qing subjects, and citizens of Republican China. The shifting meanings of Manchu clothing in Qing drama, I suggest, most conspicuously signify the changing relations between costuming, personhood, and the state.

Beginning in the mid-Qing period, Manchu clothing started to appear more frequently in theatrical works, not as part of an alien culture but as a theatrical trope for self-fashioning. *The Ganoderma Shrine* (*Zhikan ji* 芝龕記, 1751) is one of the earliest dramas that explicitly feature Manchu attire.[1] *The Ganoderma Shrine* represents female generals Qin Liangyu 秦良玉 and Shen Yunying 沈雲英 fighting against rebel armies in the late Ming period. The author claims to have strictly based the drama on history, with each and every character corresponding to a real historical person.[2] The use of clothing substantiates the author's commitment to historical authenticity. In scene 54, the wife of a military commissioner (總兵) commits suicide during an attack by the rebel army. The lady introduces herself as a Mongolian surnamed Liu, and the costume instructions indicate that she appears wearing Manchu clothing. This is one of the earliest playscripts that use Manchu clothing to represent women of non-Han ethnicity. In the penultimate scene (59), four eunuchs from the Manchu palace arrive to deliver an imperial edict. The costume instructions indicate that they appear in *shizhuang* 時裝, namely, clothing of the Qing dynasty—followed immediately by the specification "uniforms with badges" (*bufu*), the uniform of the Manchu court. The Qianlong and Jiaqing emperors openly prohibited the use of *benchao fuse* (attire of the current dynasty) in drama performances because official uniforms in the Manchu style symbolized the power of the Manchu state. *The Ganoderma Shrine*, however, uses Manchu clothing for both a Mongolian woman and eunuchs from the Manchu court. The possible rationale for the explicit use of Manchu uniforms is that the drama represents the Manchu royal palace and a noble lady of the Mongolians—allies of the Manchus in the Qing dynasty. The drama eulogizes the Manchus as saviors of the defeated Han Chinese and thus employs Manchu clothing to dress the noble characters.

In addition to representing ethnic characters, Manchu clothing appeared in other dramas as a symbol of loyalty to the Qing regime. *The Frost of Guilin* (*Guilin shuang* 桂林霜, preface dated 1771), by Jiang Shiquan 蔣士銓 (1725–1784), is based on the life of Ma Xiongzhen 馬雄鎮 and his family. The history of the Ma family reflects the development of ethnic relations between Manchus and Han Chinese from the early to the mid-Qing periods.[3] A century earlier, Ma's ancestors had sacrificed themselves to protect the Ming dynasty against the Manchu invasion. Later, as a Qing official and Han bannerman, Ma Xiongzhen considered himself a loyal subject of the Manchu regime. When the Ming general Wu Sangui revolted against the Manchu government, Ma confronted Wu's rebel army.[4] Unwilling to surrender to Wu after being captured, he and his entire family committed suicide.

Following the tradition of Chinese drama, *The Frost of Guilin* opens with the hero's self-introduction. What is unique about the drama is that the costume instructions indicate that the hero wears an official uniform of the Qing dynasty (*guochao guanfu* 國朝官服) upon his first appearance. The first scene features the Ma family's sacrificial ritual, in which the ancestors of the past three generations appear together "with white beards, wearing official robes with badges and caps with knobs" (*baixu dingmao bufu* 白鬚頂帽補服)—official uniforms of the Qing dynasty. In my discussion in chapter 3 of *A Ten-Thousand-Li Reunion*, I showed how Huang Xiangjian's bare body preserved his fundamental connection with his family. As described in *The Frost of Guilin*, it is not one's body but rather the Manchu state attire that serves as the ceremonial dress in the ancestral ritual of the Ma family.

Subsequent scenes of *The Frost of Guilin* frequently describe the official uniforms of the hero and other role types representing Qing officials. Among these official uniforms, a robe bestowed upon Ma by the emperor serves as the drama's through line. In scene 3, Ma enters with his servant holding the robe, which he later entrusts to his wife for safekeeping. Still later, this piece of clothing displays magical powers against the ghost troops conjured up by the rebel army. After Ma's death, the robe remains intact and becomes a symbol of the hero's loyalty as a Qing official.

As shown in figure 6.1, in a woodblock print of the drama, a space is reserved before the words *yuyi* 御衣 (imperial dress), a typical way of showing respect at the mention of subjects connected to the emperor.[5] The author's contemporaneous readers readily recognized this message. On the next page, a marginal commentary remarks on the drama's depiction of the robe: "Highlighting the dragon robe and adding such unusual iridescence—we can clearly see the literary mind is like fine damask."[6] *The Frost of Guilin* is also titled *A Record of Bestowed Dress* (*Ciyi ji* 賜衣記),

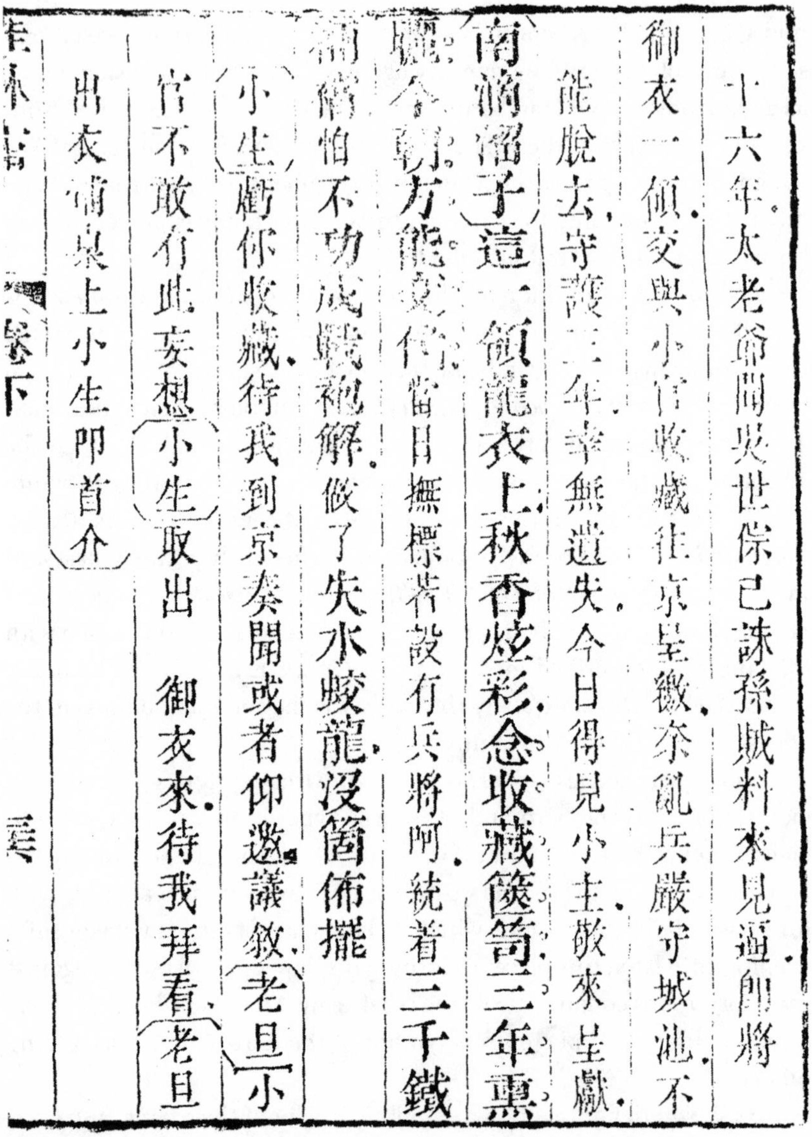

十六年太老爺間哭世俗已誅賊料來見通即將
御衣一領．交與小官收藏往京呈徽．奈亂兵嚴守城池不
能脫去守護三年幸無遺失今日得見小主敬來呈獻
南澗溜子這一領龍衣上秋香炫彩念收藏篋笥三年熏
聽令郎方能愛你當日撫標若設有兵將阿統着三千鐵
禰備怕不功成戰袍解做了失水蛟龍沒箇術擺
〔小生〕虧你收藏待我到京奏開或者仰邀議敘〔老旦〕小
官不敢有此妄想〔小生〕取出 御衣來待我拜看〔老旦
出衣捧泉上小生叩首介〕

FIGURE 6.1 A woodblock page related to the imperial robe in *The Frost of Guilin*. Jiang Shiquan 蔣士銓, *Guilin shuang* 桂林霜, Hongxuelou print edition, preface dated 1781, *juan b*, 36a, in *Budeng daya wenku zhenben xiqu congkan* 不登大雅文庫珍本戲曲叢刊, ed. Beijing Daxue Tushuguan 北京大學圖書館 (Beijing: Xueyuan chubanshe, 2003), 20:69.

indicating the central role and symbolic meaning of the imperial robe. The imperial robe and other official Manchu attire have become a sartorial language with which the drama's protagonist claims his identity as a loyal subject to the Manchu regime.

In contrast to the Manchu clothing celebrated in the drama, Ming official attire appears as a symbol of betrayal. In scene 9, "Demanding a Surrender" (Xiexiang 脅降), the rebellious general Wu Sangui sends the hero an official uniform in the style of the previous Ming dynasty. A clownish character delivers the uniform and says, "I have brought with me a round-collared gown and a black silk cap—a design fabricated in Yunnan."[7] For Wu and his fellow rebels, Yunnan was the proclaimed center of the newly restored Ming dynasty, but for the Qing regime and its loyalists Yunnan was the restless periphery. In the drama, since the round-collared robe and black silk cap are "fabricated" in Yunnan, they do not represent the state attire of the previous Ming dynasty but instead a forgery by Wu's rebel army.

The drama's characters regard the newly produced uniform as equivalent to theatrical costumes rather than Ming state attire. After introducing the uniform, the clownish character continues, "If [Ma] refuses to accept it, I cannot simply discard it. I will banish it to theater trunks and sell it for a handful of cash."[8] His speech indicates the resemblance between the Ming uniform and theatrical costumes: the newly fabricated Ming attire can be conveniently used by a theatrical troupe for stage performances. The soldiers in the Ma mansion make another comment on the theatrical nature of Ming uniforms. Upon seeing the set of clothing, one soldier says, "Ah, you have brought a drama performance to entertain our master. Why haven't you carried with you the costume trunks and brought only this silk cap."[9] As this conversation indicates, the Ming uniform produced in Yunnan is reduced to nothing but a piece of costume that can be mingled with the other pieces in a troupe's costume trunks. In chapter 5 on *Peach Blossom Fan*, I discussed the theatricalization of Ming state attire. *The Frost of Guilin* illustrates the consequence of that transformation, that the Ming uniform was no longer a symbol of loyalty but of betrayal.

Some of the play's mid-Qing readers interpreted the meaning of clothing in the same way as the characters themselves. The Hongxuelou edition of *The Frost of Guilin* begins with a series of poems written by the author's friends. One of them reads,

How can unfilial beasts understand repaying a favor—
[Wu] removes his peacock feather and aspires to a black silk cap.
Suiyang had not fallen, yet Nan and Lei were dead.
On the same day we have witnessed two true men.

枭獍何曾解報恩，花翎不戴想烏巾。
睢陽未陷南雷死，同日男兒有兩人。[10]

The peacock feather mentioned in the poem refers to the cap of the Manchu uniform, whereas the black cap refers to the official Ming uniform. The poem recapitulates the play's message that Manchu and Han clothing represent, respectively, loyalty and betrayal.

In addition to this historical drama, Jiang Shiquan composed a group of four *zaju* plays to celebrate the birthday of the Qianlong emperor's mother. In the opening scene of *Auspicious Sign of Peace* (*Shengping rui* 昇平瑞), the hero enters wearing the "cap and belt of the Qing dynasty" (*guochao guandai* 國朝冠帶).[11] In the second scene, a *jing* role features a summer hat and a cloth gown (*liangmao bupao* 涼帽布袍), followed by a group of three characters wearing caps with tassels (*weimao* 緯帽), and a group of officials wearing uniforms with badges (*bufu* 補服). These items include official uniforms and everyday clothing, all in the Manchu style of the Qing dynasty. At least to the literati playwright Jiang Shiquan, it was completely reasonable to use Manchu clothing in dramas to represent the Manchu regime and its subjects.

As in drama scripts, Manchu clothing also appeared in drama illustrations produced in the Qianlong era. The Manchu government in early Qing China assigned Manchu clothing to the space of reality and Han clothing to the space of theatricality. The logic applied not only to actual clothes and costumes but also to different genres of visual representation. In addition to prohibiting its male subjects from wearing Han clothing in society, the Manchu government considered it a crime to portray someone wearing traditional Han clothing in a portrait.[12] In drama illustrations of the early Qing period, in contrast, all the characters are depicted wearing Han-style clothing, including the portraits of the

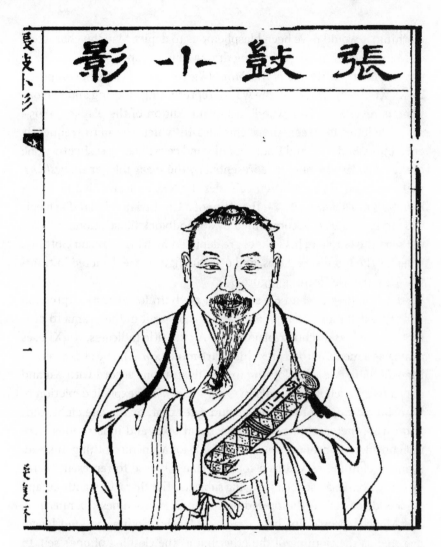

FIGURE 6.2 Portrait of Zhang Lan in his drama *Terrace of Ten-Thousand Flowers*. Zhang Lan 張瀾, *Terrace of Ten-Thousand Flowers* (*Wanhua tai* 萬花臺), preface dated 1711, in *Guben xiqu congkan* 古本戲曲叢刊 (Shanghai: Shanghai guji chubanshe, 1986), ser. 5, front matter.

playwrights. For instance, Zhang Lan 張瀾 (b. 1662), a playwright and county magistrate, included his portrait at the beginning of a woodblock print of his drama, where he is dressed in scholarly clothing in the Han style, obviously contradictory to what he should have been wearing in early Qing society (figure 6.2).[13] Just as it was taboo to stage Manchu clothing, it would have been blasphemous to depict Manchu characters or Manchu clothing in early Qing drama illustrations.

In *Theatrical Voices of My Mind* (*Xiexin zaju* 寫心雜劇), composed by Xu Xi 徐爔 (1732–1807), the way of representing clothing and personhood is reversed.[14] One woodblock-print edition of the play (ca. 1805–1807) includes eighteen short episodes in which the hero frequently encounters Buddhist and Daoist monks and celestial figures. In every one of the episodes, the hero is represented by the *sheng* role (or *zhengsheng*, male lead), and in at least ten episodes the text indicates that he wears *rufu* 儒服 or *ruzhuang* 儒裝—the attire of a Confucian scholar. Each episode in the series is accompanied by a woodblock illustration. In many of them, the hero and his fellows are depicted wearing Manchu clothing, whereas the monks, recluses, and celestial figures are depicted in traditional Han-style clothing (figure 6.3).

Both figures 6.2 and 6.3 serve as a medium for identity expression and representation. Zhang Lan places his portrait in the drama to promote himself as a scholar-playwright. As the title indicates, Xu Xi uses drama as a medium to express his heart-mind (*xin* 心). The characters in Manchu hairstyle and clothing in the illustrations accord with Xu and his fellows as scholar-officials in Qing society. The explicit depiction of Manchu clothing in these images indicates that, by the late eighteenth and early nineteenth centuries, theatrical texts and illustrations were not considered a profane space unsuitable for Manchu clothing. Instead, Manchu clothing served as a tool for Han Chinese to represent themselves as Confucian scholars or Qing subjects. The characters, authors, and readers discussed in the preceding included Han Chinese, bannermen, and Manchu people. In these dramas, Manchu clothing was no longer depicted as the clothing of the other but as the clothing of one's self. In contrast, Ming state attire had become an alien artifact, its destined space located only within costume trunks.

MANCHU CLOTHING ONSTAGE

As discussed earlier, there was overall an absence of Manchu clothing on the early Qing stage with the possible exception of Manchu-style armor in drama performances within the Manchu court. The late Qianlong

FIGURE 6.3 Drama illustrations with scholars and officials wearing Manchu hair-style and clothing. Xu Xi 徐熙, *Xiexin zaju* 寫心雜劇, ca. 1805–1807, in *Zhongguo gudai zaju wenxian jilu* 中國古代雜劇文獻輯錄, ed. Jiang Yasha 姜亞沙, Jing Li 經莉, and Chen Zhanqi 陳湛綺 (Beijing: Quanguo tushuguan wenxian suowei fuzhi zhongxin, 2006), 9:299, 364.

reign in the late nineteenth century was a turning point in Chinese drama performances. The refined *kunqu* performances had gradually lost favor and in their stead, different performance genres, collectively referred to as the flower section (*huabu* 花部), competed for popularity in cities like Beijing, leading to the maturation of a new performance genre—Beijing opera.[15] The new performance genres inherited costumes from the preceding theatrical traditions and incorporated new pieces from contemporary society. Existing evidence suggests that various pieces of Manchu clothing started to appear in performance records of the mid-Qing period, both inside and outside the court.

Yangzhou huafang lu 揚州畫舫錄 includes one group of the earliest records pertaining to theatrical costumes used in popular perfor-mances.[16] The section titled "Costumes of Itinerant Troupes" (Jianghu

FIGURE 6.4 Illustration of the scene "Listening to Wind Chimes," from *Palace of Lasting Life*. Qinyinweng 琴隐翁, ed., *Shenyin jiangu lu* 審音鑑古錄, in *Kunqu yishu dadian* 崑曲藝術大典, ed. Wang Wenzhang 王文章 et al. (Hefei: Anhui wenyi chubanshe, 2016), *biaoyan dian*, 4:920.

xingtou 江湖行頭) reflects the status quo of costuming in popular drama performances of the late Qianlong era. The document lists a group of costumes, including the archer's jacket with horseshoe-shaped cuffs (*jianxiu* 箭袖), horse jacket (*magua* 馬褂), and summer hat (*liangmao* 涼帽). Whereas the archer's jacket was already used in early Qing drama, the latter two, especially the horse jacket, started to appear in performance records only during the Qianlong era.[17] Another document, *Shenyin jiangu lu* 審音鑑古錄, is a collection of popular scenes with particular instructions about their performances onstage. Although the extant print copy was produced in 1834, scholars argue that the script was completed between 1751 and 1795.[18] *Shenyin jiangu lu* includes a scene titled "Listening to Wind Chimes" (Wenling 聞鈴) from *Palace of Lasting Life* (*Changsheng dian* 長生殿), in which an imperial retainer accompanies the Xuanzong emperor of Tang China in flight from the capital. The costume instruction indicates that the retainer wears an archer's jacket with dragon decoration (*long jianyi* 龍箭衣), a horse jacket with dragon decoration (*long magua* 龍馬褂), and a bead string (*suzhu* 素珠, more commonly referred to as *shuzhu* 數珠).[19] In figure 6.4, the string of beads and the horseshoe-shaped cuffs worn by the retainer guiding the horse are clearly visible.[20] Both documents illustrate the use of garments considered typical Manchu clothing in popular drama performances. It is possible that by the late Qianlong era, despite the explicit governmental prohibition, Manchu-style costumes had begun to appear in popular drama performances outside the court.

Comparing *Shenyin jiangu lu* with *A Register of Costumes* (*Chuandai tigang* 穿戴題綱, a document listing the personnel, costumes, and props used in court performances during the Daoguang reign), Song Junhua concludes that by the Daoguang reign, the costumes for court performances and those for popular performances were quite similar to each other.[21] In records of court performances of the nineteenth century, there are possible references to Manchu clothing beyond military uniforms. In a drama titled "Niannian kangtai" 年年康泰 performed by Shengping Shu 升平署 during or after the Daoguang reign, the provincial governors and governors-general (*xunfu zongdu* 巡撫總督) of the Qing government appear to welcome a group of kings from foreign countries. One of the Qing officials sings, "A troupe of red tassels hurry along amid songs" (一簇紅纓趨唱頻), indicating that the officials might be wearing the red-tassel caps—part of the Manchu official uniform.[22] This performance is more orchestrated ritual than theatrical. The solemnity of the ritual occasion rendered it legitimate to demonstrate state attire in the Manchu style.

Another document most clearly points to the lifting of the ban on using Manchu state attire onstage. During the Qianlong emperor's campaign of drama censorship (1780s), *The Temple of the Red Gate* (*Hongmen si* 紅門寺) was banned because it used Qing state attire for its characters. The Xianfeng emperor, ironically, issued an edict (1855) stipulating that all the male characters in the drama should wear the attire of the Qing dynasty and that the protagonist, Yu Chenglong, in particular, should wear the official uniform, including a cap with a red knob (*hongding* 紅頂), an official robe with a square badge (*fangbu* 方補), a court bead string (*chaozhu* 朝珠), and a horse jacket.[23] As Ye Xiaoqing notes, after the Xianfeng emperor's 1855 edict, "it then became a convention that all nomadic characters in drama wore Manchu costumes."[24] By the mid-nineteenth century, Manchu rulers no longer considered the stage unfit for the attire of the Manchu dynasty. Manchu clothing started to be used onstage for Manchu people as well as for officials of the Manchu state.

If it is understandable that court performances featured Manchu clothing for Manchu characters, it is surprising to see Manchu clothing employed to represent northern "barbarians." As recorded in *A Register of Costumes*, the performance of the popular scene "Zhaojun" 昭君 used yellow horse jackets (*huang magua* 黃馬褂) for two "barbarians" (*dazi* 達子), possibly because the two retainers were from the Hungarian court.[25] In the early Qing period, the yellow horse jacket was a highly regarded item of Manchu clothing, available only as a gift from the emperor. Its use as a theatrical costume in the Daoguang reign indicates first that the yellow horse jacket was more commonly used in the late Qing period and, second, that using Manchu clothing onstage, even to dress "barbarian" characters, was an accepted practice in the court.

Finally, we can gain a clearer understanding of the increasing use of Manchu clothing in Qing drama through different plays about the Song–Liao conflicts in the tenth century.[26] Some Ming-dynasty dramas about the Yang family resisting the Khitan invasion used fur hats and coats to dress Khitan characters. The grand play *Sagely Songs of a Peaceful*

Time (*Zhaodai xiaoshao* 昭代簫韶), produced during the Jiaqing reign (1796–1820), already employed the horse jacket for some military characters.[27] However, in the drama Manchu clothing is not employed for female characters. Two prominent female figures include Empress Dowager Xiao of the Liao dynasty and her daughter, Princess Tiejing (full name Yelü Qionge 耶律瓊娥). At their first appearance in book 1, their costumes are listed as follows: "*Dan* performs Yelü Qionge, wearing a seven-star-diadem helmet, pheasant and parrot-tail feathers, armor, commanding flags, python robe, belt, and a horse whip. *Dan* performs Empress Dowager Xiao, wearing a Mongolian cap with drooping straps, armor, commanding flags, python robe, belt, and a horse whip."[28] In the drama, Princess Tiejing wears a military uniform featuring armor and pheasant feathers, a typical costume for minority military generals without explicit connection to the Manchus. The descriptions also state that Empress Dowager Xiao is dressed in Mongolian-style garb, following the tradition in Ming *zaju* dramas.

In the late nineteenth century, Empress Dowager Cixi ordered that the grand play *Sagely Songs of a Peaceful Time*, which was originally written for *kunqu*, be adapted for the more popular genre of Beijing opera.[29] *The Yanmen Pass* (*Yanmen guan* 雁門關) is a representative Beijing opera performance based on the same story.[30] Mei Qiaoling 梅巧玲 (1842–1882), one of the thirteen most celebrated performers of Beijing opera in the late Qing period, was well known for performing Empress Dowager Xiao.[31] As shown in figure 6.5, the empress dowager wears a Manchu uniform with a string of beads and her hair done in the Manchu style.[32] From *Sagely Songs of a Peaceful Time* to the late Qing renditions of the play, we witness Manchu clothing replacing Mongolian dress as the costume for the Khitan ruling family and high officials.

These Manchu-style costumes in performances of Beijing opera were collectively referred to as Manchu costumes (*qiyi* 旗衣). Qi Rushan writes, "Manchu costumes were used specifically for performing Manchu, Mongolian, Jurchen, and Khitan women."[33] Qi points out the predominant use of these costumes for female characters. Further, Manchu uniforms for men were also employed in the performances of Beijing opera. As one of many examples, a late Qing drama painting *Returning the Arrow of Command After Visiting His Mother* (*Tanmu huiling* 探母回令) features

FIGURE 6.5 Painting of Mei Qiaoling dressed as Empress Dowager Xiao. Detail of Shen Rongpu 沈容圃, *Tong Guang mingling shisan jue* 同光名伶十三絕, in *Zhongguo jingju tushi* 中國京劇圖史, ed. Zhou Chuanjia 周傳家, Liu Wenfeng 劉文峰, and Wu Gansheng 吳贛生 (Beijing: Beijing shiyue wenyi chubanshe, 1996), 40.

another scene of the story (figure 6.6).[34] It depicts all the members in the Khitan court, male and female, wearing attire in the Manchu style.

The Manchu, Mongolian, Jurchen, and Khitan peoples all hailed from northern China and were referred to as barbarians in the discourses of the Ming dynasty. As discussed in chapter 1, the "barbaric" dancing of northern minorities was considered taboo on the early Qing stage, and only Han-style costumes were retained in the performance space. By the

FIGURE 6.6 Qing-dynasty drama painting *Returning the Arrow of Command After Visiting His Mother*. Liao Ben 廖奔, *Zhongguo xiju tushi* 中國戲劇圖史 (Zhengzhou: Daxiang chubanshe, 2000), 289.

late Qing period, Manchu clothing was used not only as stage costumes but also to dress characters who would have fallen into the category of "barbarians" prior to the Qing dynasty. These changes indicate a further transformation in the nature of theatrical space—a space where Manchu clothing was displayed as a symbol of rule by ethnic peoples. The theatricalization of Manchu clothing was possible because of a new role of theater in society together with a decrease in anti-Manchu sentiments. As scholars have suggested, by the nineteenth century Chinese drama, especially Beijing opera, had become a distinct element of Manchu culture.[35] When opera was integrated with the Manchu state and Manchu ethnicity, Manchu clothing naturally appeared on the late Qing stage—it was no longer constitutive of a sacred dress code unbefitting the theatrical space.

China underwent unprecedented social and political reforms in the early twentieth century with the fall of the Qing dynasty, the establishment of the Republic of China, and impending threats from Japan and the Western powers. When China turned from an imperial dynasty to a nation-state, Manchu hairstyle once again became a target of anti-Manchu campaigns and was eventually abolished in society.[36] Meanwhile, both Manchu clothing and traditional Chinese drama went through continuous reforms and became associated with Chinese identity in intricate ways—both inside and beyond mainland China.[37] Against this background, drama costumes in the Manchu style received a completely new interpretation. The *National Drama Pictorial* (*Guoju huabao* 國劇畫報), a magazine specifically about Beijing opera, published two special issues in 1932 on Manchu-style costumes (*qizhuang* 旗裝). Figure 6.7 shows a photograph published in the *National Drama Pictorial*, depicting three actors wearing costumes used in the performance of *The Yanmen Pass*. The characters in the center and on the right, respectively, showcase the onstage use of Manchu-style costumes for female and male figures. In their prefatory address of this special issue, the editors wrote, "Needless to say, today when we see Manchu costumes, every one of us will immediately realize that this is clothing of Manchuria, a style of fashion with its own aesthetic qualities. However, currently Manchuria has been occupied by others. What a significant provocation! What a pervasive provocation! How appropriate it is that our pictorial uses it to commemorate the day of national shame."[38] Against the threat from foreign enemies, the *National Drama Pictorial* did not use Manchu-style costumes to invoke hatred for the Manchus, who had been foreign rulers in centuries past. Instead, the editors tried to provoke nationalist emotion about lost Chinese land and concerns about preserving the territory of a modern nation-state, Republican China.[39]

Behind these changes in sartorial spectacles lies a constantly shifting boundary between self and others. In the early Qing period, Manchu rulers regarded drama as an alien art form; correspondingly, Han Chinese playwrights, performers, and audiences treated Manchu clothing as a foreign element intruding into the existing sartorial system. In the following centuries, the Manchus increasingly accepted drama and

FIGURE 6.7 Performance photo of *The Yanmen Pass*. *National Drama Pictorial* (*Guoju huabao* 國劇畫報), no. 35 (September 16, 1932), 138.

theater as an art form of the Qing state; Manchu clothing appeared in drama texts and performances to represent non-Han characters, Qing loyalists, and to serve as an instrument for Han scholars' self-expression and self-fashioning. The social changes in the last decades of the Qing dynasty destabilized the received meanings of clothing in Qing drama, reassociating clothing with conceptions of nation-states and racial relations in the modern world. The increasing dramatization of Manchu clothing indicated a new relation among Manchus, Han Chinese, drama, and China transitioning from an empire to a nation-state.

Just as clothing is a fluid interface between one's body and the outside world, so was clothing a shifting boundary between the perceived self and others in Qing China. Historians have debated the nature of Manchu rule during the Qing dynasty. Many of those debates boil down to a fundamental question: does it matter to our understanding of Qing China that it was ruled by an ethnic group other than Han Chinese?

Whereas historians tend to answer the question positively, literary scholars tend to reply negatively. Literary scholars stress the fact that most Manchu authors in the Qing dynasty actually wrote their works in Chinese; and they consider Manchu-language literature a subcategory of ethnic minority literatures. In fact, the Manchu state policed Chinese drama as scripts and performances not least out of concern for the differences between the Manchu and Han cultures. The Manchu regulations on hairstyle and clothing, in particular, were translated into explicit and implicit censorship of costuming in theatrical practices.

It is my argument in this book that the dynastic transition influenced Chinese drama in more ways than one: different dress codes onstage and in society created unique sartorial spectacles at drama performances; state censorship limited and shaped the ways in which theatrical practices represented people's hairstyle, clothing, and activities in daily life. Meanwhile, traditional Chinese drama enabled individuals and communities in early Qing China to probe multiple dimensions of the dynastic change. Since hairstyle and clothing were at the center of ethnic conflicts, theatrical costuming served as an effective—if not the only—venue for theatrical practitioners to respond to changing ethnic and gender relations. As I have shown in the epilogue, the tensions between theater and the Manchu state ironically metamorphosed into the integration between theater and Manchu ethnicity toward the late Qing era. In that sense, the book delineates a new history of Qing drama, one complicating and shifting away from the Han-centered narrative of Qing literature. Through the prism of costuming, *Staging Personhood* has explored the entanglements between Chinese drama and nascent Manchu rule. The methods employed in this study promise refreshing perspectives on literature and society well beyond seventeenth-century China.

Appendix 1: Extant Editions of
A Ten-Thousand-Li Reunion
(*Wanli yuan* 萬里圓)

I have organized the list items as referred to in the book. Unless otherwise indicated, the scene scripts include both arias and dialogues.

THE FULL DRAMA

GBXQ: Li Yu 李玉, *Wanli yuan*, purportedly nineteenth-century edition; 27 numbered scenes (*chu* 出), with 3 missing. In *Guben xiqu congkan*, 古本戲曲叢刊, ser. 3. Shanghai: Wenxue guji kanxingshe, 1957. Scenes in the *GBXQ* edition most closely resemble those in the Shengping Shu edition produced in the nineteenth century.

Li Yu xiqu ji 李玉戲曲集: Li Yu 李玉, *Wanli yuan*; 27 numbered scenes (*chu* 齣), with 3 missing. In *Li Yu xiqu ji*, ed. Chen Guyu 陳古虞, Chen Duo 陳多, and Ma Shenggui 馬聖貴. 3 vols. Shanghai: Shanghai guji chubanshe, 2004.

The Player's Press (*Liyuan gongbao* 梨園公報): Li Yu 李玉, *Wanli yuan*, purportedly based on a 1716 edition; 22 numbered scenes (*chu* 齣) and one opening scene, "Jiamen" 家門. In *Liyuan gongbao*, ed. Sun Yusheng 孫玉聲 [1864–1940], issue no. (*hao* 號) 56 (February 23, 1929) to no. 170 (February 17, 1930); microform PN2876.S4L5, reel no. 1, University of Chicago Library, http://pi.lib.uchi cago.edu/1001/cat/bib/5849459.

SCENES FROM THE DRAMA

Chinese National Academy of Arts 中國藝術研究院: "Dachai" 打差, manuscript, 1866, produced by Caoshi Chude Tang 曹氏處得堂. Collected in the Chinese National Academy of Arts, 夕羊戲140.651.0.213 善本123237.

Illustrated Patched White Fur (*Huitu zhuibaiqiu* 繪圖綴白裘): "Sanxi" 三溪, "Dachai" 打差, "Diexue" 跌雪. In *Huitu zhuibaiqiu*, ed. Wanhua Zhuren 玩花主人 and Qian Decang 錢德蒼, 6:9a–10a; 8:2b–3a, 7b; 9:10a, 12b–13a. 12 vols. Shanghai: Shanghai shuju, 1895.

Kunju chuanshi yanchu zhenben quanbian 崑劇傳世演出珍本全編: "Yuhu diexue" 遇虎跌雪, "Sanxi" 三溪, "Dachai" 打差. In *Kunju chuanshi yanchu zhenben quanbian*, ed. Suzhou Kunju Chuanxi Suo 蘇州崑劇傳習所, ser. 2, *han* 函 2, *juan* 7, 1a–10a. 3 ser. Shanghai: Shanghai renmin chubanshe, 2011.

Nashuying qupu 納書楹曲譜: "Sanxi" 三溪. In *Nashuying qupu*, comp. Ye Tang 葉堂, *waiji* 外集, *juan* 1. In *Shanben xiqu congkan* 善本戲曲叢刊, ed. Wang Qiugui 王秋桂, ser. 6, 2:1441–44. Taipei: Taiwan xuesheng shuju, 1987.

National Library of China 中國國家圖書館: "Dachai" 打差; undated ms. In the collection of the National Library of China, Shanben Gujibu 善本古籍部, no. 33705.

Patched White Fur (*Zhui baiqiu* 綴白裘): "Sanxi" 三溪, "Dachai" 打差, "Diexue" 跌雪. In *Zhui baiqiu xinji hebian* 綴白裘新集合編, ed. Wanhua Zhuren 玩花主人 and Qian Decang 錢德蒼. Hongwentang 鴻文堂 woodblock print, 1777. In *Shanben xiqu congkan* 善本戲曲叢刊, ed. Wang Qiugui 王秋桂, ser. 5, 1:2513–20, 3343–58, 3853–60. Taipei: Taiwan xuesheng shuju, 1987.

Shengping Shu 昇平署: "Sanxi" 三溪 (aria only), "Sanxi" 三溪 A, "Yuhu" 遇虎, "Sanxi" 三溪 B; manuscripts for Qing court performance, ca. nineteenth century. In *Zhongguo guojia tushuguan cang Qinggong Shengpingshu dang'an jicheng* 中國國家圖書館藏清宮昇平署檔案集成, ed. Zhongguo Guojia Tushuguan 中國國家圖書館, 88:51509–43, 102: 59823–36. 108 vols. Beijing: Zhonghua shuju, 2011.

Takemura Noriyuki 竹村則行: *Wanli yuan* 萬理圓, 7 scenes; undated ms. In the collection of Takemura Noriyuki.

Yougu Xuan 猶古軒: "Dachai" 打差, "Yuhu" 遇虎 and "Diexue" 跌雪 (respectively, for two halves of one scene), "Sanxi" 三溪. Yougu Xuan manuscript edition, ed. Zhang Zidong 張紫東, 1890s. In *Kunju shouchao quben yibaiche* 崑劇手抄曲本一百冊, ed. Kunju Shouchao Quben Yibaice Bianji Weiyuanhui 崑劇手抄曲本一百冊編輯委員會 and Zhongguo Kunqu Bowuguan 中國崑曲博物館, 56:23a–40a. 101 vols. Yangzhou: Guangling shushe, 2009.

Zhuiyuxuan qupu 綴玉軒曲譜: Scene(s) of *Wanli yuan*. In *Zhuiyuxuan qupu*. Formerly in the collection of Mei Lanfang 梅蘭芳, currently in the collection of the National Library of China but unavailable.

Appendix 2: Scene Synopsis of *A Ten-Thousand-Li Reunion*

No.	Title	Time	Space	Dress style	Plot elements
1	Jiamen 家門				Summary of the story
2	Songbie 送別	1643	Suzhou	Han	Huang Kongzhao leaves Suzhou
3	Qiuyuan 求援	1644	Boat on Yangzi River	Han	Ming officials Shi Kefa and Huang Degong discuss how to protect the Southern Ming court
4	Zuzou/Mianxiang 阻奏/面相	1644	Nanjing court	Han	Ma Shiying prevents Shi and Huang from meeting with the emperor; northern armies march southward
5	Baojing 報警	1644	Dayao, Yunnan	Han	Huang Kongzhao meets local students; minority leader Wu Bikui rebels
6	Changluan 倡亂	Soon after	Yunnan	Han	After quelling Wu, another minority leader, Sha Dingzhou, rebels and captures the provincial capital of Yunnan
7	Jiaoyin 交印	Later	Dayao, Yunnan	Han	After Sha, Sichuan army takes all of Yunnan; Huang Kongzhao resigns from office
8	Biejia 別家	1651	Suzhou	Manchu	Huang Xiangjian informs his wife about his journey to Yunnan

9	Shanglu 上路	1651	Suzhou	Manchu	Huang Xiangjian's cousin and son-in-law see him off
10	Baojing 報警	ca. 1651	Baiyanjing, Yunnan	Han	A traveling veteran recounts the Manchu intrusion into Suzhou
11	Kedian 客店	New Year's Eve, 1651	Local inn at Xuwan, on way to Yunnan	Manchu	Travelers perform a scene from the drama *Jiexiao ji*, in which a filial son travels far to find his mother
12	Yujie 遇劫 (Diexue 跌雪)	ca. 1652	Zhuangyuanling, Fuzhou, on way to Yunnan	Manchu	Huang Xiangjian encounters a bandit, who robs him of his clothes; Huang is later saved by a monk
13	Suanming 算命	ca. 1652	Suzhou	Manchu	Huang's mother-in-law visits his wife; a comic scene of fortune-telling performed by some clown characters
14	Sanxi 三溪	1652	On way to Yunnan	Manchu	Huang Xiangjian crosses three rivers with the help of boatmen
15		1652	Yunnan	Han	Huang Kongzhao's former students pay their respects to him

(continued)

No.	Title	Time	Space	Dress style	Plot elements
16	Jizha 給劄	1652	Puding in Guizhou	Han	The general of Yunnan captures Huang Xiangjian and provides him with a travel permit
17	Miaohui 廟會	1652	Guansuoling in Yunnan	Han	In a Daoist temple Huang Xiangjian encounters his father's former colleagues, who help him travel to his parents
18	Missing scene				
19	Qingyi 請醫				Huang Xiangjian's son visits a doctor to treat his mother's illness
20	Missing scene				
21	Chairao 差擾	1652	Suzhou	Manchu	Local government runner tries to arrest Huang Xiangjian's wife and son because of Huang Kong-zhao's service in the Ming court and is stopped by neighbors

No.	Scene title	Date	Location	Ethnicity	Description
22	Dachai 打差	1652	Suzhou	Manchu	Huang Xiangjian's cousin Huang Chengyou beats two Qing officers who come to harass the Huang family
23		1652	Baiyanjing in Yunnan	Han	Huang Kongzhao reads stories about filial sons looking for their parents
24	Yuqin 遇親	1652	Baiyanjing in Yunnan	Han	Huang Xiangjian runs into his cousin Huang Xiangyan; the family finally reunites
25	Wengua 問卦	ca. 1653	Suzhou	Han	Huang Xiangjian's wife visits a fortune-teller to inquire about the family
26		1653	Border pass in Yunnan	Han	Huang Xiangjian and his parents cross the border between Yunnan and Manchu territory
27	Tuanyuan 團圓	1653	Suzhou	Manchu	The entire family reunites

Note: The order of scenes is based on the modern edition of *Wanli yuan* in *Li Yu xiqu ji*, which is based on the *GBXQ* edition. Scene titles are taken from *The Player's Press* edition since the *GBXQ* edition does not have scene titles. The scene "Qingyi" exists only in *The Player's Press* edition.

Notes

INTRODUCTION

1. You Tong's autobiography is titled *Nianpu tushi* 年譜圖詩 or *Nianpu tuyong* 年譜圖詠 in its different editions. The editions of You Tong's works are extremely complicated. For recent studies of You Tong's writings, see Sun Shulei 孫書磊, *Xiqu wenxian yu lilun yanjiu* 戲曲文獻與理論研究 (Taipei: Guojia chubanshe, 2014), 328–71, and Xu Kun 徐坤, *You Tong yanjiu* 尤侗研究 (Shanghai: Shanghai wenhua chubanshe, 2008).

2. The image is from Judith T. Zeitlin, Yuhang Li, and Richard A. Born, eds., *Performing Images: Opera in Chinese Visual Culture* (Chicago: Smart Museum of Art, University of Chicago, 2014), 141. It is based on a Kangxi edition of You Tong's *Xitang quanji* 西堂全集. For an almost identical image, see You Tong 尤侗, "Caotang xicai tu" 草堂戲彩圖, in *Nianpu tushi* 年譜圖詩, *Xitang yuji* 西堂餘集, in *Beijing tushuguan cang zhenben nianpu congkan* 北京圖書館藏珍本年譜叢刊, ed. Beijing Tushuguan 北京圖書館 (Beijing: Beijing tushuguan chubanshe, 1999), 73:646. The performance this image depicts took place in the twelfth month of the fourteenth year of the Shunzhi reign (January 1658). See You Tong, *Huian nianpu* 悔菴年譜, in *Beijing tushuguan cang zhenben nianpu congkan*, 74:27. Judith Zeitlin has discussed the image in several places. See her articles "Music and Performance in Hong Sheng's *Palace of Lasting Life*," in *Trauma and Transcendence in Early Qing Literature*, ed. Wilt L. Idema, Wai-yee Li, and Ellen Widmer (Cambridge, Mass.: Harvard University Asia Center, 2006), 454–87; "Spirit Writing and Performance in the Work of You Tong 尤侗

(1618–1704)," *T'oung Pao* 84 (1998): 102–35; and a catalogue entry with a translation of the caption in *Performing Images*.

3. The image shows a typical *tanghui* performance, which Andrea Goldman translates as "salon performance," one of three main venues of drama performances in the Qing dynasty. See Andrea S. Goldman, *Opera and the City: The Politics of Culture in Beijing, 1770–1900* (Stanford, Calif.: Stanford University Press, 2012), 97–112.

4. The image in *Beijing tushuguan cang zhenben nianpu congkan* includes eleven visible audience members. The hairstyle and clothing of the three extra ones resemble those of the rest.

5. For a description of the clothing in the image, see Zeitlin, Li, and Born, *Performing Images*, 141.

6. It is possible that in this performance at a private household the troupe members alternately played the roles of performers and musicians. Otherwise, the professional musicians and other offstage staff members would have been wearing Manchu clothing.

7. Dorothy Ko, "The Body as Attire: The Shifting Meanings of Footbinding in Seventeenth-Century China," *Journal of Women's History* 8, no. 4 (1997): 12.

8. Records concerning clothing were usually included in the *Treatise on Ritual and Music* (*Liyue zhi* 禮樂志) and *Treatise on Carriages and Clothing* (*Yufu zhi* 輿服志) in official histories. For a comprehensive list of studies on Chinese clothing, see Li Zhitan 李之檀, ed., *Zhongguo fushi wenhua cankao wenxian mulu* 中國服飾文化參考文獻目錄 (Beijing: Zhongguo fangzhi chubanshe, 2001), 227–80.

9. These practices related to dynastic transition are commonly referred to as *gai zhengshuo yi fuse* 改正朔易服色 (changing the commencement of the year and month and altering the color of attire). See Zhuang Qingmei 莊慶美, "Qiangu Zhonghua fushi zhidu 'gaizhengshuo yifushe' de lishi botao" 千古中華服飾制度「改正朔、易服色」的歷史波濤, *Lishi wenwu: Guoli lishi bowuguan guankan* 14, no. 11 (2004): 32–39. See also Wang Yu-ching 王宇清, *Liyun fuse kao* 歷運服色考 (Taipei: Guoli lishi bowuguan, 1971).

10. As scholars have pointed out, the concepts of both Han and Manchu ethnicities were historically formed and constantly shifting. In this book, I refer to Han and Manchu ethnicities as they were perceived and discursively presented in early Qing history. For a collection of articles on the topic, see Thomas S. Mullaney, James Leibold, Stéphane Gros, and Eric Vanden Bussche, eds., *Critical Han Studies: The History, Representation, and Identity of China's Majority* (Berkeley: University of California Press, 2012).

11. On the first day the Manchu army penetrated the Great Wall through the Shanhai pass (山海關) in northeastern China in 1644, Manchu rulers ordered

the surrendering Han people to shave their heads. The policy was suspended one month later because of intense resistance from Han residence near Beijing. After the Manchu army captured the southern capital, Nanjing, in 1645, Manchu rulers resumed the policy and enforced it stringently. Feng Erkang 馮爾康 outlines the issue in "Qingchu de tifa yu yiyiguan—jianlun minzu guanxi shi yanjiu neirong" 清初的剃髮與易衣冠—兼論民族關係史研究內容, *Shixue jikan* 2 (1985): 32–42. Recent studies on the topic include Weikun Cheng, "Politics of the Queue: Agitation and Resistance in the Beginning and End of Qing China," in *Hair: Its Power and Meaning in Asian Cultures*, ed. Alf Hiltebeitel and Barbara D. Miller (Albany: State University of New York Press, 1998), 123–42. Tobie Meyer-Fong, *What Remains: Coming to Terms with Civil War in 19th Century China* (Stanford, Calif.: Stanford University Press, 2013), chap. 3, discusses hair and clothes, among other factors, as markers of identities during the Taiping Rebellion.

12. For one explanation of the punishment, see Gao Shaoxian 高紹先, *Zhongguo xingfashi jingyao* 中國刑法史精要 (Beijing: Falü chubanshe, 2001), 407.

13. Lin Li-yueh published a group of papers on clothing in late Ming and early Qing societies. Those concerning the sartorial transition in early Qing China include "Guguo yiguan: Dingge yifu yu Ming Qing zhiji de yimin xintai" 故國衣冠: 鼎革易服與明清之際的遺民心態, *Taiwan shida lishi xuebao* 30 (2002): 39–56, and "Wanfa juqi—wangjin yu Mingdai shehui wenhua de jige mianxiang" 萬髮俱齊—網巾與明代社會文化的幾個面向, *Taida lishi xuebao* 33 (2004): 133–60.

14. The Qianlong emperor personally ordered the scholar executed and the printing blocks of his books to be destroyed. See "Liu Zhenyu *Zhiping xince* an" 劉震宇治平新策案, in *Qingdai wenziyu dang* 清代文字獄檔, ed. Shanghai Shudian Chubanshe 上海書店出版社 (Shanghai: Shanghai shudian chubanshe, 2007), vol. 1.

15. Eva Shan Chou, *Memory, Violence, Queues: Lu Xun Interprets China* (Ann Arbor, Mich.: Association for Asian Studies, 2012); Fan Xueqing 樊學慶, *Bianfu fengyun: Jianfa yifu yu Qingji shehui bian'ge* 辮服風雲: 剪髮易服與清季社會變革 (Beijing: Sanlian shudian, 2014).

16. For a study of the Han clothing movement, see Kevin Carrico, *The Great Han: Race, Nationalism, and Tradition in China Today* (Oakland: University of California Press, 2017).

17. The Qing court also required the "cooked savages" in Taiwan to adopt the queue and wear proper clothes (1758). See Emma Jinhua Teng, *Taiwan's Imagined Geography: Chinese Colonial Travel Writing and Pictures, 1683–1895* (Cambridge, Mass.: Harvard University Asia Center, 2004), 228–30.

18. In their discourses on ethnic culture, Manchu rulers occasionally regarded Manchu clothing as one of the qualities that defined the "Manchu Way." See

Mark C. Elliott, *The Manchu Way: The Eight Banners and Ethnic Identity in Late Imperial China* (Stanford, Calif.: Stanford University Press, 2001), 276. For a general introduction to Manchu clothing, see Wang Yunying 王雲英, *Zaitian xiuse—Manzu guanmin fushi* 再添秀色—滿族官民服飾 (Shenyang: Liaohai chubanshe, 1997). See also Evelyn S. Rawski, *The Last Emperors: A Social History of Qing Imperial Institutions* (Berkeley: University of California Press, 1998), 39–43.

19. For a comprehensive discussion of how the Manchu government regulated clothing, especially the use of fur, see Jonathan Schlesinger, *A World Trimmed with Fur: Wild Things, Pristine Places, and the Natural Fringes of Qing Rule* (Stanford, Calif.: Stanford University Press, 2017), chap. 1. On Manchu regulation of women's dress, see Rawski, *The Last Emperors*, 41.

20. The Qing court is said to have adopted a proposal of "ten exemptions"—proposed by Jin Zhijun 金之俊, a Han official—that summarized these specifics with ten paired lines. For a discussion of the policy, especially regarding women, see Xia Xiaohong 夏曉虹, *Wan Qing nüxing yu jindai Zhongguo* 晚清女性與近代中國 (Hong Kong: Zhonghe chuban youxian gongsi, 2011), chap. 4.

21. Ge Zhaoguang 葛兆光, "Da Ming yiguan jin hezai" 大明衣冠今何在, *Shixue yuekan* 10 (2005): 44, explains the preservation of Han clothing onstage: "Perhaps because people were accustomed to Han clothing onstage, even performances in Manchu noble households used Han clothing. As a result, drama performances 'escaped the net' and were exempt from the clothing regulations."

22. As Song Junhua 宋俊華, *Zhongguo gudai xiju fushi yanjiu* 中國古代戲劇服飾研究 (Guangzhou: Guangdong gaodeng jiaoyu chubanshe, 2003), 106–19, points out, drama costumes in the Ming dynasty generally were inspired by clothing in society, and the Manchu regime forcefully severed the correlation.

23. Lu Eting, *Kunju yanchu shigao* 崑劇演出史稿 (Shanghai: Shanghai jiaoyu chubanshe, 2005), 213.

24. The translation is from Ye Xiaoqing, *Ascendant Peace in the Four Seas: Drama and the Qing Imperial Court* (Hong Kong: Chinese University Press, 2012), 207.

25. For an introduction to hair and dress policies of conquest dynasties in Chinese history, see Herbert Franke and Denis Twitchett, eds., *The Cambridge History of China, Volume 6: Alien Regimes and Border States, 907–1368* (Cambridge: Cambridge University Press, 1994), 46, 182, 281.

26. Yuming He, "Difficulties of Performance: The Musical Career of Xu Wei's *The Mad Drummer*," *Harvard Journal of Asiatic Studies* 68, no. 2 (2008): 77–114 shows the pervasive sense of performance in late imperial China. Chun Mei, *The Novel and Theatrical Imagination in Early Modern China* (Leiden: Brill,

2011), examines how theatrical imagination—especially through the dynamics of the viewer-viewed relationship—can serve as historical and theatrical context for what she calls theatrical novels.

27. Jonathan Hay, "World-Making in Performance and Painting: An Intertwined History," in Zeitlin, Li, and Born, *Performing Images*, 32.

28. Sophie Volpp, *Worldly Stage: Theatricality in Seventeenth-Century China* (Cambridge, Mass.: Harvard University Asia Center, 2011), 84.

29. For a brief discussion of these terms, see Song, *Zhongguo gudai xiju fushi yanjiu*, 75.

30. Alexandra B. Bonds, *Beijing Opera Costumes: The Visual Communication of Character and Culture* (Honolulu: University of Hawai`i Press, 2008).

31. Song, *Zhongguo gudai xiju fushi yanjiu*, 106–30.

32. Robert I. Lublin, *Costuming the Shakespearean Stage: Visual Codes of Representation in Early Modern Theatre and Culture* (Farnham, Surrey, U.K.: Ashgate Publishing, 2011), 5–7.

33. The concept of epitheatre, Mark Stevenson suggests, could capture "a longer series of translations between performance, player, playing-about, and page" and "provide a finer understanding of the playing out of cultural and social processes, social change, aesthetics, and public space" ("One as Form and Shadow: Theater and the Space of Sentimentality in Nineteenth-Century Beijing," *Frontiers of History in China* 9, no. 2 [2014]: 232).

34. In this book, I intend "drama scripts" and "drama texts" to refer to written plays and "drama performance" and "theater" to indicate the staging of plays. "Theatrical works" include written and staged plays; "theatrical practices" refer to the largest group of activities—textual, performance, and pictorial—that exemplify the sense of theatricality. This terminology helps us understand drama in late imperial China, including playwriting, drama printing, and theatrical performance in different social settings. It also illuminates the various aspects of what I define as theatrical costuming.

35. Most notably, the classical saying *shi yan zhi* 詩言志 (poetry articulates the mind) regards writing as the exteriorization of one's innerness. Mengzi proposed sophisticated methods of interpreting a piece of writing, such as *zhiren lunshi* 知人論世 (knowing the persons and the ages they lived in) and *yiyi nizhi* 以意逆志 (meeting the intent [of the authors] with sympathetic understanding).

36. Wilt L. Idema, "Drama After the Conquest: An Introduction," in Idema, Li, and Widmer, *Trauma and Transcendence*, 377.

37. For instance, a large portion of studies on *Peach Blossom Fan* discuss whether the drama expresses Kong Shangren's anti-Manchu sentiments. Other playwrights frequently discussed include Li Yu 李玉, Ding Yaokang 丁耀亢, Wu Weiye 吳偉業, and Wang Fuzhi 王夫之, among others.

38. In the case of *Celestial Court Music*, scholars argue that the hero and other characters in the drama correspond with You Tong and a few of his literati friends, and accordingly that the frustrations depicted in the drama reflect the discontent experienced by early Qing scholars. For some examples, see Guo Yingde 郭英德, "'Ruoda qiankun wuchu zhu'—tan You Tong de *Juntian yue* chuanqi" "偌大乾坤無處住"—談尤侗的《鈞天樂》傳奇, *Mingzuo xinshang* 1 (1988): 20, 58–62, and Han Li 韓莉, "You Tong *Juntian yue* zhong zhuyao renwu yuanxing kaozheng" 尤侗《鈞天樂》中主要人物原型考證, *Lanzhou wenli xueyuan xuebao* 30, no. 5 (2014): 93–96.

39. Kang-I Sun Chang, "The Idea of the Mask in Wu Wei-yeh (1609–1671)," *Harvard Journal of Asiatic Studies* 48, no. 2 (1988): 291.

40. Michel Foucault, "What Is an Author," in *Aesthetics, Method, and Epistemology: Essential Works of Foucault (1954–1984)*, ed. James D. Faubion, trans. Robert Hurley et al. (New York: New Press, 1998), 210.

41. Foucault, "What Is an Author," 220.

42. Foucault, "What Is an Author," 216.

43. Foucault is certainly not the only Western thinker who has discussed the issue of authorship. Here I limit my discussion to Foucault's article because it is most directly related to my discussion of costuming.

44. Patricia Sieber, *Theaters of Desire: Authors, Readers, and the Reproduction of Early Chinese Song-Drama, 1300–2000* (New York: Palgrave Macmillan, 2003), xvii–xx.

45. For two related studies of the production of Yuan drama, see Wilt L. Idema, "Why You Never Have Read a Yuan Drama: The Transformation of *Zaju* at the Ming Court," in *Studi in onore di Lionello Lanciotti*, ed. S. M. Carletti, M. Sacchetti, and P. Santangelo (Naples: Istituto Universitario Orientale, Dipartimento di Studi Asiatici, and Istituto Italiano per il Medio ed Estremo Oriente, 1996), 765–91, and Stephen H. West, "Text and Ideology: Ming Editors and Northern Drama," in *Ming Qing xiqu guoji yantaohui luwen ji* 明清戲曲國際研討會論文集, ed. Hua Wei 華瑋 and Wang Ayling 王璦玲 (Taipei: Zhongyang yanjiuyuan Zhongguo wenzhe yanjiusuo, 1998), 329–73.

46. Judith Milhous and Robert D. Hume, *Producible Interpretation: Eight English Plays, 1675–1707* (Carbondale: Southern Illinois University Press, 1985), 10.

47. Andrew Sofer, *The Stage Life of Props* (Ann Arbor: University of Michigan Press, 2003), 3–6.

48. Andrew Sofer, *Dark Matter: Invisibility in Drama, Theater, and Performance* (Ann Arbor: University of Michigan Press, 2013).

49. Stephen Orgel, "What Is a Text?," in *Staging the Renaissance: Reinterpretations of Elizabethan and Jacobean Drama*, ed. David Scott Kastan and Peter Stallybrass (New York: Routledge, 1991), 83.

50. Richard Schechner suggests a model of concentric, overlapping circles—drama, script, theater, and performance—to understand different types of human activities. As Schechner discusses, a drama and script correspond, respectively, with the author/composer and teacher/interpreter of a piece of work; and theater and performance are in turn the domains of the performers and audience. See Richard Schechner, "Drama, Script, Theatre, and Performance," *Drama Review* 17, no. 3 (1973): 7–9. The article is included as a chapter in Richard Schechner, *Performance Theory* (New York: Routledge Classics, 2003).

51. Tina Lu, *Persons, Roles, and Minds: Identity in* Peony Pavilion *and* Peach Blossom Fan (Stanford, Calif.: Stanford University Press, 2001); Stephen Owen, " 'I Don't Want to Act as Emperor Any More': Finding the Genuine in *Peach Blossom Fan*," in Idema, Li, and Widmer, *Trauma and Transcendence*, 488–511.

52. In the caption of the image, You explains that he "instructed a number of young actors" (教小伶數人) to perform the drama.

53. In the early eighteenth century, the Yongzheng emperor prohibited women from performing onstage, triggering the large-scale practice of male actors performing female characters, or male *dan* (*nandan* 男旦). However, most of the dramas discussed in this book were composed before the eighteenth century.

54. See Yufu Huang, "Chinese Women's Status as Seen Through Peking Opera," in *Holding Up Half the Sky: Chinese Women Past, Present, and Future*, ed. Tao Jie, Zheng Bijun, and Shirley L. Mow (New York: Feminist Press, 2004), 30–38.

55. Stephen Greenblatt, *Shakespearean Negotiations: The Circulation of Social Energy in Renaissance England* (Berkeley: University of California Press, 1988), 4–5.

56. Rogers Brubaker and Frederick Cooper, "Beyond 'Identity,' " *Theory and Society* 29, no. 1 (2000): 11. In the article, Brubaker and Cooper suggest alternative terms, such as "self-understanding," "self-representation," "connectedness," and "groupness." For convenience, I use such terms as "identities," "identity expression," and "identity negotiation," but I use "personhood" as an overarching concept to capture different parties involved in theatrical practices, an individual person's multiple roles, and the incoherence between different aspects of a person—actual or represented.

57. Stephen Greenblatt, *Renaissance Self-Fashioning: From More to Shakespeare* (Chicago: University of Chicago Press, 2005), 9: "Self-fashioning is always, though not exclusively, in language."

58. Based on the use of digital tools, Paul Vierthaler, "Quasi-History and Public Knowledge: A Social History of Late Ming and Early Qing Unofficial Historical Narratives" (PhD diss., Yale University, 2014), discusses the border between

news and fiction in quasi-historical narratives about the corrupt eunuch Wei Zhongxian. Ironically, historical dramas were also employed to serve the most urgent needs of political struggle in modern China, especially during the Cultural Revolution.

59. For one example, Guan Hanqing's *Baiyue ting* 拜月亭 unfolds during the Mongolian army's attack on Beijing in 1214 and the Jin court's flight south. For an overview of such dramas in Chinese history, see Li Jiangjie 李江傑, *Ming Qing shishiju yanjiu* 明清時事劇研究 (Jinan: Qi Lu shushe, 2014), 7–17.

60. A Qing-dynasty scholar, Zhao Yi 趙翼 (1727–1814), observed, "When people of the Ming dynasty staged drama performances, they frequently made use of events in their own dynasty" (明人演戲多有用本朝事者). See Zhao Yi 趙翼, *Gaiyu congkao* 陔餘叢考 (Beijing: Zhonghua shuju, 2006), 20:397. In the entry, Zhao records three examples to support his statement.

61. For example, Qi Biaojia 祁彪佳 (1602–1645) mentioned this term a few times in his work of drama commentary; see Qi Biaojia, *Yuanshantang Ming qupin jupin jiaolu* 遠山堂明曲品劇品校錄, ed. Huang Shang 黃裳 (Shanghai: Shanghai gudian wenxue chubanshe, 1957), 34, 36, 113–14, 127, 129–30.

62. One early Qing drama based on the Yang family stories is Li Yu's 李玉 *Haotian ta* 昊天塔.

63. Early Qing dramas featuring Yue Fei, who led the resistance against the Jurchen invasion of Song China, include Li Yu's 李玉 *Niutou shan* 牛頭山 and Shen Dafu's 沈大復 *Rushi guan* 如是觀. Selected scenes of the latter play were possibly performed in the Qianlong court, where derogative expressions against the "barbarians" were deleted or altered. See Isobe Yūko 磯部祐子, "Riben suocang neifu chaoben *Rushi guan* sizhong juben zhi yanjiu" 日本所藏內府鈔本《如是觀》四種劇本之研究, *Wenxue yichan* 4 (2012): 130–35.

64. Wang Fan-sen, *Quanli de maoxiguan zuoyong: Qingdai de sixiang xueshu yu xintai* 權力的毛細管作用: 清代的思想、學術與心態 (Taipei: Lianjing chuban shiye gufen youxian gongsi, 2013), 394.

65. In the early Qing period, drama censorship was part of a general censorship on all kinds of writings. The Qing dynasty did not establish an institution for drama censorship like the Lord Chamberlain's Office in England. For studies on drama censorship in British history, see L. W. Conolly, *The Censorship of English Drama 1737–1824* (San Marino, Calif.: Huntington Library, 1976) and John Russell Stephens, *The Censorship of English Drama, 1824–1901* (Cambridge: Cambridge University Press, 1980).

66. For recent studies of these dramas, see Li, *Ming Qing shishiju yanjiu*, and Wu Jen-shu 巫仁恕, "Ming Qing zhiji jiangnan shishiju de fazhan jiqi suo fanying de shehui xintai" 明清之際江南時事劇的發展及其所反映的社會心態, *Zhongyang yangjiuyuan jindaishi yanjiusuo jikan* 31 (1999): 1–48.

67. The numbers are based on research published in Guo Yingde 郭英德, *Ming Qing chuanqi zonglu* 明清傳奇綜錄 (Shijiazhuang: Hebei jiaoyu chubanshe, 1997), and Du Guiping 杜桂萍, *Qingchu zaju yanjiu* 清初雜劇研究 (Beijing: Renmin wenxue chubanshe, 2005). Lu Eting considers the century between 1621 and 1722 as a period when *kun* opera directly responded to the dynastic transition; see Lu, *Kunju yanchu shigao*, 77.

68. The missing dramas on the dynastic change include *Guangyuan shu* 廣爰書, *Xifeng chun* 喜逢春, *Wuse shi* 五色石, and *Yuanyang tao* 鴛鴦縧. See Ding Shumei 丁淑梅, *Qingdai jinhui xiqu shiliao biannian* 清代禁毀戲曲史料編年 (Chengdu: Sichuan daxue chubanshe, 2010), 77.

69. As an example, *Xihu shan* 西湖扇, a drama composed by Ding Yaokang 丁耀亢 in the early years of the Qing dynasty, recounts a romantic story between a couple who encountered each other at West Lake, soon parted because of war, and finally reunited. The drama's preface discloses that it was based on a real event during the Ming–Qing transition, but Ding Yaokang sets it against the backdrop of wars between the Song dynasty and the Jurchen Jin dynasty. For an example of fantastic literature, see *Huaren you* 化人遊, discussed in Xiaoqiao Ling, "Home and Imagined Stage in Ding Yaokang's *Huaren you* (Ramblings with Magicians): The Communal Reading of a Seventeenth-Century Play," *CHINOPERL: Journal of Chinese Oral and Performing Literature* 33, no. 1 (2014): 1–36.

70. Paize Keulemans, "Onstage Rumor, Offstage Voices: The Politics of the Present in the Contemporary Opera of Li Yu," *Frontiers of History in China* 9, no. 2 (2014): 172.

71. The only extant dramas printed in the Yuan dynasty include no dialogue. Scholars accordingly argue that playwrights of the Yuan dynasty composed only the arias, and that it was literati scholars of the Ming dynasty who added dialogue. For further discussion of the Yuan collection, see Idema, "Why You Never." See also Min Tian, "Stage Directions in the Performance of Yuan Drama," *Comparative Drama* 39, nos. 3, 4 (2005): 397–443.

72. There are a large number of studies in Chinese on these materials. For a recent English study, see Jeehee Hong, *Theater of the Dead: A Social Turn in Chinese Funerary Art, 1000–1400* (Honolulu: University of Hawai`i Press, 2016).

73. See Li-ling Hsiao, *The Eternal Present of the Past: Illustration, Theater, and Reading in the Wanli Period, 1573–1619* (Leiden: Brill, 2007).

74. Such records include the list of costumes (*chuanguan* 穿關) appended to *Maiwangguan chaojiaoben gujin zaju* 脈望館抄校本古今雜劇, edited in the late Ming dynasty. Scholars have regarded this document as reflecting the stage costumes used in the Yuan and early Ming periods. A similar document, *Chuandai tigang* 穿戴題綱, arguably dated to the Daoguang reign of the Qing dynasty

(1821–1850), reflects the type of costumes prepared for performances at the Qing court. Another important list incorporated into *Yangzhou huafang lu* 揚州畫舫錄 records costumes used in commercial troupe performances in the mid-Qing period.

75. Jonathan Hay, "Toward a Disjunctive Diachronics of Chinese Art History," *RES: Anthropology and Aesthetics* 40 (Autumn 2001): 107.

1. WAYS TO DRESS AND WAYS TO SEE

1. John Francis Davis, *The Chinese: A General Description of the Empire of China and Its Inhabitants* (New York: Harper, 1836), 188–89. On Davis's writings and translations, see Patricia Sieber, *Theaters of Desire: Authors, Readers, and the Reproduction of Early Chinese Song-Drama, 1300–2000* (New York: Palgrave Macmillan, 2003), 11–12, 17–18.

2. Liu Yuemei has published a series of books on costumes in different performance genres. See *Zhongguo jingju yixiang* 中國京劇衣箱 (Shanghai: Shanghai cishu chubanshe, 2002), *Zhongguo xiqu yixiang—juese chuandai* 中國戲曲衣箱—角色穿戴 (Beijing: Zhongguo xiju chubanshe, 2006), and *Zhongguo kunqu yixiang* 中國崑曲衣箱 (Shanghai: Shanghai cishu chubanshe, 2010).

3. Alexandra B. Bonds, *Beijing Opera Costumes: The Visual Communication of Character and Culture* (Honolulu: University of Hawai`i Press, 2008), 265.

4. Song Junhua 宋俊華, *Zhongguo gudai xiju fushi yanjiu* 中國古代戲劇服飾研究 (Guangzhou: Guangdong gaodeng jiaoyu chubanshe, 2003). The first half of the book studies the diachronic changes in theater costumes and the second half discusses long-standing features of stage costumes.

5. Scholars usually trace the origin of Chinese theater to early ritual and religious performances involving masks and dance costumes. Since this book is concerned with costuming as a means of interpreting contemporary history, it focuses on dramas about worldly affairs rather than costumes used in ritual and religious performances.

6. Sima Qian 司馬遷, "Huaji liezhuan" 滑稽列傳, in *Shiji* 史記 (Beijing: Zhonghua shuju, 1982), 10:3201.

7. Song, *Zhongguo gudai xiju fushi yanjiu*, 31–32; Ren Zhongmin 任中敏, *Tang xinong* 唐戲弄, ed. Yang Xiaoai 楊曉靄 and Xiao Yuxia 肖玉霞 (Nanjing: Fenghuang chubanshe, 2013), 702.

8. Liao Ben 廖奔 and Liu Yanjun 劉彥君, *Zhongguo xiqu fazhan shi* 中國戲曲發展史 (Beijing: Zhongguo xiju chubanshe, 2013), 1:293–96.

9. D. C. Lau, trans., *The Analects* (Harmondsworth, Middlesex, U.K.: Penguin Books, 1979), 14.17. See the discussions in Weikun Cheng, "Politics of the Queue: Agitation and Resistance in the Beginning and End of Qing China," in

Hair: Its Power and Meaning in Asian Cultures, ed. Alf Hiltebeitel and Barbara D. Miller (Albany: State University of New York Press, 1998), 127, and Tobie Meyer-Fong, *What Remains: Coming to Terms with Civil War in 19th Century China* (Stanford, Calif.: Stanford University Press, 2013), 67, 227.

10. On ethnic confrontation and integration during the non-Han dynasties, see Francesca Fiaschetti and Julia Schneider, eds., *Political Strategies of Identity Building in Non-Han Empires in China* (Wiesbaden: Harrassowitz, 2014).

11. Zhang Jia 張佳, "Chongzheng guanshang: Hongwu shiqi de fushi gaige" 重整冠裳: 洪武時期的服飾改革, *Zhongguo wenhua yanjiusuo xuebao* 58 (2014): 116–17. The article is included in Zhang Jia, *Xin tianxia zhi hua—Mingchu lisu gaige yanjiu* 新天下之化—明初禮俗改革研究 (Shanghai: Fudan daxue chubanshe, 2014).

12. Focusing on the fifth to seventh centuries, Kate A. Lingley delineates a process whereby some features of foreign dress became part of ordinary dress in Tang society, ceasing to function as ethnic markers; "Naturalizing the Exotic: On the Changing Meanings of Ethnic Dress in Medieval China," *Ars Orientalis* 38 (2010): 50–80. For a recent discussion of the "cosmopolitanism" in the Tang empire seen through fashion, see BuYun Chen, *Empire of Style: Silk and Fashion in Tang China* (Seattle: University of Washington Press, 2019), chap. 1.

13. Shen Qian 沈倩, "Cong xiqu wenwu kan Songdai de yanchu fushi" 從戲曲文物看宋代的演出服飾, *Quxue* 3 (2015): 314–15.

14. Zhu Hengfu 朱恆夫, *Lun xiqu de lishi yu yishu* 論戲曲的歷史與藝術 (Shanghai: Xuelin chubanshe, 2008), 94. It is not clear whether drama performances in the Jurchen Jin and the Khitan Liao dynasties featured different costumes in the style of their ethnic clothing. Song Junhua, *Zhongguo gudai xiju fushi yanjiu*, 33–64, discusses drama performances in the Song–Jin period but does not address the minority dynasties in particular. Song seems to suggest that drama performances across geographical districts in that long period were all based on everyday clothes of the Song dynasty.

15. Song, *Zhongguo gudai xiju fushi yanjiu*, 78.

16. Regarding the *zaju* performance scene (dated 1324) on the southeastern wall of the main hall of the Water God's Temple in Hongdong, Shanxi province, see Zhou Yibai 周貽白, *Zhongguo xiqu lunji* 中國戲曲論集 (Beijing: Zhongguo xiju chubanshe, 1960), 397, and Zhu, *Lun xiqu de lishi yu yishu*, 99.

17. The Ming court did not simply eliminate Yuan cultural legacies. Related studies include David M. Robinson, *Martial Spectacles of the Ming Court* (Cambridge, Mass.: Harvard University Asia Center, 2013), and David M. Robinson, "The Ming Court and the Legacy of the Yuan Mongols," in *Culture, Courtiers, and Competition: The Ming Court (1368–1644)*, ed. David M. Robinson (Cambridge, Mass.: Harvard University Asia Center, 2008), 365–422.

18. Dong Meikan 董每戡, "Shuo xingtou" 說行頭, in *Dong Meikan wenji* 董每戡文集 (Guangzhou: Guangdong gaodeng jiaoyu chubanshe, 1999), 1:625.

19. Liao and Liu, *Zhongguo xiqu fazhan shi*, 3:138.

20. Zhou Xibao 周錫保, *Zhongguo gudai fushi shi* 中國古代服飾史 (Beijing: Zhongguo xiju chubanshe, 1984), 381.

21. Song Junhua 宋俊華, "Mangyi kaoyuan jiantan Ming gongting yanju de wujiang zhuangban" 蟒衣考源兼談明宮廷演劇的武將裝扮, *Zhongshan daxue xuebao* 41, no. 4 (2001): 61. Later, *kunqu* performances replaced *mangyi yesa* for military generals with *zhajia* 扎甲 (bound armor). See Gong Hede 龔和德, *Wutai meishu yanjiu* 舞台美術研究 (Beijing: Zhongguo xiju chubanshe, 1987), 347.

22. Zhao Qimei 趙琦美, ed., *Maiwangguan chaojiaoben gujin zaju* 脈望館抄校本古今雜劇, in *Guben xiqu congkan* 古本戲曲叢刊, ser. 4 (Shanghai: Shangwu yinshuguan, 1958).

23. *Shi tanzi da'nao Yan'anfu* 十探子大鬧延安府, in *Maiwangguan chaojiaoben gujin zaju*, 62:45a–47b. These costumes do not necessarily reflect historical clothing. For example, the use of rank badges on official uniforms started in the Ming dynasty, not the Song dynasty.

24. *Yang Liulang diaobing po tianzhen* 楊六郎調兵破天陣, in *Maiwangguan chaojiaoben gujin zaju*, 61:45a–49a.

25. *Deng Furen kutong ku Cunxiao* 鄧夫人苦痛哭存孝, in *Maiwangguan chaojiaoben gujin zaju*, 7:25a–b. Other plays in the anthology about the Five Dynasties generals Li Cunxiao 李存孝, Li Cunxin 李存信, and Li Keyong 李克用 involve a large number of costumes in different ethnic styles.

26. *Song dajing Yue Fei jingzhong* 宋大將岳飛精忠, in *Maiwangguan chaojiaoben gujin zaju*, 61:39a–40b. Modern-day Beijing opera performances still use two white foxtails attached to the headpiece to indicate a character's "barbarian" identity. See Bonds, *Beijing Opera Costumes*, 37.

27. For an English introduction to drama performances in the Qing court, see Mei Mei Rado, "Images of Opera Characters Related to the Qing Court," in *Performing Images: Opera in Chinese Visual Culture*, ed. Judith T. Zeitlin, Yuhang Li, and Richard A. Born (Chicago: Smart Museum of Art, University of Chicago, 2014), 58–73.

28. Jonas A. Barish, *The Antitheatrical Prejudice* (Berkeley: University of California Press, 1981).

29. Regarding the (ineffective) prohibition against performing the emperor onstage in the Ming, see Tian Yuan Tan, "Prohibition of *Jiatou Zaju* in the Ming Dynasty and the Portrayal of the Emperor on Stage," *Ming Studies* 49 (2004): 82–111. For general studies of antitheatrical practices in Chinese history, see Wang Liqi 王利器, *Yuan Ming Qing sandai jinhui xiaoshuo xiqu shiliao* 元明清三代禁毀小說戲曲史料 (Shanghai: Shanghai guji chubanshe, 1981),

and, more recently, Ding Shumei 丁淑梅, *Zhongguo gudai jinhui xiju shilun* 中國古代禁毀戲劇史論 (Beijing: Zhongguo shehui kexue chubanshe, 2008). Occasionally, however, drama performances were elevated to be an example of Confucian ritual and music, especially in the early Ming period. See Li Shunhua 李舜華, *Liyue yu Ming qianzhongqi yanju* 禮樂與明前中期演劇 (Shanghai: Shanghai guji chubanshe, 2006).

30. Their antagonism stemmed from various sources: drama texts and performances were considered morally corrupting; drama performances provided an illicit space for promiscuity between men and women, gambling, and other types of social disturbance; and drama performances led to the squander of wealth.

31. For a discussion on Rousseau's antitheatrical attitudes and writings, see Barish, *The Antitheatrical Prejudice*, chap. 9. For a chronological anthology of records on antitheatrical practices in the Qing dynasty, see Ding Shumei 丁淑梅, *Qingdai jinhui xiqu shiliao biannian* 清代禁毀戲曲史料編年 (Chengdu: Sichuan daxue chubanshe, 2010). For an English study on drama censorship in the Qing dynasty, see Ye Xiaoqing, *Ascendant Peace in the Four Seas: Drama and the Qing Imperial Court* (Hong Kong: Chinese University Press, 2012), chap. 4.

32. As the *Jin History* (*Jinshi* 金史) recounts, "When performers occasionally undertake the task of receiving guests at banquets, they are allowed temporarily to don decorated dress; their personal attire should be the same as that for commoners" (倡優遇迎接、公筵承應，許暫服繪畫之服，其私服與庶人同). See Tuo Tuo 脫脫 et al., eds., *Jinshi* 金史 (Beijing: Zhonghua shuju, 1975), *juan* 43, 987. There are similar entries in the "Chariot and Clothing" section in *Yuanshi* 元史. On the social status of musicians in traditional China, especially the Qing dynasty, see Ye Xiaoqing, "The Legal and Social Status of Theatrical Performers in Beijing during the Qing," *East Asian History* 25/26 (2003): 69–84, and Zhang Hanmo, "Property of the State, Prisoners of Music: Identity of the Song Drama Players and Their Roles in the *Washi* Pleasure Precincts," *Bulletin of the Jao Tsung-I Academy of Sinology* 2 (2015): 277–326.

33. *Ming Taizu shilu* 明太祖實錄, *juan* 126, 5b, in *Ming shilu* 明實錄 (Taipei: Zhongyang yanjiuyuan lishi yuyan yanjiusuo, 1962), 1:2018. For a discussion of these policies, see Zhang Jia, "Chongzheng guanshang," 143. Green headgear had been associated with low-status groups, especially prostitutes and performers, in the Yuan dynasty. It then became a general term for a cuckold.

34. *Huangchao wenxian tongkao* 皇朝文獻通考, *juan* 141, in *Yingyin Wenyuange Siku quanshu* 影印文淵閣四庫全書 (Taipei: Taiwan shangwu yinshuguan, 1983), *shibu, zhengshu*, 141:36b.

35. *Shizu Zhanghuangdi shilu* 世祖章皇帝實錄, *juan* 78, 11a–b, in *Qing shilu* 清實錄 (Beijing: Zhonghua shuju, 1985), 3:619.

36. Gugong Bowuyuan Wenxianguan 故宮博物院文獻館, ed., *Shiliao xunkan* 史料旬刊 19 (1930–31): 697. For another case of children performers keeping their hair to impersonate women onstage, see Ding, *Qingdai jinhui xiqu shiliao biannian*, 88–90.

37. *Gaozong Chunhuangdi shilu* 高宗純皇帝實錄, *juan* 1118, in *Qing shilu* 清實錄 (Beijing: Zhonghua shuju, 1986), 22:939. See the discussion of this campaign in Ding Shumei 丁淑梅, *Zhongguo gudai jinhui xiju biannian shi* 中國古代禁毀戲劇編年史 (Chongqing: Chongqing daxue chubanshe, 2014), 413–19.

38. In a 1781 report, an official, Quan De 全德, explained that some scenes depicting the defeat of the Jurchens during the Song–Jin confrontation were inappropriately performed. The report indicates that negative depictions of the Jurchens were considered improper. See Zhu Jiajin 朱家溍 and Ding Ruqin 丁汝芹, *Qingdai neiting yanju shimo kao* 清代內廷演劇始末考 (Beijing: Zhongguo shudian, 2007), 65.

39. Zhu and Ding, *Qingdai neiting yanju shimo kao*, 58.

40. Zhongguo Diyi Lishi Dang'anguan 中國第一歷史檔案館, ed., *Zuanxiu Siku quanshu dang'an* 纂修四庫全書檔案 (Shanghai: Shanghai guji chubanshe, 1997), 1398.

41. Ye, *Ascendant Peace*, 208.

42. *Shiliao xunkan* 22 (1931): 793b. The report also includes the expression "performing the attire of our dynasty" (扮演本朝服色).

43. Mark C. Elliott, *The Manchu Way: The Eight Banners and Ethnic Identity in Late Imperial China* (Stanford, Calif.: Stanford University Press, 2001), chap. 7, discusses the Manchu identity crisis in the eighteenth century, caused not least by the decline in military practice and the use of the Manchu language.

44. Andrea S. Goldman, *Opera and the City: The Politics of Culture in Beijing, 1770–1900* (Stanford, Calif.: Stanford University Press, 2012), 112.

45. Liu Ruiyu 劉汭嶼, "Wan Qing jingju qizhuangxi yu danhang huashan de xingqi" 晚清京劇旗裝戲與旦行花衫的興起, *Zhongguo xiqu xueyuan xuebao* 36, no. 4 (2015): 64–71.

46. Qi Rushan 齊如山, *Xingtou kuitou* 行頭盔頭 (Beiping: Beiping guoju xuehui, 1935), 8, 26, 36.

47. Qi Rushan, *Qi Rushan lun jingju yishu* 齊如山論京劇藝術, ed. Liang Yan 梁燕 (Shanghai: Shanghai wenyi chubanshe, 2014), 20–21.

48. Liu, *Zhongguo jingju yixiang*, 129–33, and *Zhongguo kunqu yixiang*, 45–49.

49. Concerning the painting and Qianlong's armor, see Huang Nengfu 黃能馥, *Zhongguo fushi tongshi* 中國服飾通史 (Beijing: Zhongguo fangzhi chubanshe, 2007), 232.

50. On the time of production of these costumes, see Wang Hebei, "Liushi yuwai de Qinggong xiyi" 流失域外的清宮戲衣, *Zhonghua wenhua huabao* 中華文化畫報

01 (2018): 84–95. The article introduces other items of court costume collected in China and America.

51. Wang, "Liushi yuwai de Qinggong xiyi," 89. Immediately following the establishment of the Qing dynasty, the inner court used existing textiles from the Ming dynasty to manufacture theatrical costumes. Later, the Jiangnan General Manufacturing Bureau undertook the task of providing the court theater with costumes.

52. For more images of these costumes, see Wang Wenzhang 王文章 et al., eds., *Kunqu yishu dadian* 崑曲藝術大典 (Hefei: Anhui wenyi chubanshe, 2016), *meishu dian*, vol. 8.

53. I thank Qin Wenbao 秦文寶 for providing his professional evaluation of the two costumes.

54. Fan Limin 范麗敏, *Qingdai Beijing xiqu yanchu yanjiu* 清代北京戲曲演出研究 (Beijing: Renmin wenxue chubanshe, 2007), 57–62.

55. The Shengping Shu was established in 1827. Dating these texts is extremely difficult. My argument in this section is based on the assumption that some of the texts discussed here could have been produced at an early time of the Qing dynasty. Even if they were produced at a later stage, they still support my argument that Manchu clothing was not widely used in drama performances in the court during the early Qing period.

56. Gugong Bowuyuan 故宮博物院, ed., *Gugong zhenben congkan* 故宮珍本叢刊 (Haikou: Hainan chubanshe, 2000), 660:31.

57. Gugong Bowuyuan, *Gugong zhenben congkan*, 660:121.

58. Gugong Bowuyuan, *Gugong zhenben congkan*, 661:249.

59. Ye Xiaoqing, "Ascendant Peace in the Four Seas: Tributary Drama and the Macartney Mission of 1793," *Late Imperial China* 26, no. 2 (2005): 97.

60. Gugong Bowuyuan, *Gugong zhenben congkan*, 661:250. Other examples include *Wanguo songhu* 萬國嵩呼, *Sihai shengping* 四海昇平, and *Sihai qingning* 四海清寧 in vols. 661, 270, and 380. Ye, "Ascendant Peace," 97, points out that the Qing court produced "a collection of drawings of the costumes of all tributary delegations" in the 1750s.

61. Song, *Zhongguo gudai xiju fushi yanjiu*, 399.

62. Zhang Jingqiu 張淨秋, unpublished study of *Shengping baofa* 昇平寶筏, in *Guben xiqu congkan* 古本戲曲叢刊, ser. 9 (Shanghai: Shangwu yinshuguan, 1964).

63. Fan, *Qingdai Beijing xiqu yanchu yanjiu*, 64.

64. Zhu and Ding, *Qingdai neiting yanju shimo kao*, 40–46. Other documents of the Bureau of Internal Affairs indeed include mention of Manchu clothes, such as *liangmao* (summer hat), but they were most probably worn by the actors in everyday life instead of onstage (12, 15).

65. In a drama performed at the Chongyang festival, the *sheng* role features Tao Yuanming wearing the traditional Han-style clothes for scholars, whereas the *fumo* role presents an old runner appearing in an archer's robe. See Gugong Bowuyuan, *Gugong zhenben congkan*, 660:124–25. Similarly, in *A Gathering of Kings in an Era of Great Tranquility*, the Manchu-style archer's robe is used together with the gauze hat and round-collar uniform for Chinese officials.

66. For a brief introduction to the garment, see Qi, *Xingtou kuitou*, 36. For a list of *jianxiu* 箭袖 in Qing grand plays, see Song, *Zhongguo gudai xiju fushi yanjiu*, 397.

67. For a comparison of these two works, see Song, *Zhongguo gudai xiju fushi yanjiu*, 141.

68. *Yulan ji* 魚籃記, late Ming edition, *juan* b, 27a, in *Guben xiqu congkan* 古本戲曲叢刊, ser. 2 (Shanghai: Shangwu yinshuguan, 1955). Zhang Dai 張岱 recorded a hunting event in 1638 where the female attendants were wearing *jianyi* as a military uniform. See "Niushou shan dalie" 牛首山打獵 in Zhang Dai 張岱, *Tao'an mengyi* 陶庵夢憶, ed. Ma Xingrong 馬興榮 (Beijing: Zhonghua shuju, 2007), 47.

69. Most studies treat the two terms in Qing drama indiscriminately, considering both to have originated in the mid-Qing performances. See Gao Xin 高新, *Zhongguo jingju shuyao* 中國京劇述要 (Jinan: Shandong daxue chubanshe, 2001), 130–31. For some images of *jianyi*, see Zhongguo Xiqu Xueyuan 中國戲曲學院 and Tan Yuanjie 譚元傑, eds., *Zhongguo jingju fuzhuang tupu* 中國京劇服裝圖譜 (Beijing: Beijing gongyi meishu chubanshe, 2008), 168–79.

70. Liu, *Zhongguo jingju yixiang*, 158, and *Zhongguo kunqu yixiang*, 73.

71. Robert I. Lublin, *Costuming the Shakespearean Stage: Visual Codes of Representation in Early Modern Theatre and Culture* (Farnham, Surrey, U.K.: Ashgate Publishing, 2011), 10, 83.

72. Relevant studies include Margaret Rose Jaster, "'Out of All Frame and Good Fashion': Sartorial Resistance as Political Spectacle," *Irish Review* 34 (2006): 44–57, and Lou Taylor, *The Study of Dress History* (Manchester, U.K.: Manchester University Press, 2002), 214–17.

73. Goldman, *Opera and the City*, chap. 2.

74. For an introduction to ethnic segregation in early Qing cities, see Elliott, *The Manchu Way*, 98–116.

75. Hui Zhong 慧中 et al., eds., *Qinding taigui* 欽定臺規, 1743, *juan* 5, 26a–b, in *Siku weishoushu jikan* 四庫未收書輯刊 (Beijing: Beijing chubanshe, 2000), ser. 2, 26:232. The entry is also included in Yan Xu 延煦 et al., eds., *Qinding taigui* 欽定臺規, 1892, *juan* 25.

76. *Shizong Xianhuangdi shilu*, *juan* 18, 4a–b, in *Qing shilu* (Beijing: Zhonghua shuju, 1985), 7:297.

77. *Qinding baqi tongzhi* 欽定八旗通志, *juan* 30, in *Siku quanshu, shibu, zhengshu*, 422:762–63.

78. *Renzong Ruihuangdi shilu, juan* 313, 14a–b, in *Qing shilu* (Beijing: Zhonghua shuju, 1986), 32:165.

79. Such titles include imperially commissioned compendia such as *Qinding libu chufen zeli* 欽定吏部處分則例 (*juan* 45), *Huangchao wenxian tongkao* 皇朝文献通考 (*juan* 202), *Daqing huidian shili* 大清會典事例, and official histories of the Manchu people such as *Baqi tongzhi* 八旗通志. These books were all categorized as administrative manuals (*zhengshu* 政書) in *Siku quanshu zongmu tiyao*. See also privately edited manuals such as Shen Shucheng 沈書城, ed., *Zeli bianlan* 則例便覽, 1791, *juan* 29, in *Siku weishoushu jikan* 四庫未收書輯刊 (Beijing: Beijing chubanshe, 2000), ser. 2, vol. 27.

80. The regulations should have applied to Manchus in particular, not banner people in general. Quite a few Han bannermen in early Qing were well-known playwrights, such as Cao Yin 曹寅 (1658–1712) and Tang Ying 唐英 (1682–1756).

81. Goldman, *Opera and the City*, 72.

82. Ding, *Qingdai jinhui xiqu shiliao biannian*, 82.

83. Goldman, *Opera and the City*, 98.

84. Goldman, *Opera and the City*, 65.

85. For brief histories of the institutes responsible for court performances in the Qing dynasty, see Fan, *Qingdai Beijing xiqu yanchu yanjiu*, chap. 1, and Ye, *Ascendant Peace*, chap. 1.

86. Wu Hung, "Beyond Stereotypes: The Twelve Beauties in Qing Court Art and the *Dream of the Red Chamber*," in *Writing Women in Late Imperial China*, ed. Ellen Widmer and Kang-i Sun Chang (Stanford, Calif.: Stanford University Press, 1997), 363.

87. There are a number of studies on the composition of the imperial troupe. For example, see Ye, *Ascendant Peace*, chap. 3, and Ye Xiaoqing, "Imperial Institutions and Drama in the Qing Court," *European Journal of East Asian Studies* 2, no. 2 (2003): 336.

88. On drama performances at temple fairs in and near Beijing, see Goldman, *Opera and the City*, 87–97.

89. *Wanshou tu* 萬壽圖, 1799 painting, based on similar paintings and woodblock prints produced in the 1710s, in *Putian tongqing: Qingdai wanshou shengdian* 普天同慶：清代萬壽盛典, ed. Gugong Bowuyuan 故宮博物院 (Beijing: Gugong chubanshe, 2015), 78–79. For a similar image featuring the three immortals of "bliss, fortune, and longevity" (福祿壽), see *Wanshou shengdian chuji* 萬壽盛典初集, ed. Wang Yuanqi 王原祁 et al., 1717, *juan* 41, 62a, reprinted in *Wanshou shengdian* 萬壽盛典 (Beijing: Beijing guji chubanshe, 1996).

90. Xu Ke, comp., *Qingbai leichao* 清稗類鈔 (Beijing: Zhonghua shuju, 2010), 11:5034.

91. For both the poem and figure 1.4, see Liu Cheng, *Yitong shiji* 嶧桐詩集, 1893, *juan* 7, 30a, in *Siku jinhuishu congkan* 四庫禁燬書叢刊 (Beijing: Beijing chubanshe, 2000), *jibu*, 121:621. Another late Qing edition of the poem preserves the word "barbarian" (*hu* 胡). See Liu Cheng, *Yitong shiji*, in *Guichi ermiao ji* 貴池二妙集, ed. Liu Shiheng 劉世珩, 1902, in *Congshu jicheng xubian* 叢書集成續編 (Taipei: Xinwenfeng chuban gongsi, 1991), 162:695. In the poem, Young Master Zhou alludes to Zhou Yu 周瑜 of the Three Kingdoms era, who was a military general and an expert on music.

92. In the Qianlong reign alone, *Yitong shiji* was officially banned three times. See Wang Ping 王平, "Liu Cheng he tade sishou guichi 'guannuo shi'" 劉城和他的四首貴池"觀儺詩," *Chizhou shizhuan xuebao* 18, no. 4 (2004): 52–54.

93. Li Shengguang, "Guanxi" 觀戲, in *Xishange bi* 西山閣筆, in *Siku weishoushu jikan* 四庫未收書輯刊 (Beijing: Beijing chubanshe, 2000), *jibu*, ser. 8, 16:346.

94. Xu, *Qingbai leichao*, 5049. The couplet at the end of the record reads, 十公班內諸公子, 故國衣冠拜冕旒.

95. Wang Wei, *Wang Wei ji jiaozhu* 王維集校注, ed. Chen Tiemin 陳鐵民 (Beijing: Zhonghua shuju, 1997), 488.

96. For a recent study on the interactions between sartorial cultures in East Asia, see Zhu Xiaoen 竺小恩 and Ge Xiaohong 葛曉弘, *Zhongguo yu dongbeiya fushi wenhua jiaoliu yanjiu* 中國與東北亞服飾文化交流研究 (Hangzhou: Zhejiang daxue chubanshe, 2015).

97. Yi Yo, *Yŏndo kihaeng* 燕途紀行, in *Kugyŏk Yŏnhaengnok sŏnjip* 國譯燕行錄选集 (Seoul: Sŏnggyun'gwan Taehakkyo Taedong Munhwa Yŏn'guwŏn, 1962), 2:234.

98. Yi Tŏkmu, *Ibyŏn'gi* 入燕記 b, in *Kugyŏk Ch'ŏngjanggwan chŏnsŏ* 國譯青莊館全書, *Yŏnhaengnok chŏnjip* 燕行錄全集, ed. Im Ki-jung 林基中 (Seoul: Tongguk Taehakkyo Ch'ulp'anbu, 1992), 57:287.

99. Daphne Pi-Wei Lei, *Operatic China: Staging Chinese Identity across the Pacific* (New York: Palgrave Macmillan, 2006), 168. Lei discusses the "revolution-theatre" (chap. 3), which involves the Taiping Rebellion, the Boxer Rebellion, and the rebellion led by the Cantonese opera actor Li Wenmao 李文茂. In her book, Lei points out that even for the diasporic communities in nineteenth-century California, "Theatre was the place to see and to be the real Chinese" (141).

100. Chen Qubing, *Chen Qubing shiwen ji* 陳去病詩文集 (Beijing: Shehui kexue wenxian chubanshe, 2009), a:414.

101. Scholars have paid increasing attention to the writings about the Ming–Qing transition in Asian countries other than China. For a thorough study of writings by Korean scholars, see Wu Zhengwei 吳政緯, *Juanjuan Mingchao:*

Chaoxian shiren de Zhongguo lunshu yu wenhua xintai (1600–1800) 眷眷明朝: 朝鮮士人的中國論述與文化心態 (1600–1800) (Taipei: Guoli Taiwan shifan daxue lishixuexi, 2015).

102. Kim Ch'ang-ŏp, *Yŏnhaeng ilgi* 燕行日記, in *Yŏnhaengnok chŏnjip*, 32:167.

103. Hong Taeyong, *Tamhŏn yŏn'gi* 湛軒燕記, in *Yŏnhaengnok chŏnjip*, 42:217.

104. Hong Taeyong, *Yŏnhaeng chapki* 燕行雜記, in *Yŏnhaengnok chŏnjip*, 42:412–17.

105. Yi Hŏnmuk, *Yŏnhaeng illok* 燕行日錄, in *Yŏnhaengnok sokchip* 燕行錄續集, ed. Im Ki-jung 林基中 (Seoul: Sangsŏwŏn, 2008), vol. 118; cited from Cheng Yun 程芸, ed., "*Yanxinglu xubian* jingju shiliao" 《燕行錄續編》京劇史料, in *Jingju lishi wenxian huibian Qingdai juan xubian* 京劇歷史文獻彙編清代卷續編, ed. Fu Jin 傅謹 (Nanjing: Fenghuang chubanshe, 2013), 4:593.

106. In the Ming and Qing dynasties, Korean intellectuals often used the phrase *hanguan weiyi* 漢官威儀 to refer to traditional Chinese clothing. The expression first appeared in *Houhan shu* 後漢書, when an old official says, "I had not expected to be able to see the Han might and demeanor again on this day" (不圖今日復見漢官威儀). See "Guangwu di ji" 光武帝紀 in Fan Ye 范曄, comp., *Houhan shu* 後漢書 (Beijing: Zhonghua shuju, 1965), 10. Thus, the phrase *hanguan* in Yi's words could be short for *hanguan weiyi*—Han attire.

107. Ge Zhaoguang 葛兆光, *Xiangxiang yiyu: Du Lichao Chaoxian hanwen yanxing wenxian zhaji* 想像異域: 讀李朝朝鮮漢文燕行文獻箚記 (Beijing: Zhonghua shuju, 2014), chap. 9. For a similar argument, see Wang Zhengyao 王政堯, *Qingdai xiju wenhua kaobiao* 清代戲劇文化考辨 (Beijing: Beijing yanshan chubanshe, 2014), chaps. 4 and 5.

108. Nakagawa Tadateru, *Shinzoku kibun* 清俗紀聞, 1800, vol. 12, "Sairei" 祭禮, 15b–16a (repr., Taipei: Dali chubanshe, 1982), 522–23.

109. See Antonia Finnane, *Changing Clothes in China: Fashion, History, Nation* (New York: Columbia University Press, 2008), 19.

110. For a thorough study of this drama performance, especially the political message in it, see Ye, "Ascendant Peace."

111. William Alexander, *Picturesque Representations of the Dress and Manners of the Chinese* (London: Bulmer, 1814), plate 30, "A Female Comedian." The book includes another image of a performer, plate 45, "A Stage Player."

112. William Alexander, "A Chinese Comedian," in *The Costume of China, Illustrated in Forty-eight Coloured Engravings* (London: Miller, 1805).

113. Sir George Staunton, *An Authentic Account of an Embassy from the King of Great Britain to the Emperor of China* (London: Bulmer, 1797), 1:xxiv. See also Finnane's discussion of Staunton's works in *Changing Clothes in China*, 23.

114. John Barrow, *Travels in China* (London: Strahan, 1804), 147.

115. Quoted in Clark Worswick, *Sheying: Shades of China, 1850–1900* (Madrid: Turner, 2008), 61.

116. Jeehee Hong, *Theater of the Dead: A Social Turn in Chinese Funerary Art, 1000–1400* (Honolulu: University of Hawai`i Press, 2016), 6. See also Fan Jeremy Zhang, "'Drama Sustains the Spirit': Art, Ritual, and Theater in Jin and Yuan Period Pingyang, 1150–1350" (PhD diss., Brown University, 2011).

2. ACROSS GENDERS AND ETHNICITIES

1. Qu Dajun, "Jiren shuo" 髻人說, in *Qu Dajun quanji* 屈大均全集, ed. Ou Chu 歐初 and Wang Guichen 王貴忱 (Beijing: Renmin wenxue chubanshe, 1996), 3:472. Martin Huang briefly discusses this piece in *Negotiating Masculinities in Late Imperial China* (Honolulu: University of Hawai`i Press, 2006), 83.

2. Martin W. Huang 黃衛總, "Guonan yu shiren de xingbie jiaolü" 國難與士人的性別焦慮, in *Ming Qing wenxue yu sixiang zhong zhi zhuti yishi yu shehui* 明清文學與思想中之主體意識與社會, ed. Wang Ayling 王璦玲 (Taipei: Zhongyang yanjiuyuan Zhongguo wenzhe yanjiusuo, 2004), 385–412.

3. Zhu Ying, *Dao yuanyang chuanqi* 倒鴛鴦傳奇, preface dated 1650, in *Guben xiqu congkan* 古本戲曲叢刊, ser. 3 (Shanghai: Wenxue guji kanxingshe, 1957).

4. Dramas attributed to Zhu Ying include *Zui Yangzhou* 醉揚州, *Nao Wujiang* 鬧烏江, *Dao yuanyang* 倒鴛鴦, *Yehu chan* 野狐禪. and *Lin'ge dai* 麟閣待. In addition to *Lovebirds*, a copy of the first half of *Nao Wujiang* was recently recovered in Japan and is reproduced in *Riben suocang xijian Zhongguo xiqu wenxian congkan* 日本所藏稀見中國戲曲文獻叢刊, ed. Huang Shizhong 黃仕忠, Qiao Xiuyan 喬秀岩, and Kin Bunkyō 金文京 (Guilin: Guangxi shifan daxue chubanshe, 2006), ser. 1, vol. 3. An edited edition of the drama is included in *Ming Qing guben xijian xiqu huikan* 明清孤本稀見戲曲彙刊, ed. Huang Shizhong 黃仕忠 (Guilin: Guangxi shifan daxue chubanshe, 2014), vol. 2. A single woodblock-print edition of *Xinbian lin'ge dai chuanqi* 新編麟閣待傳奇 is in the collection of the Suzhou Library; a few copies made from that edition are available in different libraries (my citations are from this edition). Qu Qijia 瞿啟甲 (1873–1939) produced a manuscript copy based on the early Qing print edition of *Lin'ge dai* and presented it to the Qing court. The manuscript edition was recently reproduced in *Guben xiqu congkan* 古本戲曲叢刊, ser. 7 (Beijing: Guojia tushuguan chubanshe, 2018).

5. The most direct evidence is the author's signature at the end of the preface to *Lovebirds*: 雲間朱英寄林氏識於江寧玉嘯堂. See Liu Zhizhong 劉致中, "Guben *Lin'ge dai chuanqi* de zuozhe he chengshu niandai" 孤本《麟閣待傳奇》的作者和成書年代, *Wenxian* 2 (2000): 108–12, 131. A revised and enlarged version of this article is included in Liu Zhizhong, *Ming Qing xiqu kaolun* 明清戲曲考論 (Taipei: Guojia chubanshe, 2009). *Wuxian zhi* 吳縣志 (1933, *juan* 56) also records Zhu Jilin (Zhu Ying) as the author of three dramas. It is possible that Zhu Ying lived in Suzhou sometime during his life.

6. The woodblock pages of *Disturbance at the Wu River* and *Lovebirds* follow the same format in terms of the number of lines on each page and characters per line, and the styles of the characters in the main texts and the prefaces, indicating they were probably produced at the same time. The format of *Unicorn Pavilion Awaiting* is slightly different from that of the other two. Most notably, it does not have the name Yuxiao Tang between the two half-folio pages.

7. Based on such evidence, Liu Zhizhong regards the drama as alluding to the resistance led by Zheng Chenggong 鄭成功 against the Manchu invasion, especially Zheng's failed foray into the lower Yangzi delta in 1659. See Liu, "Guben *Lin'ge dai chuanqi* de zuozhe he chengshu niandai." However, the drama itself does not indicate any connection with Zheng. As my earlier discussion shows, the drama was likely completed before 1650.

8. For a detailed account of Southern Ming history, see Lynn A. Struve, *The Southern Ming, 1644–1662* (New Haven, Conn.: Yale University Press, 1984), chap. 2.

9. *Shizu Zhanghuangdi shilu* 世祖章皇帝實錄, *juan* 17, 5a–b, in *Qing shilu* 清實錄 (Beijing: Zhonghua shuju, 1985), 3:151.

10. *Shizu Zhanghuangdi shilu, juan* 19, 4b–5a, in *Qing shilu*, 3:168.

11. Ge Zhaoguang 葛兆光, "Da Ming yiguan jin hezai" 大明衣冠今何在, *Shixue yuekan* 10 (2005): 43.

12. For a representative discussion on late Ming fashion, see Lin Li-yueh 林麗月, "Yishang yu fengjiao—Wan Ming de fushi fengshang yu 'fuyao' yilun" 衣裳與風教—晚明的服飾風尚與「服妖」議論, *Xin shixue* 10, no. 3 (1999): 111–57.

13. According to Song Junhua 宋俊華, *Zhongguo gudai xiju fushi yanjiu* 中國古代戲劇服飾研究 (Guangzhou: Guangdong gaodeng jiaoyu chubanshe, 2003), 374, 386, Jin-style headgear appeared in both *chuanqi* and *zaju* dramas of the Ming dynasty.

14. Zhao Yuan 趙園, *Ming Qing zhiji shidafu yanjiu* 明清之際士大夫研究 (Beijing: Beijing daxue chubanshe, 1999), 308–17.

15. Preface to *Lovebirds*, in *Guben xiqu congkan*, ser. 3.

16. Expressions such as *"yiguan* can be used to fend off violence" (衣冠可以止暴) have appeared in scholarly studies of the *Yijing* 易經. For example, see Sun Qifeng 孫奇逢, *Du Yi dazhi* 讀易大旨, *juan* 1 and 2, in *Yingyin Wenyuange Siku quanshu* 影印文淵閣四庫全書 (Taipei: Taiwan shangwu yinshuguan, 1983), *jingbu*, vol. 39.

17. *Disturbance at the Wu River*, scene 2, in *Riben suocang xijian Zhongguo xiqu wenxian congkan*, ser. 1, 3:223–24.

18. *Disturbance at the Wu River*, scene 12, in *Riben suocang xijian Zhongguo xiqu wenxian congkan*, ser. 1, 3:294.

19. For one explanation, see Gao Shaoxian 高紹先, *Zhongguo xingfa shi jingyao* 中國刑法史精要 (Beijing: Falü chubanshe, 2001), 407.

20. Wang Yunying 王雲英, *Zaitian xiuse—Manzu guanmin fushi* 再添秀色—滿族官民服飾 (Shenyang: Liaohai chubanshe, 1997), 42–43.

21. To avoid an early meeting between the mother and daughter, the drama does not include Shui Suyue in the group sent by the Hua family to receive the two brides in the Shui family, although the *dan* appears in that scene as a musician (scene 33).

22. Tina Lu has discussed in detail how the father as well as the emperor in *Peony Pavilion* together guarantee a stable moral order and identity for each of the characters; *Persons, Roles, and Minds: Identity in* Peony Pavilion *and* Peach Blossom Fan (Stanford, Calif.: Stanford University Press, 2001), chap. 3, esp. 140–41.

23. Charlotte Furth, "Androgynous Males and Deficient Females: Biology and Gender Boundaries in Sixteenth- and Seventeenth-Century China," *Late Imperial China* 9, no. 2 (1988): 25.

24. Richard E. Strassberg, "The Authentic Self in 17th Century Chinese Drama," *Tamkang Review* 8, no. 2 (1977): 69. In the article, Strassberg uses "lyric capsule" in reference to a group of Chinese dramas including *Peony Pavilion* and *Peach Blossom Fan.*

25. For a discussion of the scene and the term, see Cyril Birch, "A Comparative View of Dramatic Romance: *The Winter's Tale* and *The Peony Pavilion*," in *Interpreting Culture Through Translation: A Festschrift for D. C. Lau*, ed. Roger T. Ames, Chan Sin-wai, and Mau-sang Ng (Hong Kong: Chinese University Press, 1991), 67–70.

26. For a list of Chinese dramas that involve cross-dressing, see Xu Wei, "Nandan: Xingbie fanchuan" 男旦: 性別反串 (PhD diss., Xiamen Daxue, 2007), 76–78.

27. Xu Wei 徐渭, *Sisheng yuan* 四聲猿, ed. Zhou Zhongming 周中明 (Shanghai: Shanghai guji chubanshe, 1984). For a recent translation and study of the four plays including *Ci Mulan*, see Shiamin Kwa, *Strange Eventful Histories: Identity, Performance, and Xu Wei's* Four Cries of a Gibbon (Cambridge, Mass.: Harvard University Asia Center, 2012).

28. *Zengshu ji*, in *Liushizhong qu* 六十種曲, ed. Mao Jin 毛晉 (Beijing: Zhonghua shuju, 1958).

29. Sophie Volpp, *Worldly Stage: Theatricality in Seventeenth-Century China* (Cambridge, Mass.: Harvard University Asia Center, 2011), chap. 4.

30. Robert I. Lublin, *Costuming the Shakespearean Stage: Visual Codes of Representation in Early Modern Theatre and Culture* (Farnham, Surrey, U.K.: Ashgate Publishing, 2011), 5.

31. For a discussion on this topic, see Zeng Yongyi 曾永義, "Nanban nüzhuang yu nüban nanzhuang" 男扮女妝與女扮男妝, in *Shuo xiqu* 說戲曲 (Taipei: Lianjing

chuban shiye gongsi, 1976), 31–47. For a recent study, see Wang Anqi 王安祈, *Xingbie zhengzhi yu jingju biaoyan wenhua* 性別、政治與京劇表演文化 (Taipei: Taida chuban zhongxin, 2011), 2–5. For a brief summary and discussion of female impersonation, see Min Tian, "Male *Dan*: The Paradox of Sex, Acting, and Perception of Female Impersonation in Traditional Chinese Theatre," *Asian Theatre Journal* 17, no. 1 (2000): 78–97.

32. For example, the Yuan-dynasty document *Qinglou ji* 青樓集 records a large number of actresses who performed male characters onstage.

33. A professional troupe of *kunqu* performers in the Ming dynasty was made up mostly of male performers. The Yongzheng emperor prohibited women from performing onstage in the Manchu court. Beijing opera, when it arose in the mid-Qing era, was performed mostly by male actors.

34. Zhongguo Xiqu Xueyuan 中國戲曲學院 and Tan Yuanjie 譚元傑, eds., *Zhongguo jingju fuzhuang tupu* 中國京劇服裝圖譜 (Beijing: Beijing gongyi mei-shu chubanshe, 1990), 324. The specific term for this type of costume is "cap with two pendulous strands of hair" (*kuimao chui fabian* 盔帽垂髮辮).

35. Maram Epstein, *Competing Discourses: Orthodoxy, Authenticity, and Engendered Meanings in Late Imperial Chinese Fiction* (Cambridge, Mass.: Harvard University Asia Center, 2001), 34.

36. Epstein, *Competing Discourses*, 30–31.

37. The preface mentions not only the plotline in *Lovebirds* but also characters in *Unicorn Pavilion Awaiting* such as the pirates. It is possible that this is a preface to a group of Zhu's dramas published at a similar time.

38. Judith T. Zeitlin, *Historian of the Strange: Pu Songling and the Chinese Classical Tale* (Stanford, Calif.: Stanford University Press, 1997), 116.

39. The term *nannü* is subject to different interpretations. In a recent publication, scholars have discussed the possibility of viewing *nannü* as a critical category that extends beyond the man-woman binary; See "Introduction: Toward a Transnational Feminist Theory," in *The Birth of Chinese Feminism: Essential Texts in Transnational Theory*, ed. Lydia H. Liu, Rebecca E. Karl, and Dorothy Ko (New York: Columbia University Press, 2013).

40. Marjorie B. Garber, *Vested Interests: Cross-Dressing and Cultural Anxiety* (New York: Routledge, 2011), 16.

3. BETWEEN FAMILY AND STATE

1. For a detailed introduction to the story of the Huang family, see Elizabeth Kindall, *Geo-Narratives of a Filial Son: The Paintings and Travel Diaries of Huang Xiangjian (1609–1673)* (Cambridge, Mass.: Harvard University Asia Center, 2016), 19, 97–101. A brief introduction is also available in Lynn A. Struve,

ed., *Voices from the Ming–Qing Cataclysm: China in Tigers' Jaws* (New Haven, Conn.: Yale University Press, 1993), 162–65. On the dates of birth and death for the father and son, see Guo Yingde 郭英德, "Duochong kongjian de xinggou, bingzhi yu yanyi—Li Yu *Wanli yuan* chuanqi de 'kongjian' jiedu" 多重空間的形構、並置與演繹—李玉《萬里圓》傳奇的"空間"解讀, in *Hai neiwai Zhongguo xijushi jia zixuanji Guo Yingde juan* 海內外中國戲劇史家自選集郭英德卷 (Zhengzhou: Daxiang chubanshe, 2017), 152. Guo dates the drama as composed between 1654 and 1660 because the earliest known performance of the drama took place in 1661 (153).

2. About half of these dramas still exist. See Yan Changke 顏長珂 and Zhou Chuanjia 周傳家, *Li Yu pingzhuan* 李玉評傳 (Beijing: Zhongguo xiju chubanshe, 1985), 7–11. See also Zhuang Yifu 莊一拂, *Gudian xiqu cunmu huikao* 古典戲曲存目彙考 (Shanghai: Shanghai guji chubanshe, 1982), 1145–60. For a recent summary of Li Yu's biography and drama composition, see Liu Zhizhong 劉致中, *Ming Qing xiqu kaolun* 明清戲曲考論 (Taipei: Guojia chubanshe, 2009), 196–205.

3. The full titles of the four plays are *A Handful of Snow* (*Yipeng xue* 一捧雪), *Between Man and Monster* (*Renshou guan* 人獸關), *Eternal Reunion* (*Yong tuanyuan* 永團圓), and *Flower Queen* (*Zhan huakui* 占花魁). The late Ming print editions of these plays are reproduced in *Guben xiqu congkan* 古本戲曲叢刊, ser. 3 (Shanghai: Wenxue guji kanxingshe, 1957).

4. In general, woodblock-print editions of Li Yu's dramas include relatively more detailed stage directions, whereas some manuscript copies of his dramas—such as *Qilin ge* 麒麟閣, include few stage directions. The difference can be clearly seen in comparing the print and manuscript editions of Li Yu's drama *Qingzhong pu* 清忠譜.

5. *Reunion* and another work, *Two Manly Heroes* (*Liang xumei* 兩鬚眉), are set during the Ming–Qing transition. *Flower Queen* and *Mount Ox Head* (*Niutou shan* 牛頭山) are set against the military conflicts between the Song dynasty and the Jurchen Jin dynasty. *The Slaughter of the Thousand Loyal Ones* (*Qianzhong lu* 千忠錄) represents the usurpation of the throne within the imperial family in the early Ming. Some scholars have questioned the authorship of the *Thousand Loyal Ones*; see Liu Zhizhong, *Ming Qing xiqu kaolun*, 203.

6. For the numbers in the table, I considered all available editions of *Reunion* (see appendix 1). For the other dramas, I referred to the edited plays in Li Yu 李玉, *Li Yu xiqu ji* 李玉戲曲集, ed. Chen Guyu 陳古虞, Chen Duo 陳多, and Ma Shenggui 馬聖貴 (Shanghai: Shanghai guji chubanshe, 2004), without considering all existing editions of the dramas.

7. In addition to composing individual plays, Li Yu also edited the music score *Beici guangzheng pu* 北詞廣正譜.

8. Catherine Swatek discovered and discussed this edition of the play. For a brief introduction, see her English translation "Beating the Officers," *Renditions* 70 (Autumn 2008): 105.

9. See the editorial note by Shushi 漱石 at the beginning of the first issue. Shushi (short for Haishang Shushi Sheng 海上漱石生) is the style name of Sun Yusheng 孫玉聲 (1864–1940).

10. In the discussion of the drama's plotlines, I have considered the differences in its various editions. See the scene synopsis of the drama in appendix 2. The modern edited *Reunion* in *Li Yu xiqu ji* is based on the *GBXQ* edition. Unless otherwise noted, my quotations are from the drama's *Li Yu xiqu ji* edition.

11. The residents of Yunnan during the Ming–Qing transition included ethnic groups, Muslim Chinese, and military settlers deployed by the Ming government. See Charles Patterson Giersch, *Asian Borderlands: The Transformation of Qing China's Yunnan Frontier* (Cambridge, Mass.: Harvard University Press, 2006), chap. 3. Anthropologists have discussed the "semistate spaces" of Guizhou, the province adjacent to Yunnan. See Jodi L. Weinstein, *Empire and Identity in Guizhou: Local Resistance to Qing Expansion* (Seattle: University of Washington Press, 2014), chap. 3. For a recent study of the southwestern frontiers in the Ming–Qing literary imagination, see Hu Siao-chen 胡曉真, *Ming Qing wenxue zhong de xinan xushi* 明清文學中的西南敘事 (Taipei: Taida chuban zhongxin, 2017).

12. Paize Keulemans, "Onstage Rumor, Offstage Voices: The Politics of the Present in the Contemporary Opera of Li Yu," *Frontiers of History in China* 9, no. 2 (2014): 192–93, discusses the structure of *Reunion* based on geographical space.

13. For the length of Huang's journey, see Kindall, *Geo-Narratives*, 97. Kindall points out that Huang's reputation as a filial son and the family tale of filial piety were partly a result of the Huang family's campaign to promote the story (chap. 3).

14. Wanhua Zhuren 玩花主人 and Qian Decang 錢德蒼, eds., *Huitu zhuibaiqiu* 繪圖綴白裘 (Shanghai: Shanghai shuju, 1895), vol. 9, 10a.

15. Scholars of Huang Xiangjian's time frequently described him as carrying an umbrella during his journey. Kindall, *Geo-Narratives*, 254, points out that every extant painting of Huang Xiangjian on his Yunnan trip shows him carrying an umbrella.

16. For one example, see the discussion in Jessica Munns and Penny Richards, eds., *The Clothes That Wear Us: Essays on Dressing and Transgressing in Eighteenth-Century Culture* (Newark: University of Delaware Press, 1999).

17. A particularly representative case involving the performance of nudity is Xu Wei's *zaju* drama *The Mad Drummer* (*Kuang gushi* 狂鼓史). Yuming He,

"Difficulties of Performance: The Musical Career of Xu Wei's *The Mad Drummer*," *Harvard Journal of Asiatic Studies* 68, no. 2 (2008): 77–114, discusses the challenges of staging the drama in late Ming society from the perspective of music structure. Another difficulty in performing the drama involves the protagonist, Mi Heng's, naked body. Some illustrations in late Ming print editions of the drama depict Mi Heng half naked—with exposed chest, belly, and feet and wearing underclothes and a hat. Nudity is also an important theme for female characters in other plays by Xu Wei, such as *Nü zhuangyuan* 女狀元 and *Ci Mulan* 雌木蘭. Some Ming-dynasty illustrations depict the female protagonist of *Dou E yuan* 竇娥冤 as half naked upon her execution. In contemporary China, actors of traditional Chinese drama usually leave the upper body unclothed or wear white to perform nudity.

18. Huang Xiangjian, *Xunqin jicheng* 尋親紀程, in *Huang Xiaozi jicheng* 黃孝子紀程, *Zhibuzu zhai congshu* 知不足齋叢書, ed. Bao Tingbo 鮑廷博, Qianlong edition (repr., Shanghai: Gushu liutong chu, 1921), ser. 5, vol. 6, 7b, 12a.

19. Huang, *Xunqin jicheng*, 6a–b, 11b.

20. Gui Zhuang, "Huang Xiaozi zhuan," in *Huang Xiaozi jicheng, Zhibuzu zhai congshu*, ser. 5, vol. 6, *fuzhuan* 附傳, 2b.

21. Huang, *Xunqin jicheng*, 13b.

22. Some distinctions between Han and Manchu clothes related to Huang Xiangjian involve wide and narrow sleeves, the shape of the collar, the use of buttons, and different types of headgear. See figure 3.7 for a portrait of Huang wearing Manchu clothing.

23. Chen Hu 陳瑚 [1613–1675], *Quean wengao* 確庵文稿, in *Siku jinhuishu congkan* 四庫禁燬書叢刊 (Beijing: Beijing chubanshe, 1997), *jibu*, 184:327.

24. Wang Bian, *Wang Chaosong nianpu* 王巢松年譜, in *Congshu jicheng xubian* 叢書集成續編 (Shanghai: Shanghai shudian, 1994), *shibu*, 37:796.

25. See James Legge, trans., *The Sacred Books of China: The Texts of Confucianism*; *The Hsiao King*, 2nd ed. (Oxford: Clarendon Press, 1899), 466.

26. The earliest manuscript edition of the *Thousand Loyal Ones* (1708) is reproduced in Wang Wenzhang 王文章 and Liu Wenfeng 劉文峰, eds., *Fu Xihua cang gudian xiqu zhenben congkan* 傅惜華藏古典戲曲珍本叢刊 (Beijing: Xueyuan chubanshe, 2010), vol. 17. Another manuscript edition of this work and one of *Reunion* were collected by Cheng Yanqiu and reproduced in one volume in *Guben xiqu congkan*. For the purpose of comparison with *Reunion* in this chapter, I have used the *GBXQ* edition of the *Thousand Loyal Ones*. For a detailed discussion of the drama, see Liu Chiung-yun 劉瓊云, "Qingchu *Qianzhong lu* lide shenti shengqing yu zhongchen jiyi" 清初《千忠錄》裡的身體、聲情與忠臣記憶," *Xiju yanjiu* 17 (2016): 1–39. Other examples of changes in

clothing in Li Yu's dramas include Shi Kefa in *Two Manly Heroes*, Yue Fei in *Mount Ox Head*, and the traitor officers in *Flower Queen*.

27. In the late Ming and early Qing periods, the Jianwen emperor's loss of the throne became a heated topic among Chinese literati, with many considering it a prelude to the decline of the Ming dynasty. See Zhao Yuan 趙園, *Ming Qing zhiji shidafu yanjiu* 明清之際士大夫研究 (Beijing: Beijing daxue chubanshe, 1999), chap. 3. Whereas the Jianwen emperor's later whereabouts remained a mystery in history, Li Yu provides a reconciliation between the rivaling parties in the *Thousand Loyal Ones*. As the Jianwen event is analogous with the Ming–Qing transition, Li Yu's rendering in the drama could be interpreted as a commentary on contemporary history.

28. One scene of their trip home in between the last two scenes might be missing, because the opening aria of the drama, which summarizes the play, references a storm the father and son encountered on their way home, but that part of the story is missing in the existing editions; still, the action after the family leave Yunnan is rather hasty.

29. Legge, *The Hsiao King*, 466–67. This order reverses what we see in the Confucian classic *The Great Learning* (*Daxue* 大學), that a person must first cultivate himself before successfully administering the duties of the family and state. *The Great Learning* defines a person's self as the basis of all his social and political relations.

30. Catherine Swatek has translated "Beating the Officers" into English based on different editions of the drama. In her translation, Swatek demonstrates the textual variations in different editions of the scene. As her study shows, it is impossible to produce a standard collated text of the scene because of the radical differences in its existing editions. The title "Chairao" 差擾 exists only in *The Player's Press* edition.

31. For a brief introduction to the adjutant play, see William Dolby, "Early Chinese Plays and Theater," in *Chinese Theater: From Its Origins to the Present Day*, ed. Colin Mackerras (Honolulu: University of Hawai`i Press, 1983), 13–14. For a detailed study, see Ren Zhongmin 任中敏, *Tang xinong* 唐戲弄, ed. Yang Xiaoai 楊曉靄 and Xiao Yuxia 肖玉霞 (Nanjing: Fenghuang chubanshe, 2013), 226–92.

32. The Chinese National Academy of Arts edition includes the line, "(*Jing*) Who is the one wearing a fucking *jinzi* on the head?" The Youguxuan edition includes a similar line: "Who is that one wearing a *jinzi*?"

33. Lin Li-yueh 林麗月, "Wanfa juqi—wangjin yu Mingdai shehui wenhua de jige mianxiang" 萬髮俱齊—網巾與明代社會文化的幾個面向, *Taida lishi xuebao* 33 (2004): 133–60.

34. *Reunion*, in *GBXQ*, *juan* b, 7b, 8b, 9b, 14b.

35. Li Yu, *Mount Ox Head*, in *Guben xiqu congkan*, ser. 3. For example, scene 3 provides a description of the Jurchen characters: "*Wai* performs a barbarian official and enters holding an imperial decree; *chou*, *lao*, and *jing* enter wearing helmets and armor, holding knives and axes; *tie*, *zheng*, *xiaosheng*, and *fu* perform barbarian officers and enter holding flags" (外扮番官捧詔上; 丑老与淨戴盔甲鉞斧, 貼正小生付扮番將執旗上).

36. Li Yu, *Flower Queen*, in *Guben xiqu congkan*, ser. 3, scene 13.

37. Illustration to scene 13, "Returning from the North," of *Flower Queen*, in *Guben xiqu congkan*, ser. 3. The two feathers on the cap of the other Jurchen soldier in the picture might also indicate his ethnic identity, although in traditional Chinese theater such feathers were also used to portray military men and women of Chinese ethnicity.

38. Liu Yuemei 刘月美 holds that the *saozi* hat and *shaozi* hat refer to the same headgear in *kunqu* performance; see Liu Yuemei, *Zhongguo kunqu yixiang* 中國崑曲衣箱 (Shanghai: Shanghai cishu chubanshe, 2010), 117. On *saozi* hats used for performing Li Yu's *Thousand Loyal Ones*, see Liu Yuemei 劉月美, *Zhongguo kunqu zhuangban yishu* 中國崑曲裝扮藝術 (Shanghai: Shanghai cishu chubanshe, 2009), 246. For a dictionary entry on *shaozi* hats, see Wu Xinlei 吳新雷, Yu Weimin 俞爲民, and Gu Lingsen 顧聆森, eds., *Zhongguo kunju da cidian* 中國崑劇大辭典 (Nanjing: Nanjing daxue chubanshe, 2002), 630.

39. According to some studies, one edition of *Patched White Fur* with a preface dated 1739 includes the scene "Beating the Officers" from *Wanli yuan* 萬里緣. See Wu Gan 吳敢, "*Zhui baiqiu* xukao (A)" 綴白裘敘考上, *Xuzhou jiaoyu xueyuan xuebao* 15, no. 4 (2000): 45. The expanded edition of *Patched White Fur* edited by Qian Decang and continually printed from 1764 to 1773 includes three scenes from *Reunion*. The quoted text is from a 1777 edition of *Patched White Fur* produced by Hongwentang 鴻文堂 and reprinted in *Shanben xiqu congkan* 善本戲曲叢刊, ed. Wang Qiugui 王秋桂 (Taipei: Taiwan xuesheng shuju, 1987), ser. 5, 1:3357.

40. "Fake Tiger Hills" (*jia Huqiu* 假虎丘) is part of a Suzhou idiom that refers to the calligraphic work *Huqiu jianchi* 虎丘劍池 originally written by Yan Zhenqing in the Tang dynasty. It is said that later the two characters representing *Huqiu* faded away and were redone by someone in the late Ming era, hence the idiom.

41. "Introduction: Rethinking Theories of the State in an Age of Globalization," in *The Anthropology of the State: A Reader*, ed. Aradhana Sharma and Akhil Gupta (Malden, Mass.: Blackwell Publishing, 2006), 19; emphasis in original.

42. Kindall, *Geo-Narratives*, 342.

43. Kindall, *Geo-Narratives*, 342.

44. Early Qing scholar-artists frequently depicted themselves wearing Han-style clothing in their landscape paintings. For a discussion of the paintings by Chen Hongshou 陳洪綬 and other early Qing scholars, see Peter C. Sturman and Susan S. Tai, eds., *The Artful Recluse: Painting, Poetry, and Politics in Seventeenth-Century China* (Santa Barbara, Calif.: Santa Barbara Museum of Art; Munich: DelMonico Books / Prestel, 2012).

45. Gu Yuan et al., eds., *Wujun wubai mingxian tuzhuanzan* 吳郡五百名賢圖傳贊, 1829 (repr., Taipei: Guangwen shuju, 1978). Gu Yuan began collecting materials in 1824. The shrine was completed by 1828 and the book was published around 1829. The portraits in the book were produced by Kong Jiyao 孔繼垚. For a detailed study of the collection, see Seunghyun Han, *After the Prosperous Age: State and Elites in Early Nineteenth-Century Suzhou* (Cambridge, Mass.: Harvard University Asia Center, 2016), chap. 5. This chapter is based on Seunghyun Han, "Shrine, Images, and Power: The Worship of Former Worthies in Early Nineteenth Century Suzhou," *T'oung Pao* 95, nos. 1–3 (2009): 167–95.

46. The editors explained in one of the prefatory pieces, "These portraits are either copied from ancient albums or collected from descendants of different families. All the caps and attire follow their original appearance with authentic evidence. None have been fabricated."

47. "Editorial Principles," in Gu, *Wujun wubai mingxian tuzhuanzan.*

48. Gu, *Wujun wubai mingxian tuzhuanzan, juan* 14, 17a, and *juan* 16, 30a. Historians in the Qing dynasty usually determined a person's dynastic belonging based on whether he held a degree or served in an office in the Ming dynasty. Based on this standard, Huang Kongzhao belonged to the Ming since he served as a magistrate, whereas Huang Xiangjian belonged to the Qing since he did not take office in the Ming.

49. Keulemans, "Onstage Rumor, Offstage Voices," 165. Keulemans argues that the use of reports and rumors in *Reunion* contributes to the sense of "a poignant political urgency" (194).

50. This point is taken up in greater detail in the epilogue.

51. On the performance of "Beating the Officers" in modern China (in Jiangsu and Shanghai), see Zhou Qin 周秦, ed., *Kunxi jicun* 崑戲集存 (Hefei: Huangshan shushe, 2011), A:60, and Liu, *Zhongguo kunqu zhuangban yishu*, 241.

52. See the introduction in Kunju Shouchao Quben Yibaice Bianji Weiyuanhui 崑劇手抄曲本一百冊編輯委員會 and Zhongguo Kunqu Bowuguan 中國崑曲博物館, eds., *Kunju shouchao quben yibaice* 崑劇手抄曲本一百冊 (Yangzhou: Guangling shushe, 2009). The undated manuscript preserved in the National Library of China (中國國家圖書館), Beijing, was also finely produced with beautiful calligraphy, detailed musical notations, and copious stage instructions.

53. Catherine Swatek has pointed out, on different occasions, the nuanced meaning of the Wu dialect in the drama to audiences with knowledge of the dialect. Discussing a Yuan-dynasty southern play, Stephen H. West also points out that the use of southern dialect in the play "creates a bond of intimacy between audience and stage and simultaneously creates a mentality of inner and outer" ("Shifting Spaces: Local Dialect in *A Playboy from a Noble House Opts for the Wrong Career*," *Journal of Theater Studies* 1, no. 1 [2008]: 102.)

54. *A Register of Costumes*, in *Gugong zhenben congkan* 故宮珍本叢刊, ed. Gugong Bowuyuan 故宮博物院 (Haikou: Hainan chubanshe, 2000), 690:267.

55. This edition is undated, but the use of the term "horse jacket" (*magua* 馬褂) came rather late in Qing drama. One of the earliest records of "horse jacket" as part of a stage costume appears in *Yangzhou huafang lu* 揚州畫舫錄, produced in the late Qianlong period.

56. Hu Sanqiao 胡三橋, drama painting of "Beating the Officers," 1879, in Lu Eting 陸萼庭, *Kunju yanchu shigao* 崑劇演出史稿 (Shanghai: Shanghai jiaoyu chubanshe, 2005). Scholars believe that the two characters' costumes are strictly based on stage performances of the scene in late Qing China. Recent studies on drama painting include Zhou Huabin 周華斌, "Xiqu wenxian: Zhou Yibai suo-cang Qinggong xihua" 戲曲文獻：周貽白所藏清宮戲畫, *Xiqu xuebao* 9 (2011): 225–33, and Zhang Daxia 張大夏, *Xihua xihua* 戲畫戲話 (Taipei: Chongguang wenyi chubanshe, 1971).

57. Xuan Ding 宣鼎, drama painting of "Beating the Officers," 1873, in *Kunqu yishu dadian* 崑曲藝術大典, ed. Wang Wenzhang 王文章 et al. (Hefei: Anhui wenyi chubanshe, 2016), 146:2164.

58. Suzhoushi Xiqu Yanjiu Shi 蘇州市戲曲研究室, comp., *Kunju chuandai* 崑劇穿戴 (Suzhou: Suzhoushi xiqu yanjiu shi, 1963), 1:48. See a similar entry in Liu, *Zhongguo kunqu zhuangban yishu*, 242.

59. Fang Jiaji 方家驥 and Zhu Jianming 朱建明, eds., *Shanghai kunju zhi* 上海崑劇志 (Shanghai: Shanghai wenhua chubanshe, 1998), 85.

60. Catherine Swatek, "Beating the Officers and Cursing the Manchus: Suzhou Dialect and *Kun* Opera" (unpublished paper). As an example of the "anti-Manchu digs," Swatek discusses Wang Zhenglong's words in one edition of the scene. When the two officers threaten to flay and pull out his tendons, Wang responds, "Aiyo! What wonderful Manchu torture" (阿唷, 好滿州刑法).

61. One possible reason that Manchu clothing was used in performing clownish characters in front of Manchu rulers is that the two officers in the drama are not real Manchus but Han Chinese serving the Manchu government.

62. Timothy Mitchell, "Society, Economy, and the State Effect," in Sharma and Gupta, *Anthropology of the State*, 178.

63. On censorship as a productive force in shaping Chinese drama, see Ling Hon Lam, "The Matriarch's Private Ear: Performance, Reading, Censorship, and the Fabrication of Interiority in *The Story of the Stone*," *Harvard Journal of Asiatic Studies* 65, no. 2 (2005): 357–415.

4. THE CHASTE LADY IMMORTAL OF SEAMLESS STITCHING

1. Whereas most sources record the couple's names as Chen Youliang and Lady Hai, only "Hai Liefu zhuan" 海烈婦傳 by Lu Ciyun 陸次雲 renders Chen's name Chen Zaiyi 陳再益 (*Chaste Lady Hai, juanshou*, 19a); in the drama *Jieyi xian chuanqi* 節義仙傳奇, Chen's name is Zaiyi 再益 and style name Wufang 無方. *Xuzou fuzhi* 徐州府志 (1874 edition) lists Chen's name as Rong 容 and style name Youliang, the same as in the novel *Bailianzhen Hai Liefu* 百煉真海烈婦. Lady Hai is referred to as Hai Fenggu 海鳳姑 in some biographies (*Chaste Lady Hai, juanshou*, 20b) and Hai Wuxia 海無瑕 in *Bailianzhen Hai Liefu*. For consistency, I refer to the couple as Chen Youliang and Lady Hai throughout this chapter. Full bibliographic information for the aforementioned titles is given in the notes that follow.

2. In different sources, Lin Xianrui has been described as a soldier for canal transport (旗丁運卒) (*Chaste Lady Hai*, scene 2) and a canal transport corporal (伍長旗丁) (*Jieyi xian*, scene 5). The profession was hereditary and similar to the Manchu banner system, hence the name *qiding* (banner laborer).

3. Susan Mann, *Precious Records: Women in China's Long Eighteenth Century* (Stanford, Calif.: Stanford University Press, 1997), 25. See also Janet M. Theiss, *Disgraceful Matters: The Politics of Chastity in Eighteenth-Century China* (Berkeley: University of California Press, 2004), 27.

4. Susan Mann has discussed the term *zongjiaohua* (literally, "become a religion") as coined by some Chinese scholars in the 1930s; "Widows in the Kinship, Class, and Community Structures of Qing Dynasty China," *Journal of Asian Studies* 46, no. 1 (1987): 37–38.

5. Ju-k'ang T'ien, *Male Anxiety and Female Chastity: A Comparative Study of Chinese Ethical Values in Ming–Ch'ing Times* (Leiden: Brill, 1988), 42.

6. For example, one biographical writing collected in *Chaste Lady Hai* indicates that "her statue was cast and placed near the bank of the canal" (範像於運河之畔) (*juanshou*, 24a).

7. He Qie 何焭 [1620–1696], "Bai Hai Liefu ci" 拜海烈婦祠, in *Qingjiangge ji* 晴江閣集, preface dated 1670s, *juan* 8, 10b, in *Siku weishoushu jikan* 四庫未收書輯刊 (Beijing: Beijing chubanshe, 2000), ser. 7, 30:69.

8. Zhou Rong 周容, "Hai Liefu zhuan" 海烈婦傳, in *Chunjiutang wencun* 春酒堂文存, *Chunjiutang yishu* 春酒堂遺書, *juan* 2, 23a, in *Siming congshu* 四明叢書, ser. 1, vol. 37.

9. Unfortunately, there is not a portrait of Lady Hai preserved in any format.

10. Sanwu Molang Zhuren 三吳墨浪主人, ed., *Xinjuan xiuxiang Bailianzhen Hai Liefu zhuan* 新鎸繡像百煉真海烈婦傳, ca. 1667–1668, chap. 8, in *Guben xiaoshuo congkan* 古本小說叢刊 (Beijing: Zhonghua shuju, 1991), ser. 26, 5:2236–37; also in *Guben xiaoshuo jicheng* 古本小說集成 (Shanghai: Shanghai guji chubanshe, 1994), ser. 4, vol. 106. For a brief study of the novel, see Huang Yishu 黃義樞, "Qingchu xiaoshuo *Bailianzhen Hai Liefu zhuan* kaoshu" 清初小說《百煉真海烈婦傳》考述, *Mingzuo xinshang* 8 (2012): 105–7.

11. Shen Shouhong, *Hai Liefu chuanqi*, 1841 print edition based on an early Qing manuscript, in *Guben xiqu congkan* 古本戲曲叢刊, ser. 7 (Beijing: Guojia tushuguan chubanshe, 2018). Different print copies of the drama include slightly different materials, especially the pieces added by the editor Jiang Wenxun 蔣文勳 in the drama's front matter. For a detailed study of the drama's composition and circulation, see Guo Yingde 郭英德, "*Hai Liefu chuanqi* zuozhe benshi yu xuba jikao" 《海烈婦傳奇》作者、本事與序跋輯考, *Wenxian* 1 (2012):191–200.

12. Hui Mu 灰木, *Piling yi jieyi xian ji* 毗陵驛節義仙記, 1668–1670. I used a copy of the drama preserved in the Shanghai Library, which is reproduced in *Guben xiqu congkan*, ser. 7; an edited edition is included in Huang Shizhong 黃仕忠, ed., *Ming Qing guben xijian xiqu huikan* 明清孤本稀見戲曲彙刊 (Guilin: Guangxi shifan daxue chubanshe, 2014), vol. 2. For a detailed introduction to the drama, see Huang Yishu 黃義樞, "Xijian chuanqi *Piling yi jieyi xian ji* shukao" 稀見傳奇《毘陵驛節義仙記》述考, *Zhongguo xiqu xueyuan xuebao* 33, no. 4 (2012): 67–70, 109. Scholars believe the drama was composed by Huang Guangye 黃光業, who served as a registrar (經歷) in Changzhou prefecture in the early Qing. Huang Shizhong dates the production of the drama as between 1668 and 1670. See his introduction to the drama in *Ming Qing guben xijian xiqu huikan*, 758.

13. For example, "An Account of Ten Days in Yangzhou" (揚州十日記; late Qing edition) provides a compelling narrative of the atrocities inflicted on people in southern China during the Ming–Qing transition. For a discussion of women's war experiences recorded in the text, see Wai-yee Li, *Women and National Trauma in Late Imperial Chinese Literature* (Cambridge, Mass.: Harvard University Asia Center, 2014), 480–85.

14. Official histories in traditional China include numerous stories about women's suicide, but very few of them involve the stitching up of clothing. The *Ming History* includes a few such stories. For example, faced with threats from

bandits, a certain Lady Fang 方 in Tongcheng, Jiangsu province, "densely stitched her upper and lower garments and, holding her daughter, entered the water and died" (密紉上下服, 抱女赴水死). Caught in the turmoil of the late Ming, a Lady Lü 呂 "tightly fastened her body with a fishing net" (取魚網結其體甚固) to guard against sexual assault. See Zhang Tingyu 張廷玉 et al., eds., *Mingshi* 明史 (Beijing: Zhonghua shuju, 1974), 7761, 7757.

15. The last scene is missing from the existing copy. The scene title in the table of contents is also missing, possibly scrapped by a book dealer to pass the drama off as a complete copy.

16. *Immortal*, scene 24, 27b–28a. These official titles were commonly used in the Tang dynasty but were later abandoned.

17. *Immortal*, scene 15, 41b–42a. The original word at the end of this line is *zhu* 銖, which must be a mistake for *shu* 姝.

18. *Mengzi yizhu* 孟子譯注, ed. Yang Bojun 楊伯峻 (Beijing: Zhonghua shuju, 2003), 6.10. Lady Hai refers to Wuling (in Shandong province) possibly because her husband is surnamed Chen, the same as Chen Zongzi 陳仲子 in the paragraph from *Mengzi*.

19. For example, the phrase echoes Qu Yuan's well-known line in *Lisao* 離騷: 製芰荷以為衣兮, 集芙蓉以為裳. See Hong Xingzu 洪興祖, comp., *Chuci buzhu* 楚辭補注, ed. Bai Huawen 白化文, Xu Denan 許德楠, Li Ruluan 李如鸞, and Fang Jin 方進 (Beijing: Zhonghua shuju, 1983), 17.

20. Violence suffuses the second half of the drama, especially in scene 25, where the *fumo*-role actor performs as Lady Hai's nephew with Lin Xianrui's head hanging from his waist. Stage instructions make it clear that the *fumo* actor "holds the head and places it on top of the desk," as a sacrifice for the deceased Lady Hai.

21. Huang, "Xijian chuanqi *Piling yi jieyi xian ji* shukao," 69–70.

22. Robert E. Hegel, "Imagined Violence: Representing Homicide in Late Imperial Crime Reports and Fiction," *Zhongguo wenzhe yanjiu jikan* 25 (2004): 61–89, and "Images in Legal and Fictional Texts from Qing China," *Bulletin de l'École française d'Extrême-Orient* 89 (2002): 277–90. For more studies on law and literature in late imperial China, see Robert E. Hegel and Katherine Carlitz, eds., *Writing and Law in Late Imperial China: Crime, Conflict, and Judgment* (Seattle: University of Washington Press, 2007).

23. Hegel, "Images," 278.

24. See Yi Jolan 衣若蘭, *Shixue yu xingbie:* Mingshi Lienü zhuan *yu Mingdai nüxingshi zhi jiangou* 史學與性別：《明史‧列女傳》與明代女性史之建構 (Taiyuan: Shangxi jiaoyu chubanshe, 2011), 87–98.

25. Katherine Carlitz, "The Social Uses of Female Virtue in Late Ming Editions of *Lienü zhuan*," *Late Imperial China* 12, no. 2 (1991): 141. Carlitz points out that

Ming scholars placed significant emphasis upon chaste women resisting rape, listing in *Yuan History* twice as many virtuous women as in any previous dynastic history.

26. Katherine Carlitz, "Desire, Danger, and the Body: Stories of Women's Virtue in Late Ming China," in *Engendering China: Women, Culture, and the State*, ed. Christina K. Gilmartin, Gail Hershatter, Lisa Rofel, and Tyrene White (Cambridge, Mass.: Harvard University Press, 1994), 117; emphasis in original.

27. For a detailed study of the phantom heroines in Chinese drama, see Judith T. Zeitlin, *The Phantom Heroine: Ghosts and Gender in Seventeenth-Century Chinese Literature* (Honolulu: University of Hawai`i Press, 2007), chap. 4. Zeitlin discusses the use of a "spirit kerchief" (*hun pa*) in a group of dramas, with the earliest being a 1689 manuscript (163–71, 245). *Immortal*, produced around 1668–1670, could be an earlier example, although the drama refers to the kerchief as *pa* rather than *hun pa*.

28. For an introduction to deliverance plays, see Wilt L. Idema, *The Dramatic Oeuvre of Chu Yu-Tun (1379–1439)* (Leiden: Brill, 1985), chap. 4.

29. *Jingmao* 京帽 appears in both Ming and Qing documents. It refers to hats in the style of the district of the capital, Beijing. For example, a Qing-dynasty manual for newly appointed provincial governors lists the things they need to bring from the capital to their provincial posts. The clothing section includes *jingmao* and other garments. See Yan Chang 延昌, *Zhifu xuzhi* 知府須知, *juan* 1, in *Siku weishoushu jikan*, ser. 4, 19:239.

30. Qi Rushan 齊如山, *Qi Rushan lun jingju yishu* 齊如山論京劇藝術, ed. Liang Yan 梁燕 (Shanghai: Shanghai wenyi chubanshe, 2014), 18.

31. Marginal commentary, in scene 18, "Yusui" 玉碎, *Chaste Lady Hai*. The woodblock print of the drama includes marginal commentaries throughout. A major message in the commentaries is the moral lesson the drama provides. The commentator was possibly Sheng Jing 盛敬 (1610–1685), Shen Shouhong's teacher. See Guo, "*Hai Liefu chuanqi* zuozhe benshi yu xuba jikao," 196.

32. Francesca Bray, *Technology, Gender and History in Imperial China: Great Transformations Reconsidered* (London: Routledge, 2013), 110. Bray differentiates between two translations of *nügong* 女紅, "womanly work" and "women's work," the former referring to "a moral activity linked to a gendered identity, and embodied in weaving," and the latter to female labor "operating at the level of the private household economy, within the framework of a market economy." See also Angela Sheng, "Women's Work, Virtue, and Space: Change from Early to Late Imperial China," in "Women and Textile Production Techniques in Traditional China," ed. Angela Sheng, special issue, *East Asian Science, Technology, and Medicine* 36 (2012): 9–38.

33. For example, see paragraphs in "The Pattern of the Family" (Neize 內則) 36, in *Liji zhengyi* 禮記正義, *Shisanjing zhushu* 十三經注疏, ed. Shisanjing Zhushu Zhengli Weiyuanhui 十三經注疏整理委員會 (Beijing: Beijing daxue chubanshe, 2000), vol. 6.

34. Mann, *Precious Records*, 159.

35. Mann, *Precious Records*, 144.

36. Bray, *Technology, Gender*, 117.

37. See the discussion on needlework and space in Dorothy Ko, "Epilogue: Textile, Technology, and Gender in China," in Sheng, "Women and Textile Production Techniques," 167–76.

38. A number of scholars have discussed literary writing by women in late imperial China. Representative works include Kang-I Sun Chang and Haun Saussy, eds., *Women Writers of Traditional China: An Anthology of Poetry and Criticism* (Stanford, Calif.: Stanford University Press, 1999); Ellen Widmer and Kang-I Sun Chang, eds., *Writing Women in Late Imperial China* (Stanford, Calif.: Stanford University Press, 1997); and Wilt L. Idema and Beata Grant, *The Red Brush: Writing Women of Imperial China* (Cambridge, Mass.: Harvard University Asia Center, 2004).

39. Christopher Breward, *The Culture of Fashion: A New History of Fashionable Dress* (Manchester, U.K.: Manchester University Press, 1995).

40. Gao Ming 高明, *Yuanben Pipaji jiaozhu* 元本琵琶記校注, ed. Qian Nanyang 錢南揚 (Shanghai: Shanghai guji chubanshe, 1980), 154.

41. At the same time, the expression *zhixue linli* 指血淋漓 was used in historical writings about male heroes. A well-known example is in "Zhang Zhongcheng zhuan houxu" 張中丞傳後敘, by Han Yu: 因拔所佩刀，斷一指，血淋漓，以示賀蘭. See Han Yu 韓愈, *Han Changli wenji jiaozhu* 韓昌黎文集校注, ed. Ma Qichang 馬其昶 (Shanghai: Shanghai guji chubanshe, 1986), 76. The phrase in the drama adds to Lady Hai's masculine image.

42. Dorothy Ko, "The Body as Attire: The Shifting Meanings of Footbinding in Seventeenth-Century China," *Journal of Women's History* 8, no. 4 (1997): 17.

43. Jiang Cai, "Liefu shi" 烈婦詩, in *Jingting ji* 敬亭集, Kangxi edition, *juan* 1, in *Siku quanshu cunmu congshu* 四庫全書存目叢書 (Jinan: Qi Lu shushe, 1997), *jibu*, 193:555.

44. Lu Shiyi 陸世儀, "Hai Liefu zhuan" 海烈婦傳, in *Chaste Lady Hai, juanshou*, 14a.

45. Matthew H. Sommer, *Sex, Law, and Society in Late Imperial China* (Stanford, Calif.: Stanford University Press, 2000), 79.

46. Sommer, *Sex, Law, and Society*, 89.

47. The line of verse is by Meng Yin, from Yunyang 雲陽孟媚, included in *Bailianzhen Hai Liefu*, in *Guben xiaoshuo congkan*, ser. 26, 5:2014.

48. The marginal commentary related to the scene (*juanxia*, 79a) points out that the three figures in the drama are based on the biography of the chaste lady written by Huang Guangye 黃光業.

49. For biographical information on some of the scholars in this scene, see Guo, "*Hai Liefu chuanqi* zuozhe benshi yu xuba jikao."

50. Guo Yingde 郭英德, "*Hai Liefu chuanqi* yu Qingchu jiangnan shiren de shenghuo yu sixiang" 《海烈婦傳奇》與清初江南士人的生活與思想, *Wenxue yichan* 6 (2011): 90.

51. "Introductory Remarks" (Xuyan 敘言), in *Bailianzhen Hai Liefu*, in *Guben xiaoshuo congkan*, ser. 26, 5:1928.

52. Martin W. Huang, *Negotiating Masculinities in Late Imperial China* (Honolulu: University of Hawai'i Press, 2006), 84.

53. Yu Kun 于琨 et al., eds., *Changzhou fuzhi* 常州府志, 1695, *juan* 18, 8b. See also Huang Zhijuan 黃之雋 et al., eds., *Qianlong jiangnan tongzhi* 乾隆江南通志, *juan* 39, 29a. *Wujin Yanghu xianzhi* 武進陽湖縣志 (1879, *juan* 4, 23a) records a few times when the shrine was rebuilt or renovated in 1697, 1770, and 1869, respectively.

54. *Chaste Lady Hai, juanshou*, 22b.

55. Zhou You 周右 et al., eds., *Dongtai xianzhi* 東臺縣志, 1817, *juan* 40, 6a. The gazetteer entry was based on a document of the Miao lineage.

56. Janet Theiss, "Managing Martyrdom: Female Suicide and Statecraft in Mid-Qing China," in *Passionate Women: Female Suicide in Late Imperial China*, ed. Paul S. Ropp, Paola Zamperini, and Harriet T. Zurndorfer (Leiden: Brill, 2001), 52.

57. Sommer, *Sex, Law, and Society*, 78.

58. Ellen Widmer, introduction to Widmer and Change, *Writing Women*, 10. Widmer's observation is in connection to Judith T. Zeitlin's chapter in the same book.

59. The early Qing novel *Bailianzhen Hai Liefu* also exists as a single copy housed in the Bibliothèque nationale de France.

60. He, "Bai Hai Liefu ci." A note near the line reads, "There is a *chuanqi* drama titled *Jieyi xian*" (有節義仙傳奇).

61. Shen Shouhong recorded the performance of *Chaste Lady Hai* in "Hai Liefu citang ge" 海烈婦祠堂歌, *Bailou ji* 白溇集, *juan* 1, 12a–13a, in *Qingdai shiwenji huibian* 清代詩文集彙編 (Shanghai: Shanghai guji chubanshe, 2010), 167:480.

62. See the explanation in "Hai Liefu chuanqi xiaoxu" 海烈婦傳奇小序, *Chaste Lady Hai, juanshou*, 5a–b.

63. "Hai Liefu zhuan," in *Chaste Lady Hai, juanshou*, 11a.

64. "Ci zhangfu tici" 此丈夫題辭 (b), in *Chaste Lady Hai, juanshou*, 3a.

65. *Chaste Lady Hai, juanshou*, 28 a–b.

66. *Chaste Lady Hai, juanshou*, 2 a–b.

67. Jiang Wenxun 蔣文勳, "Hai Liefu chuanqi ba" 海烈婦傳奇跋, in *Chaste Lady Hai, ba* 跋, 2a.

68. Mann, *Precious Records*, 25.

69. Other writings concerning Lady Hai include the fictional piece "Hai Liefu" 海烈婦 in *Gujin lienüzhuan yanyi* 古今列女傳演義, attributed to Feng Menglong (in *Guben xiaoshuo jicheng*, ser. 2); the folk drama *Hai Liefu ji* 海烈婦記 by Yu Zhi 余治 (in *Shujitang jinyue chuji* 庶幾堂今樂初集); the fictional work "Hai Liefu miguo liufang" 海烈婦米槨流芳, in *Jingwu zhong* 警悟鐘 (in *Guben xiaoshuo jicheng*, ser. 3, vol. 11); "Hai Liefu" 海烈婦 in *Qing Chewangfu cang quben* 清車王府藏曲本 and its edited version titled "Hai Liefu zongjiang" 海烈婦總講 in *Qing Chewangfu cang xiqu quanbian* 清車王府藏戲曲全編.

70. Zhao Erxun 趙爾巽 et al., eds., *Qingshi gao* 清史稿 (Beijing: Zhonghua shuju, 1977), *juan* 511, "Biography" (列傳) 298, 14177–78.

5. FROM STATE ATTIRE TO STAGE PROP

1. In traditional Chinese drama, *qiemo* refers to various stage props, including clothing. For a brief summary, see Chen Zhiyong 陳志勇, "Song Yuan xiqu 'qiemo' kaolun" 宋元戲曲"砌末"考論, *Yishu baijia* 2 (2006): 41, 46–49. Qi Rushan suggests a broad and a narrow definition of *qiemo*, the latter being makeshift props temporarily rented or prepared by the performers—cited and discussed in Zhou Yibai 周貽白 (given as Zhou Bai 周白 in the book), *Zhongguo juchang shi* 中國劇場史 (Taipei: Chang'an chubanshe, 1976), 85–88.

2. Kong Shangren, *Taohua shan* 桃花扇, Kangxi edition, in *Guben xiqu congkan* 古本戲曲叢刊, ser. 5 (Shanghai: Shanghai guji chubanshe, 1986), *juan* b, 138a. Unless otherwise indicated, my quotations of the drama are from this edition. English translations of the quotations are based on K'ung Shang-Jen, *The Peach Blossom Fan*, trans. Shih-hsiang Chen, Harold Acton, and Cyril Birch (New York: New York Review of Books, 2015).

3. Kong, *Peach Blossom Fan*, *juan* b, 147b.

4. Keir Elam, *The Semiotics of Theatre and Drama* (London: Routledge, 2002), 5–8.

5. Andrew Sofer, *The Stage Life of Props* (Ann Arbor: University of Michigan Press, 2003), vi, 2.

6. Countless monographs and papers in Chinese have been written on *Peach Blossom Fan* in the past century. A collection of representative studies is Liu Zhenghong 劉政宏, ed., *Ershi shiji* Taohua shan *yanjiu* 20 世紀『桃花扇』研究 (Shijiazhuang: Hebei jiaoyu chubanshe, 2010). These studies generally focus on the drama's textual production and performance, the authorial intention in its composition, and its relation to dynastic history.

7. The practice of recording stage props in drama scripts dates back to the Yuan dynasty, but it had become rare in late imperial Chinese dramas. Playwrights generally considered props less important than the libretto and did not care to mention them when composing their dramas. *Peach Blossom Fan* bears the largest number of paratextual pieces written by the author himself among late imperial Chinese dramas.

8. See, for example, Wang Jisi 王季思, Su Huanzhong 苏寰中, and Yang Deping 杨德平, eds., *Taohua shan* 桃花扇 (Beijing: Renmin wenxue chubanshe, 1959); *Taohua shan* 桃花扇, in *Kong Shangren quanji jijiao zhuping* 孔尚任全集輯校註評, ed. Xu Zhengui 徐振貴 et al. (Jinan: Qi Lu shushe, 2004).

9. To be exact, the action of the play spans a period of turmoil from the second month in the sixteenth year of the Chongzhen reign to the seventh month in the second year of the Shunzhi reign.

10. Jon McKenzie, in "The Liminal-Norm," in *The Performance Studies Reader*, ed. Henry Bial (London: Routledge, 2004), 26, introduces the concept of the "liminal-norm" to define performance as between theater and ritual, "its limen is the theatricalization of ritual and ritualization of theater." Scholars have also looked for the origins of theater in ritual practices. For a concise discussion, see Tracy C. Davis and Thomas Postlewait, eds., *Theatricality* (Cambridge: Cambridge University Press, 2003), 7.

11. Deeming theater as inauthentic in nature, J. L. Austin disqualifies theatrical practices as speech acts since they do not involve the performers' sincere intention; *How to Do Things with Words* (Cambridge, Mass.: Harvard University Press, 1962). Some scholars have used the criterion of authenticity to distinguish between theatrical and social practices, whereas others have tried to connect the two. See Davis and Postlewait, *Theatricality*, 28–29.

12. William O. Beeman, "The Anthropology of Theater and Spectacle," *Annual Review of Anthropology* 22 (1993): 380.

13. *Jinling dizhi tukao* 金陵地志圖考, in *Zhongguo fangzhi congshu* 中國方志叢書 (Taipei: Chengwen chubanshe youxian gongsi, 1983), Huazhong district, Jiangsu province, 437:70–71. The Directorate of Education (國子監) in Nanjing was renamed the Jiangning Prefecture School (江寧府學) in 1650. Since the map uses the latter name, it was likely produced after 1650.

14. According to official documents of the Ming dynasty, sacrificial worship of Confucius took place in Confucius's temples nationwide twice every month. Two of the most important dates were the *ding* days of the second and eighth months in the lunar calendar.

15. Ge Haiyan 葛海燕, "Cong *Taohua shan* kan rujia de jisi wenhua" 从《桃花扇》看儒家的祭祀文化, *Suihua xueyuan xuebao* 31, no. 1 (2011): 64–66.

16. The description of the statues of Confucius and his disciples could be counter-factual. By the Song dynasty, such a ritual in worship of Confucius included the statues of Confucius and his major disciples together with portraits of other disciples. However, when the founding Hongwu emperor of the Ming dynasty built the Imperial Academy in Nanjing, he ordered a tablet rather than a statue of Confucius to be placed there. During the iconoclastic movement in the Jiajing reign (1530s), most of the statues were replaced with tablets throughout the country. For a brief account, see Seunghyun Han, "Shrine, Images, and Power: The Worship of Former Worthies in Early Nineteenth Century Suzhou," *T'oung Pao* 95, nos. 1–3 (2009): 172, 174.

17. Catherine Bell, *Ritual Theory, Ritual Practice* (New York: Oxford University Press, 1992), 98.

18. For example, Ma Shiying makes a poignant comment on the power of theatrical paint that ruins the scholarly identity in scene 24.

19. Tina Lu, *Persons, Roles, and Minds: Identity in* Peony Pavilion *and* Peach Blossom Fan (Stanford, Calif.: Stanford University Press, 2001), 232.

20. Qian Haiyue 錢海岳, ed., *Nanming shi* 南明史 (Beijing: Zhonghua shuju, 2006), 381.

21. In Beijing opera performance, *sufu* can refer to costumes plain in color or material; see Alexander B. Bonds, *Beijing Opera Costumes: The Visual Communication of Character and Culture* (Honolulu: University of Hawai`i Press, 2008), 332.

22. Zhang Tingyu 張廷玉 et al., eds., *Mingshi* 明史 (Beijing: Zhonghua shuju, 1974), 1447.

23. According to Wu Xinlei 吳新雷, "Lun Kong Shangren *Taohua shan* de chuang-zuo sixiang" 論孔尚任《桃花扇》的創作思想, *Nanjing daxue xuebao* 3 (1997): 107–14, White Cloud Temple was a Buddhist temple. The Daoist Zhang (a historical person) lived there as an individual Daoist practitioner, not part of the temple personnel.

24. Right after this map, *Jinling dizhi tukao* includes a map for comparison titled "Lidai huxian tu" 歷代互見圖, where the name Rose-Cloud-Dwelling Temple (Qixia Si 棲霞寺) appears next to Sheshan.

25. The official robe with a crane badge is a typical costume for officials in today's Beijing opera performances; see Bonds, *Beijing Opera Costumes*, 36. Another interpretation is that Zhang Wei is performing a Daoist ritual, in which case the clothes are a Daoist ritual costume resembling the Ming state uniform.

26. The drama uses Yang Xiong's 揚雄 phrase *xianglei* 湘纍 (the person banished to the Xiang River) in allusion to Qu Yuan (scene 38).

27. There are other records of the seal stamps in Shi's clothing. For an example in a Republican-era novel, see Fei Zhiyuan 費只園, *Qingchao sanbainian yanshi*

yanyi 清朝三百年艷史演義 (Beijing: Dazhong wenyi chubanshe, 1999), chap. 5. Another understanding of the plot is that there is an official seal hidden in the clothing. The English translation by Shih-hsiang Chen, Harold Acton, and Cyril Birch follows the latter reading. However, the "Stage Items" section does not list a seal for this scene.

28. Coincidentally, the cover of the 2015 edition of *The Peach Blossom Fan* features a painting by the Ming loyalist Chen Hongshou, in which the entire desolate landscape appears to be red with the exception of Chen himself in black and white leaning against a tree.

29. Xu Zhengui et al., *Kong Shangren quanji jijiao zhuping*, 1094.

30. Li-ling Hsiao, *The Eternal Present of the Past: Illustration, Theatre, and Reading in the Wanli Period, 1573–1619* (Leiden: Brill, 2007), 176.

31. See Ann Rosalind Jones and Peter Stallybrass, "Introduction: Fashion, Fetishism, and Memory in Early Modern England and Europe," in *Renaissance Clothing and the Materials of Memory* (Cambridge: Cambridge University Press, 2000). See also Marvin Carlson, *The Haunted Stage: The Theatre as Memory Machine* (Ann Arbor: University of Michigan Press, 2003).

32. For a discussion of these marginal characters in the drama, see Maria Franca Sibau, "Maids, Fishermen, and Storytellers: Rewriting Marginal Characters in Early Qing Drama and Fiction," *CHINOPERL: Journal of Chinese Oral and Performing Literature* 35, no. 1 (2016): 15–26.

33. The date was in fact the birthday of Kong Shangren himself. In popular belief in traditional China, the god of wealth was born on the twenty-second day of the seventh month or the seventeenth day of the ninth month.

34. Lin Li-yueh 林麗月, "Guguo yiguan: Dingge yifu yu Ming Qing zhiji de yimin xintai" 故國衣冠: 鼎革易服與明清之際的遺民心態, *Taiwan shida lishi xuebao* 30 (2002): 50–54.

35. Guojun Wang, "Dressing Self and Others in Kong Shangren's (1648–1718) Poetry," *Chinese Literature: Essays, Articles, Reviews*, vol. 41 (2019).

36. Some editions of the drama render 五年戊子 in the quote as 歲在戊子. For example, see *Taohua shan chuanqi* 桃花扇傳奇, ed. Hehu Sanren 賀湖散人 (Shanghai: Shanghai huiwentang xinji shuju, 1924), 131.

37. Liu Yuemei 劉月美, *Zhongguo kunqu yixiang* 中國崑曲衣箱 (Shanghai: Shanghai cishu chubanshe, 2010), 123.

38. In the Republican edition of the drama edited by Hehu Sanren, the phrase reads "a runner in red and black" (紅黑皂隸).

39. James Laver, *Costume in the Theatre* (New York: Hill and Wang, 1965), 13.

40. The Ming–Qing transition also involved the change of dynastic time. As the Manchus marched southward in the 1640s, they issued a new calendar based on a new imperial reign. In the second year of the Shunzhi reign, when

the Southern Ming dynasty was still struggling in southern China, the Qing court decided to compile the *Ming History* as a means to end the existence of the lingering Ming dynasty, thereby pushing it into the historical past.

41. Li Desheng 李德生, *Lihua yizhi chundaiyu—shuobujin de qizhuangxi* 梨花一支春帶雨—說不盡的旗裝戲 (Beijing: Renmin ribao chubanshe, 2012), 8–9. This proposition is incorrect because, first, the textual record of *shifu* does not ensure the stage use of Manchu clothing proper and, second, I have found occurrences of Manchu clothing in drama texts produced much earlier than *Peach Blossom Fan* (see my discussion of *Dao yuanyang* in chapter 2).

42. Kong Shangren, *Qing caihuiben Taohua shan* 清彩繪本桃花扇, illustrated by Jianbai Daoren 堅白道人 (Beijing: Zuojia chubanshe, 2009), 181. The crossing collars, in particular, resemble a Ming-style garment. The narrow sleeves and the pouch hanging on the waist belt, though, might indicate some elements of Manchu-style clothing. *Qing caihuiben Taohua shan* includes forty-four paintings based on the forty-four scenes of the drama. One of the prefaces to the collection is dated 1810. See the introduction by Shen Naiwen 沈乃文 in the book.

43. Kong Shangren, *Taohua shan* 桃花扇, in *Nuanhongshi huike chuanju* 暖紅室彙刻傳劇, ed. Liu Shiheng 劉世珩, Wu Mei 吳梅, and Li Xiang 李詳 (repr., Yangzhou: Jiangsu guangling guji keyinshe, 1979), 128a. For some similar images of Qing runners' uniforms, see Zhou Xibao 周錫保, *Zhongguo gudai fushi shi* 中國古代服飾史 (Beijing: Zhongguo xiju chubanshe, 1984), 480, nos. 8 and 11.

44. The editors of a major modern edition of the drama have adopted the latter reading; see *Peach Blossom Fan* in Xu Zhengui et al., *Kong Shangren quanji jijiao zhuping*, 316.

45. Tina Lu (*Persons, Roles, and Minds*, 273) discusses Kong Shangren's conundrum: the theatrical world he depicts cannot uphold fixed identities, especially given theater's relation to the political world. Therefore, the stage is left empty at the end of the play.

46. Jing Shen interprets this plot as "a parody of the literati ideal of aesthetic cultivation and friendship" (*Playwrights and Literary Games in Seventeenth-Century China: Plays by Tang Xianzu, Mei Dingzuo, Wu Bing, Li Yu, and Kong Shangren* [Lanham, Md.: Lexington Books, 2010], 227).

47. On Kong's writings on the imperial visit, see Guojun Wang, "The Inconvenient Imperial Visit: Writing Clothing and Ethnicity in 1684 Qufu," *Late Imperial China* 37, no. 2 (2016): 137–70.

48. There is not much extant information about this particular theater in the early Qing period. For a general introduction to traditional Chinese theater, see Liao Ben 廖奔, *Zhongguo gudai juchang shi* 中國古代劇場史 (Zhengzhou: Zhongzhou guji chubanshe, 1997), 79–83.

49. Ethnic segregation existed in early Qing Beijing and Nanjing. In figure 5.2, we can see the term *Mancheng* 滿城, denoting the area of Manchu residence, within the space of the inner city (location D).
50. Andrea S. Goldman, *Opera and the City: The Politics of Culture in Beijing, 1770–1900* (Stanford, Calif.: Stanford University Press, 2012), 67–87.
51. Today, Daoist practitioners in Taiwan still don traditional robes in the Han style, yet some high-level clergy members have employed Manchu-style attire. My thanks go to Fong-mao Lee and Fu-ming Lee for this information.
52. Xu Zhengui et al., *Kong Shangren quanji jijiao zhuping*, 1057.
53. Some scholars have pointed out that the summer hat (*liangmao* 涼帽) and bamboo hat (*li* 笠) were typical Manchu clothing items in the Qing dynasty. See Zeng Hui 曾慧, *Manzu fushi wenhua yanjiu* 滿族服飾文化研究 (Shenyang: Liaoning minzu chubanshe, 2010), 155.
54. Sophie Volpp, *Worldly Stage: Theatricality in Seventeenth-Century China* (Cambridge, Mass.: Harvard University Asia Center, 2011), 240–44.
55. Note that this audience might not be the same as that in the House of Great Serenity, where the *fumo* actor watched the performance of *Peach Blossom Fan* "yesterday." The *fumo* does not specify the setting of "today's" performance.
56. *Qing caihuiben Taohua shan*, 9, 97.
57. In 2006, director Tian Qinxin 田沁鑫 produced an experimental performance of *Peach Blossom Fan* set in the year 1699, when the drama was completed. In this avant-garde production, the director had troupe members sit around the stage to perform as the audience. In the production, both the Ceremonial Assistant and the audience wear traditional Han clothing, which contradicts the actual situation in early Qing theater because an early Qing drama audience would have comprised mostly men wearing Manchu instead of Han clothing.
58. Wai-yee Li, "The Representation of History in *The Peach Blossom Fan*," *Journal of the American Oriental Society* 115, no. 3 (1995): 421–33.
59. Volpp, *Worldly Stage*, 60.
60. Kong Shangren, "Yantai zaxing sishi shou youxu" 燕臺雜興四十首有序, no. 8, in Xu Zhengui et al., *Kong Shangren quanji jijiao zhuping*, 1771.
61. Temple fairs, a third venue for theatrical performance, usually did not stage dramas on current affairs such as *Peach Blossom Fan*.
62. Scholars often refer to Kong's statement that *Peach Blossom Fan* was performed by the Jindou 金斗 troupe. As he explains in his postscript, however, the troupe was private and belonged to prime minister Li Tianfu 李天馥 (sobriquet Xiangbei 湘北), not a commercial theater proper; "Benmo" 本末, in *Guben xiqu congkan*, ser. 5, *juan* b, 147a. Jiang Xingyu 蔣星煜, *Taohua shan yanjiu yu xinshang* 《桃花扇》研究與欣賞 (Shanghai: Shanghai renmin chubanshe,

2008), 160–80, provides a thorough account of performances of *Peach Blossom Fan* in Qing China, and almost all took place in relatively private settings.

63. Kong, "Benmo," 147b.

64. Kong, "Benmo," 148a.

65. Wu Mu, "Taohua shan houxu" 桃花扇後序, in *Guben xiqu congkan*, ser. 5, *juan* b, "Houxu," 3a.

66. Yi In-sang 李麟祥 [1710–1760], "Tohwasŏnchi" 桃花扇識, in *Nŭngho chip* 凌壺集, 1779, *juan* 4, in *Han'guk munjip ch'onggan* 韓國文集叢刊 (Seoul: Min-jok Munhwa Ch'ujinhoe, 2001), vol. 225.

67. For one example, see Yuan Shishuo 袁世碩, *Kong Shangren nianpu* 孔尚任年譜 (Jinan: Qi Lu shushe, 1987), 156–58.

68. Kong Shangren, "Youshi Weiyang zhu kaifu daliao zhaoyan guanju" 有事維揚諸開府大僚招讌觀劇, in Xu Zhengui et al., *Kong Shangren quanji jijiao zhuping*, 711.

69. Ye Tang 葉堂, comp., *Nashuying qupu* 納書楹曲譜, in *Shanben xiqu congkan* 善本戲曲叢刊, ed. Wang Qiugui 王秋桂 (Taipei: Taiwan xuesheng shuju, 1987), ser. 6, 2:427–46.

70. Volpp, *Worldly Stage*, 86–87, takes *Peach Blossom Fan* as an example reflecting the second mode of theatricality.

71. For a thorough examination of theatricality in traditional Chinese literature, see Ling Hon Lam, *The Spatiality of Emotion in Early Modern China: From Dreamscapes to Theatricality* (New York: Columbia University Press, 2018).

72. See, for example, Guo Yingde 郭英德, *Ming Qing chuanqi shi* 明清傳奇史 (Nanjing: Jiangsu guji chubanshe, 1999), 491–92.

EPILOGUE: DRESSING OTHER AND SELF

1. Dong Rong 董榕 [1711–1760], *Zhikan ji*, 1751, in *Fu Xihua cang gudian xiqu zhenben congkan* 傅惜華藏古典戲曲珍本叢刊, ed. Wang Wenzhang 王文章 and Liu Wenfeng 劉文峰 (Beijing: Xueyuan chubanshe, 2010), vol. 35.

2. Regarding the representation and commentary on Ming–Qing history in the drama, see Wang Ayling 王璦玲, "'Suiming chuanqi, que shishi yiduan yousheng youse Mingshi'—lun Dong Rong *Zhikan ji* chuanqi zhong zhi yanshi pingshi yu quanshi"「雖名傳奇，卻實是一段有聲有色明史」—論董榕《芝龕記》傳奇中之演史、評史與詮史, *Xiju yanjiu* 13 (2014): 61–98.

3. Gao Lan 高嵐, "Yuhe de shanghen yu chongsu de jiyi—cong *Guilin shuang* kan Qianlong chao minzu rentong bianqian" 癒合的傷痕與重塑的記憶—从《桂林霜》看乾隆朝民族認同變遷, *Minzu wenxue yanjiu* 1 (2008): 31–35.

4. The historical figure Wu Sangui appeared in several dramas discussed in this book. He was a Ming official entreating help from the Manchus in *Hukou*

yusheng 虎口餘生 and was mentioned as a general of Yunnan in one edition of *Wanli yuan*. In early Qing history, the turncoat official Wu Sangui became de facto ruler of Yunnan in the 1640s. In the early 1670s, after three decades serving the Manchus, Wu revolted against the Qing court for the purpose of restoring the Ming dynasty. For a note on the changing images of Wu Sangui in early Qing China, see Ying Zhang, *Confucian Image Politics: Masculine Morality in Seventeenth-Century China* (Seattle: University of Washington Press, 2017), 183.

5. Jiang Shiquan 蔣士銓, *Guilin shuang* 桂林霜, Hongxuelou print edition, preface dated 1781, *juan b*, 36a, in *Budeng daya wenku zhenben xiqu congkan* 不登大雅文庫珍本戲曲叢刊, ed. Beijing Daxue Tushuguan 北京大學圖書館 (Beijing: Xueyuan chubanshe, 2003), 20:69.

6. Jiang, *Guilin shuang, juan b*, 36b, in *Budeng daya wenku zhenben xiqu congkan*, 20:170.

7. Jiang Shiquan 蔣士銓, *Jiang Shiquan xiqu ji* 蔣士銓戲曲集, ed. Zhou Miaozhong 周妙中 (Beijing: Zhonghua shuju, 1993), 108.

8. Jiang, *Jiang Shiquan xiqu ji*, 108.

9. Jiang, *Jiang Shiquan xiqu ji*, 109.

10. Jiang Shiquan, *Guilin shuang*, "Tici," 9b, in *Budeng daya wenku zhenben xiqu congkan*, 20:28. The poem compares Ma Xiongzhen to the two heroes Nan Jiyun and Lei Wanchun, who fought to the death when defending Suiyang during the An Lushan Rebellion in the Tang dynasty.

11. Jiang, *Jiang Shiquan xiqu ji*, 751.

12. In the early Qing period, a scholar surnamed Li, in Deqing of Zhejiang province, had himself depicted in Han clothing for his portrait. The Qing government regarded it as a severe violation and it cost Li thousands of taels of silver to escape punishment. See Zhou Xibao 周錫保, *Zhongguo gudai fushi shi* 中國古代服飾史 (Beijing: Zhongguo xiju chubanshe, 1984), 451. At the same time, however, early Qing scholar-artists frequently depicted themselves wearing Han clothing in their landscape paintings.

13. Zhang Lan, *Terrace of Ten-Thousand Flowers* (*Wanhua tai* 萬花臺), preface dated 1711, in *Guben xiqu congkan*, ser. 5 (Shanghai: Shanghai guji chubanshe, 1986).

14. The composition, revision, and publication of this drama took several decades, with the earliest woodblock-print edition in 1789. The edition I use here is *Xiexin zaju* 寫心雜劇, in *Guben xiqu congkan* 古本戲曲叢刊, ser. 7 (Beijing: Guojia tushuguan chubanshe, 2018). According to Du Guiping, this collection was completed and printed between 1805 and 1807; see Du Guiping 杜桂萍, "Xu Xi *Xiexin zaju* banben xinkao" 徐爔《寫心雜劇》版本新考, *Wenxian* 4 (2007): 177–83.

15. Andrea S. Goldman, *Opera and the City: The Politics of Culture in Beijing, 1770–1900* (Stanford, Calif.: Stanford University Press, 2012), chap. 3, discusses the development of musical genres, especially the competition between *huabu* and *yabu* throughout the Qing dynasty.

16. Li Dou 李斗, *Yangzhou huafang lu*, ed. Wang Beiping 汪北平 and Tu Yugong 涂雨公 (Beijing: Zhonghua shuju, 1960), 133–36. For a recent study of the author and book, see Sun Shulei 孫書磊, *Xiqu wenxian yu lilun yanjiu* 戲曲文獻與理論研究 (Taipei: Guojia chubanshe, 2014), 180–245.

17. Similar to horseshoe-shaped cuffs, horse jackets were worn in the Ming dynasty by soldiers. The Manchus in the Qing dynasty expanded the use of the jackets as everyday clothes, turning them into a marker of Manchu ethnicity.

18. Hu Yajuan 胡亞娟, "*Shenyin jiangu lu* banben ji niandai zuozhe kao" 《審音鑒古錄》版本及年代作者考, *Yishu baijia* 3 (2007): 46–49.

19. Qinyinweng 琴隐翁, ed., *Shenyin jiangu lu* 審音鑑古錄, in *Shanben xiqu congkan* 善本戲曲叢刊, ed. Wang Qiugui 王秋桂 (Taipei: Taiwan xuesheng shuju, 1987), ser. 5, 2:897.

20. For a photocopy of the image, see Wang Wenzhang 王文章 et al., eds., *Kunqu yishu dadian* 崑曲藝術大典 (Hefei: Anhui wenyi chubanshe, 2016), *biaoyan dian*, 4:920–21.

21. Song Junhua 宋俊華, *Zhongguo gudai xiju fushi yanjiu* 中國古代戲劇服飾研究 (Guangzhou: Guangdong gaodeng jiaoyu chubanshe, 2003), 267.

22. Gugong Bowuyuan 故宮博物院, ed., *Gugong zhenben congkan* 故宮珍本叢刊 (Haikou: Hainan chubanshe, 2001), 661:367. In an article titled "Zuizao de qizhuangxi" 最早的旗裝戲, Li Desheng 李德生 considers the drama *Niannian kangtai* as one of the earliest examples of the use of Manchu uniforms in a drama performance; *Lihua yizhi chundaiyu—shuobujin de qizhuangxi* 梨花一支春帶雨—說不盡的旗裝戲 (Beijing: Renmin ribao chubanshe, 2012), 8.

23. Cited from Zhu Jiajin 朱家溍 and Ding Ruqin 丁汝芹, *Qingdai neiting yanju shimo kao* 清代內廷演劇始末考 (Beijing: Zhongguo shudian, 2007), 267. Another Shengping Shu document lists three entries of *Hongmen si* (three performances or rehearsals) in the eleventh month of the fifth year of the Xianfeng reign (1855); see Zhongguo Guojia Tushuguan 中國國家圖書館, ed., *Zhongguo guojia tushuguan cang Qinggong Shengpingshu dang'an jicheng* 中國國家圖書館藏清宮昇平署檔案集成 (Beijing: Zhonghua shuju, 2011), 15:7757.

24. Ye Xiaoqing, *Ascendant Peace in the Four Seas: Drama and the Qing Imperial Court* (Hong Kong: Chinese University Press, 2012), 208. Ye points out that the censorship of drama was especially strict during the Qianlong reign and was discontinued afterward. The confiscated drama scripts ironically became reference books for court performances beginning in the Jiaqing reign.

25. *Chuandai tigang*, in *Gugong zhenben congkan*, 690:259.

26. For an introduction to this group of dramas in the Yuan and Ming dynasties, see Wilt L. Idema [伊維德], "Yuan Ming xitai shang de Yangjiajiang" 元明戲臺上的楊家將, in *Zhongguo xiqu yanjiu de xin fangxiang* 中國戲曲研究的新方向, ed. John C. Y. Wang 王靖宇 and Wang Ayling 王璦玲 (Taipei: Guojia chubanshe, 2015), 115–47.

27. The drama's original edition was composed by Wang Tingzhang 王廷章. See *Zhaodai xiaoshao*, preface dated 1813, in *Guben xiqu congkan* 古本戲曲叢刊, ser. 9 (Shanghai: Shangwu yinshuguan, 1964). For a list of costumes in the play, see Hao Chengwen 郝成文, "Yangjiajiang xiqu ji *Zhaodai xiaoshao* yanjiu" 楊家將戲曲暨《昭代簫韶》研究 (master's thesis, Shanxi Shifan Daxue, 2009), 98–100.

28. *Zhaodai xiaoshao*, book 1, *juan* b, scene 16. In book 2 (*juan* a, scene 1), the drama provides another description of Empress Dowager Xiao's costume as Mongolian court dress.

29. The adaptation began in 1888 and was interrupted by the Boxer Rebellion in 1900, with 105 scenes completed. See Beijing Shi Yishu Yanjiusuo 北京市藝術研究所 and Shanghai Yishu Yanjiusuo 上海藝術研究所, eds., *Zhongguo jingju shi* 中國京劇史 (Beijing: Zhongguo xiju chubanshe, 1999), 1:235.

30. A group of Beijing operas of the late Qing period were based on this story. For a discussion of the complex relation between *Yanmen guan*, *Tanmu huiling*, and *Silang tanmu*, see Hao Chengwen 郝成文, "Jingju *Silang tanmu* yu *Yanmen guan* zhi guanxi bian" 京劇《四郎探母》與《雁門關》之關係辨, *Zhongguo xiqu xueyuan xuebao* 33, no. 1 (2012): 77–81.

31. For a brief biography of Mei Qiaoling, see *Zhongguo jingju shi*, book 1, 481–85.

32. The image is a detail of *Tong Guang mingling shisan jue* 同光名伶十三絕 attributed to Shen Rongpu 沈容圃, reproduced in *Zhongguo jingju tushi* 中國京劇圖史, ed. Zhou Chuanjia 周傳家, Liu Wenfeng 劉文峰 and Wu Gansheng 吳贛生 (Beijing: Beijing shiyue wenyi chubanshe, 1996), 40.

33. Qi Rushan 齊如山, *Xingtou kuitou* 行頭盔頭 (Beiping: Beiping guoju xuehui, 1935), 26.

34. Liao Ben 廖奔, *Zhongguo xiju tushi* 中國戲劇圖史 (Zhengzhou: Daxiang chubanshe, 2000), 289.

35. Two representative discussions on this topic can be found in Goldman, *Opera and the City*, 86, and Mark C. Elliott, *The Manchu Way: The Eight Banners and Ethnic Identity in Late Imperial China* (Stanford, Calif.: Stanford University Press, 2001), 288.

36. Eva Shan Chou, *Memory, Violence, Queues: Lu Xun Interprets China* (Ann Arbor, Mich.: Association for Asian Studies, 2012); Fan Xueqing 樊學慶, *Bianfu fengyun: Jianfa yifu yu Qingji shehui bian'ge* 辮服風雲：剪髮易服與清季社會變革 (Beijing: Sanlian shudian, 2014).

37. On the social history of clothing in modern China, see Antonia Finnane, *Changing Clothes in China: Fashion, History, Nation* (New York: Columbia University Press, 2008), chaps. 4–7. On the relation between Beijing opera and nationhood in late Qing and Republican China, see Joshua Goldstein, *Drama Kings: Players and Publics in the Re-creation of Peking Opera, 1870–1937* (Berkeley: University of California Press, 2007). On the connection between Chinese drama, Chinese clothing, and diasporic Chinese identity, see Daphne Pi-Wei Lei, *Operatic China: Staging Chinese Identity Across the Pacific* (New York: Palgrave Macmillan, 2006).

38. *National Drama Pictorial* (*Guoju huabao* 國劇畫報), no. 35 (September 16, 1932), 138.

39. In the same editorial note, the editors of the *National Drama Pictorial* admit that Manchu-style costume was a "special product" invented at a relatively late point in history.

Works Cited

Alexander, William. *The Costume of China, Illustrated in Forty-eight Coloured Engravings*. London: Miller, 1805.

——. *Picturesque Representations of the Dress and Manners of the Chinese*. London: Bulmer, 1814.

Austin, J. L. *How to Do Things with Words*. Cambridge, Mass.: Harvard University Press, 1962.

Barish, Jonas A. *The Antitheatrical Prejudice*. Berkeley: University of California Press, 1981.

Barrow, John. *Travels in China*. London: Straham, 1804.

Beeman, William O. "The Anthropology of Theater and Spectacle." *Annual Review of Anthropology* 22 (1993): 369–93.

Beijing Shi Yishu Yanjiusuo 北京市藝術研究所 and Shanghai Yishu Yanjiusuo 上海藝術研究所, eds. *Zhongguo jingju shi* 中國京劇史. Beijing: Zhongguo xiju chubanshe, 1999.

Beiping Guoju Xuehui 北平國劇學會, ed. *Guoju huabao* 國劇畫報, no. 35 (September 16, 1932). Reprint, Beijing: Xueyuan chubanshe, 2010.

Bell, Catherine. *Ritual Theory, Ritual Practice*. New York: Oxford University Press, 1992.

Birch, Cyril. "A Comparative View of Dramatic Romance: *The Winter's Tale* and *The Peony Pavilion*." In *Interpreting Culture Through Translation: A Festschrift for D. C. Lau*, ed. Roger T. Ames, Chan Sin-wai, and Mau-sang Ng, 59–77. Hong Kong: Chinese University Press, 1991.

Bonds, Alexandra B. *Beijing Opera Costumes: The Visual Communication of Character and Culture*. Honolulu: University of Hawai`i Press, 2008.

Bray, Francesca. *Technology and Gender: Fabrics of Power in Late Imperial China*. Berkeley: University of California Press, 1997.

——. *Technology and Society in Ming China, 1368–1644*. Washington, D.C.: American Historical Association, 2000.

——. *Technology, Gender and History in Imperial China: Great Transformations Reconsidered*. London: Routledge, 2013.

Breward, Christopher. *The Culture of Fashion: A New History of Fashionable Dress*. Manchester, U.K.: Manchester University Press, 1995.

Brubaker, Rogers, and Frederick Cooper. "Beyond 'Identity.'" *Theory and Society* 29, no. 1 (2000): 1–47.

Cao Yunyuan 曹允源 et al., eds. *Wuxian zhi* 吳縣志. 1933. In *Zhongguo fangzhi congshu* 中國方志叢書, Huazhong district, Jiangsu province, vol. 18. Taipei: Chengwen chubanshe youxian gongsi, 1970.

Carlitz, Katherine. "Desire, Danger, and the Body: Stories of Women's Virtue in Late Ming China." In *Engendering China: Women, Culture, and the State*, ed. Christina K. Gilmartin, Gail Hershatter, Lisa Rofel, and Tyrene White, 101–24. Cambridge, Mass.: Harvard University Press, 1994.

——. "The Social Uses of Female Virtue in Late Ming Editions of *Lienü zhuan*." *Late Imperial China* 12, no. 2 (1991): 117–48.

Carlson, Marvin. *The Haunted Stage: The Theatre as Memory Machine*. Ann Arbor: University of Michigan Press, 2003.

Carrico, Kevin. *The Great Han: Race, Nationalism, and Tradition in China Today*. Oakland: University of California Press, 2017.

Chang, Kang-I Sun. "The Idea of the Mask in Wu Wei-yeh (1609–1671)." *Harvard Journal of Asiatic Studies* 48, no. 2 (1988): 289–320.

Chang, Kang-I Sun, and Haun Saussy, eds. *Women Writers of Traditional China: An Anthology of Poetry and Criticism*. Stanford, Calif.: Stanford University Press, 1999.

Chen, BuYun. *Empire of Style: Silk and Fashion in Tang China*. Seattle: University of Washington Press, 2019.

Chen Guyu 陳古虞 et al., eds. *Li Yu xiqu ji* 李玉戲曲集. Shanghai: Shanghai guji chubanshe, 2004.

Chen Hu 陳瑚. *Quean wengao* 確庵文稿. In *Siku jinhuishu congkan* 四庫禁燬書叢刊, *jibu*, vol. 184. Beijing: Beijing chubanshe, 1997.

Chen Qubing 陳去病. *Chen Qubing shiwen ji* 陳去病詩文集. Beijing: Shehui kexue wenxian chubanshe, 2009.

Chen Zhiyong 陳志勇. "Song Yuan xiqu 'qiemo' kaolun" 宋元戲曲"砌末"考論. *Yishu baijia* 2 (2006): 41, 46–49.

Cheng, Weikun. "Politics of the Queue: Agitation and Resistance in the Beginning and End of Qing China." In *Hair: Its Power and Meaning in Asian Cultures*, ed. Alf Hiltebeitel and Barbara D. Miller, 123–42. Albany: State University of New York Press, 1998.

Cheng Yun 程芸, ed. "*Yanxinglu xubian* jingju shiliao" 《燕行錄續編》京劇史料. In *Jingju lishi wenxian huibian Qingdai juan xubian* 京劇歷史文獻彙編清代卷續編, ed. Fu Jin 傅謹, vol. 4. Nanjing: Fenghuang chubanshe, 2013.

Chou, Eva Shan. *Memory, Violence, Queues: Lu Xun Interprets China*. Ann Arbor, Mich.: Association for Asian Studies, 2012.

Chuandai tigang 穿戴題綱. In *Gugong zhenben congkan* 故宮珍本叢刊, ed. Gugong Bowuyuan 故宮博物院, 690:236–84. Haikou: Hainan chubanshe, 2000.

Conolly, L. W. *The Censorship of English Drama 1737–1824*. San Marino, Calif.: Huntington Library, 1976.

Crossley, Pamela Kyle. *A Translucent Mirror: History and Identity in Qing Imperial Ideology*. Berkeley: University of California Press, 1999.

Davis, John Francis. *The Chinese: A General Description of the Empire of China and Its Inhabitants*. New York: Harper, 1836.

Davis, Tracy C., and Thomas Postlewait, eds. *Theatricality*. Cambridge: Cambridge University Press, 2003.

Ding Shumei 丁淑梅. *Qingdai jinhui xiqu shiliao biannian* 清代禁毀戲曲史料編年. Chengdu: Sichuan daxue chubanshe, 2010.

——. *Zhongguo gudai jinhui xiju biannian shi* 中國古代禁毀戲劇編年史. Chongqing: Chongqing daxue chubanshe, 2014.

——. *Zhongguo gudai jinhui xiju shilun* 中國古代禁毀戲劇史論. Beijing: Zhongguo shehui kexue chubanshe, 2008.

Dolby, William. "Early Chinese Plays and Theater." In *Chinese Theater: From Its Origins to the Present Day*, ed. Colin Mackerras, 7–31. Honolulu: University of Hawai`i Press, 1983.

Dong Meikan 董每戡. *Dong Meikan wenji* 董每戡文集. Guangzhou: Guangdong gaodeng jiaoyu chubanshe, 1999.

Dong Rong 董榕. *Zhikan ji* 芝龕記. 1751. In *Fu Xihua cang gudian xiqu zhenben congkan* 傅惜華藏古典戲曲珍本叢刊, ed. Wang Wenzhang 王文章 and Liu Wenfeng 劉文峰, vol. 35. Beijing: Xueyuan chubanshe, 2010.

Du Guiping 杜桂萍. *Qingchu zaju yanjiu* 清初雜劇研究. Beijing: Renmin wenxue chubanshe, 2005.

——. "Xu Xi *Xiexin zaju* banben xinkao" 徐爔《寫心雜劇》版本新考." *Wenxian* 4 (2007): 177–83.

Elam, Keir. *The Semiotics of Theatre and Drama*. London: Routledge, 2002.

Elliott, Mark C. *The Manchu Way: The Eight Banners and Ethnic Identity in Late Imperial China*. Stanford, Calif.: Stanford University Press, 2001.

Epstein, Maram. *Competing Discourses: Orthodoxy, Authenticity, and Engendered Meanings in Late Imperial Chinese Fiction*. Cambridge, Mass.: Harvard University Asia Center, 2001.

Fan Limin 范麗敏. *Qingdai Beijing xiqu yanchu yanjiu* 清代北京戲曲演出研究. Beijing: Renmin wenxue chubanshe, 2007.

Fan Xueqing 樊學慶. *Bianfu fengyun: Jianfa yifu yu Qingji shehui bian'ge* 辮服風雲：剪髮易服與清季社會變革. Beijing: Sanlian shudian, 2014.

Fan Ye 范曄, comp. *Houhan shu* 後漢書. Beijing: Zhonghua shuju, 1965.

Fang Jiaji 方家驥 and Zhu Jianming 朱建明, eds. *Shanghai kunju zhi* 上海崑劇志. Shanghai: Shanghai wenhua chubanshe, 1998.

Fei Zhiyuan 費只園. *Qingchao sanbainian yanshi yanyi* 清朝三百年艷史演義. Beijing: Dazhong wenyi chubanshe, 1999.

Feng Erkang 馮爾康. "Qingchu de tifa yu yiyiguan—jianlun minzu guanxi shi yanjiu neirong" 清初的剃髮與易衣冠—兼論民族關係史研究內容. *Shixue jikan* 2 (1985): 32–42.

Fiaschetti, Francesca, and Julia Schneider, eds. *Political Strategies of Identity Building in Non-Han Empires in China*. Wiesbaden: Harrassowitz, 2014.

Finnane, Antonia. *Changing Clothes in China: Fashion, History, Nation*. New York: Columbia University Press, 2008.

Foucault, Michel. "What Is an Author." In *Aesthetics, Method, and Epistemology: Essential Works of Foucault (1954–1984)*, ed. James D. Faubion., trans. Robert Hurley et al., 205–22. New York: New Press, 1998.

Franke, Herbert, and Denis Twitchett, eds. *The Cambridge History of China, Volume 6: Alien Regimes and Border States, 907–1368*. Cambridge: Cambridge University Press, 1994.

Fulungga 福隆安 et al., eds. *Qinding baqi tongzhi* 欽定八旗通志. In *Yingyin Wenyuange Siku quanshu* 影印文淵閣四庫全書, *shibu*, vol. 422. Taipei: Taiwan shangwu yinshuguan, 1983.

Furth, Charlotte. "Androgynous Males and Deficient Females: Biology and Gender Boundaries in Sixteenth- and Seventeenth-Century China." *Late Imperial China* 9, no. 2 (1988): 1–31.

Gao Lan 高嵐. "Yuhe de shanghen yu chongsu de jiyi—cong *Guilin shuang* kan Qianlong chao minzu rentong bianqian" 瘉合的傷痕與重塑的記憶—从《桂林霜》看乾隆朝民族認同變遷. *Minzu wenxue yanjiu* 1 (2008): 31–35.

Gao Ming 高明. *Yuanben Pipaji jiaozhu* 元本琵琶記校注. Ed. Qian Nanyang 錢南扬. Shanghai: Shanghai guji chubanshe, 1980.

Gao Shaoxian 高紹先. *Zhongguo xingfashi jingyao* 中國刑法史精要. Beijing: Falü chubanshe, 2001.

Gao Xin 高新. *Zhongguo jingju shuyao* 中國京劇述要. Jinan: Shandong daxue chubanshe, 2001.

Garber, Marjorie B. *Vested Interests: Cross-Dressing and Cultural Anxiety.* New York: Routledge, 2011.

Ge Haiyan 葛海燕. "Cong *Taohua shan* kan rujia de jisi wenhua" 从《桃花扇》看儒家的祭祀文化. *Suihua xueyuan xuebao* 31, no. 1 (2011): 64–66.

Ge Zhaoguang 葛兆光. "Da Ming yiguan jin hezai" 大明衣冠今何在. *Shixue yuekan* 10 (2005): 41–48.

——. *Xiangxiang yiyu: Du Lichao Chaoxian hanwen yanxing wenxian zhaji* 想像異域: 讀李朝朝鮮漢文燕行文獻箚記. Beijing: Zhonghua shuju, 2014.

——. *Zhaizi Zhongguo: Chongjian youguan Zhongguo de lishi lunshu* 宅兹中國: 重建有關中國的歷史論述. Beijing: Zhonghua shuju, 2011.

Giersch, Charles Patterson. *Asian Borderlands: The Transformation of Qing China's Yunnan Frontier.* Cambridge, Mass.: Harvard University Press, 2006.

Goldman, Andrea S. *Opera and the City: The Politics of Culture in Beijing, 1770–1900.* Stanford, Calif.: Stanford University Press, 2012.

Goldstein, Joshua. *Drama Kings: Players and Publics in the Re-creation of Peking Opera, 1870–1937.* Berkeley: University of California Press, 2007.

Gong Hede 龔和德. *Wutai meishu yanjiu* 舞台美術研究. Beijing: Zhongguo xiju chubanshe, 1987.

Greenblatt, Stephen. *Renaissance Self-Fashioning: From More to Shakespeare.* Chicago: University of Chicago Press, 2005.

——. *Shakespearean Negotiations: The Circulation of Social Energy in Renaissance England.* Berkeley: University of California Press, 1988.

Gu Yuan 顧沅 et al., eds. *Wujun wubai mingxian tuzhuanzan* 吳郡五百名賢圖傳贊. 1829. Reprint, Taipei: Guangwen shuju, 1978.

Gugong Bowuyuan Wenxianguan 故宮博物院文獻館, ed. *Shiliao xunkan* 史料旬刊 19 (1930–1931).

Guo Yingde 郭英德. "Duochong kongjian de xinggou, bingzhi yu yanyi—Li Yu *Wanli yuan* chuanqi de 'kongjian' jiedu" 多重空間的形構、並置與演繹—李玉《萬里圓》傳奇的"空間"解讀. In *Hai neiwai Zhongguo xijushi jia zixuanji Guo Yingde juan* 海內外中國戲劇史家自選集郭英德卷. Zhengzhou: Daxiang chubanshe, 2017.

——. "*Hai Liefu chuanqi* yu Qingchu jiangnan shiren de shenghuo yu sixiang" 《海烈婦傳奇》與清初江南士人的生活與思想. *Wenxue yichan* 6 (2011): 84–94.

——. "*Hai Liefu chuanqi* zuozhe benshi yu xuba jikao" 《海烈婦傳奇》作者、本事與序跋輯考. *Wenxian* 1 (2012): 191–200.

——. *Ming Qing chuanqi shi* 明清傳奇史. Nanjing: Jiangsu guji chubanshe, 1999.

——. *Ming Qing chuanqi zonglu* 明清傳奇综錄. Shijiazhuang: Hebei jiaoyu chubanshe, 1997.

——. "'Ruoda qiankun wuchu zhu'—tan You Tong de *Juntian yue* chuanqi" "偌大乾坤無處住"—談尤侗的《鈞天樂》傳奇. *Mingzuo xinshang* 1 (1988): 20, 58–62.

"Hai Liefu" 海烈婦. In *Gujin lienüzhuan yanyi* 古今列女傳演義, ed. Feng Menglong 馮夢龍. In *Guben xiaoshuo jicheng* 古本小說集成, ser. 2, vol. 14, 425–36. Shanghai: Shanghai guji chubanshe, 1994.

"Hai Liefu" 海烈婦. In *Qing Chewangfu cang quben* 清車王府藏曲本, ed. Shoudu Tushuguan 首都圖書館, vol. 11, 320–29. Beijing: Xueyuan chubanshe, 2001.

"Hai Liefu miguo liufang" 海烈婦米梆流芳. In *Jingwu zhong* 警悟鐘, ed. Chichi Daoren 嗤嗤道人. In *Guben xiaoshuo jicheng* 古本小說集成, ser. 3, vol. 11, 165–213. Shanghai: Shanghai guji chubanshe, 1994.

"Hai Liefu zongjiang" 海烈婦總講. In *Qing Chewangfu cang xiqu quanbian* 清車王府藏戲曲全編, ed. Huang Shizhong 黃仕忠 et al., vol. 15, 238–57. Guangzhou: Guangdong renmin chubanshe, 2013.

Han Li 韩莉. "You Tong *Juntian yue* zhong zhuyao renwu yuanxing kaozheng" 尤侗《鈞天樂》中主要人物原型考證. *Lanzhou wenli xueyuan xuebao* 30, no. 5 (2014): 93–96.

Han, Seunghyun. *After the Prosperous Age: State and Elites in Early Nineteenth-Century Suzhou*. Cambridge, Mass.: Harvard University Asia Center, 2016.

——. "Shrine, Images, and Power: The Worship of Former Worthies in Early Nineteenth Century Suzhou." *T'oung Pao* 95, nos. 1–3 (2009): 167–95.

Han Yu 韓愈. *Han Changli wenji jiaozhu* 韓昌黎文集校注. Ed. Ma Qichang 馬其昶. Shanghai: Shanghai guji chubanshe, 1986.

Hao Chengwen 郝成文. "Jingju *Silang tanmu* yu *Yanmen guan* zhi guanxi bian" 京劇《四郎探母》與《雁門關》之關係辨. *Zhongguo xiqu xueyuan xuebao* 33, no. 1 (2012): 77–81.

——. "Yangjiajiang xiqu ji *Zhaodai xiaoshao* yanjiu" 楊家將戲曲暨《昭代簫韶》研究. Master's thesis, Shanxi Shifan Daxue, 2009.

Hay, Jonathan. "Toward a Disjunctive Diachronics of Chinese Art History." *RES: Anthropology and Aesthetics* 40 (Autumn 2001): 101–11.

——. "World-Making in Performance and Painting: An Intertwined History." In *Performing Images: Opera in Chinese Visual Culture*, ed. Judith T. Zeitlin, Yuhang Li, and Richard A. Born, 30–43. Chicago: Smart Museum of Art, University of Chicago, 2014.

He Qie 何垍. *Qingjiangge ji* 晴江閣集. Preface dated 1670s. In *Siku weishoushu jikan* 四庫未收書輯刊, ser. 7, vol. 30. Beijing: Beijing chubanshe, 2000.

He, Yuming. "Difficulties of Performance: The Musical Career of Xu Wei's *The Mad Drummer*." *Harvard Journal of Asiatic Studies* 68, no. 2 (2008): 77–114.

Hegel, Robert E. "Images in Legal and Fictional Texts from Qing China," *Bulletin de l'École française d'Extrême-Orient* 89 (2002): 277–90.

——. "Imagined Violence: Representing Homicide in Late Imperial Crime Reports and Fiction." *Zhongguo wenzhe yanjiu jikan* 25 (2004): 61–89.

Hegel, Robert E., and Katherine Carlitz, eds. *Writing and Law in Late Imperial China: Crime, Conflict, and Judgment.* Seattle: University of Washington Press, 2007.

Hong, Jeehee. *Theater of the Dead: A Social Turn in Chinese Funerary Art, 1000–1400.* Honolulu: University of Hawai`i Press, 2016.

Hong Taeyong 洪大榮. *Tamhŏn yŏn'gi* 湛軒燕記 and *Yŏnhaeng chapki* 燕行雜記. In *Yŏnhaengnok chŏnjip* 燕行錄全集, ed. Im Ki-jung 林基中, vol. 42. Seoul: Tongguk Taehakkyo Ch'ulp'anbu, 1992.

Hong Xingzu 洪興祖, comp. *Chuci buzhu* 楚辭補注. Ed. Bai Huawen 白化文, Xu Denan 許德楠, Li Ruluan 李如鸞, and Fang Jin 方進. Beijing: Zhonghua shuju, 1983.

Hsiao, Li-ling. *The Eternal Present of the Past: Illustration, Theatre, and Reading in the Wanli Period, 1573–1619.* Leiden: Brill, 2007.

Hu Siao-chen 胡曉真. *Ming Qing wenxue zhong de xinan xushi* 明清文學中的西南敘事. Taipei: Taida chuban zhongxin, 2017.

Hu Yajuan 胡亞娟. "*Shenyin jiangu lu* banben ji niandai zuozhe kao"《審音鑒古錄》版本及年代作者考. *Yishu baijia* 3 (2007): 46–49.

Hua Wei 華瑋, ed. *Ming Qing xiqu guoji yantaohui lunwenji* 明清戲曲國際研討會論文集. Taipei: Zhongyang yanjiuyuan Zhongguo wenzhe yanjiusuo choubeichu, 1998.

Huang, Martin W. [黃衛總]. "Guonan yu shiren de xingbie jiaolü" 國難與士人的性別焦慮. In *Ming Qing wenxue yu sixiang zhong zhi zhuti yishi yu shehui* 明清文學與思想中之主體意識與社會, ed. Wang Ayling 王瓊玲, 385–412. Taipei: Zhongyang yanjiuyuan Zhongguo wenzhe yanjiusuo, 2004.

——. *Negotiating Masculinities in Late Imperial China.* Honolulu: University of Hawai`i Press, 2006.

Huang Nengfu 黃能馥. *Zhongguo fushi tongshi* 中國服飾通史. Beijing: Zhongguo fangzhi chubanshe, 2007.

Huang Shizhong 黃仕忠, ed. *Ming Qing guben xijian xiqu huikan* 明清孤本稀見戲曲彙刊. Guilin: Guangxi shifan daxue chubanshe, 2014.

Huang Xiangjian 黃向堅. *Huang Xiaozi jicheng* 黃孝子紀程. In *Zhibuzu zhai congshu* 知不足齋叢書, ed. Bao Tingbo 鮑廷博, Qianlong edition, ser. 5, vol. 6. Reprint, Shanghai: Gushu liutong chu, 1921.

Huang Yishu 黃義樞. "Qingchu xiaoshuo *Bailianzhen Hai Liefu zhuan* kaoshu" 清初小說《百煉真海烈婦傳》考述. *Mingzuo xinshang* 8 (2012): 105–7.

——. "Xijian chuanqi *Piling yi jieyi xian ji* shukao" 稀見傳奇《毗陵驛節義仙記》述考. *Zhongguo xiqu xueyuan xuebao* 33, no. 4 (2012): 67–70, 109.

Huang, Yufu. "Chinese Women's Status as Seen Through Peking Opera." In *Holding Up Half the Sky: Chinese Women Past, Present, and Future,* ed. Tao Jie, Zheng Bijun, and Shirley L. Mow, 30–38. New York: Feminist Press, 2004.

Huang Zhijuan 黃之雋 et al., eds. *Qianlong jiangnan tongzhi* 乾隆江南通志. Qianlong edition. Reprint, Yangzhou: Guangling shushe, 2010.

Hui Mu 灰木. *Piling yi jieyi xian ji* 毗陵驛節義仙記. 1668–1670. In *Guben xiqu congkan* 古本戲曲叢刊, ed. Guben Xiqu Congkan Bianji Weiyuanhui 古本戲曲叢刊編輯委員會, ser. 7. Beijing: Guojia tushuguan chubanshe, 2018.

Hui Zhong 慧中 et al., eds. *Qinding taigui* 欽定臺規. Duchayuan 都察院, 1743 print edition, expanded reprint in the Qianlong era. In *Siku weishoushu jikan* 四庫未收書輯刊, ser. 2, vol. 26. Beijing: Beijing chubanshe, 2000.

Idema, Wilt L. "Drama After the Conquest: An Introduction." In *Trauma and Transcendence in Early Qing Literature*, ed. Wilt L. Idema, Wai-yee Li, and Ellen Widmer, 375–85. Cambridge, Mass.: Harvard University Asia Center, 2006.

——. *The Dramatic Oeuvre of Chu Yu-Tun (1379–1439)*. Leiden: Brill, 1985.

——. "Why You Never Have Read a Yuan Drama: The Transformation of *Zaju* at the Ming Court." In *Studi in onore di Lionello Lanciotti*, ed. S. M. Carletti, M. Sacchetti, and P. Santangelo, 765–91. Naples: Istituto Universitario Orientale, Dipartimento di Studi Asiatici, and Istituto Italiano per il Medio ed Estremo Oriente, 1996.

—— [伊維德]. "Yuan Ming xitai shang de Yangjiajiang" 元明戲臺上的楊家將. In *Zhongguo xiqu yanjiu de xin fangxiang* 中國戲曲研究的新方向, ed. John C. Y. Wang 王靖宇 and Wang Ayling 王璦玲, 115–47. Taipei: Guojia chubanshe, 2015.

Idema, Wilt L., and Beata Grant. *The Red Brush: Writing Women of Imperial China*. Cambridge, Mass.: Harvard University Asia Center, 2004.

Idema, Wilt L., Wai-yee Li, and Ellen Widmer, eds. *Trauma and Transcendence in Early Qing Literature*. Cambridge, Mass.: Harvard University Asia Center, 2006.

Isobe Yūko 磯部祐子. "Riben suocang neifu chaoben *Rushi guan* sizhong juben zhi yanjiu" 日本所藏內府鈔本《如是觀》四種劇本之研究. *Wenxue yichan* 4 (2012): 130–35.

Jaster, Margaret Rose. "'Out of All Frame and Good Fashion': Sartorial Resistance as Political Spectacle." *Irish Review* 34 (2006): 44–57.

Jiang Cai 姜埰. *Jingting ji* 敬亭集. Kangxi edition. In *Siku quanshu cunmu congshu* 四庫全書存目叢書, *jinbu*, vol. 193. Jinan: Qi Lu shushe, 1997.

Jiang Shiquan 蔣士銓. *Guilin shuang* 桂林霜. 1781. In *Budeng daya wenku zhenben xiqu congkan* 不登大雅文庫珍本戲曲叢刊, ed. Beijing Daxue Tushuguan 北京大學圖書館, vol. 20. Beijing: Xueyuan chubanshe, 2003.

——. *Jiang Shiquan xiqu ji* 蔣士銓戲曲集. Ed. Zhou Miaozhong 周妙中. Beijing: Zhonghua shuju, 1993.

Jiang Xingyu 蔣星煜. Taohua shan *yanjiu yu xinshang* 《桃花扇》研究與欣賞. Shanghai: Shanghai renmin chubanshe, 2008.

Jiao Xun 焦循. *Mengzi zhengyi* 孟子正義. Beijing: Zhonghua shuju, 1987.

Jones, Ann Rosalind, and Peter Stallybrass. *Renaissance Clothing and the Materials of Memory*. Cambridge: Cambridge University Press, 2000.

Kastan, David Scott, and Peter Stallybrass, eds. *Staging the Renaissance: Reinterpretations of Elizabethan and Jacobean Drama*. New York: Routledge, 1991.

Keulemans, Paize. "Onstage Rumor, Offstage Voices: The Politics of the Present in the Contemporary Opera of Li Yu." *Frontiers of History in China* 9, no. 2 (2014): 165–201.

Kim Ch'ang-ŏp 金昌業. *Yŏnhaeng ilgi* 燕行日記. In *Yŏnhaengnok chŏnjip* 燕行錄全集, ed. Im Ki-jung 林基中, vol. 32. Seoul: Tongguk Taehakkyo Ch'ulp'anbu, 1992.

Kindall, Elizabeth. *Geo-Narratives of a Filial Son: The Paintings and Travel Diaries of Huang Xiangjian (1609–1673)*. Cambridge, Mass.: Harvard University Asia Center, 2016.

Ko, Dorothy. "The Body as Attire: The Shifting Meanings of Footbinding in Seventeenth-Century China." *Journal of Women's History* 8, no. 4 (1997): 8–27.

——. "Epilogue: Textile, Technology, and Gender in China." In "Special Issue on Women and Textile Production Techniques in Traditional China," ed. Angela Sheng, special issue, *East Asian Science, Technology, and Medicine* 36 (2012): 167–76.

——. *Teachers of the Inner Chambers: Women and Culture in Seventeenth-Century China*. Stanford, Calif.: Stanford University Press, 1994.

Kong Shangren 孔尚任. *Kong Shangren quanji jijiao zhuping* 孔尚任全集輯校註評. Ed. Xu Zhengui 徐振貴 et al. Jinan: Qi Lu shushe, 2004.

——. *Qing caihuiben Taohua shan* 清彩繪本桃花扇. Illustrated by Jianbai Daoren 堅白道人. Beijing: Zuojia chubanshe, 2009.

——. *Taohua shan* 桃花扇. Ed. Wang Jisi 王季思, Su Huanzhong 苏寰中, and Yang Deping 杨德平. Beijing: Renmin wenxue chubanshe, 1959.

——. *Taohua shan* 桃花扇. In *Nuanhongshi huike chuanju* 暖紅室彙刻傳劇, ed. Liu Shiheng 劉世珩, Wu Mei 吳梅, and Li Xiang 李詳. Reprint, Yangzhou: Jiangsu guangling guji keyinshe, 1979.

——. *Taohua shan* 桃花扇. Kangxi edition. In *Guben xiqu congkan* 古本戲曲叢刊, ser. 5. Shanghai: Shanghai guji chubanshe, 1986.

——. *Taohua shan chuanqi* 桃花扇傳奇. Ed. Hehu Sanren 賀湖散人. Shanghai: Shanghai huiwentang xinji shuju, 1924.

K'ung, Shang-jen [Kong Shangren]. *The Peach Blossom Fan*. Trans. Shih-hsiang Chen, Harold Acton, and Cyril Birch. New York: New York Review of Books, 2015.

Kunju Shouchao Quben Yibaice Bianji Weiyuanhui 崑劇手抄曲本一百冊編輯委員會 and Zhongguo Kunqu Bowuguan 中國崑曲博物館, eds. *Kunju shouchao quben yibaice* 崑劇手抄曲本一百冊. Yangzhou: Guangling shushe, 2009.

Kwa, Shiamin. *Strange Eventful Histories: Identity, Performance, and Xu Wei's Four Cries of a Gibbon*. Cambridge, Mass.: Harvard University Asia Center, 2012.

Lam, Ling Hon. "The Matriarch's Private Ear: Performance, Reading, Censorship, and the Fabrication of Interiority in *The Story of the Stone*." *Harvard Journal of Asiatic Studies* 65, no. 2 (2005): 357–415.

——. *The Spatiality of Emotion in Early Modern China: From Dreamscapes to Theatricality*. New York: Columbia University Press, 2018.

Lau, D. C., trans. *The Analects*. Harmondsworth, Middlesex, U.K.: Penguin Books, 1979.

Laver, James. *Costume in the Theatre*. New York: Hill and Wang, 1965.

Legge, James, trans. *The Sacred Books of China: The Texts of Confucianism; The Hsiao King*. 2nd ed. Oxford: Clarendon Press, 1899.

Lei, Daphne Pi-Wei. *Operatic China: Staging Chinese Identity Across the Pacific*. New York: Palgrave Macmillan, 2006.

Li Desheng 李德生. *Lihua yizhi chundaiyu—shuobujin de qizhuangxi* 梨花一支春帶雨—說不盡的旗裝戲. Beijing: Renmin ribao chubanshe, 2012.

Li Dou 李斗. *Yangzhou huafang lu* 揚州畫舫錄. Ed. Wang Beiping 汪北平 and Tu Yugong 涂雨公. Beijing: Zhonghua shuju, 1960.

Li Jiangjie 李江傑. *Ming Qing shishiju yanjiu* 明清時事劇研究. Jinan: Qilu shushe, 2014.

Li Shengguang 李生光. *Xishange bi* 西山閣筆. In *Siku weishoushu jikan* 四庫未收書輯刊, *jibu*, ser. 8, vol. 16. Beijing: Beijing chubanshe, 2000.

Li Shunhua 李舜華. *Liyue yu Ming qianzhongqi yanju* 禮樂與明前中期演劇. Shanghai: Shanghai guji chubanshe, 2006.

Li, Wai-yee. "The Representation of History in *The Peach Blossom Fan*." *Journal of the American Oriental Society* 115, no. 3 (1995): 421–33.

——. *Women and National Trauma in Late Imperial Chinese Literature*. Cambridge, Mass.: Harvard University Asia Center, 2014.

Li Yu 李玉. *Li Yu xiqu ji* 李玉戲曲集. Ed. Chen Guyu 陳古虞, Chen Duo 陳多, and Ma Shenggui 馬聖貴. 3 vols. Shanghai: Shanghai guji chubanshe, 2004.

——. *Qianzhong lu* 千忠錄. In *Fu Xihua cang gudian xiqu zhenben congkan* 傅惜華藏古典戲曲珍本叢刊, ed. Wang Wenzhang 王文章 and Liu Wenfeng 劉文峰. Beijing: Xueyuan chubanshe, 2010.

——. *Qianzhong lu* 千鍾祿. In *Guben xiqu congkan* 古本戲曲叢刊, ser. 3. Shanghai: Wenxue guji kanxingshe, 1957.

——. *Wanli yuan* 萬里圓. In *Guben xiqu congkan* 古本戲曲叢刊, ser. 3. Shanghai: Wenxue guji kanxingshe, 1957.

——. *Wanli yuan* 萬里圓. In *Liyuan gongbao* 梨園公報. Shanghai: Beiping guoju xuehui, 1929–1930.

——. *Zhan huakui* 占花魁. In *Guben xiqu congkan* 古本戲曲叢刊, ser. 3. Shanghai: Wenxue guji kanxingshe, 1957.

Li Zhitan 李之檀, ed. *Zhongguo fushi wenhua cankao wenxian mulu* 中國服飾文化參考文獻目錄. Beijing: Zhongguo fangzhi chubanshe, 2001.

Liao Ben 廖奔. *Zhongguo gudai juchang shi* 中國古代劇場史. Zhengzhou: Zhongzhou guji chubanshe, 1997.

——. *Zhongguo xiju tushi* 中國戲劇圖史. Zhengzhou: Daxiang chubanshe, 2000.

Liao Ben 廖奔 and Liu Yanjun 劉彥君. *Zhongguo xiqu fazhan shi* 中國戲曲發展史. Beijing: Zhongguo xiju chubanshe, 2013.

Liji zhengyi 禮記正義. In *Shisanjing zhushu* 十三經注疏, ed. Shisanjing Zhushu Zhengli Weiyuanhui 十三經注疏整理委員會. Vol. 6. Beijing: Beijing daxue chubanshe, 2000.

Lin Li-yueh 林麗月. "Guguo yiguan: Dingge yifu yu Ming Qing zhiji de yimin xintai" 故國衣冠：鼎革易服與明清之際的遺民心態. *Taiwan shida lishi xuebao* 30 (2002): 39–56

——. "Wanfa juqi—wangjin yu Mingdai shehui wenhua de jige mianxiang" 萬髮俱齊—網巾與明代社會文化的幾個面向. *Taida lishi xuebao* 33 (2004): 133–60.

——. "Yishang yu fengjiao—Wan Ming de fushi fengshang yu 'fuyao' yilun" 衣裳與風教—晚明的服飾風尚與「服妖」議論. *Xin shixue* 10, no. 3 (1999): 111–57.

Ling, Xiaoqiao. "Home and Imagined Stage in Ding Yaokang's *Huaren you* (Ramblings with Magicians): The Communal Reading of a Seventeenth-Century Play." *CHINOPERL: Journal of Chinese Oral and Performing Literature* 33, no. 1 (2014): 1–36.

Lingley, Kate A. "Naturalizing the Exotic: On the Changing Meanings of Ethnic Dress in Medieval China." *Ars Orientalis* 38 (2010): 50–80.

Liu Cheng 劉城. *Yitong shiji* 嶧桐詩集. 1893. In *Siku jinhuishu congkan* 四庫禁燬書叢刊, *jibu*, vol. 121. Beijing: Beijing chubanshe, 2000.

——. *Yitong shiji* 嶧桐詩集. In *Guichi ermiao ji* 貴池二妙集, ed. Liu Shiheng 劉世珩, 1902. In *Congshu jicheng xubian* 叢書集成續編, vol. 162. Taipei: Xinwenfeng chuban gongsi, 1991.

Liu Chiung-yun 劉瓊云. "Qingchu *Qianzhong lu* lide shenti shengqing yu zhongchen jiyi" 清初《千忠錄》裡的身體、聲情與忠臣記憶. *Xiju yanjiu* 17 (2016): 1–39.

Liu, Lydia H., Rebecca E Karl, and Dorothy Ko, eds. *The Birth of Chinese Feminism: Essential Texts in Transnational Theory.* New York: Columbia University Press, 2013.

Liu Ruiyu 劉汭嶼. "Wan Qing jingju qizhuangxi yu danhang huashan de xingqi" 晚清京劇旗裝戲與旦行花衫的興起. *Zhongguo xiqu xueyuan xuebao* 36, no. 4 (2015): 64–71.

Liu Yuemei 劉月美. *Zhongguo jingju yixiang* 中國京劇衣箱. Shanghai: Shanghai cishu chubanshe, 2002.

——. *Zhongguo kunqu yixiang* 中國崑曲衣箱. Shanghai: Shanghai cishu chubanshe, 2010.

——. *Zhongguo kunqu zhuangban yishu* 中國崑曲裝扮藝術. Shanghai: Shanghai cishu chubanshe, 2009.

——. *Zhongguo xiqu yixiang—juese chuandai* 中國戲曲衣箱—角色穿戴. Beijing: Zhongguo xiju chubanshe, 2006.

Liu Zhenghong 劉政宏, ed. *Ershi shiji* Taohua shan *yanjiu* 20 世紀『桃花扇』研究. Shijiazhuang: Hebei jiaoyu chubanshe, 2010.

Liu Zhizhong 劉致中. "Guben *Lin'ge dai chuanqi* de zuozhe he chengshu niandai" 孤本《麟閣待傳奇》的作者和成書年代. *Wenxian* 2 (2000): 108–12, 131.

——. *Ming Qing xiqu kaolun* 明清戲曲考論. Taipei: Guojia chubanshe, 2009.

Lu Eting 陸萼庭. *Kunju yanchu shigao* 崑劇演出史稿. Shanghai: Shanghai jiaoyu chubanshe, 2005.

Lu, Tina. *Persons, Roles, and Minds: Identity in* Peony Pavilion *and* Peach Blossom Fan. Stanford, Calif.: Stanford University Press, 2001.

Lublin, Robert I. *Costuming the Shakespearean Stage: Visual Codes of Representation in Early Modern Theatre and Culture.* Farnham, Surrey, U.K.: Ashgate Publishing, 2011.

Macartney, George. *Embassy to China; being the journal kept by Lord Macartney during his embassy to the Emperor Ch'ien-lung.* London: Longmans, 1962.

Mann, Susan. *Precious Records: Women in China's Long Eighteenth Century.* Stanford, Calif.: Stanford University Press, 1997.

——. "Widows in the Kinship, Class, and Community Structures of Qing Dynasty China." *Journal of Asian Studies* 46, no. 1 (1987): 37–56.

McKenzie, Jon. "The Liminal-Norm." In *The Performance Studies Reader*, ed. Henry Bial, 26–31. London: Routledge, 2004.

Mei, Chun. *The Novel and Theatrical Imagination in Early Modern China.* Leiden: Brill, 2011.

Mengzi yizhu 孟子譯注. Ed. Yang Bojun 楊伯峻. Beijing: Zhonghua shuju, 2003.

Meyer-Fong, Tobie. *What Remains: Coming to Terms with Civil War in 19th Century China.* Stanford, Calif.: Stanford University Press, 2013.

Milhous, Judith, and Robert D. Hume. *Producible Interpretation: Eight English Plays, 1675–1707.* Carbondale: Southern Illinois University Press, 1985.

Mitchell, Timothy. "Society, Economy, and the State Effect." In *The Anthropology of the State: A Reader*, ed. Aradhana Sharma and Akhil Gupta, 169–86. Malden, Mass.: Blackwell Publishing, 2006.

Mullaney, Thomas S., James Leibold, Stéphane Gros, and Eric Vanden Bussche, eds. *Critical Han Studies: The History, Representation, and Identity of China's Majority.* Berkeley: University of California Press, 2012.

Munns, Jessica, and Penny Richards, eds. *The Clothes That Wear Us: Essays on Dressing and Transgressing in Eighteenth-Century Culture.* Newark: University of Delaware Press, 1999.

Orgel, Stephen. "What Is a Text?" In *Staging the Renaissance: Reinterpretations of Elizabethan and Jacobean Drama*, ed. David Scott Kastan and Peter Stallybrass, 83–87. New York: Routledge, 1991.

Owen, Stephen. "'I Don't Want to Act as Emperor Any More': Finding the Genuine in *Peach Blossom Fan*." In *Trauma and Transcendence in Early Qing Literature*, ed. Wilt L. Idema, Wai-yee Li, and Ellen Widmer, 488–511. Cambridge, Mass.: Harvard University Asia Center, 2006.

Qi Biaojia 祁彪佳. *Yuanshantang Ming qupin jupin jiaolu* 遠山堂明曲品劇品校錄. Ed. Huang Shang 黃裳. Shanghai: Shanghai gudian wenxue chubanshe, 1957.

Qi Rushan 齊如山. *Qi Rushan lun jingju yishu* 齊如山論京劇藝術. Ed. Liang Yan 梁燕. Shanghai: Shanghai wenyi chubanshe, 2014.

——. *Xingtou kuitou* 行頭盔頭. Beiping: Beiping guoju xuehui, 1935.

Qian Haiyue 錢海岳, ed. *Nanming shi* 南明史. Beijing: Zhonghua shuju, 2006.

Qing shilu 清實錄. Beijing: Zhonghua shuju, 1985–1987.

Qinyinweng 琴隐翁, ed. *Shenyin jiangu lu* 審音鑑古錄. 1834. In *Shanben xiqu congkan* 善本戲曲叢刊, ed. Wang Qiugui 王秋桂, ser. 5, vol. 2. Taipei: Taiwan xuesheng shuju, 1987.

Qu Dajun 屈大均. *Qu Dajun quanji* 屈大均全集. Ed. Ou Chu 歐初 and Wang Guichen 王貴忱. Beijing: Renmin wenxue chubanshe, 1996.

Rado, Mei Mei. "Images of Opera Characters Related to the Qing Court." In *Performing Images: Opera in Chinese Visual Culture*, ed. Judith T. Zeitlin, Yuhang Li, and Richard A. Born, 58–73. Chicago: Smart Museum of Art, University of Chicago, 2014.

Rawski, Evelyn S. *The Last Emperors: A Social History of Qing Imperial Institutions*. Berkeley: University of California Press, 1998.

Ren Zhongmin. 任中敏. *Tang xinong* 唐戲弄. Ed. Yang Xiaoai 楊曉靄 and Xiao Yuxia 肖玉霞. Nanjing: Fenghuang chubanshe, 2013.

Robinson, David M. *Martial Spectacles of the Ming Court*. Cambridge, Mass,: Harvard University Asia Center, 2013.

——. "The Ming Court and the Legacy of the Yuan Mongols." In *Culture, Courtiers, and Competition: The Ming Court (1368–1644)*, ed. David M Robinson, 365–422. Cambridge, Mass.: Harvard University Asia Center, 2008.

Sanwu Molang Zhuren 三吳墨浪主人, ed. *Xinjuan xiuxiang Bailianzhen Hai Liefu zhuan* 新鐫繡像百煉真海烈婦傳. Ca. 1667–1668. In *Guben xiaoshuo congkan* 古本小說叢刊, ser. 26, vol. 5. Beijing: Zhonghua shuju, 1991.

Schechner, Richard. "Drama, Script, Theatre, and Performance." *Drama Review* 17, no. 3 (1973): 5–36.

——. *Performance Theory*. New York: Routledge Classics, 2003.

Schlesinger, Jonathan. *A World Trimmed with Fur: Wild Things, Pristine Places, and the Natural Fringes of Qing Rule*. Stanford, Calif.: Stanford University Press, 2017.

Shanghai Shudian Chubanshe 上海書店出版社, ed. *Qingdai wenziyu dang* 清代文字獄檔. Shanghai: Shanghai shudian chubanshe, 2007.

Sharma, Aradhana, and Akhil Gupta, eds. *The Anthropology of the State: A Reader*. Malden, Mass.: Blackwell Publishing, 2006.

Shen Congwen 沈從文, ed. *Zhongguo gudai fushi yanjiu* 中國古代服飾研究. Hong Kong: Shangwu yinshuguan, 1981.

Shen, Jing. *Playwrights and Literary Games in Seventeenth-Century China: Plays by Tang Xianzu, Mei Dingzuo, Wu Bing, Li Yu, and Kong Shangren*. Lanham, Md.: Lexington Books, 2010.

Shen Qian 沈倩. "Cong xiqu wenwu kan Songdai de yanchu fushi" 從戲曲文物看宋代的演出服飾. *Quxue* 3 (2015): 299–329.

Shen Shouhong 沈受宏. *Bailou ji* 白溇集. In *Qingdai shiwenji huibian* 清代詩文集彙編, vol. 167. Shanghai: Shanghai guji chubanshe, 2010.

——. *Hai Liefu chuanqi* 海烈婦傳奇. 1841. In *Guben xiqu congkan* 古本戲曲叢刊, ser. 7. Beijing: Guojia tushuguan chubanshe, 2018.

Shen Shucheng 沈書城, ed. *Zeli bianlan* 則例便覽. 1791. In *Siku weishoushu jikan* 四庫未收書輯刊, ser. 2, vol. 27. Beijing: Beijing chubanshe, 2000.

Sheng, Angela. "Women's Work, Virtue, and Space: Change from Early to Late Imperial China." In "Women and Textile Production Techniques in Traditional China," ed. Angela Sheng, special issue, *East Asian Science, Technology, and Medicine* 36 (2012): 9–38.

Shoudu Tushuguan 首都圖書館, ed. *Qing Chewangfu cang quben* 清車王府藏曲本. Beijing: Xueyuan chubanshe, 2001.

Sibau, Maria Franca. "Maids, Fishermen, and Storytellers: Rewriting Marginal Characters in Early Qing Drama and Fiction." *CHINOPERL: Journal of Chinese Oral and Performing Literature* 35, no. 1 (2016): 1–27.

Sieber, Patricia. *Theaters of Desire: Authors, Readers, and the Reproduction of Early Chinese Song-Drama, 1300–2000*. New York: Palgrave Macmillan, 2003.

Sima Qian 司馬遷. *Shiji* 史記. Beijing: Zhonghua shuju, 1982.

Smith, Paul J., and Richard Von Glahn, eds. *The Song-Yuan-Ming Transition in Chinese History*. Cambridge, Mass.: Harvard University Press, 2003.

So Hosu 徐浩修. *Yŏnhaenggi* 燕行記. In *Yŏnhaengnok chŏnjip* 燕行錄全集, ed. Im Kijung 林基中, vol. 51. Seoul: Tongguk Taehakkyo Ch'ulp'anbu, 1992.

Sofer, Andrew. *Dark Matter: Invisibility in Drama, Theater, and Performance*. Ann Arbor: University of Michigan Press, 2013.

——. *The Stage Life of Props*. Ann Arbor: University of Michigan Press, 2003.

Sommer, Matthew H. *Sex, Law, and Society in Late Imperial China*. Stanford, Calif.: Stanford University Press, 2000.

Song Junhua 宋俊華. "Mangyi kaoyuan jiantan Ming gongting yanju de wujiang zhuangban" 蟒衣考源兼談明宮廷演劇的武將裝扮. *Zhongshan daxue xuebao* 41, no. 4 (2001): 56–62.

——. *Zhongguo gudai xiju fushi yanjiu* 中國古代戲劇服飾研究. Guangzhou: Guangdong gaodeng jiaoyu chubanshe, 2003.

Staunton, Sir George. *An Authentic Account of an Embassy from the King of Great Britain to the Emperor of China*. London: Bulmer, 1797.

Stephens, John Russell. *The Censorship of English Drama, 1824–1901*. Cambridge: Cambridge University Press, 1980.

Stevenson, Mark. "One as Form and Shadow: Theater and the Space of Sentimentality in Nineteenth-Century Beijing." *Frontiers of History in China* 9, no. 2 (2014): 225–46.

Strassberg, Richard E. "The Authentic Self in 17th Century Chinese Drama." *Tamkang Review* 8, no. 2 (1977): 61–100.

Struve, Lynn A. *The Southern Ming, 1644–1662*. New Haven, Conn.: Yale University Press, 1984.

——, ed. *Voices from the Ming–Qing Cataclysm: China in Tigers' Jaws*. New Haven, Conn.: Yale University Press, 1993.

Sturman, Peter C., and Susan S. Tai, eds. *The Artful Recluse: Painting, Poetry, and Politics in Seventeenth-Century China*. Santa Barbara, Calif.: Santa Barbara Museum of Art; Munich: DelMonico Books/Prestel, 2012.

Sun Qifeng 孫奇逢. *Du Yi dazhi* 讀易大旨. In *Yingyin Wenyuange Siku quanshu* 影印文淵閣四庫全書, *jingbu*, vol. 39. Taipei: Taiwan shangwu yinshuguan, 1983.

Sun Shulei 孫書磊. *Xiqu wenxian yu lilun yanjiu* 戲曲文獻與理論研究. Taipei: Guojia chubanshe, 2014.

Suzhoushi Xiqu Yanjiu Shi 蘇州市戲曲研究室, comp. *Kunju chuandai* 崑劇穿戴. Suzhou: Suzhoushi xiqu yanjiu shi, 1963.

Swatek, Catherine Crutchfield, trans. "Beating the Officers." *Renditions* 70 (Autumn 2008): 101–13.

——. "Beating the Officers and Cursing the Manchus: Suzhou Dialect and Kun Opera." Unpublished paper.

Tan, Tian Yuan. "Prohibition of *Jiatou Zaju* in the Ming Dynasty and the Portrayal of the Emperor on Stage." *Ming Studies* 49 (2004): 82–111.

Tang Chenglie 湯成烈 et al., eds. *Wujin Yanghu xianzhi* 武進陽湖縣志. 1879. In *Zhongguo difangzhi jicheng* 中國地方志集成, *Jiangsu fujianzhi ji* 江蘇府縣志輯, vol. 37. Nanjing: Fenghuang chubanshe, 2008.

Taylor, Lou. *The Study of Dress History*. Manchester, U.K.: Manchester University Press, 2002.

Teng, Emma Jinhua. *Taiwan's Imagined Geography: Chinese Colonial Travel Writing and Pictures, 1683–1895*. Cambridge, Mass.: Harvard University Asia Center, 2004.

Theiss, Janet M. *Disgraceful Matters: The Politics of Chastity in Eighteenth-Century China*. Berkeley: University of California Press, 2004.

——. "Managing Martyrdom: Female Suicide and Statecraft in Mid-Qing China." In *Passionate Women: Female Suicide in Late Imperial China*, ed. Paul S. Ropp, Paola Zamperini, and Harriet T. Zurndorfer, 47–76. Leiden: Brill, 2001.

Tian, Min. "Male *Dan*: The Paradox of Sex, Acting, and Perception of Female Impersonation in Traditional Chinese Theatre." *Asian Theatre Journal* 17, no. 1 (2000): 78–97.

——. "Stage Directions in the Performance of Yuan Drama." *Comparative Drama* 39, nos. 3, 4 (2005): 397–443.

T'ien, Ju-k'ang. *Male Anxiety and Female Chastity: A Comparative Study of Chinese Ethical Values in Ming–Ch'ing Times*. Leiden: Brill, 1988.

Tuo Tuo 脫脫 et al., eds. *Jinshi* 金史. Beijing: Zhonghua shuju, 1975.

Vierthaler, Paul. "Quasi-History and Public Knowledge: A Social History of Late Ming and Early Qing Unofficial Historical Narratives." PhD diss., Yale University, 2014.

Volpp, Sophie. *Worldly Stage: Theatricality in Seventeenth-Century China*. Cambridge, Mass.: Harvard University Asia Center, 2011.

Wang Anqi 王安祈. *Xingbie zhengzhi yu jingju biaoyan wenhua* 性別、政治與京劇表演文化. Taipei: Taida chuban zhongxin, 2011.

Wang Ayling 王瓈玲. "'Suiming chuanqi, que shishi yiduan yousheng youse Mingshi'—lun Dong Rong *Zhikan ji* chuanqi zhong zhi yanshi pingshi yu quanshi" 「雖名傳奇，卻實是一段有聲有色明史」—論董榕《芝龕記》傳奇中之演史、評史與詮史. *Xiju yanjiu* 13 (2014): 61–98.

Wang Bian 王抃. *Wang Chaosong nianpu* 王巢松年譜. In *Congshu jicheng xubian* 叢書集成續編, *shibu*, vol. 37. Shanghai: Shanghai shudian, 1994.

Wang Fan-sen 王汎森. *Quanli de maoxiguan zuoyong: Qingdai de sixiang xueshu yu xintai* 權力的毛細管作用: 清代的思想、學術與心態. Taipei: Lianjing chuban shiye gufen youxian gongsi, 2013.

Wang, Guojun. "Absent Presence: Costuming and Identity in the Qing Drama *A Ten-Thousand Li Reunion*." *Harvard Journal of Asiatic Studies* 79, no. 1 (2019).

——. "Dressing Self and Others in Kong Shangren's (1648–1718) Poetry." *Chinese Literature: Essays, Articles, Reviews* 41 (2019).

——. "The Inconvenient Imperial Visit: Writing Clothing and Ethnicity in 1684 Qufu." *Late Imperial China* 37, no. 2 (2016): 137–70.

Wang Hebei 王鶴北. "Liushi yuwai de Qinggong xiyi" 流失域外的清宮戲衣. *Zhonghua wenhua huabao* 01 (2018): 84–95.

Wang Liqi 王利器. *Yuan Ming Qing sandai jinhui xiaoshuo xiqu shiliao* 元明清三代禁毀小說戲曲史料. Shanghai: Shanghai guji chubanshe, 1981.

Wang Ping 王平. "Liu Cheng he tade sishou guichi 'guannuo shi'" 劉城和他的四首貴池"觀儺詩." *Chizhou shizhuan xuebao* 18, no. 4 (2004): 52–54.

Wang Tingzhang 王廷章 and Fan Wenxian 范聞賢. *Zhaodai xiaoshao* 昭代簫韶. 1813. In *Guben xiqu congkan* 古本戲曲叢刊, ser. 9. Shanghai: Shangwu yinshuguan, 1964.

Wang Wei 王維. *Wang Wei ji jiaozhu* 王維集校注. Ed. Chen Tiemin 陳鐵民. Beijing: Zhonghua shuju, 1997.

Wang Wenzhang 王文章 et al., eds. *Kunqu yishu dadian* 崑曲藝術大典. Hefei: Anhui wenyi chubanshe, 2016.

Wang Yuanqi 王原祁 et al., eds. *Wanshou shengdian chuji* 萬壽盛典初集. 1717. Reprint, *Wanshou shengdian* 萬壽盛典. Beijing: Beijing guji chubanshe, 1996.

Wang Yu-ching 王宇清. *Liyun fuse kao* 歷運服色考. Taipei: Guoli lishi bowuguan, 1971.

Wang Yunying 王雲英. *Zaitian xiuse—Manzu guanmin fushi* 再添秀色—滿族官民服飾. Shenyang: Liaohai chubanshe, 1997.

Wang Zhengyao 王政堯. *Qingdai xiju wenhua kaobiao* 清代戲劇文化考辨. Beijing: Beijing yanshan chubanshe, 2014.

Wanhua Zhuren 玩花主人 and Qian Decang 錢德蒼, eds. *Huitu zhuibaiqiu* 繪圖綴白裘. 12 vols. Shanghai: Shanghai shuju, 1895.

——, eds. *Zhui baiqiu xinji hebian* 綴白裘新集合編. 1777. In *Shanben xiqu congkan* 善本戲曲叢刊, ed. Wang Qiugui 王秋桂, ser. 5, vol. 1. Taipei: Taiwan xuesheng shuju, 1987.

Weinstein, Jodi L. *Empire and Identity in Guizhou: Local Resistance to Qing Expansion*. Seattle: University of Washington Press, 2014.

West, Stephen H. "Shifting Spaces: Local Dialect in *A Playboy from a Noble House Opts for the Wrong Career*." *Journal of Theater Studies* 1, no. 1 (2008): 83–108.

—— [奚如谷]. "Text and Ideology: Ming Editors and Northern Drama." In *Ming Qing xiqu guoji yantaohui luwen ji* 明清戲曲國際研討會論文集, ed. Hua Wei 華瑋 and Wang Ayling 王璦玲, 329–73. Taipei: Zhongyang yanjiuyuan Zhongguo wenzhe yanjiusuo, 1998.

Widmer, Ellen, and Kang-I Sun Chang, eds. *Writing Women in Late Imperial China*. Stanford, Calif.: Stanford University Press, 1997.

Worswick, Clark. *Sheying: Shades of China, 1850–1900*. Madrid: Turner, 2008.

Wu Gan 吳敢. "*Zhui Baiqiu* xukao (A)" 綴白裘敘考上. *Xuzhou jiaoyu xueyuan xuebao* 15, no. 4 (2000): 44–48.

Wu Hung. "Beyond Stereotypes: The Twelve Beauties in Qing Court Art and the *Dream of the Red Chamber*." In *Writing Women in Late Imperial China*, ed. Ellen Widmer and Kang-i Sun Chang, 306–96. Stanford, Calif.: Stanford University Press, 1997.

Wu Jen-shu 巫仁恕. "Ming Qing zhiji jiangnan shishiju de fazhan jiqi suo fanying de shehui xintai" 明清之際江南時事劇的發展及其所反映的社會心態. *Zhongyang yangjiuyuan jindaishi yanjiusuo jikan* 31 (1999): 1–48.

Wu Xinlei 吳新雷. "Lun Kong Shangren *Taohua shan* de chuangzuo sixiang" 論孔尚任《桃花扇》的創作思想. *Nanjing daxue xuebao* 3 (1997): 107–14.

Wu Xinlei 吳新雷, Yu Weimin 俞爲民, and Gu Lingsen 顧聆森, eds. *Zhongguo kunju da cidian* 中國崑劇大辭典. Nanjing: Nanjing daxue chubanshe, 2002.

Wu Zhengwei 吳政緯. *Juanjuan Mingchao: Chaoxian shiren de Zhongguo lunshu yu wenhua xintai (1600–1800)* 眷眷明朝: 朝鮮士人的中國論述與文化心態 (1600–1800). Taipei: Guoli Taiwan shifan daxue lishixuexi, 2015.

Xia Tingzhi 夏庭芝 *Qinglou ji jianzhu* 青樓集笺注. Ed. Sun Chongtao 孫崇涛 and Xu Hongtu 徐宏图. Beijing: Zhongguo xiju chubanshe, 1990.

Xia Xiaohong 夏曉虹. *Wan Qing nüxing yu jindai Zhongguo* 晚清女性與近代中國. Hong Kong: Zhonghe chuban youxian gongsi, 2011.

Xu Ke 徐珂, comp. *Qingbai leichao* 清稗類鈔. Beijing: Zhonghua shuju, 2010.

Xu Kun 徐坤. *You Tong yanjiu* 尤侗研究. Shanghai: Shanghai wenhua chubanshe, 2008.

Xu Wei 徐蔚. "Nandan: Xingbie fanchuan" 男旦: 性別反串. PhD diss., Xiamen Daxue, 2007.

Xu Wei 徐渭. *Sisheng yuan* 四聲猿. Ed. Zhou Zhongming 周中明. Shanghai: Shanghai guji chubanshe, 1984.

Xu Xi 徐爔. *Xiexin zaju* 寫心雜劇. Ca. 1805–1807. In *Guben xiqu congkan* 古本戲曲叢刊, ser. 7 (Beijing: Guojia tushuguan chubanshe, 2018).

——. *Xiexin zaju* 寫心雜劇. Ca. 1805– 1807. In *Zhongguo gudai zaju wenxian jilu* 中國古代雜劇文獻輯錄, ed. Jiang Yasha 姜亞沙, Jing Li 經莉, and Chen Zhanqi 陳湛綺, vol. 9. Beijing: Quanguo tushuguan wenxian suowei fuzhi zhongxin, 2006.

Yan Chang 延昌. *Zhifu xuzhi* 知府須知. In *Siku weishoushu jikan* 四庫未收書輯刊, ser. 4, vol. 19. Beijing: Beijing chubanshe, 2000.

Yan Changke 顏長珂 and Zhou Chuanjia 周傳家. *Li Yu pingzhuan* 李玉評傳. Beijing: Zhongguo xiju chubanshe, 1985.

Yan Xu 延煦 et al., eds. *Qinding taigui* 欽定臺規. Duchayuan 都察院, l892.

Ye Tang 葉堂, comp. *Nashuying qupu* 納書楹曲譜. In *Shanben xiqu congkan* 善本戲曲叢刊, ed. Wang Qiugui 王秋桂, ser. 6, vol. 2. Taipei: Taiwan xuesheng shuju, 1987.

Ye Xiaoqing. *Ascendant Peace in the Four Seas: Drama and the Qing Imperial Court.* Hong Kong: Chinese University Press, 2012.

——. "Ascendant Peace in the Four Seas: Tributary Drama and the Macartney Mission of 1793." *Late Imperial China* 26, no. 2 (2005): 89–113.

——. "Imperial Institutions and Drama in the Qing Court." *European Journal of East Asian Studies* 2, no. 2 (2003): 329–64.

——. "The Legal and Social Status of Theatrical Performers in Beijing during the Qing." *East Asian History* 25/26 (2003): 69–84.

Yi Hŏnmuk 李憲默. *Yŏnhaeng illok* 燕行日錄. In *Yŏnhaengnok sokchip* 燕行錄續集, ed. Im Ki-jung 林基中, vol. 118. Seoul: Sangsŏwŏn, 2008.

Yi In-sang 李麟祥. *Nŭngho chip* 凌壺集. 1779. In *Han'guk munjip ch'onggan* 韓國文集叢刊, vol. 225. Seoul: Minjok Munhwa Ch'ujinhoe, 2001.

Yi Jolan 衣若蘭. *Shixue yu xingbie:* Mingshi Lienü zhuan *yu Mingdai nüxingshi zhi jiangou* 史學與性別：《明史・列女傳》與明代女性史之建構. Taiyuan: Shangxi jiaoyu chubanshe, 2011.

Yi Tŏkmu 李德懋. *Ibyŏn'gi* 入燕記 b. In *Kugyŏk Ch'ŏngjanggwan chŏnsŏ* 國譯青莊館全書, *Yŏnhaengnok chŏnjip* 燕行錄全集, ed. Im Ki-jung 林基中, vol. 57. Seoul: Tongguk Taehakkyo Ch'ulp'anbu, 1992.

Yi Yo 李漵. *Yŏndo kihaeng* 燕途紀行. In *Kugyŏk Yŏnhaengnok sŏnjip* 國譯燕行錄选集, vol. 2. Seoul: Sŏnggyun'gwan Taehakkyo Taedong Munhwa Yŏn'guwŏn, 1962.

You Tong 尤侗. *Huian nianpu* 悔菴年譜. In *Beijing tushuguan cang zhenben nianpu congkan* 北京圖書館藏珍本年譜叢刊, ed. Beijing Tushuguan 北京圖書館, vol. 74. Beijing: Beijing tushuguan chubanshe, 1999.

——. *Juntian yue* 鈞天樂. Kangxi edition. In *Guben xiqu congkan* 古本戲曲叢刊, ser. 5. Shanghai: Shanghai guji chubanshe, 1986.

——. *Xitang yuji* 西堂餘集. In *Beijing tushuguan cang zhenben nianpu congkan* 北京圖書館藏珍本年譜叢刊, ed. Beijing Tushuguan 北京圖書館, vol. 73. Beijing: Beijing tushuguan chubanshe, 1999.

Yu Kun 于琨 et al., eds. *Changzhou fuzhi* 常州府志. 1695. In *Zhongguo difangzhi jicheng* 中國地方志集成, *Jiangsu fujianzhi ji* 江蘇府縣志輯, vol. 36. Nanjing: Fenghuang chubanshe, 2008.

Yu Zhi 余治. *Hai Liefu ji* 海烈婦記. In *Shujitang jinyue* 庶幾堂今樂. Daihezhai edition, 1880.

Yuan Shishuo 袁世碩. *Kong Shangren nianpu* 孔尚任年譜. Jinan: Qi Lu shushe, 1987.

Yulan ji 魚籃記. Late Ming edition. In *Guben xiqu congkan* 古本戲曲叢刊, ser. 2. Shanghai: Shangwu yinshuguan, 1955.

Zeitlin, Judith T. *Historian of the Strange: Pu Songling and the Chinese Classical Tale.* Stanford, Calif.: Stanford University Press, 1997.

——. "Music and Performance in Hong Sheng's *Palace of Lasting Life.*" In *Trauma and Transcendence in Early Qing Literature*, ed. Wilt L. Idema, Wai-yee Li, and Ellen Widmer, 454–87. Cambridge, Mass.: Harvard University Asia Center, 2006.

——. *The Phantom Heroine: Ghosts and Gender in Seventeenth-Century Chinese Literature.* Honolulu: University of Hawai`i Press, 2007.

——. "Spirit Writing and Performance in the Work of You Tong 尤侗 (1618–1704)." *T'oung Pao* 84 (1998): 102–35.

Zeitlin, Judith T., Yuhang Li, and Richard A. Born, eds. *Performing Images: Opera in Chinese Visual Culture.* Chicago: Smart Museum of Art, University of Chicago, 2014.

Zeng Hui 曾慧. *Manzu fushi wenhua yanjiu* 滿族服飾文化研究. Shenyang: Liaoning minzu chubanshe, 2010.

Zeng Yongyi 曾永義. *Shuo xiqu* 說戲曲. Taipei: Lianjing chuban shiye gongsi, 1976.

Zengshu ji 贈書記. In *Liushizhong qu* 六十種曲, ed. Mao Jin 毛晉. Beijing: Zhonghua shuju, 1958.

Zhang Dai 張岱. *Tao'an mengyi* 陶庵夢憶. Ed. Ma Xingrong 馬興榮. Beijing: Zhonghua shuju, 2007.

Zhang Daxia 張大夏. *Xihua xihua* 戲畫戲話. Taipei: Chongguang wenyi chubanshe, 1971.

Zhang, Fan Jeremy. "'Drama Sustains the Spirit': Art, Ritual, and Theater in Jin and Yuan Period Pingyang, 1150–1350." PhD diss. Brown University, 2011.

Zhang, Hanmo. "Property of the State, Prisoners of Music: Identity of the Song Drama Players and Their Roles in the *Washi* Pleasure Precincts." *Bulletin of the Jao Tsung-I Academy of Sinology* 2 (2015): 277–326.

Zhang Jia 張佳. "Chongzheng guanshang: Hongwu shiqi de fushi gaige" 重整冠裳：洪武時期的服飾改革. *Zhongguo wenhua yanjiusuo xuebao* 58 (2014): 114–59.

——. *Xin tianxia zhi hua—Mingchu lisu gaige yanjiu* 新天下之化—明初禮俗改革研究. Shanghai: Fudan daxue chubanshe, 2014.

Zhang Lan 張瀾. *Wanhua tai* 萬花臺. Preface dated 1711. In *Guben xiqu congkan* 古本戲曲叢刊, ser. 5. Shanghai: Shanghai guji chubanshe, 1986.

Zhang Tingyu 張廷玉 et al., eds. *Huangchao wenxian tongkao* 皇朝文獻通考. In *Yingyin Wenyuange Siku quanshu* 影印文淵閣四庫全書, *shibu*, vol. 141. Taipei: Taiwan shangwu yinshuguan, 1983.

——, eds. *Mingshi* 明史. Beijing: Zhonghua shuju, 1974.

Zhang, Ying. *Confucian Image Politics: Masculine Morality in Seventeenth-Century China*. Seattle: University of Washington Press, 2017.

Zhao Erxun 趙爾巽 et al., eds. *Qingshi gao* 清史稿. Beijing: Zhonghua shuju, 1977.

Zhao Qimei 趙琦美, ed. *Maiwangguan chaojiaoben gujin zaju* 脈望館抄校本古今雜劇. In *Guben xiqu congkan* 古本戲曲叢刊, ser. 4. Shanghai: Shangwu yinshuguan, 1958.

Zhao Yi 趙翼. *Gaiyu congkao* 陔餘叢考. Beijing: Zhonghua shuju, 2006.

Zhao Yuan 趙園. *Ming Qing zhiji shidafu yanjiu* 明清之際士大夫研究. Beijing: Beijing daxue chubanshe, 1999.

Zhongguo Diyi Lishi Dang'anguan 中國第一歷史檔案館, ed. *Zuanxiu Siku quanshu dang'an* 纂修四庫全書檔案. Shanghai: Shanghai guji chubanshe, 1997.

Zhongguo Guojia Tushuguan 中國國家圖書館, ed. *Zhongguo guojia tushuguan cang Qinggong Shengpingshu dang'an jicheng* 中國國家圖書館藏清宮昇平署檔案集成. 108 vols. Beijing: Zhonghua shuju, 2011.

Zhongguo Xiqu Xueyuan 中國戲曲學院 and Tan Yuanjie 譚元傑, eds. *Zhongguo jingju fuzhuang tupu* 中國京劇服裝圖譜. Beijing: Beijing gongyi meishu chubanshe, 1990.

Zhongyang Yanjiu Yuan Lishi Yuyan Yanjiusuo 中央研究院歷史語言研究所, ed. *Ming shilu* 明實錄. Taipei: Zhongyang yanjiuyuan lishi yuyan yanjiusuo, 1962.

Zhou Chuanjia 周傳家, Liu Wenfeng 劉文峰, and Wu Gansheng 吳贛生, eds. *Zhongguo jingju tushi* 中國京劇圖史. Beijing: Beijing shiyue wenyi chubanshe, 1996.

Zhou Huabin 周華斌. "Xiqu wenxian: Zhou Yibai suocang Qinggong xihua" 戲曲文獻: 周貽白所藏清宮戲畫. *Xiqu xuebao* 9 (2011): 225–33.

Zhou Qin 周秦, ed. *Kunxi jicun* 崑戲集存. Hefei: Huangshan shushe, 2011.

Zhou Rong 周容. *Chunjiutang yishu* 春酒堂遺書. In *Siming congshu* 四明叢書, ed. Zhang Shouyong 張壽鏞, ser. 1, vol. 37. 1932.

Zhou Xibao 周錫保. *Zhongguo gudai fushishi* 中國古代服飾史. Beijing: Zhongguo xiju chubanshe, 1984.

Zhou Yibai 周貽白. *Zhongguo juchang shi* 中國劇場史. Taipei: Chang'an chubanshe, 1976.

——. *Zhongguo xiqu lunji* 中國戲曲論集. Beijing: Zhongguo xiju chubanshe, 1960.

Zhou You 周右 et al., eds. *Dongtai xianzhi* 東臺縣志. 1817. In *Zhongguo difangzhi jicheng* 中國地方志集成, *Jiangsu fujianzhi ji* 江蘇府縣志輯, vol. 60. Nanjing: Feng-huang chubanshe, 2008.

Zhu Hengfu 朱恒夫. *Lun xiqu de lishi yu yishu* 論戲曲的歷史與藝術. Shanghai: Xuelin chubanshe, 2008.

Zhu Jiajin 朱家溍 and Ding Ruqin 丁汝芹. *Qingdai neiting yanju shimo kao* 清代內廷演劇始末考. Beijing: Zhongguo shudian, 2007.

Zhu Xiaoen 竺小恩 and Ge Xiaohong 葛曉弘. *Zhongguo yu dongbeiya fushi wenhua jiaoliu yanjiu* 中國與東北亞服飾文化交流研究. Hangzhou: Zhejiang daxue chu-banshe, 2015.

Zhu Ying 朱英. *Dao yuanyang chuanqi* 倒鴛鴦傳奇. Preface dated 1650. In *Guben xiqu congkan* 古本戲曲叢刊, ser. 3. Shanghai: Wenxue guji kanxingshe, 1957.

——. *Nao Wujiang* 鬧烏江. Preface dated 1650. In *Riben suocang xijian Zhongguo xiqu wenxian congkan* 日本所藏稀見中國戲曲文獻叢刊, ed. Huang Shizhong 黃仕忠, Qiao Xiuyan 喬秀岩, and Kin Bunkyō 金文京, ser. 1, vol. 3. Guilin: Guangxi shifan daxue chubanshe, 2006.

——. *Xinbian Lin'ge dai chuanqi* 新編麟待傳奇. Ed. Qu Qijia 瞿啟甲. Manuscript edition, ca. 1908–1911. In *Guben xiqu congkan* 古本戲曲叢刊, ser. 7. Beijing: Guo-jia tushuguan chubanshe, 2018.

——. *Xinbian Lin'ge dai chuanqi* 新編麟待傳奇. Print edition, ca. 1645–1650.

Zhuang Qingmei 莊慶美. "Qiangu Zhonghua fushi zhidu 'gaizhengshuo yifushe' de lishi botao" 千古中華服飾制度「改正朔、易服色」的歷史波濤. *Lishi wenwu: Guoli lishi bowuguan guankan* 14, no. 11 (2004): 32–39.

Zhuang Yifu 莊一拂. *Gudian xiqu cunmu huikao* 古典戲曲存目彙考. Shanghai: Shanghai guji chubanshe, 1982.

Index

"Account of Ten Days in Yangzhou, An," 248*n*13

Alexander, William, 55, *56, 57*

anti-Manchu resistance: and beating scenes, 109–11; decrease in, 205; and dialect, 122, 246*n*60; and Han dress, 51, 234*n*99; and Manchu dress onstage, 110, 113, 115, 122, 246*n*61; Wu Sangui, 193, 195, 259–60*n*4; Zheng Chenggong, 237*n*7

audiences: foreign observers in, 52–55, *54, 56, 57,* 58–59; Manchu dress of, 3, 218*n*4; Manchu participation bans, 6–7, 43–44, 233*nn*79–80; participation of, 17; in *Peach Blossom Fan,* 183, 258*n*55; and political nostalgia, 46–48, 49, 51, 187; and stage architecture, 9. *See also* spectatorship

Auspicious Sign of Peace (Shengping rui) (Jiang Shiquan), 196

Austin, J. L., 254*n*11

authenticity/inauthenticity, 160, 163, 189, 254*n*11

author function, 13–14

authorship, 12–14, 17, 221*n*37, 222*n*43

Bailianzhen Hai Liefu, 126, 130

Baiyue ting (Guan Hanqing), 224*n*59

Baojian ji, 127

Baqi tongzhi, 233*n*79

"barbarian" characters: and anti-Manchu resistance, 110–11, 224*n*63; and drama censorship, 48–49; in Manchu court performances, 40; and Manchu dress onstage, 202, 204–5. *See also* ethnic identity

"barbarian" dances, 47

Barish, Jonas, 32

Barrow, John, 58

Beici guangzheng pu (Li Yu), 240*n*7

Beijing opera: as ahistorical, 24–25, 26; cross-dressing in, 87, 239*n*33; ethnic dress, 228*n*26; Manchu dress onstage in, 37, 41, 58, 134, 199, 203–4, *204, 205, 206, 207,* 263*n*39; and *Peach Blossom Fan* costuming, 255*n*25; performer gender in, 87; *sufu* in, 255*n*21

affairs, 19, 224*n*60; ethnic dress in, 30; and Manchu court performances, 39; scholarly dress in, 237*n*13. *See also Chaste Lady Hai; Lovebirds Reversal; Ten-Thousand-Li Reunion, A*

Ci Mulan (Xu Wei), 242*n*17

Cixi (Empress Dowager), 203

Classic of Filial Piety (*Xiaojing*), 105, 108

clothing, cultural significance of, 4–5

Confucianism: and androgyny, 83; and ethnic identity, 28, 29; head-shaving as violation of, 92, 104; Ming theater as example of, 229*n*29; on needlework, 135; on nudity, 98; on political allegiance, 108; and ritual performances, 162–63, 254*n*14, 255*n*16; and scholarly dress, 72; on self, 243*n*29

Cooper, Frederick, 223*n*56

costume instructions: absent for *A Ten-Thousand-Li Reunion*, 94, 95, 98, 105, 106, 107, 119; for *Chaste Lady Hai*, 133–34; in Li Yu's works, 93, 94, 95, 240*n*4; and Manchu dress onstage, 201; for ritual performances, 39; as source, 21. *See also* Manchu dress in drama scripts

Costume in the Theatre (Laver), 174

costume registers, 21, 225–26*n*74

costuming, 10–11. *See also* theatrical costuming

court performances. *See* Manchu court performances

crime plays, 132

cross-dressing, 16; and androgyny, 80–81, 83; in Beijing opera, 87, 239*n*33; and female performance

prohibition, 223*n*53; and filial piety, 67–68, 81–82; and gender ambiguity, 85, 87; and Manchu dress regulations, 62; and Ming–Qing transition, 83, *83*, 87; Mulan story as archetype of, 84–85; as obstacle, 79–80; and performer offstage dress, 33; and public display of Manchu dress, 76–77; reversal of, 78–79, 82–83, 84, 85; and scholarly dress, 66, 67, 69, 72, 82–83; and sexual assault, 67, 69, 71; and social order, 72–74, 82; stage challenges of, 85, *86*, 87–88, 239*n*34; in traditional drama, 66, 84, 88; and voice, 68

Cultural Revolution, 224*n*58

Daoist ritual dress, 6, 167, 181, 255*n*25, 258*n*51

Daqing huidian shili, 233*n*79

Davis, John Francis, 25, 58

daxi (grand plays), 40

deliverance plays, 131

diachronics, 23

dialect, 119, 122, 246*n*53, 246*n*60

diaodun, 29

Ding Yaokang, 221*n*37

Disturbance at the Wu River (*Nao Wujiang*) (Zhu Ying), 62, 63, 71–72, 89–90, 237*n*6

Dong Zhongshu, 88

Dou E yuan, 242*n*17

Draft History of Qing (*Qingshi gao*), 155

drama censorship, 19, 34–36, 48–49, 224*nn*63, 65, 234*n*91, 261*n*24. *See also* Ming–Qing transition as taboo subject

drama on current affairs. *See shishi ju*

drama scripts: and author function, 13–14; authorial intention in, 12–13, 17, 221*n*37, 222*nn*38, 43; costume instructions in, 21; instability of, 15; stage props in, 254*n*7. *See also Lovebirds Reversal*; Manchu dress in drama scripts; production analysis

drama terminology, 221*n*34

dynastic transition practices, 4–5, 218*n*9. *See also* Ming–Qing transition

embroidery. *See* needlework

epitheatre, 10–11, 221*n*33

Epstein, Maram, 88

Eternal Reunion (*Yong tuanyuan*) (Li Yu), 240*n*3

ethnic identity: censorship of, 47, 48–49, 234*n*91; fluid nature of, 218*n*10; importance of, 207–8; Manchu, 6, 36, 230*n*43; and Manchu dress regulations, 5, 6, 219–20*n*18; and pre-Qing theatrical costuming, 28, 30–31, 35, 228*nn*23, 25; in Qing tributary dramas, 40, 231*n*60; and segregation, 43, 181, 258*n*49; Tang period assimilation process, 227*n*12. *See also* "barbarian" characters

eunuchs, 16, 44–45

expression model of drama studies, 12–13, 221*n*37

Female Mulan Goes to War on Behalf of Her Father (*Ci Mulan tifu congjun*) (Xu Wei), 84–85

Feng Menglong, 253*n*69

filial piety: and bodily suffering, 104; and cross-dressing, 67–68, 81–82; and head-shaving, 92, 104; and political allegiance, 108; in portrait paintings, 117; in *A Ten-Thousand-Li Reunion*, 98, 100, 103, 104, 107. *See also* Confucianism

Flower Queen (*Zhan huakui*) (Li Yu), 94, 110–11, *112*, 240*nn*3, 5, 243*n*27, 244*n*37

flower section (*huabu*), 199

foot-binding, 140

Foucault, Michel, 13–14, 222*n*43

Frost of Guilin, The (*Guilin shuang*) (Jiang Shiquan), 192–93, *194*, 195–96, 260*n*10

Furth, Charlotte, 83

gai zhengshuo yi fuse. See dynastic transition

Ganoderma Shrine, The (*Zhikan ji*), 192

Garber, Marjorie, 90

Gathering of Kings in an Era of Great Tranquility, A (*Taiping wanghui*), 40

gender: ambiguity of, 84, 85, 87; androgyny, 80–81; crisis of, 90–91; and eunuchs, 16; and Manchu dress regulations, 61; and Ming–Qing transition, 83, 135; and needlework, 134–35, 250*n*32; *yinyang* balance, 88–90, 92, 239*n*37. *See also* cross-dressing

geo-narrative painting, 116–17, *116*

gewu xi, 27

Ge Zai, 156

Ge Zhaoguang, 65, 220*n*21

Goldman, Andrea, 36, 43, 44, 181, 218*n*3

Great Learning, The (*Daxue*), 243*n*29

Greenblatt, Stephen, 17, 223*n*57

Guangyuan shu, 225*n*67

Guan Hanqing, 13, 224*n*59

guanshang (cap and gown), 183, 185

Gugong zhenben congkan, 39

Gui Zhuang, 100–101, 118
Guo Yingde, 240*n*1
Gupta, Akhil, 115
Gu Yanwu, 118
Gu Yuan, 117–18, *118*, 245*n*45

Han-clothing movement, 5
Handful of Snow, A (*Yipeng xue*)
  (Li Yu), 240*n*3
Han dress: features of, 242*n*22; foreign
  reactions to, 52–55, *54, 56, 57,* 58–59,
  235*n*106; in landscape paintings,
  116–17, *116*, 245*n*44, 260*n*10; in
  portrait paintings, 44, 118, *118*,
  196–97, *197*, 245*n*46, 260*n*12; and
  recluses, 5, 173, 182; shifting
  reactions to, 51; as symbol of
  subordination, 6. *See also* Han dress
  onstage; Manchu dress regulations;
  Ming state attire
Han dress onstage: and anti-Manchu
  resistance, 51, 234*n*99; in *Celestial
  Court Music* illustrations, 3, 5; in
  kun opera, 110, 244*n*38; in Manchu
  court performances, 39–41; as
  Manchu dress regulation
  exemption, 7, 220*n*21; and Ming
  loyalists as performers, 49–50; and
  Ming–Qing transition shame, 147;
  as obstacle, 79; and political
  nostalgia, 46–48, 49, 51, 187; as
  symbol of subordination, 44–46, *45,*
  53, 69; in *A Ten-Thousand-Li
  Reunion, 114,* 115. *See also* Manchu
  dress regulations; Ming state attire
Hao Shuo, 35
Haotian ta (Li Yu), 224*n*62
Hay, Jonathan, 8, 23
head-shaving requirement, 5, 65,
  218–19*n*11; and androgyny, 80–81;

and Buddhism, 100, 148; and dynastic
  time, 173–74; in *Lovebirds Reversal,*
  62, 67, 80–81; and performer offstage
  dress, 33; resistance against, 5, 67,
  218–19*n*11; and social order, 73; stage
  challenges of, *86, 87*–88, 239*n*34; and
  turncoat officials, 177; as violation of
  civility, 5, 67, 92, 104
Hegel, Robert, 130
historical drama (*lishi ju*), 18, 223–24*n*58;
  Li Yu's works as, *94, 95,* 240*n*5; and
  Manchu dress onstage, 134, 192;
  Peach Blossom Fan as, 160, 180, 186,
  254*n*9; *A Ten-Thousand-Li Reunion*
  as, 92–93, 100–101, 103; twentieth-
  century uses of, 224*n*58. *See also
  Chaste Lady Hai; specific dramas*
History of the Southern Ming, The
  (*Nanming shi*), 165
Hong, Jeehee, 59
Hong Taeyong, 52–53
Hongwu emperor, 32–33
Houhan shu, 235*n*106
Hsiao, Li-ling, 171
Huangchao wenxian tongkao, 233*n*79
Huang Guangye, 252*n*48
Huang Kongzhao: dynastic belonging of,
  245*n*48; historical story of, 92–93;
  portraits of, 117–18, *118. See also
  Ten-Thousand-Li Reunion, A*
Huang, Martin, 147
Huang Xiangjian: dynastic belonging
  of, 245*n*48; historical story of,
  92–93; paintings by, 116–17, *116*;
  portraits of, 117–18, *118*; travelogue
  by, 100–101. *See also Ten-
  Thousand-Li Reunion, A*
Hukou yusheng, 259–60*n*4
Hume, Robert, 14
Huqiu jianchi (Yan Zhenqing), 244*n*40

Manchu dress in drama scripts, 14, 63, 192–98; *The Frost of Guilin*, 192–93, *194*, 195–96; *The Ganoderma Shrine*, 192; and identity, 198, *199*, *200*; and Manchu court performances, 41; and portrait illustrations, 196–98, *197*

Manchu dress onstage, *120*, 198–207; and anti-Manchu resistance, 110, 113, 115, 122, 246*n*61; archer's robe, 37, 40, 41, 201, 232*n*69; and "barbarian" characters, 202, 204–5; in Beijing opera, 37, 41, 58, 134, 199, 203–4, *204*, *205*, *206*, *207*, 263*n*39; in *Chaste Lady Hai*, 133–34; costume production, 37–38, 231*n*51; extant costumes, *38*, *39*; horse jacket, 37, 121–22, 201, 202, 203, 246*n*55; and Manchu court performances, 38–41, 42, 201–2, 231*n*51, 261*n*22; and nation-state transition, 206, 207, *207*, 263*n*39; and popular theater, 41, 232*nn*65, 68; prohibitions on, 7, 14, 33–34, 42, 87, 192, 202; and Song-Liao conflicts, 202–3; sources for, 36–37; suggestions of, 174–75, *175*, *176*, 182, 257*nn*41–42, 258*n*53; in *A Ten-Thousand-Li Reunion*, *120*, 121–22, 246*nn*55–56; in twentieth-century theater, 121–22; in Zhu Ying's works, 63

Manchu dress regulations: and *Celestial Court Music* illustrations, 3; as challenge to social order, 92; as drama topic, 20; enforcement of, 5, 33, 65, 219*n*14; and ethnic identity, 5, 6, 219–20*n*18; exemptions to, 6, 7, 220*n*20; and Han dress as symbol of subordination, 46; in *Lovebirds*

Reversal, 20, 62, 70, 73; as method of control, 6; and Ming loyalists as performers, 49–50; performer offstage dress, 33; and portrait paintings, 196–97, 260*n*12; productive effects of, 123; and public display of Manchu dress, 74–78; resistance against, 5, 67, 76, 218–19*n*11; satirization of, 70; and stage challenges, 85, *86*, 87–88, 122, 147, 239*n*34; as taboo subject, 18, 50–51, 106; and Taiwan, 219*n*17. *See also* head-shaving; Manchu dress onstage

Manchu ethnic identity, 6, 36, 230*n*43

Manchu restrictions: and animosity towards theater, 6–7, 16, 32, 43; drama censorship, 19, 34–36, 48–49, 224*nn*63, 65, 234*n*91, 261*n*24. *See also* Manchu dress regulations; Ming–Qing transition as taboo subject

Mann, Susan, 125, 135, 155

Ma Xiongzhen, 192–93, 260*n*10

Mei Qiaoling, 203

Mengzi, 128, 155, 221*n*35

Miao Ming, 149

Milhous, Judith, 14

Ming dynasty: court apparel, 38, 231*n*51; drama regulation, 32, 228–29*n*29; ethnic dress, 30–31, 228*n*23; Jianwen emperor, 104–5, 243*n*27; onstage-offstage sartorial relationship, 32, 220*n*22; performer offstage dress, 32–33, 229*n*33. *See also* Ming–Qing transition; Yuan–Ming transition

Ming History (*Mingshi*), 130, 165, 248–49*n*14, 257*n*40

regulations; Manchu restrictions; Ming–Qing transition

Qingzhong pu (Li Yu), 109

Qin Liangyu, 192

Qi Rushan, 37, 134, 203, 253*n*1

Quanshan jinke, 40, 41

Qu Dajun, 61

Qu Yuan, 128, 168, 255*n*26

Record of a Book Gift (*Zengshu ji*), 85

Register of Costumes, A (*Chuandai tigang*), 40, 121, 201–2, 225–26*n*74

represented characters, 15, 223*n*50

Returning the Arrow of Command After Visiting His Mother (*Tanmu huiling*), 203–4, 205

Reunion. See Ten-Thousand-Li Reunion, A

ritual performances: and authenticity, 160; and bodily performance, 163; and changing clothes, 167; and Confucianism, 162–63, 254*n*14, 255*n*16; and liminal-norm, 254*n*10; and Manchu court performances, 39; theatrical disruption of, 163–64, 165–66, 167–68, 189, 255*n*18

Rousseau, Jean-Jacques, 32

Rushi guan (Shen Dafu), 224*n*63

Sagely Songs of a Peaceful Time (*Zhaodai xiaoshao*), 202–3, 262*n*29

salon performances, 44

Schechner, Richard, 223

scholarly dress: and Confucianism, 72; critique of, 71–72; and cross-dressing, 66, 67, 69, 72, 82–83; features of, 30; function of, 66–67; and Han dress as symbol of subordination, 69, 70–71; in landscape paintings, 116, 117,

245*n*44; in Manchu court performances, 39–40; in Ming drama, 237*n*13; and Ming–Qing transition shame, 147; as protection, 71, 237*n*16; and social-theatrical boundary, 178–79, 257*n*46; in *A Ten-Thousand-Li Reunion*, 100; and theatrical disruption, 164. *See also* Han dress

Searching for My Parents (*Xunqin tujuan*), 116–17, *116*

self-fashioning, 17, 223*n*57

sexual assault: cross-dressing as protection from, 67, 69, 71; during Ming–Qing transition, 126–27, 248*n*13; and reputation, 143–44. *See also* Lady Hai story

Shakespearean theater, 10, 17, 42, 87

Sharma, Aradhana, 115

Sheath of Heaven and Earth (*Qiankun qiao*), 35

Shen Dafu, 224*n*63

Sheng, Angela, 134–35

Sheng Jing, 250*n*31

Shengping baofa, 40

Shengping Shu (Bureau of Ascendant Peace), 39, 40, 119, 201

Shen Shouhong. *See Chaste Lady Hai*

Shenyin jiangu lu, 201–2

Shen Yunying, 192

shifu, 174, *176*, 257*n*41

shishi ju (drama on current affairs), 18–20, 224*nn*59–60. *See also specific dramas*

Shi tanzi da'nao Yan'anfu, 30, 228*n*23

shi yan zhi (poetry articulates the mind), 221*n*35

Sieber, Patricia, 13